W9-BQK-288

Informal Education, Childhood and Youth

Informal Education, Childhood and Youth

Geographies, Histories, Practices

Edited by

Sarah Mills
Department of Geography, Loughborough University, UK

and

Peter Kraftl
Department of Geography, University of Leicester, UK

palgrave
macmillan

Selection and editorial matter © Sarah Mills and Peter Kraftl 2014
Individual chapters © Respective authors 2014

All rights reserved. No reproduction, copy or transmission of this
publication may be made without written permission.

No portion of this publication may be reproduced, copied or transmitted
save with written permission or in accordance with the provisions of the
Copyright, Designs and Patents Act 1988, or under the terms of any licence
permitting limited copying issued by the Copyright Licensing Agency,
Saffron House, 6–10 Kirby Street, London EC1N 8TS.

Any person who does any unauthorized act in relation to this publication
may be liable to criminal prosecution and civil claims for damages.

The authors have asserted their rights to be identified as the authors of this
work in accordance with the Copyright, Designs and Patents Act 1988.

First published 2014 by
PALGRAVE MACMILLAN

Palgrave Macmillan in the UK is an imprint of Macmillan Publishers Limited,
registered in England, company number 785998, of Houndmills, Basingstoke,
Hampshire RG21 6XS.

Palgrave Macmillan in the US is a division of St Martin's Press LLC,
175 Fifth Avenue, New York, NY 10010.

Palgrave Macmillan is the global academic imprint of the above companies
and has companies and representatives throughout the world.

Palgrave® and Macmillan® are registered trademarks in the United States,
the United Kingdom, Europe and other countries.

ISBN 978–1–137–02772–6

A catalogue record for this book is available from the British Library.

A catalog record for this book is available from the Library of Congress.

Transferred to Digital Printing in 2014

For Mom, Dad and Edward
SM

For Mum, Dad and Martin
PK

Contents

Part V   Conclusion

Figures

Acknowledgements

We both wish to express our thanks to all the chapter authors, as well as to the original presenters and participants of a co-organised session at the Annual Meeting of the Association of American Geographers, Seattle, WA, in 2011 entitled 'Beyond School: Informal and Alternative Learning Practices'. Several of those presenters have contributed to this volume and have shaped the collection. This session was part of Sarah's ESRC postdoctoral fellowship (ES/I031189/1) during 2011–12 hosted at the Department of Geography, University of Leicester, where Peter acted as her mentor. We would both like to thank the ESRC for the financial support and the department for hosting the fellowship. We would also like to thank Palgrave Macmillan, in particular Andrew James, Maryam Rutter and Beth O'Leary, for their editorial support. Finally, thanks to Jacky Tivers for permission to include one of the book cover images from her father's collection.

Sarah would first like to thank Peter for his incredible support and guidance over the last few years. Three institutions have shaped and guided her early career and she would like to thank the Institute of Geography and Earth Sciences, Aberystwyth University; Department of Geography, University of Leicester; and the Department of Geography, Loughborough University. Each institutional 'home' has been a supportive and intellectually stimulating environment to work in. There are too many academic staff and postgraduate students to name here individually across each institution, but she would like to extend special thanks to her PhD supervisors Rhys Jones and Peter Merriman for their encouragement to pursue a doctorate, and to Sarah Holloway, Darren Smith and Katherine Gough for their advice and support in starting her lectureship. Finally, Sarah would like to thank all of her family and friends for their love and support, as well as their patience in enduring her constant excitement about all things geographical and 'book-related'. She feels truly blessed to have found and pursued a job she loves that has learning at its heart.

Peter would like to thank Sarah, for her energy, enthusiasm and intellectual verve, and for the ever-stimulating conversations about young people, education and learning. He would like to thank all of the participants who took part in his alternative education research at 59 learning spaces in the United Kingdom, who have inspired an interest in informal learning in its many guises and, indeed, were part of the inspiration for this book. The Department of Geography at the University of Leicester is a supportive, rich and vibrant place to work. Peter is particularly grateful to several human geographers at Leicester with whom he has enjoyed discussions about learning and social change: Gavin Brown, Jenny Pickerill, Clare Madge, Jen Dickinson, Adam Barker, Grace Sykes and Tom Grant. Many others have shaped his approach to researching childhood, youth and education, including Isabel Cartwright, Clotilde Houchon, John Horton and Pia Christensen. Finally, Peter would like thank his family and friends for their ongoing love and support.

Contributors

Dena Aufseeser is an assistant professor in the Department of Geography and Environmental Systems at the University of Maryland, Baltimore County.

Catherine Bannister is a PhD student in the Department of Sociological Studies at the University of Sheffield, UK.

Mireia Baylina is an associate professor at the Department of Geography, Universitat Autònoma de Barcelona, Spain.

Sophie Bowlby is Visiting Research Fellow at the University of Reading, where she was, before retirement, Senior Lecturer in Human Geography.

Simon Bradford is Reader in Social Sciences in the School of Health Sciences and Social Care at Brunel University, London, UK.

Richard Davies is a lecturer in the School of Education and Lifelong Learning, Aberystwyth University, UK.

Luke Dickens is a research associate in the Department of Geography at The Open University, UK.

Shanene Ditton is a PhD student at Griffith University on Australia's Gold Coast in the School of Humanities and the Griffith Centre for Cultural Research.

Ian Donnachie is Emeritus Professor in History at The Open University, author of *Robert Owen – Social Visionary* and Chair of Friends of New Lanark World Heritage Site.

Gregory T. Donovan is Assistant Professor of Sociology and Urban Studies at Saint Peter's University, founder of the OpenCUNY Academic Medium and a researcher at the Public Science Project.

Kate Edwards is Head of Research and Development for the School Improvement division of Pearson UK and a senior research associate in the Office of Sir Michael Barber, Chief Education Advisor, Pearson.

Denise Goerisch is a research fellow at the Center for Interdisciplinary Study of Youth and Space at San Diego State University.

Louise Holt is Senior Lecturer in Human Geography at the Department of Geography, Loughborough University, UK.

Peter Kraftl is Professor of Human Geography at the Department of Geography, University of Leicester, UK.

Richard G. Kyle is a lecturer in the School of Nursing, Midwifery and Health at the University of Stirling, UK.

Jennifer Lea is Lecturer in Human Geography at the University of Exeter, UK.

Douglas Lonie is Research and Evaluation Manager at the National Foundation for Youth Music.

Sarah Mills is Lecturer in Human Geography at the Department of Geography, Loughborough University, UK.

Maria Rodó-de-Zárate is a PhD student at the Department of Geography, Universitat Autònoma de Barcelona, Spain.

Stephen T. Sadlier, an English Language Lecturer at the University of Washington Educational Outreach, USA, is a 2013 Fulbright fellow at Pontificia Universidad Católica de Chile.

Jean Spence has recently retired as a lecturer in Community and Youth Work at Durham University, UK.

1
Introduction: Geographies, Histories and Practices of Informal Education

Sarah Mills and Peter Kraftl

In a 1943 survey of British youth work, Arthur Morgan described a range of youth clubs and organisations as 'training place[s] in the social art of citizenship' (p.102). Seventy years later, these types of voluntary and publicly funded spaces of non-formal or informal education 'beyond school' continue to occupy an important place in civil society as part of young people's leisure activities, learning and wider socialisation. Simultaneously, these spaces are seen as addressing the needs of the state, as they are used to mobilise wider political and policy-based discourses around participation, citizenship and engagement. For example, in 2014 the coalition government of the United Kingdom continues to roll out its National Citizen Service (NCS) scheme – 'for the lessons they can't teach you in class' – via a network of recently established charities and social businesses such as Catch22 that run alongside pilot programmes with long-standing youth organisations such as the Jewish Lads' Brigade founded in 1895. In bringing together these varied youth partnerships, the very make-up of the NCS represents a kaleidoscope of informal education spaces in the United Kingdom and a sustained focus on 'training places' for children and young people.

The United Kingdom is not alone in its continued focus on young people's citizenship education, moral fortitude and leisure activities that are part of much wider global historical trends (e.g., Gagen, 2000, on these themes in early twentieth-century New York; Alexander, 2009, on imperial Canada and India through the lens of Girl Guiding; and Verschelden et al., 2009, on the internationalisation of youth work practices across Europe). What then are the wider landscapes of informal education across diverse geographical settings and international contexts? Indeed, the diversity of informal education relates to a whole series of everyday and spontaneous learning experiences that vary across different local, national and global contexts. And how have these spaces been understood, experienced and practised over time?

1

It is these questions that frame this edited collection and its exploration of informal education, childhood and youth.

In beginning our editorial introduction with a point of connection between the past and present day, we illustrate one of the central aims of this book: to examine the geographies of informal education through both contemporary and historical examples. While a number of issues and popular understandings about children and young people have changed dramatically during the vast social, political and economic changes of the last few centuries, others remain strikingly similar, not least a series of powerful connections between youth and education. Childhood and youth are complex terms: socially constructed, historically contingent and variously located (Holloway and Valentine, 2000). Childhood continues to be used as a potent metaphor for hope (Kraftl, 2008), and 'youth' is constantly utilised as a mechanism for narrating wider global anxieties (Katz, 2008). In the context of debates surrounding informal education, there are a series of important relationships with childhood and youth: how are young people positioned within philosophies of informal education? In what ways do adult practitioners draw on notions of childhood? How do young people's identities shape their experiences of informal learning? And how have young people established and organised their own informal learning spaces? This edited collection brings together a range of studies that critically engage with these and other questions in a number of original contexts. Overall, the book examines a variety of learning spaces, practices and performances from diverse international setting and different historical epochs to explore, and in many cases push, the boundaries of definitions and understandings of informal education. The primary aims of the edited book are four fold:

1. To examine the *geographies* of informal learning and why these matter.
2. To examine the *histories* of informal learning and why these matter.
3. To compile an engaging resource of case studies for critical reflection on *practices* of informal education for students, academics and practitioners.
4. To enhance our understandings of informal learning environments through informative and engaging examples that draw on recent theoretical developments in social and cultural geography and related disciplines.

In this brief editorial introduction, we define informal education and map out some key debates surrounding its meanings and use, before speaking about the subtitle of the book: *Geographies, Histories, Practices*. Taking each in turn, we outline why geographies, histories and practices matter in the context of academic debates on informal education, expanding on the aims of the book while locating them in the relevant bodies of literature. Finally, we introduce the structure of the book and its chapters.

Defining informal education

Since the term refers to forms of learning that occur in and through everyday life, informal education can conceivably happen in an infinite array of situations, geographical and historical contexts. Understood thus, without wishing to recourse to essentialism, informal learning is an enduring and widespread facet of human experience (for an excellent resource containing many such examples, see www.infed.org). Yet, in particular times and places, informal learning has taken on rather more specific meanings. As Cartwright (2012) charts, informal education became a defined, deliberative and professionalised practice when philanthropic institutions such as the YMCA engaged in a variety of activities designed to support young people's 'personal and social development' (Merton et al., 2004, p.5; cited in Cartwright, 2012, p.152). Informal education thus accompanied the rise of professionalised youth work, in particular in the United Kingdom after the Second World War. The relationships and tensions between youth work and informal education have been debated at length. Significant attention has been paid to the progressive professionalisation of youth work and its gendering (see Chapters 12 and 13 in this volume, respectively); by extension, critical discussion has centred around the colonisation of youth work by and for education policies that seek to manage the behaviour of 'at risk' youth and accord them responsibility for becoming self-governing, neoliberal subjects (for instance, Jeffs, 2007; Davies and Merton, 2009). In all of these contexts, there is a perception that informal learning – and professional practices of informal education that seek to foster that learning – is being squeezed out.

Yet, these important debates notwithstanding, it is possible to identify at least three features of informal education that retain their significance in many contemporary contexts (after Cartwright, 2012). Firstly, informal learning is and should be a process that flows from the *everyday* concerns of young people (Falk et al., 2009). While an individual or group of young people may be identified as being somehow 'in need' of intervention, they should willingly engage in informal educational programmes and themselves identify the issues that should be addressed. Very often, therefore, space matters – informal education (ideally) takes place in locales where young people themselves choose to be and are most comfortable – be they youth clubs, street corners, bus stops or religious institutions. Indeed, it may be that those spaces themselves present the very everyday issues that foster further learning – whether around bullying, sexual relationships, music, sports or something else entirely. However, informal learning need not necessarily take place in 'informal' settings. Increasingly in the United Kingdom and other contexts, informal education takes place within mainstream schools (Jeffs, 2007) and, as several chapters in this volume show, within other institutional contexts, such as scouting organisations, youth volunteering, alternative and non-formal education (see especially Part I and Chapter 11 by Dickens and Lonie). Secondly, informal education relies heavily on *dialogue* and conversation. Informal education requires the building-up of trust, affinity, respect and even affection between educators and learners (Jeffs and Smith, 2005). Clearly, this is also a process that takes time. It requires a process of listening to young people's everyday concerns and directing conversation (and related activities) in such a way that young people can reflect upon their own lives in a supportive environment (Young, 2006). Against charges that youth work in neoliberal contexts is being forced to become evermore instrumental, while simultaneously fire-fighting the 'problematic' or 'anti-social' behaviours displayed by young people, the dialogical nature of informal learning is meant to be non-teleological, although not necessarily *anti*-teleological. That is to say, the outcomes of informal learning – which as Cartwright (2012) shows can be as diverse as a collective film or a change in a young person's emotional outlook – are not necessarily determined in advance, are contingent and seek *some kind* of positive change.

Thirdly, informal education can involve some kind of (sometimes weakly) *political* edge. Informal educators may deliberately position themselves against the grain of apparent deficiencies of mainstream education, especially where their work is inspired by radical critiques of schooling (see Fielding and Moss, 2011; Kraftl, 2013). However, more commonly deriving influence from Paolo Freire (2008), informal education is conceived as a kind of learning from life, through dialogue, that enables a form of consciousness-raising (*conscientização*) among dispossessed groups to identify and seek means to overcome the social relations that dehumanise them. Thus, to take another key geographical term, informal education may inevitably involve a degree of *upscaling*, from the personal and the local through to issues of 'wider' socio-political concern. Key examples of this process of upscaling can be found in several chapters in this book, not least Sadlier's evocative analysis of the tarpaulin and the tablecloth as microspaces that are productive of 'politics of play, love and concern' in the public spaces of Oaxaca, Mexico.

In itself, the definition provided above is neither all-encompassing nor indicative of the many subtleties of informal education. The key aims of this text are, however, as indicated in the previous section, to both explore and push at the boundaries of the above definition in terms of the geographies, histories and practices that comprise informal education. It is our hope that the chapters in this text not only provide examples of the three features listed above in practice but also critically interrogate the role of informal education in a range of geographical and historical contexts, and through a range of theoretical perspectives. The next sections of this chapter provide some context as to our understanding of three key terms for this edited collection: geographies, histories and practices. While dealing with each in turn for the sake of clarity, we should stress that this volume brings together chapters that often interweave these three elements, as well as engage with disciplinary debates in geography and history.

Geographies of informal education

In this volume, we use the term 'geographies' to refer to a range of perspectives on how informal educational practices operate in, through and as *spaces*. In some cases, the term refers to the particular geographical contexts in which informal education happens, and which are fundamental to our understanding of the situated nature of informal education. For instance, this volume includes chapters based in Mexico, the United Kingdom, Peru, Australia, Spain and the United States. In each country, informal education may flow from particular sets of social concerns, political currents and accepted ways of relating between (for instance) adults and young people.

It is, however, not sufficient to acknowledge that practices of informal education may vary across space as well as time, and to collate examples from around the world (indeed, this book is quite partial in terms of its geographical coverage). Rather, several of the chapters in this book seek to explore how practices of informal education are woven into and implicated in the complex social, political and cultural textures that make up particular places. This book is, then, based on an understanding of 'geography' that does not see educational processes as merely derivative of other, somehow more fundamental processes. Indeed, Hanson Thiem (2009) argues that for too long geographical analyses of education have sought to emphasise how, for instance, school distribution is an outcome of some contemporary policy imperative, or how ethnic segregation in school catchments reflects wider social trends (cf. Bondi, 1991; Johnston et al., 2008). She contends that, despite their absolute significance, such approaches 'neglect education's constitutive properties – that is, how educational systems, institutions, and practices (and the political struggles that surround them) effect change *beyond* the sector' (Hanson Thiem, 2009, p.157, original emphasis).

In the above light, the ambition of a geographical approach to education is manifest not only in mapping the effects of political or economic currents at various spatial scales – as if geographical processes like distribution, segregation or migration were somehow separate from and a mere result of those currents. Rather, as Gulson and Symes (2007, p.3) point out, geographies of education require attentiveness to *spatiality*: to 'complex theorizations of material and symbolic life' where educational and spatial processes are indistinguishable from one another. Thus, Gulson and Symes build on decades of theorising about spatiality in disciplinary geography, wherein the term

> capture[s] the ways in which the *social* and *spatial* are inextricably realized in one another; [and] conjure[s] up the circumstances in which society and space are simultaneously realized by thinking, feeling, doing

individuals and [...] the many different conditions in which such
realizations are experienced.

(Pile and Keith, 1993, p.6)

An acknowledgement of spatiality brings with it a requirement to exceed
what immediately *seems* 'geographical' about education processes. Herein,
the geographies of education (as both a scholarly endeavour and facets of
the social world) may be conceived as complex, multifaceted and multi-
scaled. In effect, from within disciplinary human geography alone, the
geographies of education have increased and diversified enormously since
the early 2000s, due in part to approaches developed by those working in
'children's geographies'. In a relatively early review, Collins and Coleman
(2008) distinguished between studies that sought to examine the spaces
within schools and those beyond school boundaries – a schematic that
remains pertinent. On the former, a raft of studies has examined micro-
scale interactions and power relations in dining halls (Pike, 2008), the design
of school spaces and pupil participation therein (Kraftl, 2006; den Besten
et al., 2011) and the classroom as a microcosm of larger imperatives for
nation-building or citizenship education (e.g. Gruffudd, 1996; Pykett, 2012).
On the latter, important research by geographers and others has critically
examined the relationships between schools and their communities, and in
particular the articulation of pedagogic linkages between home and school
that may, frequently, be implicitly class-biased (see, in particular, Holloway
and Pimlott-Wilson, 2011; Wainwright and Marandet, 2011). Here, there are
clear parallels with the ways in which informal educators seek both to carve
out spaces *within* formal/mainstream settings and to transcend boundaries
between environments designated for learning and those apparently outside
that design (Mills, 2013). In other words – as Cartwright (2012) has ably
shown – an understanding of spaces within and beyond formally designated
schools is arguably central for any analysis of informal education.

   Geographical studies of education have also developed parallel to – and in
conversation with – the so-called New Social Studies of Childhood (NSSC)
(James and James, 2004; Jenks, 2005). Bridging sociology, anthropology,
geography, education studies and a range of other disciplines, NSSC have
been premised upon a commitment to interrogate the socially constituted
elements of childhood experience and to foreground the agency, participation and voices of young people in both research and social life. It has been
repeatedly shown that both the construction and experience of childhood
are inherently spatial – from the rules that undergird intergenerational interactions in public spaces to the ways in which children seek to carve out
niches in overwhelmingly adult-controlled environments (Holloway and
Valentine, 2000; Matthews et al., 2000; for a review, see Kraftl et al., 2012).
Although subject to a range of critiques (e.g. Prout, 2005; King, 2007; Philo,
2011), an understanding of children's experiences of education – as some

of the many *subjects* of educational practices – has remained a significant component of research on education spaces (see Holloway et al., 2010, for an excellent review and examples). Critically, while focussing on the subjects of education, Holloway et al. argue that geographers themselves need to extend their repertoire of what 'count' as education spaces:

> [W]e need to expand our interpretation of what count as spaces of education [...to] pay greater attention to the home, pre-school provision, neighbourhood spaces and after-school care, as well as thinking more deeply about the ways in which people learn in subsistence agriculture, family businesses, paid work and so on.
>
> (Holloway et al., 2010, p.595)

Resonating with some definitions of informal education (especially Falk et al., 2009), this statement can be reinterpreted as a call for greater interrogation of the spatialities of informal education, with a particular focus on the teachers, practitioners, parents, young people and others who populate them. This is, in fact, a driving principle for the current volume. While not all of the chapters draw directly upon the experiences of young people, many do attend to the ways in which childhoods/youth are constructed through informal education spaces, and/or are based on empirical research with practitioners – who are clearly also key 'subjects' in education spaces (Holloway et al., 2010).

Of final and equal significance is a need to attune to the ways in which geographies of education may both draw on and inform key contemporary conceptual debates. Two excellent edited collections, notable for their development of social-scientific understandings of embodiment and emotion, are pertinent to the present volume. In one, Cook and Hemming (2011) curate a collection of papers on the multisensuous, *embodied* dynamics of education spaces – from the evocative sounds of a primary school corridor (Gallagher, 2011) to the disruptive aesthetic potential presented by the reorganisation of common design conventions in Higher Education classrooms (Lambert, 2011). In the second, Kenway and Youdell (2011) attend to some of the multiple intersections between *emotion* and educational spaces – from how 'emotional geographies are manifest in the formation and maintenance of particular racialisation and ethnicisation processes within a multicultural primary school' (Zembylas, 2011, p.151) to the production of feelings of alienation among young people excluded from mainstream school spaces (Nairn and Higgins, 2011). As we highlighted in the previous section, definitions of informal education highlight the importance of both interpersonal relationships and carefully managed situations, through which feelings such as trust, comfort and affection may emerge. Thus, many of the chapters in this volume also interrogate questions of emotion and embodiment, applying and developing these concepts through Scout and Guide camps, Care Farms, socio-emotional differences, music and information technologies. At the same time, many chapters develop a range of other theoretical perspectives, including feminist, radical and materialist perspectives on childhood, youth and pedagogy.

Geographies of education are becoming evermore diverse, arguably more disparate, and yet constitute an increasing presence across disciplinary human geography and beyond (Holloway and Jöns, 2012). This edited collection – which includes contributions from geographers and non-geographers – bears witness to some of that diversity. At the same time, it foregrounds the importance of geographical context, space, place and spatiality for understanding informal education. In particular, it demonstrates how informal education spaces are not merely derivative of, but may produce, inform, relate to *and* resist, contemporary socio-political processes.

Histories of informal education

In exploring the geographies of informal learning outlined above, this volume draws on both contemporary and, notably, historical examples. In doing so, this edited collection also contributes more broadly to *histories* of informal education. Significantly, this historical element is relatively new within the subdiscipline of children's geographies and geographies of education, discussed in the previous section. While there have been historical studies of formal schooling and children's built environments within geography (Ploszajska, 1998; Gagen, 2000), the presence and activities of alternative and informal learning spaces over time have been hitherto neglected (although see Mills, 2013, on scouting, and Cameron, 2006, on an experimental school). In excavating some of the hidden historical geographies of informal education, this text highlights the need to consider informal education over *time* as well as space.

The history of informal education has also been a marginal but sustained interest for historians of childhood, leisure and youth (e.g., Springhall, 1977; Proctor, 2002). Much of this scholarly focus – notably by informal educators and practitioners themselves – has been on the history of youth work, often as part of wider studies on community work and voluntarism. Notably, a now well-established series of edited volumes based on conference proceedings has brought together histories of youth work, mainly focusing on nineteenth- and twentieth-century Britain (Gilchrist et al., 2001, 2003, 2006, 2009, 2011). There have also been more in-depth historical accounts of the institutional structures and wider social and political changes that have shaped youth work over time (Davies 1999a, 1999b), as well as studies charting the contribution of religious communities (e.g., 1975, on Jewish youth work).

In more recent years, a much-needed wider lens has been cast over the history of youth work through a comparative European perspective. Three insightful edited volumes have sought to forge connections between the history of youth work in Europe and contemporary youth policy (Coussée et al., 2010, 2012; Verschelden et al., 2009). The volumes are both academically engaging and practical, with Coussée remarking in his own chapter that

> [t]racing back the roots of youth work and identifying different evolutions within and between countries must help us to initiate a fundamental discussion on nowadays youth work identity and cope in a constructive way with the recurrent youth work paradoxes.
>
> (Coussée, 2009, p.7)

In many ways, the policies and practices of youth work today are a legacy of the historical development of informal education, its related political motivations and the national (and international) policy contexts that have shaped its characteristics (see, e.g., Smith and Doyle, 2002, on the impact of the Albemarle Report [1960] on youth work in England and Wales). However, for us, a focus on the histories of informal education extends beyond the social, political and economic factors that frame the historical development of youth work to include *multiple* and *enlivened histories* of informal education that consider the fragmented, embodied and diverse experiences of informal learning across different spaces over time.

In opening up the histories of informal education to include but also *go beyond* youth work, this volume captures some of the past activities and influential legacies of educational thinkers (Donnachie, Chapter 6, on Robert Owen) as well as offers a unique contribution on the gendered dimensions of post-war youth work and professional practice (Bradford, Chapter 12; Spence, Chapter 13). Furthermore, some authors explore the past philosophies and performances of different voluntary youth organisations (Kyle, Chapter 2; Mills Chapter 5). As Tony Jeffs notes:

> [o]verwhelmingly, the historical material [relating to youth work] focuses on policy and agencies, and far too infrequently on what it meant to be a member or a 'client'. Few historians have moved beyond the study of youth work as an ongoing process to undertake the primary research required to understand how boys' and girls' clubs, uniformed groups, youth projects, and detached and outreach programmes worked *in practice*.
>
> (Jeffs, 2010, p.16, emphasis added)

This volume therefore highlights some potential conceptual and methodological entry points that begin to address Jeffs' call for what is clearly an important but much-larger project. For example, one potential avenue is to follow Kyle's unique approach in Chapter 2 of weaving contemporary *and* historical accounts of an informal learning space – the camp – together in one study. Overall, we contend that there is a pressing need to bring such enlivened histories into wider academic conversations about informal education, childhood and youth. The methodological innovations that have been utilised in diverse geographies of education, in particular within children's geographies, could be further enhanced through historical approaches and source materials. Indeed, a number of historians of childhood, leisure and gender are engaging with diverse historical sources to gain insight into young people's (past) experiences of spaces 'beyond school'. For example, Tebbutt's (2012) recent monograph uses a range of historical sources (including her own father's diaries) to explore the activities and practices of 'the Boys' Brigade' in Northampton, England, drawing on recent theorisations and writings in geography on mobility and place.

In terms of the present volume there is not one particular decade or historical period that the authors focus upon; neither do we seek to claim a 'definitive history' of informal education (if indeed there can be such a thing) – but rather, the collection presents selected *histories* of informal education that are intimately entwined with the *geographies* of informal education. Indeed, the contributions do not simply chart developments or policies but rather push at some of the geographical sensibilities and spatialities (outlined in the previous section), either at a particular 'critical moment' in history or over a longer period of time. Finally, it is also worth noting here that the book is structured thematically, rather than chronologically. This again highlights our (and the authors') commitment to exploring informal education, childhood and youth based on conceptual, thematic and analytical connections over time and space, rather than constructing a linear trajectory or particular national or regional focus. While seemingly disparate in terms of historical context, the chapters are united in their focus within structured parts (explored later in this introduction). Furthermore, the authors make their own connections between historical and contemporary-focused contributions. Taken together then, the chapters – while moving between different decades and indeed the present day – are complementary in their aim to explore the geographies of informal education and why these matter, as well as critically reflect on the *practices* of informal education.

Practices of informal education

In addition to contributing to geographical and historical studies of informal education, there is something in the way that the contributors to this volume critically reflect on *practice*, which is worthy of further attention and indeed comprises the third and final element of the volume's subtitle. Here, and in the following chapters, practices are understood and addressed in three central ways, which resonate with the definition of informal education we provided above.

First, in terms of the people – practitioners, volunteers, educators, teachers or young people themselves – that literally 'do', 'enable' or 'facilitate' informal education. While education scholars and youth workers have acknowledged the need to critically reflect on professional practice and create space for 'voices of practice' (Spence and Devanney, 2006; see also Richardson and Wolfe, 2001), this text extends this call through a number of contributions that reflect on the motivations, experiences and challenges for adult practitioners, as well as young people as educators themselves. In doing so, several authors reflect on how informal education is actually performed, rehearsed and experienced *in practice* (see Jeffs' quote in the previous section).

Second, there is a focus within this text in most, if not all, chapters on the diverse *material* practices and technologies that enable informal education to take 'place' (see also Bekerman et al., 2005). At various points in the book, authors discuss young people's embodied practices of camping, crafting, dancing, singing, mending, gardening, writing and blogging. Furthermore, a number of chapters highlight the role of material objects used by adults and young people to facilitate such activities and create a space for informal learning, for example firewood, tents or a computer. Elsewhere, in his study of alternative education in the United Kingdom, Kraftl has described the contingent and 'messy' practices of learning, arguing that 'alternative learning spaces are constantly characterised by an interplay between mess and order (or *dis/order*)' (2013: 119–120), and in some cases are understood through the *absence* of certain material objects associated with 'artefacts of school'. The authors in this volume attend to some of these materialities, highlighting how a range of technologies enable and negotiate experiences of informal education. This text therefore also contributes to some wider debates in social and cultural geography on childhood, materiality and embodiment.

Third, there is a need to focus on the everyday praxes – combinations of everyday pedagogic practice and political motivation – that drive informal education. Several of the chapters are situated within, or rub up against, both historical and contemporary political imperatives. They chart how some informal educators seek to make space for childhoods *other* than the flexible subjects by neoliberal regimes, while others wish to address inequalities in terms of gender or class. Commonly, the broader political goals of informal education are entwined with and produced by the everyday practices of dialogue and interpersonal interaction that we have identified above. In many ways, then, informal educators experiment with the hopeful, if not utopian, potentialities of everyday practice in order to raise the consciousness of young people so that – if only in a minor way – the seeds of social or political transformation may be sown (Cartwright, 2012; also Gardiner, 2004).

Overall, informal education itself can be seen as an 'alternative practice'; as Kraftl notes, 'there exist many alternative education practices that knowingly distance themselves from mainstream and especially state-sponsored schooling, whether or not they acknowledge that mainstream schooling can be massively diverse' (2012, p.2; also Woods and Woods, 2009). While the main focus of this book is not to interrogate the relationship between formal and informal learning, or critically evaluate the professional practices of informal educators, several chapters do address related themes in their examination of the geographies and histories of informal education. We now turn our focus to introducing these individual chapters, positioning them within the wider thematic structure of the book.

The structure of the book

Part I – 'Nature Spaces' – examines four separate organisations or informal learning spaces whose imaginative geographies draw upon nature, or whose 'alternative' learning activities occur outside, usually in rural environments. Historical and contemporary connections between youth, nature, morality and the 'great outdoors' are powerful (see, e.g., Philo, 1992; Matless, 1998). In Part I, the authors discuss several of these ideas, pushing conceptual understandings of 'inside/outside', while also making some broader arguments about the geographies and practices of informal education, specifically in a UK context. In Chapter 2, Richard Kyle draws on historical and contemporary data on 'the Boys' Brigade' in Scotland to explore the 'extraordinary geographies' of camp. Using the joint metaphor of 'cocoon' and 'chrysalis' to explain how volunteers and the organisation have understood camp over time, he also argues that outdoor and indoor spaces of informal learning are 'locked in continual processes of co-creation'. Chapter 3, by Catherine Bannister, also interrogates the spaces and practices of camp, but this time in a contemporary sociological investigation of rituals and performances on Scout and Guide camps in England. By uniquely examining these two uniformed organisations together, Bannister argues that camp can be seen as a 'liminal' space where certain 'rites of passage' characterise these informal learning landscapes. Chapter 4, by Peter Kraftl, explores a small but growing number of Care Farms in the United Kingdom that operate, in part, as 'alternative' educational spaces to mainstream schools. Through interviews with Care Farm practitioners, Kraftl teases out the complex understandings of the 'local' within this community of informal educators. The varied types of local connectedness he discusses involve different relationships with the Care Farm's 'constitutive outsides', or 'inside and outside the farm gate'. In Chapter 5, Sarah Mills echoes earlier arguments for a closer interrogation of outdoor *and* indoor spaces of informal education. In her study of the Woodcraft Folk between 1925 and 1975, Mills draws on archival material to consider the ways in which 'nature' (broadly conceived) was utilised not just 'on camp' but through a range of specific arts-based performances within indoor meeting places. In particular, she explores the role of music and dance as part of a wider examination of the pedagogical practices of this British youth movement. Part II, 'Negotiating In/formal Education Spaces', explores some of the multiple sites within which informal education takes place. It highlights the connectedness of informal education *within* formal school spaces to informal education practices taking place *without*. In other words, informal education is often a mobile practice, which travels and may seek to transgress boundaries as much as constitute them, in multiple ways (see Collins and Coleman, 2008). In Chapter 6, Ian Donnachie examines the educational achievements of a social reformer – Robert Owen – whose work has influenced both formal and informal education practices. With particular emphasis upon the relative microscale of the classrooms and playgrounds at New Lanark, Scotland, Donnachie nevertheless demonstrates how Owen's ideas travelled well beyond Scotland, helping to stimulate educational reform both nationally and internationally. In Chapter 7, Stephen Sadlier focuses on Oaxaca City, Mexico, and the pedagogic projects of teachers in response to contemporary governance and rule in the country. He uses the tarpaulin and the tablecloth as both material case studies and metaphors for the extension of informal education beyond the school to small niches carved out in public space. In particular, these material-and-metaphorical spaces – these spatialities – become sites for the expression of love, concern and empathy (cf. Freire, 2008). In Chapter 8, Dena Aufseeser focuses on the child workers' movement in Peru. She explores the potential for informal education with children *outside* formal, mainstream institutions, and especially on the streets where they work. However, she places informal education in a symbiotic relationship with formal education: Peruvian children value formal schooling, but indicate that it is their street work that enables them to attend school and to acquire other, complementary 'life' skills. Chapter 9, by Sophie Bowlby, Jennifer Lea and Louise Holt, explores the attempts to intervene in, manage and regulate the 'socially unacceptable' behaviour of young people with socio-emotional differences. They examine how school teachers seek to 'teach' such young people to make and keep friendships, to develop empathy and to socialise with other 'desirable' children. They argue in particular that the constitution of space-times, where predominant schooling norms are relaxed, may provide an opportunity for young people to develop the above kinds of emotional intelligence, but also reinforce a sense in which they are 'different' from other pupils. Chapter 10, by Kate Edwards, explores how current developments in e-learning may afford the potential for unsettling traditional conceptions of learning space. Drawing on research with school students, she demonstrates how, for instance, the presence of laptops affords a 'liberating' quality for students, which enables greater freedom in their interactions with other young people. She critically conceives of the 'third spaces' of e-learning, emphasising the importance of interaction and dialogue rather than the wholesale transferral of learning resources to online, bite-size repositories.

In Part III, 'Youth Work Spaces', the book turns to the long-standing relationship between youth work and informal education. In Chapter 11, Luke Dickens and Douglas Lonie explore music rehearsal spaces as catalysts for addressing the problems faced by young people living in disadvantaged neighbourhoods. They carefully seek to distinguish between non-formal and informal education, principally because the activities they describe involve a greater measure of planning and structure than most definitions of informal education allow. Drawing on the voices of young people, they articulate a disjuncture between the aims of the non-formal rehearsal spaces in which they worked (inclusion, regeneration) and a sense that for young people the rehearsal spaces afforded an opportunity for informal, collaborative music-making that was unavailable elsewhere. In Chapter 12, Simon Bradford examines the professionalisation of youth work after the Second World War. He examines some of the embodied geographies of youth work, where young people's bodies (and their fitness) were conceived as a key medium for a rapidly developing profession. He also argues that the sequestration of particular leisure and public spaces as the 'proper places' of youth work was key, in particular because these were viewed as settings where young people's capacities to act responsibly could be developed. In Chapter 13, Jean Spence examines the period just after the 1960s and focuses upon single-sex spaces of feminist youth work. Examining the period 1975–85, and through an analysis of contemporary newsletters, conference and research reports produced by feminist youth workers, she discusses how single-sex youth work spaces were viewed as critical to girls' development. She highlights how a key principle of informal education – Freire's 'practice of freedom' – was deployed via activities that sought to raise girls' consciousness about the gender inequalities that led to the marginalisation of women. In Chapter 14, Richard Davies explores some of the wider relationships between youth workers and school teachers through an analysis of the material arrangements of 'the school'. Through a philosophical approach, drawing on his experience as a youth worker in schools in England, Davies argues that co-located working can disrupt the school, its borders and social geography.

Part IV, 'Youth-Led Spaces', brings an explicit focus on spaces of informal learning organised, negotiated and in some cases established by young people themselves. Across a diverse set of geographical contexts (Australia, Spain and two US cities), the authors in this final part of the volume explore the ways in which youth-led schemes and projects are shaped and experienced by a range of young people, in particular through various technologies, materialities and public space. In Chapter 15, Shanene Ditton explores the different practices of a range of young people who seek to challenge the representations, cultural stigma and 'moral panic' surrounding Australia's Gold Coast youth. She outlines processes of youth-led cultural change, drawing on Freire's notion of 'cultural voice' (1970) and through an in-depth analysis of initiatives established by local young people, notably a zine and blog. In Chapter 16, Maria Rodó-de-Zárate and Mireia Baylina offer a rich account of the practices of a youth-led feminist group in Barcelona. Using participatory methods, the authors focus on girls' use of public space for various forms of social action and learning. In doing so, they highlight varied processes and practices of informal education, in particular around issues of self-management, knowledge exchange and empowerment. In Chapter 17, Denise Goerisch focuses on a popular and well-established non-formal youth organisation in the United States – the Girl Scouts. Her study specifically explores the annual fundraiser of Girl Scout Cookie Sales, locating the scheme within wider neoliberal constructions of citizenship and debates surrounding financial literacy. Goerisch draws out the gendered ideologies espoused in the scheme, while importantly exploring how its leadership roles are understood and negotiated by young people themselves. In Chapter 18, Gregory T. Donovan explores young people's consumption, production and governance of social and digital media. In particular, he interrogates shared understandings of privacy, property and security while also examining the varied learning practices surrounding the MyDigitalFootprint.ORG project, drawing on his participatory action design research with the Youth Design and Research Collective in New York City.

Overall, this volume brings together scholars from a range of diverse disciplinary backgrounds to consider the explicit, complex and diverse geographies of informal education. In our conclusion (Chapter 19), we reflect on the possible future directions of academic research on informal education that could be developed around recurring and important themes expressed in this collection.

References

K. Alexander (2009) 'The girl guide movement and imperial internationalism in interwar England, Canada and India', *Journal of the History of Childhood and Youth*, 2, 37–63.
Z. Bekerman, N. C. Burbules and D. Silberman-Keller (eds) (2005) *Learning in Places: The informal education reader* (New York: Peter Lang Publishing).
L. Bondi (1991) 'Attainment at primary schools: An analysis of variations between schools', *British Educational Research Journal*, 17, 203–17.
S. Bunt (1975) *Jewish Youth Work: Past, present and future* (London: Bedford Square Press).
L. Cameron (2006) 'Science, nature, and hatred: "finding out" at the Malting House Garden School, 1924–29', *Environment and Planning D: Society and Space*, 24, 851–72.

I. Cartwright (2012) 'Informal education in compulsory schooling in the UK', in P. Kraftl, J. Horton and F. Tucker (eds) *Critical Geographies of Childhood and Youth* (Bristol: Policy Press).

D. Collins and T. Coleman (2008) 'Social geographies of education: Looking within, and beyond, school boundaries', *Geography Compass*, 2, 281–99.

V. Cook and P. Hemming (2011) 'Education spaces: Embodied dimensions and dynamics', *Social and Cultural Geography*, 12, 1–8.

F. Coussée (2009) 'The relevance of youth work's history' in G. Verschelden, F. Coussée, T. Van de Walle and H. Williamson (eds) *The History of Youth Work in Europe – Relevance for Today's Youth Work Policy – Volume 1* (Council of Europe publishing).

F. Coussée, G. Verschelden, T. Van de Walle, M. Mędlińska and H. Williamson (2010) (eds) *The History of Youth Work in Europe – Relevance for Today's Youth Work Policy – Volume 2* (Council of Europe Publishing).

F. Coussée, H. Williamson and G. Verschelden (eds) (2012) *The History of Youth Work in Europe – Relevance for Today's Youth Work Policy – Volume 3* (Council of Europe publishing).

B. Davies (1999a) *From Voluntaryism to Welfare State. A history of the youth service in England. Volume 1: 1939–1979* (Leicester: Youth Work Press).

B. Davies (1999b) *From Thatcherism to New Labour. A history of the youth service in England. Volume 2: 1979–1999* (Leicester: Youth Work Press).

B. Davies and B. Merton (2009) *Squaring the Circle? Findings of a 'modest inquiry' into the state of youth work practice in a changing policy environment* (Leicester: De Montfort University).

O. den Besten, J. Horton, P. Adey, and P. Kraftl (2011) 'Claiming events of school (re)design: Materialising the promise of building schools for the future', *Social and Cultural Geography*, 12, 9–26.

J. Falk, J. Heimlich and S. Foutz (eds) (2009) *Free-choice Learning and the Environment* (Lanham, MD: AltaMira Press).

M. Fielding and P. Moss (2011) *Radical Education and the Common School: A democratic alternative* (London: Routledge).

P. Freire (2008) [1974] *Education for Critical Consciousness* (London: Continuum).

E. Gagen (2000) 'An example to us all: Child development and identity construction in early 20th-century playgrounds', *Environment and Planning A*, 32, 599–616.

M. Gallagher (2011) 'Sound, space and power in a primary school', *Social and Cultural Geography*, 12, 47–61.

M. Gardiner (2004) 'Everyday utopianism: Lefebvre and his critics', *Cultural Studies*, 18, 228–54.

R. Gilchrist, T. Hodgson, T. Jeffs, J. Spence, N. Stanton and J. Walker (eds) (2011) *Essays in the History of Youth and Community Work: Reflecting on the past* (Lyme Regis: Russell House Publishing).

R. Gilchrist, T. Jeffs and J. Spence (eds) (2001) *Essays in the History of Community and Youth Work* (Leicester: National Youth Agency).

R. Gilchrist, T. Jeffs and J. Spence (eds) (2003) *Architects of Change: Essays in the history of community and youth work* (Leicester: National Youth Agency).

R. Gilchrist, T. Jeffs and J. Spence (eds) (2006) *Drawing on the Past: Essays in the history of community and youth work* (Leicester: National Youth Agency).

R. Gilchrist, T. Jeffs, J. Spence and J. Walker (eds) (2009) *Essays in the History of Youth and Community Work: Discovering the past* (Lyme Regis: Russell House Publishing).

P. Gruffudd (1996) 'The countryside as educator: Schools, rurality and citizenship in inter-war Wales', *Journal of Historical Geography*, 22, 412–23.

K. Gulson and C. Symes (2007) *Spatial theories of education: Policy and geography matters* (London: Routledge).

C. Hanson Thiem (2009) 'Thinking through education: The geographies of contemporary educational restructuring', *Progress in Human Geography*, 33, 154–73.

S. Holloway, P. Hubbard, H. Jöns and H. Pimlott-Wilson (2010) 'Geographies of education and the significance of children, youth and families', *Progress in Human Geography*, 34, 583–600.

S. Holloway and H. Jöns (2012) 'Geographies of education and learning', *Transactions of the Institute of British Geographers*, 37, 482–88.

S. Holloway and H. Pimlott-Wilson (2011) 'The politics of aspiration: Neo-liberal education policy, "low" parental aspirations and primary school Extended Services in disadvantaged communities', *Children's Geographies*, 9, 79–94.

S. Holloway and G. Valentine (2000) 'Spatiality and the new social studies of childhood', *Sociology*, 34, 763–83.

A. James and A. James (2004) *Constructing Childhood: Theory, policy and practice* (Basingstoke: Palgrave Macmillan).

T. Jeffs (2007) 'Crossing the divide: School-based youth work', in R. Harrison, C. Benjamin, S. Curran and R. Hunter (eds) *Leading Work with Young People* (Milton Keynes: OUP).

T. Jeffs (2010) 'The relevance of history in youth work' in F. Coussée, G. Verschelden, T. Van de Walle, M. Mędlińska and H. Williamson (eds) *The History of Youth Work in Europe – Relevance for Today's Youth Work Policy – Volume 2* (Council of Europe Publishing).

T. Jeffs and M. Smith (2005) *Informal Education: Conversation, democracy and learning* (London: Educational Heretics Press).

C. Jenks (2005) *Childhood* (London: Routledge).

R. Johnston, S. Burgess, R. Harris and D. Wilson (2008) ' "Sleep-walking towards segregation'? The changing ethnic composition of English schools, 1997–2003: An entry cohort analysis', *Transactions of the Institute of British Geographers*, 33, 73–90.

C. Katz (2008) 'Childhood as spectacle: Relays of anxiety and the reconfiguration of the child', *Cultural Geographies*, 15, 5–17.

J. Kenway and D. Youdell (2011) 'The emotional geographies of education: Beginning a conversation', *Emotion, Space and Society*, 4, 131–6.

M. King (2007) 'The sociology of childhood as scientific communication: Observations from a social systems perspective', *Childhood*, 14, 192–213.

P. Kraftl (2006) 'Building an idea: The material construction of an ideal childhood', *Transactions of the Institute of British Geographers*, 31, 488–504.

P. Kraftl (2008) 'Young people, hope and childhood-hope', *Space and Culture*, 11, 81–92.

P. Kraftl (2012) 'Towards geographies of "alternative" education: A case study of UK home schooling families, *Transactions of the Institute of British Geographers*, earlyview online DOI: 10.1111/j.1475-5661.2012.00536.x

P. Kraftl (2013) *Geographies of Alternative Education: Diverse learning spaces for children and young people* (Bristol: Policy Press).

P. Kraftl, J. Horton and F. Tucker (2012) *Critical Geographies of Childhood and Youth: Contemporary policy and practice* (Bristol: Policy Press).

C. Lambert (2011) 'Psycho classrooms: Teaching as a work of art', *Social and Cultural Geography*, 12, 27–46.

D. Matless (1998) *Landscape and Englishness* (London: Reaktion Books).

H. Matthews, M. Limb and M. Taylor (2000) The street as 'Thirdspace' in S. Holloway and G. Valentine (eds) *Children's Geographies: Playing, living, learning* (London: Routledge).

S. Mills (2013) ' "An instruction in good citizenship": Scouting and the historical geographies of citizenship education', *Transactions of the Institute of British Geographers*, 38, 120–34.

A. E. Morgan (1943) *Young Citizen* (Harmondsworth: Penguin).

K. Nairn and J. Higgins (2011) 'The emotional geographies of neoliberal school reforms: Spaces of refuge and containment', *Emotion, Space and Society*, 4, 180–6.

C. Philo (1992) 'Neglected rural geographies: A review', *Journal of Rural Studies*, 8, 193–207.

C. Philo (2011) 'Foucault, sexuality and when not to listen to children', *Children's Geographies*, 9, 123–7.

J. Pike (2008) 'Foucault, space and primary school dining rooms', *Children's Geographies*, 6, 413–22.

S. Pile and M. Keith (1993) *Place and the Politics of Identity* (London: Routledge).

T. Ploszajska (1998) 'Down to earth? Geography fieldwork in English schools, 1870–1944', *Environment and Planning D: Society and Space*, 16, 757–74.

T. Proctor (2002) *On My Honour: Guides and scouts in interwar Britain* (Philadelphia: American Philosophical Society).

A. Prout (2005) *The Future of Childhood* (London: Routledge).

J. Pykett (2012) 'Making "youth publics" and "neuro-citizens": Critical geographies of contemporary education practice in the UK', in P. Kraftl, J. Horton and F. Tucker (eds) *Critical Geographies of Childhood and Youth* (Bristol: Policy Press).

L. D. Richardson and M. Wolfe (eds) (2001) *Principles and Practice of Informal Education* (London: Routledge).

J. Spence and C. A. Devanney (2006) *Youth Work: Voices of practice* (Leicester: National Youth Agency).

J. Springhall (1977) *Youth, Empire and Society: British youth movements 1883–1940* (Beckenham: Croom Helm).

M. K. Smith and M. E. Doyle (2002) 'The Albemarle report and the development of youth work in England and Wales', The encyclopaedia of informal education, available at: http://www.infed.org/youthwork/albemarle_report.htm, date accessed 2 February 2013.

M. Tebbutt (2012) *Being Boys: Youth, leisure and identity in the inter-war years* (Manchester: Manchester University Press).

G. Verschelden, F. Coussée, T. Van de Walle and H. Williamson (eds) (2009) *The History of Youth Work in Europe – Relevance for Today's Youth Work Policy – Volume 1* (Council of Europe Publishing).

E. Wainwright and E. Marandet (2011) 'Geographies of family learning and aspirations of belonging', *Children's Geographies*, 9, 95–110.

P. Woods and G. Woods (2009) *Alternative Education for the 21st Century* (London: Palgrave Macmillan).

K. Young (2006) *The Art of Youth Work* (Lyme Regis: Russell House).

M. Zembylas (2011) 'Investigating the emotional geographies of exclusion at a multicultural school', *Emotion, Space and Society* 4, 151–9.

Part I
Nature Spaces

2
Inside-out: Connecting Indoor and Outdoor Spaces of Informal Education through the Extraordinary Geographies of The Boys' Brigade Camp

Richard G. Kyle

Introduction

Scholarly interest in informal education stretches back several decades. Historians were the first to frame this field through studies that described the emergence of organised youth work in the Victorian era (Eager, 1953; Wilkinson, 1969; Dawes, 1975; Springhall, 1977) and charted the trajectory of youth organisations, including The Boys' Brigade (Springhall et al., 1983), Church and Jewish Lads' and Girls' Brigades (Kadish, 1995), Scouts (Warren, 1986; Proctor, 2009) and Woodcraft Folk (Davis, 2000). Only relatively recently have academic geographers begun to write *geographies* of informal education that explore the spatialities of specific youth organisations, such as The Boys' Brigade (Kyle, 2006) and Scouts (Mills, 2013). Yet, despite increased attention on the *geographical* accomplishment (Philo and Parr, 2000) of informal education, to date there has been a tendency to examine indoor and outdoor spaces of informal education in relative isolation, with little consideration of their interconnection (although see Mills, Chapter 5, this volume). This chapter challenges this approach and offers an alternative theorisation of the interrelationship between indoor and outdoor educational environments. It does so through an empirical examination of the practices, purposes, histories and geographies of camping in The Boys' Brigade (BB), a volunteer-led Christian uniformed youth organisation.

Outdoor spaces of informal education, most notably camp and adventure-based education (Sibthorp and Morgan, 2011), have received much scholarly attention, especially in the United States, where 'Summer Camps' have a culturally important role in the physical, emotional and spiritual development of American young people (Yust, 2006; Henderson et al., 2007; Garst et al., 2011). Camps also feature prominently in the organisational memory and current programme of several youth movements, not least the BB, Scouts (Bannister, Chapter 3, this volume) and Woodcraft Folk, as well as the personal accounts of those whose lives these organisations have shaped (Tebbutt, 2012).

In this chapter historical and contemporary reflections from archival research and interviews with current BB leaders (Officers) in Scotland are interwoven to examine the geographies of the BB camp. Initially the BB and the origins of camping in the organisation are introduced. Four key practices and purposes of camping in the BB described by current leaders are then discussed. This segues into the substantive focus of the chapter: writing the *geographies* of the BB camp through the twin metaphor of cocoon and chrysalis. First, as a cocoon – created from virtually nothing and characterised by isolation – camp is considered as a microcosm of practices and performances integral to the indoor materialisation of the weekly meeting. Second, as a chrysalis, camp is a site of metamorphosis from which boys, adult leaders and the affective quality of the indoor weekly meeting emerge changed. In so doing, the chapter contends that the BB camp can be theorised as an *extra*ordinary space of self-development that is both a reflection and extension of its familiar indoor incarnation. Finally, the chapter concludes by suggesting that this theorisation – alert to the crucial and complex ways indoor and outdoor spaces of informal education are locked in continual processes of co-creation – has applicability beyond the BB, and youth work more generally, to elicit nuanced understandings of other indoor and outdoor spaces of informal education.

The Boys' Brigade

Founded by Sir William Alexander Smith in 1883 in Glasgow, Scotland, the BB emerged in an era when there was a 'growing connection between religion and the military' (Springhall et al., 1983, p.25). In 1943 King George VI termed Smith's own marriage of military discipline with religious instruction the movement's 'twin pillars' (Springhall et al., 1983, p.178). These pillars continue to support the BB's work with boys and young men. Despite changes to the activities offered, the uniform worn and the approach to Christian teaching during the organisation's 130-year history, the BB remains a volunteer-led Christian uniformed youth movement with a membership of 60,000 in 1,500 local groups (Companies) across the United Kingdom. Much of the BB's work takes place weekly in a variety of indoor spaces such as church halls, schools and, occasionally, purpose-built BB halls.

However, outdoor activities such as camp also feature, the origins of which are now introduced.

Historical geographies of the BB camp

The year 1874 proved pivotal in the BB's conception. In 1874 Smith participated in the 1873–75 revival of American evangelists Dwight L. Moody and Ira D. Sankey, an event that shaped and strengthened his Christian faith and led to the formation of the Woodside Morning Branch of the Young Men's Christian Association (YMCA) with James Findlay, and later, James Moffat and James and John Hill – brothers who would become Smith's Lieutenants in the first BB company. Almost inevitably given his family's strong military roots (Springhall et al., 1983), in 1874 Smith also enlisted in the 1st Lanarkshire Rifle Volunteers. Volunteer experience undoubtedly informed his instigation of the BB camp. Although history records that Smith was not present at his regiment's first camp in August 1883, he likely joined the regiment at camp in July 1885 (Gibbs, 1986), exactly a year before the first BB camp held in Argyll, Scotland, on 16 July 1886.

For two weeks each year, industrial Glasgow ground to a halt as 'fair fortnight' began. As dawn broke on 'Fair Friday' – the first day of this holiday – the 1st Glasgow BB Company assembled for a 5:00 a.m. roll call (McFarlan, 1982). After a brief inspection, at 5:30 a.m. the march to camp commenced (Gibbs, 1986). Friends and family waved; the band played. To the tune of 'The girl I left behind me' the parade wound its way along West End streets, south towards the River Clyde. Halting at the Broomielaw docks, the company boarded the steamer *Columba* bound for Tignabruaich: 'the unpronounceable spot on the Kyles of Bute' (Peacock, 1954, p.88).

After a short march to Auchenlochan, the 1st Glasgow arrived at their campsite (McFarlan, 1983). This first camp was not, however, held under canvas, as might be expected, but rather in 'a fine public hall' (Gibbs, 1986, p.3). Roger Peacock, one of Smith's biographers, suggests that Smith 'was impelled to make a concession to public opinion' and, particularly, parents who feared that their children would 'catch their death of cold [. . .] be gored by cows, bitten by sheep, stung by wasps and tossed by bulls' (1954, p.84). However hyperbolic this account may be, it contains a modicum of truth: Smith's anxiety around the boys' resilience at least partly accounts for his accommodation choice. 'In many of our Companies', Smith wrote, 'Boys are not strong enough to run the risks of exposure to weather to which life under canvas would subject them' (quoted in Gibbs, 1986, p.3).

It was not until 1888 that the first BB camp under canvas was held by the 1st Newhaven (Edinburgh) Company at Elie in Fife (Gibbs, 1986, p.3). Gibbs records that of the six camps to take place the next year 'two or three' were under canvas (Gibbs, 1986, p.3). Smith, however, continued to err on the side of caution. One of the first articles in the BB's monthly *Gazette* for officers offering 'advice and guidance' about camping 'undoubtedly' written by Smith 'between March and May 1890' (Gibbs, 1986, p.4) notes:

> Boys' Brigade Company Camps have already been held, both under canvas and in halls. There is no doubt that, if favourable weather could be counted upon, a real 'Tent Camp' is the ideal one. The 'Hall' or 'Barn' Camp has, however, many advantages, which make it, while not 'ideal', perhaps the best and safest for the majority of Boys in the Brigade.
>
> (Quoted in Gibbs, 1986, p.4)

Subtle shifts in Smith's own (protective) attitude can be traced, such as the advice offered to officers two years later in October 1892's *Gazette*:

> While our readers will notice that most of the Camps recorded in the *Gazette* are located in a hall or other building, it is becoming very usual to pitch one or more tents, as an adjunct to the more solid structure, while in some cases the whole Camp has been quartered under canvas without any apparent harm having resulted to the Boys.
>
> (Quoted in Gibbs, 1986, p.4)

It did not, however, alter Smith's practice: so acute were his anxieties around the boys' resilience that the 1st Glasgow did not camp under campus until after his death in 1914 (Gibbs, 1986, p.4).

Notwithstanding variation in form, as camping's popularity grew its purpose was increasingly discussed. As part of his Presidential address at the fifth annual BB meeting in Glasgow on Boxing Day 1889, Major James Carfrae Alston commented upon camping's growing popularity. Gibbon added his own assessment of his speech's significance:

> It was now being recognised that camp is the officer's great opportunity. In no other way can a man get to know boys so intimately, or exert such influence over them.
>
> (Gibbon, 1953, p.93)

Exploring this early history of camping in the BB reveals that almost from the first, camp was variously accomplished. Although guidance was offered to officers, no 'model' was proposed and actively policed. Instead, the eventual unfolding of camping practice in the BB was a product of personal attitudes towards prospective campers (e.g., Smith's own 'protective' approach) and the purposes of camping (e.g., to exert influence). On one level, then, this realisation safeguards against a revisionist organisational history that valorises a particular 'ideal' form of BB camp or young Victorian man (and in this sense actively challenges the view that protective attitudes towards young people are a contemporary phenomenon with no historical provenance). On another level, it reinforces the importance of careful and critical examination of contemporary leaders' camping practice and, in particular, how the perceived purposes of camping are achieved in the present. The remainder of this chapter therefore draws upon current BB leaders' accounts of camping to understand contemporary practices and purposes, as a necessary first step to writing its geography.

Contemporary geographies of the BB camp

Practices and purposes

Thirty-three officers from 23 companies across Scotland were interviewed (Kyle, 2006). All 23 companies camped. Expectedly, form did vary: 13 of the 23 companies camped at outdoor centres; the remaining ten used campsites within the United Kingdom. International camps in Germany, France, the Netherlands, and Austria were also reported. Despite variety of form and location, four common purposes of camp emerged:

1. attracting boys within and without The BB company;
2. enabling group bonding and team working;
3. offering opportunities for life-lessons to be taught and learnt;
4. providing opportunities to gain knowledge of self and others.

Attraction

Leaders frequently conceived of camp as a 'carrot':

> They say that they come because they want to go to camp at the end of the year and that's the carrot [...]. They'll put up with all the [laughs] Christian bits and all the bits that they're not that fond of to get their camp.
>
> (Interviewee [I]7)

Yet, camp was considered to do more than simply appease. By providing something for boys to 'look forward to' (I12) with 'real excitement and enthusiasm' (I10) camp was also a subtle disciplinary mechanism ensuring compliance throughout the year by giving boys both 'something to aim for' (I13) and a 'reward' (I2) for hard work.

Camp's allure contributed to leaders' retention and recruitment strategy. 'The camp experience', one leader suggested, 'is an incentive if they were swithering about whether to come back to our BB. I think that could sway some of them' (I5). For another, the timing of camp was essential to its efficacy as an incentive. A camp at the start of the BB year in September instead of at the end of the session in May ensured a smooth transition of boys between two different 'sections' of the company for younger and older boys (I18). Camp also served as a 'recruiting sergeant': 'This year we've started [...] doing [...] more camps and our numbers have risen' (I15).

Esprit-de-corps

Leaders frequently remarked that the camp experience brought boys 'closer together' (I10) because 'they've got to get on with' and 'look after each other' in a 'different way from' the way 'they do when they're in the church hall [or] when they're at home' (I3). Other leaders stressed the importance of communal living as a mechanism to encourage collective responsibility. Responsibility for the group of boys in their tent or dormitory not only 'allows tensions to be sorted out' (I5) but, crucially, introduced the possibility that an individual can 'let the whole team down' (I18). One leader's recollection of a (fictitious) camp conversation provides insightful reflection on the purpose of 'communal living' (I18):

> That they've got to respect other people, they've got to respect that they're part of a team and if they don't do what they're supposed to do they're letting the whole team down. [...] They're in dormitories so again they've got to pull together to make sure their dormitory's tidy; 'well, that's not my mess', 'I don't care whose mess it is, it's your room, collectively it's your room, you all pull together to get it tidied'. I think they learn from that as well. (I18)

Thus, through different tasks (e.g., taking responsibility for their tent) camp is designed to both bind and teach boys how to work together by reconciling differences, recognising strengths and supporting each other. In this way the lessons learned at camp extend throughout life:

> I think for the boys it means they have got to work together. They'll have their duties to do and I think, it's to instil in them that there's certain things you've got to do in life that you maybe don't particularly want to do but if you just get them over and done with you can then move on to the better things. [...] It's about participating, taking the rough with the smooth, there'll be a few knocks, there'll be a few tears, but within that they'll be supported. So just building up that kind of team spirit, camaraderie. (I10)

Life-lessons

Several skills unique to outdoor life (e.g., tent-craft, map- and compass-reading, orienteering and expedition) were considered valuable lessons learned at camp. Although this skill set was considered 'transferable' (I21) – particularly if in later life boys pursued hill-walking or camping as leisure pursuits – through these skills generic lessons were purposefully taught (e.g., teamwork, leadership). Hence, leaders suggested that camp provided opportunities for boys to 'learn some [...] life skills as well' (I20), foremost among which was 'self-reliance' (I5):

> They've not got their parents [...], they have to rely on themselves. It's self-catering, nobody organises their food. [...] What I tend to do is I check to see what they've got [...],'what have you got for your main meal?', 'oh right, ok', and then, unofficially you make sure they get the right stuff, if they bring pot noodles or stuff like that. [...] In the morning [I] make sure that everybody's got a hot breakfast and at night [...] if I see somebody, 'what? give me that, get into this'. [...] You tend to find that they bring their own gear and they do their own thing, but under Big Brother watching you. (I9)

Promotion of 'self-reliance' is not entirely hands-off: it is a lesson, structured and controlled, purposefully designed and micro-managed. In the broadest sense, freedom, in this case to fail, is illusory.

Knowledge of 'self' and others

Camps are, in one interviewee's words, 'a great way of building relationships with the boys when you're away for 48 hours; a good chance to get to know them a lot better' (I10). Repeatedly, leaders suggested that relationships are forged and fortified through constructive chat: 'it's amazing what these wee boys'll tell you when you're away for camp and you've got quality time to sit and blether to them' (I23). Camp conversations revealed boys' social backgrounds, family problems and arguments with peers, allowing leaders to handle these sensitively and work more effectively towards (re)solutions. Conversely – and crucially – discussion also allowed boys to get to know their leaders:

> What's the value? Well I think you get to know [the boys] better. I think that when you meet them in that situation you get to live [with] them, I think you bond with them. You see what makes them tick. Sometimes they see, more importantly, what makes you tick and how you live. So if they see me being polite all the time, cleaning your teeth, washing your cup, saying please and thank you, or having grace or reading the Bible, or [that] we do think charitably, and care for them all the time; there's a Christian witness on a daily basis. (I20)

Recalling historical observations on the importance of camp as a vehicle for influence, leaders' recollections of constructive chat reverberate with Jennifer Robinson's (2000) understanding of the nuanced and negotiated workings of 'noisy' surveillance by Octavia Hill Woman Housing Managers in Victorian London. Drawing on Michel Foucault's theorisation of power as relational, always diffuse, circulatory and potentially productive (Sharp et al., 2000), Robinson (2000) suggests that moral inspection and improvement were effected by Hill and her colleagues through friendship. Simply put, through relationships influence was exerted and imbibed.

Harry Hendrick has written of the BB in similar terms: 'If discipline and religion were central to the BB philosophy, so too was friendship – it was the Trojan horse in which "influence" hid, awaiting its opportunity' (1990, p.161). Hence, time spent at camp building and sustaining relationships is central to the process of shaping boys' lives and development. 'Chat' is the subtle vehicle through which leaders' lives are subjected to scrutiny and boys decide whether or not to imitate their example:

> We can have a big influence over them when they're away from home and they're being with us. [Interviewer: 'Influence in what sense?']. Well, I mean obviously the way we live. (I6)

This process was evident not only between adult volunteers and boys. Devolving responsibility for a group of boys in a tent or dormitory to a senior boy drew older teenagers into a pastoral system underpinned by friendship. Assuming adult roles, senior boys became adult-endorsed role models.

Although leaders stressed the importance of forging productive lines of friendship between individuals (i.e., between boys, between adults and boys), interviewees also acknowledged the importance of boys learning about themselves. Camp encouraged self-knowledge and, in turn, self-discipline. Or, put another way, drawing again on Foucault, camp provides fertile terrain for cultivation of the self (Foucault, 1986) through self-surveillance and self-mastery (Foucault, 1979):

> I think it is about having the time just to be themselves. They're either at home with brothers and sisters or mum and dad, but they can go away and they can stay up all night with their mates the first night, which invariably happens. [...] There's not really any barriers on them there and I think it's about well, they can find out what their own barriers are. And then they fall asleep in their dinner on the Saturday night because they've walked 20 miles but they haven't had any sleep. [...] They learn a bit about themselves, [...] they can find out about themselves, and they can find out I can do this, but I can put limits on it myself. (I1)

Geographies

Although carefully unpacked, leaders' understandings of the practices and purposes of camping have hitherto been considered *a*spatially. Yet, as noted at the outset, the theoretical contribution of this chapter to the *geographies* of informal education is its direct challenge to such aspatial approaches through its focus on the interconnection between indoor and outdoor spaces of informal education. Thus, leaders' conceptualisations of camp as a *geographical* accomplishment (Philo and Parr, 2000) – that is, how the practices and purposes of camp are realised in and through space – are now examined through the twin metaphors of cocoon and chrysalis.

Cocoon

'Basically', one leader remarked, 'there is nothing, it's just a field, it's in the middle of nowhere and I think for city kids that's something very precious' (I8). Indeed, recalling earlier historical observations, for this leader this sense of nothingness distinguishes the indoor and outdoor camp and designates the latter as more effective:

> In the main what we tend to do is we go to outdoor centres. I don't think that's as effective as a traditional camp because I think you have to rely on yourself very much more. I think the boys can see that. If there's staff from the outdoor centre there you're not yourself, you're not running things yourself. While there's nothing wrong with it, to me there is nothing like the traditional week long camp under canvas in a field where you arrive and there's nothing and you have to dig a latrine and things like that. (I8)

At its core a canvas camp is a reconfiguration of outdoor space. In erecting tents and marquees, marking out football pitches and digging latrines (after careful consideration of drainage patterns) a camp comes into being. It is created from practically nothing or very little. A camp's geometry is demarcated to ensure its purposes permeate through not only its activities but also its distinct spatialities. As one leader remarked:

> What we enjoyed this year because we're back under canvas – because the last two years we've been indoors – it was back together because obviously with the canvas we made a square, we had the big football pitch set up outside the square but in the square we had football, tennis going and two benches and the people were more together. The last two years at indoor centres people have broken up and [gone] into their rooms or you couldn't see things because there's walls and doors. Canvas feels like we're back together and everyone was mainly within sight or within hearing distance even if they were in the marquee behind us, so yeah, literally being together. (I24)

Some measure of control over what camp can accomplish is exercised through the command of its geography. And herein lies the root of the preference for the outdoor canvas camp. Indoor spaces are merely inhabited, their spatialities worked around. Outdoor camps are actively configured, their geographies worked through.

Yet, the nothingness from which camp is created is complemented by the emptiness that surrounds it. Geographical isolation isolates boys from their everyday lives and, particularly, its technological trappings, such as televisions, mobile phones and gaming devices. In this way, camp triggers a return to 'simple' (I24) entertainment – board games and 'silly games like port and starboard' (I12) and regress to 'running about and playing boys' (I24). Indeed, it is because 'they can still have access to their radios and hairdryers and other things' that the leader quoted earlier thinks that indoor camps 'don't measure up' to the 'traditional week long camp under canvas in a field' (I8).

Thus, by taking boys elsewhere, removing them from their everyday (material) lives and shielding them, camp is a cocoon in which the purposes outlined above are achieved. Young people's lives are often characterised by time spent in, and shuttling back and forth between, 'cocoons' such as the school, formal (increasingly) private and indoor play provision (Smith and Barker, 1999) and car (Kearns et al., 2003). Conceptually, the cocoon is nothing new; camp could (albeit uncritically) be considered just another cocoon. Yet, at camp sanctioning – rather than curtailing – temporal and spatial 'freedom' is essential to its efficacy as a cocoon:

> Our camp's traditional, quite strict, disciplined, full programme, fewer and short periods of free time, quite different from when I was a boy when you would be left to your own devices for big chunks of the day. In today's world that's just going to either bore the boys or boys are going to get up to mischief, shall we say, so I'm a great believer in having a busy programme. (I24)

Thus, although free time is valued, insofar as it prises open interstices in which the previously discussed 'work' of 'getting to know each other' through constructive chat can take place, leaders often eliminated unstructured 'free time' and replaced it with structured 'free time'. What is provided, then, is 'limited freedom' (I18). Here, one leader's laughter is revealing:

> If I think back on my own experience I looked forward to the summer camps as well, whether it's just you were going away with all your pals and you could do things together on holiday instead of going with your parents. You would be able to choose in your free time what you could do; at least you thought you could anyway [laughs]. I think it's just, a start of a wee first step to a wee bit freedom away from the home. (I10)

Chrysalis

Conceived as a cocoon, camp is a protective space for (self-)development. However, this conceptualisation only partly captures leaders' understanding of camp inasmuch as it highlights the (albeit negotiated) boundaries that 'contain' a process of change, but neglects the change itself. Adding the related metaphor of a chrysalis, however, helps arrive at more complete understanding. Leaders suggested that camp triggered at least three changes.

First, leaders' preconceptions of boys in their company change. At camp leaders perceived that they not only see boys 'in a different light' (I18) but in fact see 'two different boys' (I16). A sense emerged that camp allowed boys to shed their weeknight persona and become the boys they 'are':

> You see them in a different light when they're away. You're not with them just for the two hours, you're with them from the minute they get up to the minute they go to bed. And some of the ones you think were maybe a bit like ogres are actually quite nice boys underneath and they're willing to help people [...], and the ones you think maybe are quite shy and quiet nice wee boys are, when you get them on their own, they're not nice just all the time. (I18)

Second, boys themselves emerge from camp changed. Leaders remarked that boys return 'more confident' (I11) or 'more mature' (I20):

> If you've been away with them their kind of respect, your kudos with them goes up a little bit and they sometimes act in a more responsible, a more mature manner. [...] I think sometimes they take more seriously what you will be telling them, not in a very serious way. I think you can joke easy with them, the relationship becomes more informal, it becomes more relaxed. You've built up a lot of trust, I think, between you and that person. (I20)

Fulfilling the image of a chrysalis, for others, camp is crucial for boys' *emergence*:

> You'll see some who emerge through that. Maybe one or two will surprise you. So you might see some boys maybe shine through that otherwise weren't going to shine so much. (I9)

Third, the affective quality of the company – its 'atmosphere' (Anderson, 2009; Kyle, 2009) – alters:

> It's difficult to put your finger on it, but it certainly feels as if the boys respond better and they feel more focused when they come back, more motivated. When we go away in October you'll find between October and Christmas they're very fired up, enthusiastic. (I13)

Microcosm/Metamorphosis

These reflections highlight how camp folds back into the routine operation of the company on a weekday evening. However, leaders also suggested camp was an out-folding of the company. Through camp certain familiar practices inherent to the company on a weeknight evening were replicated and adapted, and this served to amplify their effect.

To revisit the aforementioned practices and purposes of camp, a varied weekly programme of attractive activities and ancillary events such as competitions with other local companies are designed to recruit and retain boys in the company. Yet, leaders commented that camp is 'more attractive than just being in a church hall on an evening' (I10) and that it is precisely because 'it is so different from their normal programmed Friday night [...] that it's the opposite of it I think that attracts' (I22).

Similarly, the formation of smaller teams of boys in dormitories or tents under the care and charge of an older boy is a 'throwback to their parade [weekday evening meeting] night' (I22) where senior boys assume responsibility for a squad of younger boys.

Moreover, reflecting on the reciprocal process through which leaders accrued knowledge of boys and, conversely, boys learn about themselves and their leaders, interviewees suggested that this occurred in the company, but they also stressed that the extended period of time at camp and the different nature of its constituent activities open up more space and time to be filled with constructive chat. 'Camp', one leader remarked, 'really brings you together a lot more than you would do one night a week [...] because you're with them 24 hours' (I23):

> You can't do it here [in the company], albeit you're here maybe 25 weeks of the year once a week because you're so busy and the programmes so structured, you don't get the time to sit and talk to the boys, really find out about them. But when you're away at camp that's when you do. (I23)

Further, the related infusion of influence at camp is considered more effective, because at camp leaders are unmasked and boys can 'see people up clear' (I8):

> You can meet a kid for five years for three hours a week on a Friday night and not know them half as well as you will when you come back from a BB holiday. Again you're talking about that Christian example [...] that's really where they see it in action. Where the Officers don't just take a prayer at the beginning and take a Bible class every now and again, actually to do that and see their daily lives where they see people up clear, they see people what they're really like, it's seeing people who are living together and are enjoying each other's company. (I8)

Thus, extending the twin metaphors of cocoon and chrysalis still further, camp can, respectively, be considered both a microcosm of the practices and performances integral to the manifestation of the weekly indoor meeting and a place of metamorphosis which alters this indoor materialisation.

As such, the indoor and outdoor spaces of company and camp are inextricably interconnected and locked in a continual cycle of co-creation.

Conclusion

This chapter proposed a simple idea: outdoor spaces of informal education cannot be understood in isolation from their indoor incarnation. Taking the BB camp as a case study, archival and interview data from current BB leaders has been interwoven to conceptualise the BB camp as a cocoon and chrysalis simultaneously. Understood as a cocoon it is a microcosm of the company; the *company* camp is an extension of the familiar company into outdoor spaces. Or, put another way, camp is an *extra*ordinary space: that is, the 'ordinary', familiar and frequently recreated spaces of the company extended infrequently (Kyle, 2009). Captured through the metaphor of a chrysalis it is also a site of metamorphosis: that is, this extraordinary, infrequent outdoor expression of the company folds back into the company, irrevocably altering it.

However, this reading is not limited to the BB camp. Rather, it has wider application to our understanding of other spaces of informal education. Most immediately, reading and comparing the relationship between indoor and outdoor spaces of other volunteer-led youth work organisations such as the Scouts and Woodcraft Folk through this frame is warranted, especially due to the different ethos and practices that underpin these organisations *vis-à-vis* the BB. Here, longitudinal research that follows a cohort of young people or local groups through the indoor and outdoor spaces of informal education would undoubtedly add significant insight to the processes sketched cross-sectionally in this chapter.

An approach centred on the interconnection between indoor and outdoor spaces also likely has applicability even beyond the geographies of informal education to fully comprehend *formal* educational spaces, including the interplay between school, college and university classrooms and outdoor field classes, or indoor spaces in the care or youth justice systems and adventure-based activities often used to support this work. Indeed, the impact and interconnection between outdoor spaces of informal education and other educational spaces (broadly conceived) such as the home would also be fruitful areas for future research. Advancing this work will open up a new area of research that is alert to the acute association between indoor and outdoor educational spaces identified in this chapter. And, arguably, only by doing so will such spaces be understood inside-out.

References

B. Anderson (2009) 'Affective atmospheres', *Emotion, Space and Society*, 2, 77–81.
M. Davis (2000) *Fashioning a New World: A history of the Woodcraft Folk* (Loughborough: Holyoake Books).

F. Dawes (1975) *A Cry from the Streets: The boys' club movement in Britain from the 1850s to the present day* (Hove Wayland).

W. McG. Eager (1953) *Making Men: The history of Boys Clubs and related movements in Great Britain* (London: University of London Press).

M. Foucault (1979) *The Will to Knowledge: The history of sexuality, volume 1* (London: Penguin).

M. Foucault (1986) *The Care of the Self: The history of sexuality, volume 3* (London: Penguin).

B. A. Garst, L. P. Browne and M. D. Bialeschki (2011) 'Youth development and the camp experience', *New Directions for Youth Development*, 130, 73–87.

F. P. Gibbon (1953) *William A. Smith of the Boys' Brigade* (Glasgow: Collins).

M. Gibbs (1986) *Camping in the Boys' Brigade* (London: The Boys' Brigade Archive Press).

K. A. Henderson, L. S. Whitaker, M. D. Bialeschki, M. M. Scanlin and C. Thurber (2007) 'Summer camp experiences: Parental perceptions of youth development outcomes', *Journal of Family Issues*, 28, 987–1007.

H. Hendrick (1990) 'Constructions and reconstructions of British childhood: An interpretative survey, 1800 to the present' in A. James and A. Prout (eds) *Constructing and Reconstructing Childhood: Contemporary Issues in the Sociological Study of Childhood* (London: Routledge).

S. Kadish (1995) *A Good Jew and a good Englishman: The Jewish Lads' and Girls' Brigade 1895–1995* (London: Valentine Mitchell).

R. A. Kearns, D. C. A. Collins and P. M. Neuwelt (2003) 'The walking school bus: Extending children's geographies?' *Area*, 35, 285–92.

R. G. Kyle (2006) *Negotiating Youth Work: Moral geographies of the Boys' Brigade in Scotland* (University of Glasgow: Unpublished PhD thesis).

R. G. Kyle (2009) 'Familiar rooms in foreign fields: Placing the "BB atmosphere" in The Boys' Brigade's recreation Hut, Rouen, France, 1915–1919' in R. Gilchrist, T. Jeffs, J. Spence and J. Walker (eds) *Essays in the History of Youth and Community Work: Discovering the past* (Lyme Regis: Russell House).

D. M. McFarlan (1982) *First for Boys: The story of the Boys' Brigade 1883–1983* (Glasgow: Collins).

S. Mills (2013) '"An instruction in good citizenship": Scouting and the historical geographies of citizenship education', *Transactions of the Institute of British Geographers*, 38, 120–34.

R. S. Peacock (1954) *Pioneer of Boyhood: Story of Sir William A. Smith, founder of the Boys' Brigade* (London: The Boys' Brigade).

C. Philo and H. Parr (2000) 'Editorial: Institutional geographies: Introductory remarks', *Geoforum*, 31, 513–21.

T. M. Proctor (2009) *Scouting for Girls: A century of girl guides and girl scouts* (Oxford: Praeger).

J. Robinson (2000) 'Power as friendship: Spatiality, femininity and "noisy" surveillance' in J. Sharp, P. Routledge, C. Philo and R. Paddison (2000) *Entanglements of Power: Geographies of domination/resistance* (London: Routledge).

J. Sharp, P. Routledge, C. Philo and R. Paddison (2000) *Entanglements of Power: Geographies of domination/resistance* (London: Routledge).

J. Sibthorp and C. Morgan (2011) 'Adventure-based programming: Exemplary youth development practice', *New Directions for Youth Development*, 130, 105–19.

F. Smith and J. Barker (1999) 'From "Ninja Turtles" to the "Spice Girls": Children's participation in the development of out of school play environments', *Built Environment*, 25, 35–43.

J. Springhall (1977) *Youth, Empire and Society: British youth movements 1883–1940* (Beckenham: Crook Helm).

J. Springhall, B. Fraser and M. Hoare (1983) *Sure & Stedfast: A history of the Boys' Brigade, 1883–1983* (Glasgow: Collins).

M. Tebbutt (2012) *Being Boys: Youth, leisure and identity in the inter-war years* (Manchester: Manchester University Press).

A. Warren (1986) 'Sir Robert Baden-Powell, the scout movement, and citizen training in Britain, 1900–1920', *English Historical Review*, 101, 376–98.

P. Wilkinson (1969) 'English youth movement 1908–1930', *Journal of Contemporary History*, 4, 3–23.

K-M. Yust (2006) 'Creating an idyllic world for children's spiritual formation', *International Journal of Children's Spirituality*, 11, 177–188.

3
'Like a Scout Does...Like a Guide Does...': The Scout or Guide Camp's Lessons of Identity

Catherine Bannister

Camping and identity: A history

Camping has been fundamental to the Scouting and Girl Guiding programmes since Robert Baden-Powell first trialled his 'school of the woods', as he later described Scouting (1930, p.74) at an 'experimental Boy Scout camp' in 1907 (Springhall, 1977, p.61). Boys from differing social backgrounds were brought together on Brownsea Island off England's south coast and organised into small semi self-governing groups or 'patrols', spending their days performing what became identifiably 'Scouting' practices: building shelters from natural materials, playing tracking games and gathering around the campfire (Jeal, 2001, p.385). This camp was deemed so successful that the following year Scouting was introduced to British children via the ultimate adventure handbook *Scouting for Boys* (1908). Girl Guiding was a response to girls' demands to participate in the open-air activities their male peers were enjoying. Steered by Scouting's handbook, and wearing makeshift uniforms, girls were already forming patrols and embarking on expeditions before Guiding was officially established in 1910 (Proctor, 2009, pp.4–5).

Camping was the youth organisation's 'greatest attraction', offering escape for urban children from sometimes grim surroundings, and the restrictions of home and school (Springhall, 1977, p.98). Yet Baden-Powell's vision of Scouting as an informal outdoor academy indicates that Scout (and Guide) camps were more than a holiday. 'Tension' existed at the heart of the fledgling Scout movement between the adventures it promised and the 'discipline' and 'moral lesson' it intended to impart (MacDonald, 1993, p.6). Scouting was born out of a 'growing moral panic' over the condition of Britain's young people, and the fate of the nation which rested on their shoulders, says Mills (2009, p.191). If the anxieties over juvenile delinquency which validated the rise of Victorian-era movements such as the brigades were waning by the early 1900s, they were being supplanted by new fears:

that an 'over-civilised' youth weakened by modernity's conveniences was putting the nation and empire at risk (Springhall, 1977, p.57).

'Scouting' was to 'restore...."character" in the modern boy' (Springhall, 1977, p.59), 'character' being shorthand for physical and moral fitness. 'Education... counts in building character and in making men', Baden-Powell stated in the 1930 edition of *Aids to Scoutmastership* (p.51), which contrasts Scouting's 'education' favourably with conventional schooling. Averse to collective 'rote learning' (Warren, 1986, p.239), he stated that true education involved 'drawing out' individual children's innate abilities in the proper location: the 'open and breezy' campsite (1930, pp.45–9). For leaders, camping offered the opportunity to assess boys' characters and act as positive role models. The camp, he wrote, 'gives the Scoutmaster a far better opportunity than any other of getting hold of his boys and of impressing his personality upon them' (1930, p.45).

While Baden-Powell denied that Scouting had a formal 'curriculum', a blend of nature study and survival skills termed 'woodcraft' informed the camp programme. Woodcraft's underpinning philosophy was 'recapitulation theory', which proposed that, as they grew, children lived through humankind's evolutionary history, as some understood it by the turn of the twentieth century: a linear 'cultural' development from savagery to civilisation (Bowler, 1989, p.233). As the bulk of this history was pre-industrial, the countryside constituted the 'savage' child's natural habitat. There they could give their instincts free rein, learning and developing as nature intended (Armitage, 2007). For Hall, modernity had 'kidnapped' children from 'the true homes of childhood' (1920, p. xi).

Baden-Powell appreciated the idea that, by imitating cultures considered primitive within a natural landscape, boys could attain a hardy manliness that would, paradoxically, salvage western civilisation (MacDonald, 1993, pp.132–3). Woodcraft justified Scout practices: 'its rituals and secret codes... following spoor... squatting round a campfire' (MacDonald, 1993, p.133). Camp living also promised immediate results. Bridges' (c. 1909) Scout publication, *Camping Out*, suggests that camp swiftly improved 'character' (p.14):

> It is astonishing how much more tidy and considerate a boy becomes after he has had a week or two of cooking for himself, looking after his own belongings, and keeping his tent tidy.

For the Guides, parallels were drawn between camp living and household maintenance, while nature study reinforced the girl's biological destiny as a mother (Alexander, 2009). Yet Alexander's research into inter-war Guide camps also suggests that they gave girls and women leaders 'a degree of gender freedom' and the space and means to 'try out new identities' (2009, p.115).

Becoming a Scout – or Guide – entailed self-transformation. Through engaging in these organisations' activities, wearing uniform, and learning the promises, laws and language, children developed a movement identity that was also a stepping-stone to adulthood. Academics (MacDonald, 1993; Sundmark, 2009) suggest that Baden-Powell saw Scouting as an 'initiation' into manhood – a position supported by his description of an African coming-of-age ordeal in *Scouting for Boys* (1908/2005, p.152 quoted in Sundmark, 2009, p.117):

> It is a pity that all British boys cannot have the same sort of training before they are allowed to consider themselves men – and the training which we are now doing as scouts is intended to fill that want as far as possible.

The above discussion suggests that the campsite was initially framed as an educational environment for character training, assisting children's development into competent adult citizens. While 'recapitulation theory' has been consigned to history, identity issues still figure in the camp experience, with the site as both a setting and catalyst for transformation. The theory of 'rites of passage' offers a means of interpreting the modern camp experience, for Scouting and Guiding's continuing shared aim of young people's positive personal development places members in a constant transitional state (Buttignol, 2000). This chapter explores camp as a rite of passage, and the campsite as a geographical space *and* 'liminal place' for personal transformation, discussing how the camp's landscape is employed to teach contemporary Scouting and Guiding via their 'focal practices' (Young, 2005, p.43) and to construct movement identities.

Research methods

This chapter draws on fieldwork conducted among Scout and Guide groups in northern England during 2009 and 2010. Some of this data comes from interviews with past and current adult members of both organisations. As some research participants were life-long members, and as my research has a historical dimension, some interviews recorded participants' personal histories and memories. Data also comes from in-house literature and observation sessions at campsites. Two particular campsites, or Outdoor Activities Centres (OACs), served as information for this chapter. Many features typical of these sites – the flagpole and the campfire are obvious examples – are permanent fixed points, allowing some room for generalisations when discussing the ideal-typical site's geography. For despite differences in location and size, the sites' layouts are similar in some regards.

Rites of passage and liminality

Social groups accommodate the shifting statuses of their members through 'rites of passage', ritualised events marking changes in the lives or careers of groups or individuals that carry social implications (Bell, 1997). Van Gennep (1909/1960, pp.10–11) states that rites of passage consist of three sub-sets of ritual: (1) rites of separation divorcing the individual from their former role, (2) transition rituals when the individual crosses the boundary between their old and new identities and (3) incorporation rites when the individual re-enters society in their new guise. 'A rite of passage marks a recognisable cultural change', says Kearney (2009, p.74), noting that a community's ritual performances express its values. Kearney and Bell (2003) observe how the rites of passage model applies to outdoor education generally and camps specifically. Young people move from familiar environments and habitual identity roles to fresh surroundings where they undergo potentially life-changing experiences before returning home, altered by where they have been and what they have done there.

Those undergoing rites of passage are 'liminal' or 'threshold people', their identities ambiguous (Turner, 1969/2008, pp.94–5). Communal liminal identities share common features. There may be a levelling of social status, reflected in a uniform style of dress. Space and property may be shared, precedence may be given to the sacred over the profane and submission to the rule of tradition, incorporating submission by the ritual subjects to the rulings of their instructors, may be accepted (Turner, 1969, pp.106–7).

Liminal spaces are similarly ambiguous and can become spaces of 'inspiration or enchantment' (Davidson, 1993, p.9). Such places gain an aura of 'sacredness'. Durkheim suggests that places or objects deemed sacred are set apart from the 'profane' or workaday. Interacting with the sacred means conforming to prescribed behaviours and avoiding taboos, while around the sacred item grow up 'beliefs, myths... and legends' expressing its character (Durkheim, 1912/2008, p.36). The next section of this chapter considers how these concepts relate to the Scout and Guide camp experience.

The 'Sacred' campsite

Given that camping retains its 'central place in the mythology of Guiding and Scouting' (Alexander, 2009, p.108), the campsite can be seen as a 'sacred' space, its metaphorical boundaries transcending the physical. In the 1930s, one research participant's Scout Troop sang, *'I'm going back to Gilwell as quickly as I can, Back to Gilwell, Happy Land, I'm going to work my ticket if I can'*. They had sat around the campfire, he told me, 'waving their cocoa mugs' and singing about Gilwell – an historic training centre considered UK Scouting's outdoor home – not knowing what, or where, Gilwell was and with little chance of going had they known. Moreover, the camp is conjured up in unlikely locations: A Scout 'campfire leader', who facilitates campfire performances at Scout district and regional camps and events, explained how, through Scouting's indoor campfire tradition, he tries to bring the woods in to children on a hospital ward.

As symbolic storehouses, campsites construct communities through their features and artefacts. At permanent Scout and Guide campsites, or OACs, the entrances, buildings, flags and banners, and the camp shop's souvenirs feature Scout or Guide symbols, slogans or related imagery, reinforcing membership. Symbols may have local or personal significance, subtly instructing site-users in that area's organisational history and recalling past members and leaders. At one OAC, for example, carved stones memorialise leaders who have, in a Scouting euphemism drawn from tracking signs, 'gone home'.

Individuals attribute personal meanings to shared group symbols, writes Cohen, allowing them to feel part of something bigger, while retaining a sense of autonomy (Cohen, 1992, p.18). At the same time, he observes, the fuzzy polysemy of symbols promotes internal group unity, preventing conflict over the precise meanings of hazy concepts. By immersing residents in a symbolic universe, Scout and Guide campsites can create a sense of belonging among members.

Notably, campsites do not have stable identities. Places have multiple purposes and slide between being more or less profane. A footpath, for example, can be a routine path, a prosaic educational tool when covered in tracking signs, a processional route during an opening or closing ceremony or an atmospheric setting for a torch-lit return from the campfire.

The camp as a rite of passage

Rites of passage begin by separating people from their everyday environment, followed by a move into the liminal realm. Although camps usually begin with a formal opening ceremony, separation rites, and the camp itself, can begin with the journey to camp, conforming to Turner's observation that separation rituals can involve physical movement 'from one place to another' (1982, p.25). A former Guide recalling 1980s childhood coach journeys to Guide camp emphasised both the journey's significance and the liminal location of the campsite:

> I think the big thing to me when we went on ... obviously the joy of going up, we didn't go very far but to us it was like the end of the earth.

Entering the camp means crossing a physical threshold. For permanent sites like OACs, this can be a gateway bearing the site's name, an organisational symbol or a relevant image perhaps drawn from nature. Entrances declare that campers are entering movement space where Guide and Scout ways of acting *should* over-ride their off-camp behaviours. While uniform may be reserved for ceremonial occasions on the contemporary camp, larger camps for multiple Scout and Guide groups sometimes issue souvenir scarves to new arrivals, known colloquially as 'neckers'. Featuring the camp's name or logo, they are considered legitimate uniform for this camp only, emphasising membership of *this* community. Young people might also have to forgo personal possessions on camp, such as mobile phones, which would allow their owners contact with the outside world, and their 'off-camp' selves.

In pitching camp, groups divide the land into sacred and profane areas, although the boundaries between these can blur. With tents commonly pitched in a circle or horseshoe formation, with the Union Flag or group standard at the head or centre, a group camp's layout can mirror how Guides and Scouts stand together during ceremonies. The flag becomes a focal symbol, ceremonially 'broken' each morning and finally lowered when a group 'breaks camp'. A sacred object, it cannot touch the floor, and during ceremonies, the ground around the flagpole becomes subject to sacred contagion (Durkheim, 1912/2008; Douglas, 1966/2002). During this time, community members avoid the area unless on ceremonial business, receiving badges or awards, or participating in a new member's investiture, which is a popular campsite ritual and an obvious example of identity transformation.

On camp, young people are encouraged to socialise with campers from their own and other groups, in line with both Scouting and Guiding's emphasis on friendship. 'Camping', explained one Group Scout Leader, is 'a good way of teaching the kids how to live together', adding that it gives leaders a chance to teach group culture:

> ...you do it year on year on year on year, and you pass on the troop history, they can see there's a long history of doing things. And also the troop stories get passed on...

Communal living means negotiating social relationships in the context of the group members' temporary on-site personae, and recognised movement hierarchies. Some leaders suggested that an almost familial relationship between leaders and young members, grounded in respect rather than in obligation, helps children learn. 'They learn stuff from us because we're not their mums, and we're not their teachers,' said one Guide leader. 'They're talking to us about our lives as well.'

Furthermore, social groups have traditionally employed unofficial 'socializing customs' (Beck, 1987, p.3) marking a new member's entry into a group or defining a member's status within it. I learned, through interviews, of individual group customs, existing until relatively recently, which could be interpreted in this context. Two now-obsolete practices were bathing the 'baby' – or youngest Scout on camp – in a baby bath, and 'pegging out', when a young person was pinned to the ground with tent pegs and ropes by their peers. The latter was reserved for 'troublemakers' within one camp community. I heard of one active tradition apparently practised by an (unidentified) group that 'before they go camping will dunk kids in the river . . . ', said a Group Scout Leader. This leader expressed reservations over customary practices which could run 'very close to picking on people' or worry the participants.[1] Yet, if it is performed, the 'dunking' custom could be viewed as a separation ritual, with a physical feature imagined as a symbolic threshold. Recounting her Guide camp experiences, the former Guide quoted earlier explained that young people found their own ways of indicating their status on camp:

> . . . the tents . . . were . . . patrol tents with no ground sheet, so . . . if you were in the end, that was a worse position than being in the middle. So obviously if you were new to the patrol, or new to the camp . . . you . . . always started off on the outskirts, near where the pole was . . . so obviously your sleeping bag was always wet and it was always walked on more times . . .

Landscape and learning

The campsite replicates the countryside, with copses for gathering kindling and shelter-building materials, footpaths to traverse the site and features such as ponds for raft and bridge-building activities. Permanent campsites particularly can offer campers a well-maintained version of the great outdoors, with water literally on tap. On-site activities – from traditional backwoods activities to entertainments such as zip-wires, flight simulators and even ice rinks – are intended to boost children's self-confidence and encourage independent thinking. They also ideally deepen their understanding of the movements' promises and laws, fitting with the liminal period as a time of knowledge acquisition. Observing Cub Scouts (aged between around eight and ten) building shelters at an OAC revealed how knowledge was communicated on site: through allowing the Cubs, who were working in small groups, to experiment, encouraging them to discuss their decisions, suggesting solutions and praising success. They were advised not to take branches from living trees. 'You know better', said their leader or 'Akela', alluding to a body of knowledge specific to, and validating, Cub identity. Similarly, an older member of the party could use a knife 'because she's a Scout', a comment connecting Scout-specific competencies with Scout identity. Akela explained what the traditional activity conveyed to twenty-first-century children:

> . . . it's to teach them that bricks and mortar are just things we've created. . . . It teaches children that things are not just handed to them; that they can make it; they've got to work for it, that things don't cost money. It teaches them basic survival skills, gets them to use their imaginations. It also learns them about sustainability and materials.

A Guide leader suggested that the pace of camp living helped modern Guides to 'slow... down', adding:

> You know how, when you come back from camping and boil the kettle and think 'that was quick'.

The campfire as an identity-constructing performance

Even inside the liminal camp-world, the campfire's location is especially liminal, sited as they often are at the interface between the living zones and wilder places (Mechling, 1980, p.38). Reaching the fire means moving away from relative civilisation to a place of otherness. At some sites, memorials to members and leaders are situated close to the campfire circle, highlighting the location's sacred significance to the camp community. As the campfire leader cited earlier explained:

> ... there's often plaques, and... memorial-type things to people who may have either loved the campfire or had some sort of link to Scouting. And so if someone's passed away... some campfires will often be dedicated to them...

He mentioned some of the factors informing a campfire's setting:

> ... it may be a special place where people think, 'Yeah, this is where it should be'. A lot of it's practical... make sure it's not in the elements, it's quite, sort of... secluded. You're looking for acoustics as well because when you're in the open air your voice just gets lost...

The fire's sacred status means the campfire is not used for cooking, although treats like marshmallows are sometimes toasted on traditional grounds. The fire itself, although a potent symbol and focal point, is not the main event. Its lighting is a cue for the performance which follows. This performance may create feelings of 'communitas', or a temporary, near-spiritual, solidarity (Turner, 1969/2008, p.138) within the group. Furthermore, the campfire can be read as a 'ritual of symbolic reversal' (Cohen, 1992, pp.58–60) which the performers will benefit from by heeding the Scouting lesson of 'playing the game'. This phrase has its roots in the vocabulary of the Victorian public school – of which Baden-Powell was a product – that equated games on the sports field to the game of life (Mangan, 2000). 'Playing the game' meant exhibiting the attributes of 'manliness': a will to succeed, a sense of fair play, team spirit and compassion for the less successful (Mangan, 2000, p.135). Baden-Powell lifted the term for Scouting, notes Mangan (p.203), urging Scouts to 'play the game' in the empire's defence (*Scouting for Boys*, 1908, p.278). For contemporary Scouting, 'playing the game' can mean participating with as much of an impression of cheerful willingness as possible, with the possible subtext that failure to do so is failure to conform to the character of the 'good Scout'.

The campfire requires attendance and audience participation. While coming together around the fire spatially reinforces the unity of the camp community, the isolated setting and restrictive form of the campfire circle makes non-participation difficult. One tactic for engaging with non-participators is to address them directly, albeit gently, or humorously, for not 'playing the game', choosing to talk among themselves or interact with their phones rather than perform songs which require silly voices, silly actions and can feature very mild innuendo, depending on the audience's age. Sometimes, the campfire leader said, you must accept that not everyone enjoys the experience:

> Occasionally you may have to say to a group of children, if you don't want to be here either sit at the back or just tell your leader that you're not interested in being here, but you're disrupting it for everybody else... So there are times when you have to say to certain kids 'play the game', you know.

Yet 'silly' songs can be seen as a necessary part of a reversal of social symbolism, when 'people behave quite differently and collectively in ways which they supposedly abhor or which are usually proscribed' to reinforce group norms and boundaries (Cohen, 1992, p.58). Some of these songs deal directly with Scouting and Guiding. One such song is *Boom-Chicka-Boom*.

Boom-chicka-boom

This call-and-response song holds a fairground mirror up to the Scout and Guide movements, reflecting exaggerated stereotypes back to the audience. The song is lyrically malleable, as traditional songs often are, with the caricatures varying from fire to fire. The campfire leader described how he performs the song:

> I say 'a-boom chicka boom' and the kids reply back to you, and you get them to clap, right? Then it goes 'just one more time'..., 'like a Scout Leader does'. So then I put on this persona of this sort of like, you know, a Scout Leader who's very authoritarian... sort of like staid... And it's very much a stereotype, you know... the female leaders are, like, mumsy and the male leaders are like... patriarchal and stoical. And then... I'll say 'like a Guide does' and I'll say 'Does my bum look big in this?' You know, 'cause it's like vanity... And then I'll get to the Scouts and 'like a Scout does' and I'll just go 'Well I'm not doing that!'... and all the Scouts laugh because that's very much the Scouts.

Campfire songs are 'folk texts' expressing 'ideas and anxieties' potentially too difficult or damaging for discussion (Mechling, 1980, p.50). The campfire leader asserted that these stereotypes already existed, as they do within any group, and that this song brings them into the open. By laughing at exaggerated versions of themselves, Scouts and Guides puncture the power of these stereotypes, which may also allude to complexities in organisational relationships between members of all ages, and issues pertaining to Guide and Scout identities, such as gender. The Scout character is performed as male despite Scouting's co-educational status, for example, while the Guide is ludicrously feminine. But more than that, I suggest that members and leaders witness themselves as they could be if the movement values that influence their behaviour did not exist. Eradicating the positive traits Guiding and Scouting represent conversely draws attention to them, perhaps making members glad to belong to their movements rather than being like the one-dimensional characters of the song (Cohen, 1992; Mechling, 2001).

With the group values affirmed by the ritualised performance (Mechling, 2001 p.54), the campfire moves into its final phase with songs emphasising group togetherness, such as *Campfire's Burning*. They may be sung in the round, each section taking its own part to make a greater whole just as individual members make up the movements, and fade away leaving feelings of solidarity behind. Playing the game has its rewards.

Further thoughts

This chapter interprets the Scout or Guide camp experience as a rite of passage, with the campsite as a crucible of identity transformation. Movement members enter a liminal landscape where they live communally, adopt similar clothing and absorb their movement's cultures through their symbolic surroundings, through Scout and Guide ceremonial performances and activities, and by interacting with sacred artefacts. They may also pass through 'micro initiations' within this larger ritualised context.

The campsite's landscape is critical. Its features and layout demand appropriate actions and attitudes from the campers that vary from setting to setting and are integral to the activities undertaken there. These activities are presented as activities which Guides and Scouts *do*; so to engage in them and learn from them means becoming or being a Guide or Scout. One Guide leader, discussing her group's taste for campfires, said, 'I don't know whether that's more of a "we like this because it's fun", or "we feel this is what Guides should do" '.

While this chapter considers separation and transition rites, incorporation rites are not discussed. Bell (2003, p.47) contends that this stage is where many expeditions presented as rites of passage stumble. Jenkins notes that identity is more than simply a 'name or label', such as Scout or Guide. Its meaning 'lies also in the difference that it makes in individual lives'

(2008, p.99). Bell suggests that rites fail when the home community fails to acknowledge changes in those returning, and to respond accordingly; perhaps, he says, because of western society's tendency to view personal change as a lengthy process. However, he proposes that smaller groups and organisations may have the systems necessary to support rites of passage and recognise members' transformation. Kyle's discussion (Chapter 2, this volume) of camp as both 'cocoon' and 'chrysalis' for children's self-transformation, and his consideration of how an organisation's camps and indoor meetings inform and continually recreate one another, may provide a means of exploring how this final phase is recognised and acted on by youth movements returning from camp.

Acknowledgements

I am very grateful to my research participants within Scouting and Girl Guiding past and present, and those in the Department of Sociological Studies at the University of Sheffield, including my supervisor Prof. Richard Jenkins, for their invaluable assistance with this research project.

Note

1. Scout Association members are subject to its *Policy, Organisation and Rules (POR)*, which incorporates the movement's Child Protection and Anti-Bullying policies (Scout Association, 2012).

References

K. Alexander (2009) 'Similarity and difference at girl guide camps in England, Canada, and India' in N. R. Block and T. M. Proctor (eds) *Scouting Frontiers: Youth and the Scout movement's first century* (Newcastle Upon Tyne: Cambridge Scholars Publishing).

K. C. Armitage (2007) ' "The child is a born naturalist": Nature study, woodcraft Indians, and the theory of recapitulation', *The Journal of the Gilded Age and Progressive Era*, 6, 43–70.

R. Baden-Powell (1908) *Scouting for Boys: The original 1908 edition*. Elleke Boehmer (ed.), 2005, (Oxford: Oxford University Press).

R. Baden-Powell (1930) *Aids to Scoutmastership: The theory of scouting for scoutmasters*. Revised edn (London: Herbert Jenkins Ltd).

E. Beck (1987) 'Socializing customs in the castle market community', *Folklore*, 98, 3–10.

B. Bell (2003) 'The rites of passage and outdoor education: Critical concerns for effective programming', *Journal of Experiential Education*, 26, 41–9.

C. Bell (1997) *Ritual: Perspectives and Dimensions* (Oxford: Oxford University Press).

P. J. Bowler (1989) *Evolution: The history of an idea*. Revised edn (Berkeley; Los Angeles; London: University of California Press).

V. Bridges (c. 1909) *Camping Out*. 2nd edn (London: C. Arthur Pearson Ltd).

M. Buttignol (2000) 'Standing on the bank of the tenure-stream and helpful brownies: Two initiation experiences', *Teaching Education Quarterly*, Spring edn, 145–60.

A. P. Cohen (1992) *The Symbolic Construction of Community* (London: Routledge).

H. E. Davidson (1993) 'Introduction' in H. E. Davidson (ed) *Boundaries and Thresholds: Papers from a colloquium of the Katharine Briggs club* (Stroud: Thimble Press).

M. Douglas (1966/2002) *Purity and Danger* (London: Routledge).

E. Durkheim (1912) *The Elementary Forms of Religious Life*, translated by C. Cosman, 2008 (Oxford: Oxford University Press).

A. van Gennep (1909) *The Rites of Passage*, translated by M. B. Vizedom and G. L. Caffee, 1960 (Chicago: University of Chicago Press).

G. S. Hall (1920) *Adolescence, Vol I.* (New York and London: D. Appleton and Company).

T. Jeal (2001) *Baden-Powell* (New Haven and London: Yale Nota Bene).

R. Jenkins (2008) *Social Identity.* 3rd ed. (Abingdon: Routledge).

P. J. Kearney (2009) 'The Barretstown experience: A rite of passage', *Irish Journal of Sociology*, 17, 72–89.

R. H. MacDonald (1993) *Sons of the Empire: The frontier and the Boy Scout movement, 1890–1918* (Toronto, Buffalo, London: University of Toronto Press).

J. A. Mangan (2000) *Athleticism in the Victorian and Edwardian Public School: The emergence and consolidation of an educational ideology* (London: Frank Cass Publishers).

J. Mechling (1980) 'The magic of the boy scout campfire', *Journal of American Folklore*, 93, 35–56.

J. Mechling (2001) *On My Honor: Boy Scouts and the making of American youth* (Chicago: The University of Chicago Press).

S. Mills (2009) 'Youth citizenship and religious difference: Muslim scouting in the United Kingdom' in N. R. Block and T. M. Proctor (eds) *Scouting Frontiers: Youth and the scout movement's first century* (Newcastle on Tyne: Cambridge Scholars).

T. M. Proctor (2009) *Scouting for Girls: A century of girl guides and girl Scouts* (Santa Barbara, California; Denver, Colorado; Oxford, England: Praeger).

The Scout Association (2012) *Policy, Organisation and Rules* (London: The Scout Association), http://members.scouts.org.uk/documents/POR%20September%202012.pdf, date accessed 18 March 2013.

J. Springhall (1977) *Youth, Empire and Society* (London: Croom Helm Ltd).

B. Sundmark (2009) 'Citizenship and children's identity in *The wonderful adventures of nils* and *scouting for boys*', *Children's Literature in Education*, 40, 109–19.

V. Turner (1969/2008) *The Ritual Process: Structure and anti-structure* (New Brunswick: Aldine Transaction).

V. Turner (1982) *From Ritual to Theatre: The human seriousness of play* (New York: PAJ Publications).

A. Warren (1986) 'Citizens of empire: Baden-Powell, scouts and guides, and an imperial ideal' in John M. Macken (ed.) *Imperialism and Popular Culture* (Manchester: Manchester University Press).

K. Young (2005) 'Curriculum of imperialism: Good girl citizens and the making of the literary educated imagination', *Journal of the Canadian Association for Curriculum Studies*, 3, 41–53.

4

'Alternative' Education Spaces and Local Community Connections: A Case Study of Care Farming in the United Kingdom

Peter Kraftl

Introduction

This chapter focuses on education spaces that are marked as 'alternative'. Arguably, this focus is important for any book on informal education. Most scholars accept that informal education can happen in many settings: from formal learning spaces like schools to voluntary organisations, youth clubs, homes and neighbourhood streets (Falk et al., 2009). However, in this chapter, I ask what happens to the concepts, practices and spaces of informal education when one examines contexts that are designated *for* learning, but which are not part of formal education provision *per se*? In posing this question, I am referring to forms of 'alternative education' provision that constitute a small but growing context for children's learning – at least, in the United Kingdom. In order to offer one response, I focus on selected examples from the rapidly emerging UK Care Farming community.

The first section of the chapter summarises academic research on alternative education, before introducing Care Farming in the United Kingdom. It then examines some relatively detailed stories of individual Care Farmers' experiences. Drawing on interviews with Care Farm practitioners, I argue that Care Farms present an internally differentiated but indicative series of alternative education spaces, in two ways. First – despite their name – most Care Farms provide learning experiences and *not* 'care for' the children and other clients with whom they work. Very often, those learning experiences can be characterised *as* informal education. Second, important research has shown that alternative education spaces are seldom elitist, privatised, isolationist enterprises, often instead seeking some kind of engagement with their constitutive 'outsides' (Ferguson and Seddon, 2007; Woods and Woods, 2009). Yet, less attention has been paid to the ways in which alternative education spaces are multiply embedded within and connected to their *local* communities, specifically. As I will show, each case study Care Farm imagines and relates to its 'local' community in particular ways. My second and main argument will therefore be that these forms of local connection are fundamental to, and constitutive of, informal education at Care Farms.

Alternative education and care farming in the United Kingdom

Definitions of alternative education vary with context. In the Minority Global North, the best definitions focus on education institutions located outside 'the main conventions of publicly funded school education as generally understood in Western countries' (Woods and Woods, 2009, p.3). Commonly, alternative education spaces are demarcated not only by their financial or legislative separation from the 'mainstream' but by their basis in knowingly alternative, often innovative pedagogies, spiritual beliefs and philosophies (Sliwka, 2008). This means that there is enormous variation in the kinds of approaches that can be labelled alternative: in the study on which this chapter is based alone, the sample included Homeschooling, Human-Scale Schooling, Steiner Schooling, Montessori Schooling, Democratic Schooling, education-focussed spiritual communities and Forest Schooling, as well as Care Farms. In supplementing the above definition, therefore, my research has drawn upon a range of United Kingdom-based alternatives that partially (or usually, wholly) replaces attendance at mainstream schools.

According to my own secondary research, I have calculated that around 5 per cent (400,000) of the United Kingdom's compulsory-school-age-children (4–16) receive some kind of alternative education, whether part- or full-time (Kraftl, 2013). More importantly, the number of alternative education *providers* increased rapidly in the first decade of the twenty-first century. For instance, the number of Forest Schools increased from zero in the mid-1990s to 140 at the end of the 2000s (O'Brien, 2009) – and stood at over 200 at the time of the publication of this text. The UK Care Farming sector has seen a similarly impressive rise to prominence. While Care-Farm-like organisations have existed for decades in the United Kingdom, there were 76 *registered* Care Farms in the mid-2000s (Hine et al., 2008), but by early 2012, I calculated there were over 180 (taken from www.carefarminguk.org).

Academic research on alternative education has tended to be quite patchy, and often confined to education studies (for a comprehensive review, see Kraftl, 2013). It has also tended not to keep pace with the development of alternative education spaces indicated above. For the purposes of this chapter, three features of this research stand out. Firstly, significant attention has been paid to the stated *role* of alternative education spaces within the broader societies in which they are situated (Ferguson and Seddon, 2007). Thus, Woods and Woods' (2009) neat categorisation of the goals of alternative education organisations divides them thus: those that seek to *separate* themselves from the mainstream; those that seek *engagement*, especially with governments and/or funding agencies; and those that articulate an *activist* mission, aimed at engendering wider social change (also Fielding and Moss, 2011). Secondly, significant research has focused upon the internal workings of alternative education spaces. Most frequently, this research has examined processes, practices and inter-personal relationships through which educators seek to accomplish their pedagogic goals (on spirituality, classroom practice and Steiner schooling, see Oberski, 2011; on child-led learning in homeschooling, see Neuman and Aviram, 2003; Kraftl, 2013). The present chapter builds on both of the above strands of work. On the one hand, it seeks to add detail and complexity to conceptualisations of 'engagement' between alternative learning spaces and their constitutive outsides. It does so with particular regard to diverse forms of connection that Care Farmers perform on an often daily basis with their local communities. On the other, it examines how those forms of local connectedness are intrinsic to, and constitutive of, the kinds of informal learning that Care Farms promote 'inside' their organisations.

This chapter also makes a final contribution, which relates to a third feature of alternative education research. Aside from a few exceptions, there are virtually no studies of alternative education by *geographers*, nor of the role of space/place (exceptions include Kraftl, 2006; 2013; Cameron, 2006; Hanson Thiem, 2007). There is a parallel with the relative dearth of research by geographers on informal education (for an important exception, see Mills, 2013). Moreover, there have been few analyses that place alternative and informal education alongside one another (for a similar argument on non-formal education, see Dickens and Lonie, Chapter 11, this volume). Often, it is assumed that some forms of alternative education are informal somehow, because they value 'useful' forms of learning from everyday situations. This chapter's modest contribution to this large lacuna is to stress the role of spatial scale – the local scale – in the conceptualisation and practice of particular forms of informal education within and beyond the boundaries of individual Care Farms.

Care farms in the United Kingdom

As previously indicated, the number of UK Care Farms has increased dramatically since 2000. Care Farms are more established in other European countries: in the Netherlands, where the practice arguably originated, there are over 1,000 farms (Hassink et al., 2010); it is also popular in Belgium, Italy, Austria and some Scandinavian nations (Haubenhofer et al., 2010). The most straightforward definition notes that 'care farming is defined as the use of commercial farms and agricultural landscapes [...] for promoting mental and physical health, through normal farming activity' (Hine et al., 2008, p.1). In the United Kingdom, one can schematically divide between two types of farm. Firstly, conventional working farms of any type (e.g., arable, dairy) that have diversified away from their core business to provide Care Farming activities. Secondly, farms – often smaller, often located in cities – built with the express aim of becoming a Care Farm (although including other facilities, such as play and Forest School). Care Farms of either type tend to provide for a range of 'clients' (to use the sector parlance): from young people with emotional and behavioural difficulties to children and adults with special educational needs, and from school groups on day-long visits to recovering criminals or drug-users.

There are three broader influences upon Care Farming as it is practiced in the United Kingdom. The first forms part of neoliberal imperatives to transfer the responsibility for care from state institutions (like residential homes) to community organisations and families: the so-called socialisation of care (Hassink et al., 2010, p.423). The socialisation of care implies that those individuals who had previously been incarcerated in caring institutions receive care within the 'normal' spaces of everyday life. However, in practice, this has given rise to a series of new, specialist sites dedicated to providing therapy, work and life-skills experiences – including Care Farms. Secondly, notwithstanding the gradual de-institutionalisation/privatisation of care, there remains an *indirect* link between the State and organisations like Care Farms. In the United Kingdom, many Care Farms receive referrals (and attendant funding) from education authorities, social services, prisons and other statutory service providers. The third influence relates to the understandings of 'care' adopted by Care Farmers. These tend to follow the European (and especially Dutch) model of 'green care' (Hassink et al., 2010), whereby care is understood twofold: to refer to the therapeutic benefits for a client of caring *for* an animal (e.g., grooming or mucking out) or plant (e.g., potting on small plants); and to refer to the resultant habitual changes that might allow that person to better socialise with – and care for – their peers (Berget and Braastad, 2008).

Notwithstanding these three influences, UK Care Farms are diverse. While most Care Farms are affiliated with a UK-wide charity that provides advice and guidance (www.carefarminguk.org), there exists no regulatory body. In addition, Care Farmers come from varied backgrounds – from school-teaching to adult social care, and from business careers to farming itself. However, from my study of ten UK Farms, I observed a tendency to combine several kinds of activities, including maintenance work (repairing fences, pens or ditches); animal care (grooming, feeding); 'nature' experiences (pond-dipping, preparing wildlife areas); horticulture/market gardening (tending, cooking); adventure play; interaction with public visitors; and educational visits by schools.

There has been a dearth of academic research on Care Farming, especially in the United Kingdom. What research does exist outside the United Kingdom has tended to focus on the therapeutic outcomes of Care

Farming – how *care* is provided and its (likely) benefits (Berget and Braastad, 2008). There has been some limited acknowledgement that forms of eco-therapy and Care Farming could be considered 'alternative education' (Hine et al., 2008, p.248): that Care Farms provide *learning* experiences as much as care. However, beyond this assertion, there have been few attempts to crit-ically interrogate the kinds of learning that take place. This is all the more surprising given that – as I detail later – most Care Farmers see themselves as providing learning experiences as well as care.

In order to address the above gaps, I undertook research at ten Care Farms as part of a much larger project on geographies of alternative education (Kraftl, 2013). I visited each farm for between one and three days. Data col-lection took various forms, including a guided tour with farm managers; in-depth, semi-structured interviews with farm managers and employees (14 in total); semi-structured interviews with clients/learners (five in total); informal conversations with groups of clients/learners (two in total).[1] The guided tours and semi-structured interviews were tape-recorded, transcribed and subject to thematic data analysis. Clearly, the above research effort is relatively small-scale, as it formed part of a much larger body of research at nearly 60 alternative education sites. However, these methods yielded some rich qualitative insights. In particular, interviews with managers and employees provided detailed case studies, which illuminated some of the diverse ways that Care Farmers view and deal with their local communities in the provision of informal education.

Informal education inside and outside the farm gate: Care Farming and the construction of local learning communities

A key part of the definitional logic of 'alternative' education spaces is that they purport to do something separate from the 'mainstream'. However, as Woods and Woods (2009) prudently point out, this does not mean that alternative education organisations seek to separate *themselves* from either mainstream care/education institutions or wider publics who surround them. Developing Woods and Woods' contention that many providers actu-ally seek to engage the mainstream, I have argued elsewhere that alternative education spaces are constituted through carefully orchestrated processes of connection and disconnection, with *multiple* mainstreams (Kraftl, 2013). These mainstreams can include school inspectors, teacher training, National Curricula and so forth. But they can also include the local communities which are situated proximate to alternative education spaces. The rest of this chapter presents a critical analysis of the multiple ways in which Care Farmers understand and deal with their local communities, specifically in relation to the kinds of informal education that take place at Care Farms. I focus on four themes: enrolment of new clients, reducing stigma, being there 'for' the local community, local responsibilities. In each part of my analysis, I use a detailed narrative from one of four farms to bring each theme to life.

(Informal) education and the enrolment of new clients: Banbuck Farm, Scotland

Banbuck Farm is a purpose-built, 15-acre Care Farm situated in the countryside outside a small Scottish city. Tony, its owner, was a science teacher in southern England before moving to Scotland to set up his farm. Tony is typical of many Care Farmers in that – despite running a 'Care' Farm – he foregrounded the *educational* experiences that his farm provides:

> I insist that we are an educational centre. Because everyone who comes in has to come for a purpose. [...] There have to be targets, and we report on them [...] we do not provide care. [...] If someone needs care, they come with a carer. [...] Everyone who comes has to be able to make progress in some social, academic, formal or informal way.

Banbuck has a variety of different spaces: an indoor classroom within an ecological building; a kitchen garden; a small woodland with outdoor musical instruments; a wildlife area; animal enclosures with chickens, rabbits, cows and sheep; various sheds for music, relaxation and informal, one-to-one learning sessions. Tony referred to this collection of spaces as a 'tool-box that can be used and accessed for different purposes' – again, fairly typical of how many Care Farms seek to combine several kinds of spaces to provide diverse learning experiences. While carefully managed, these spaces are meant to work as relatively faithful representations of everyday life and work on a 'normal' farm – a 'real-world education', as Tony puts it.

I have argued elsewhere that this approach to education views learning as immanent to the spaces of everyday life (Kraftl, 2013); that is, where everyday *spaces* are overflowing with learning potential *because* of their very ordinariness. In many ways, this is an extension of common wisdom about informal education, which is often conceived as flowing imminently from the everyday concerns and social positioning of learners (Jeffs and Smith, 2005). A subtle but important difference is that many informal educators appear to prefer situations where there is less concern for or control over the layout of a learning space – where the environment is contrived as little as possible (Cartwright, 2012). Yet the Care Farm is a little different. It *is* – especially in cases such as Banbuck – a contrived space, albeit one that looks very different from a school classroom. It is not – *quite* – the same as an experience of informal education that is contingent and emergent from the interests of a learner at a place and time defined by them, and which could, arguably, take place *any*where. A Care Farm is a *semi*-formalised space, wherein the activities and spaces in which a young person engages are set out in advance: Tony's 'tool-box' is not limitless in scope, and was never meant to be. Yet it still represents a suite of activities from which young people may choose and wherein they can engage in the kinds of 'realistic', everyday farming work so important to the definition of Care Farming (Hine et al., 2008).

Bearing in mind the above, it should be recognised that, as an alternative *education* space, Care Farms offer a subtly different brand of informal education than that taking place in either school environments (Cartwright, 2012) or youth work settings (see Part III of this volume). For, while contriving a series of everyday-like, managed spaces in which learning can take place, Care Farms offer learning experiences that still resonate with an important tenet of informal education: *dialogue* (Richardson and Wolfe, 2001). Often working on a one-to-one basis, adult practitioners engage young people in 'everyday' tasks in order to foster conversation and to recalibrate young people's disposition to the social world. The 'tool-box' approach is key to this dialogical process: Banbuck seeks to offer a series of micro-spaces, one of which, Tony told me, will feel 'safe' enough for a young person to enter into a trusting conversation with an adult (Jeffs and Smith, 2005): 'it's very much talk to them [young people], ask them why they're here, where are they starting from? It's very much individual'. Another practitioner at Banbuck, Clive, told me of the importance of smaller spaces like sheds and shelters 'for chilling out: they're pressure valves'. While limited in several ways (as noted above), Clive explained how these spaces nevertheless engendered conversations resonant with informal educators' practices. For instance, one severely bullied teenage girl, who was at risk of dropping out of school, had found the farm (and a particular shed) a safe space, in which she was allowed to be herself in her conversational interactions with adults. As Cartwright (2012, p.157) puts it, '[c]onversation involves immediate responses – saying things in the heat of the moment and thinking out loud', and thus requires a space in which trust and mutual respect can be fostered (Jeffs and Smith, 2005). Ultimately, Clive told me, in feeling safe, the girl in question was enabled greater awareness of both her own failings and of her social positioning with regard to her peers in school, so that she eventually returned to school. This is another central goal of informal education: to use dialogue to foster critical awareness of an individual's position within relations of power or oppression (Freire, 2008).

Thus far, I have argued that Care Farms like Banbuck offer a particular brand of informal education in an alternative, life-*like*, but nevertheless semi-formalised space. The careful management of that space is, I have suggested, a fundament *for* informal education. While I could explore these issues in considerably more depth, I want in the rest of this section to focus elsewhere. For, the geographies of education at Care Farms like Banbuck extend beyond the farm gate to the ways in which they are positioned relative to their local communities, however defined.

Care Farms are not educational institutions where young people spend prolonged periods of time. In fact, they may attend for one–two days a week for six weeks before returning to school, college, work or training. They are (at least for younger clients) a temporary, liminal space – and as such cannot be understood outside of the local families, communities and/or institutions with which they are related. Banbuck was typical of this in-between-ness, situated, as Tony puts it, 'somewhere between home and school [...] where we want people to be comfortable and happy, but it's purposeful'. Later on, I will indicate how other Care Farmers imagine themselves in similar but subtly different ways. But here, I want to highlight how the relational positioning of a Care Farm *within* locally scaled geographies of family, community and statutory institutions is crucial to the internal workings of informal education on the farm, at which I hinted above.

The first point, most evident at Banbuck, relates to interaction with local families. Banbuck receives its clients through various routes, including referrals from the local Education Authority. However, having experienced Banbuck, Tony recalled how those parents who saw a positive response from their offspring suggested they continue:

> So this Mum said, my son has direct payments [State funding for parents to organize education for their child], we'll pay. I said, I don't want to make profit. But she said no, from our point of view, this is good for our son. We'll pay. Don't feel guilty. He was our first person. So suddenly we had more, paying fees, mainly through word of mouth. I felt awful, it took me years to get over the charging fees. I'd spent years in public service, and it's a different mindset. But it means employing people has become more reliable.

Thus, through word of mouth, Banbuck built up a local client base of families who were willing to pay for their children to attend. Tony's experience – and his feeling about taking money – represented for him a difficult set of practical, pedagogical and moral decisions about how he wished to position his farm within the local community. He had struggled to make the Local Authority see the value of Banbuck's work because, he told me, the latter had found his brand of education 'too nebulous', and did not fully appreciate his non-linear, informal, 'tool-box' approach. Meanwhile, as evident in the above quotation, he had struggled with how to position the farm as a business while retaining a public service mission. Ultimately, Tony has created a kind of social enterprise business model (although not his words) – which emerged through contingent sets of *local* relations: in the negotiation between active demand from local families, interaction with the Education Authority and his personal beliefs about public service and education.

Banbuck, then, represents just one example of how Care Farms position themselves locally. In the remainder of the chapter I turn to three further examples of how Care Farms elsewhere in the United Kingdom have somehow positioned themselves 'for' the local community. As I will demonstrate, in its educational work, each of the three farms uses a similar model of informal learning to Banbuck. However, each represents a different example of how a Care Farm might relate to its local community.

Reducing stigma: Hunters Farm, southern England

Hunters Farm is one of the oldest Care Farms in the United Kingdom – in fact, pre-dating the common adoption of the term. At 52 acres, it is much larger than Banbuck. It has always taken adult clients referred from the Local Authority who have ongoing learning disabilities. Some clients work at the farm every day for extended periods – in a few cases over 30 years. However, since 2000, the farm has increasingly taken younger clients (usually aged 16–18) and school-leavers. The farm offers a wide range of activities with paddocks and pens for farm animals, an extensive plant nursery and tea room, generally open to public visitors (on which more below). As Yvonne, one of the managers pointed out, '[p]eople who come here see this as coming to work. But the work we do here is therapeutic too [...] grooming, barrowing, potting up plants, mixing compost – can have both elements. The touching, the smells, the sounds.' Significantly, however, the *educational* role of Hunters Farm has gained in importance. Thus, these tactile, sensory elements of therapy are retained, but recast as elements of learning:

> Historically, people were placed here and stayed here. [...] The aim is now, they get what they want from us, and they use it as a pathway, then they move on. We do [...] look at their progress. At the moment, it's informal learning. But that's [more formal] the way we want it to be in the future. Have an aim, come in, support them, and an exit point.

Yvonne's description of learning resonated strongly with Tony's at Banbuck. He too had wrestled with the pressure to formalise the kinds of learning that were happening at his farm. Yvonne, however, was more certain that learning would become more formalised, managed and targeted in future.

A key part of the (currently informal) learning experience at Hunters Farm is the acquisition of communication/social skills, with the aim that some clients will become employable. These skills are honed in at least two ways. Firstly, through the designation of what Yvonne called 'a working ethos' – a timetable, communal tea-breaks and responsibility for completing tasks. Secondly – and of more importance for this chapter – through interaction with public visitors from the large town a couple of miles away. Most of the farm's clients spend time working at the entrance gate (visitors must pay a small entrance fee), in the nursery shop, tea room, or interacting informally with visitors while working. Arguably, a broader – but related – process of informal learning occurs through these interactions.

At the shop, we employ an adult with learning difficulties [...] and he's paid. It has to be as realistic as possible, whilst still providing the service we provide and safeguarding our clients. And it's where they pay an entrance fee. And it's important to have that [...] customer interaction – it could be formal in the shop, or informal in the car park. The community come to us, not us going out and about. It helps reduce stigma, and gets different groups of people together who never would have met. Everyone learns something who comes here, even though we never set out for that to happen (Yvonne)

The fact that Hunters is a Care Farm recedes somewhat into the background here. When considering how the farm is positioned *locally*, it is possible to see the farm as the hub of a community of learning. As Yvonne observed, learning can take place in multiple ways, deliberately or by chance, through diverse inter-personal interactions. Perhaps young children will learn about care of farm animals from an informal conversation with a client; perhaps clients will gradually acquire communication and service skills through taking entrance fees; most significantly, perhaps the very openness of the farm, and the possibility for encounter between clients and visitors, will help to reduce stigma.

On the one hand, Hunters Farm can be positioned as a working example of the socialisation of care, wherein attempts to deinstitutionalise and un-mark individuals with learning disabilities are couched in environments that are as 'naturalistic' as possible (Hassink et al., 2010). On the other, the implications for informal (as well as increasingly formalised) *learning* should not be understated. The central implication is that learning inside the farm gate is held in an inseparable relationship with learning without. It matters, profoundly, that different kinds of learning and learners come together at the farm. As an 'alternative' learning space, Hunters Farm has a permeable boundary that is controlled (for safeguarding reasons) but which is as open as possible. In this way, the tactile, *micro*-scale, therapeutic forms of learning that occur through turning soil and grooming animals are reinforced through the positioning of the farm as a learning space for the *local* community beyond the farm gate – and vice-versa.

Being 'for' the local community: Heathermount Farm, English Midlands

Opened in the mid-1980s, Heathermount Farm is one of several very small 'city farms' in the United Kingdom. It comprises a couple of acres and is located in the suburb of a large city in the English Midlands, between two low-income housing estates. Like Hunters Farm, Heathermount has several different areas, but concentrates more on animals than horticulture. Unlike Hunters Farm, it has a more diverse client group: from teenage schoolchildren on work experience to Education Authority referrals of children at risk of being excluded from school, and from children with special educational needs to adults with a range of disabilities. But of most significance to this chapter is the way Heathermount seeks to be as open as possible to *unexpected* visitors from the local community. Like Hunters Farm, Heathermount has increasingly turned its attention to its educational role, and done so through an explicit mission to constitute a resource for the local community. Significantly, the definition of the 'local' sccale has *expanded* over time to extend beyond the two most proximate housing estates to the entire northern suburb of the city. As Ursula, the Farm manager, stated, this happened for various reasons:

> As the years have gone by, it's spread further afield, particularly on the educational side. And that's because several other facilities around here have got more expensive. So we've tried to be as cost-effective as we can. For lower income groups. And that means we're literally open as a farm. There's no-one on the gate, and no entrance fee. It's a visitor problem more than anything else. On a sunny day, we have visitors with alcohol. We can set the standard with the user group, not the public. You deal with it once it's here. You have to start from being welcoming – you can't have an entry policy.

For Heathermount, then, the 'educational side' has meant being as 'open' as possible. Education is figured here as an absolutely informal process, without goals or expectations, because literally anybody is allowed to enter the farm. This is not the managed informal education of what Ursula terms the 'user group' (regular clients), but about a deliberate disposition *to* 'the community': where, as Ursula puts it, 'you have to start from being welcoming'. This attitude, in the tradition of informal education, is about *trust*. But it is not about the trust gained through long hours of conversation and gradually acquired familiarity (compare Jeffs and Smith, 2005). Rather, it is a trusting disposition that enables a sense of welcome to unknown strangers – who may be figured as potential learners – and in the ability of the farm and its workers to deal with any 'problems' as they arise.

Heathermount's approach has an important implication because it positions the local community – now spread over an entire segment of a city – as a potential client base. By being open, Ursula conceived the farm as a 'resource, just for the public', at any time they needed it. She observed that 'a lot of people want to live the good life' – self-sufficient, in terms of their food – as well as mainstream schools were displaying increasing interest in raising animals and plants on their own grounds. Ursula viewed this as an increasingly important role for UK Care Farms – where local community members and school groups could simply drop in on an *ad hoc* basis to 'learn what it's like first, learn whether they can do it, and learn about boundaries and guidelines for growing your own, be it chickens or potatoes'. It was this tacit, latent kind of connection with the local community – just existing, should they be needed – that was central to Heathermount's approach. In fact, as similar providers had lost funding or become more expensive, her definition of 'local' had expanded to one that was far more relational (Massey, 2005). As Ursula puts it, 'it's not just about the space you have inside the farm boundaries, but about just existing as a resource, having a connection with *other* places. We're a porous place really.'

Constituting an 'in-between' space with ever-increasing local responsibilities: Oldrow Farm, eastern England

My final example is taken from another 'city farm', this time located in a medium-sized city in eastern England. Oldrow is, even compared with Heathermount, a very small Care Farm. It, too, is located within a deprived outer suburb and has also had to re-imagine its role several times following changes to funding elsewhere. In fact, it is this point that I will pick up below. Oldrow differs from Heathermount, however, in terms of the services it offers. Its 'farm' element is (very) limited – to a few geese and chickens, a pig and some rabbits. It also has a small patch of trees for Forest School, an adventure playground and a large indoor space for playgroups and parenting classes.

My reason for finishing with Oldrow is that it encapsulates how forms of informal learning within the micro-scale, intimate spaces of the farm itself operate in an iterative and ineluctable relationship with the positioning of the farm within its local community. Like Forest School, Oldrow emphasises un-directed (but adult-supervised), child-led play as an important facet of informal learning, even for teenagers (Knight, 2009). It was through play – not only in the farm's adventure playground spaces but in its animal area – that dialogue was fostered. Again, *space* mattered. Maura, a Care Farm practitioner/playworker, told me that the different physical spaces on the farm enabled different kinds of dialogue.

> The outside area, the adventure playground, the quietest of child [...] they become more vocal, happier. The eco garden, they would become quieter but more chatter, because it's more relaxed. It's important in any space like this to have different kinds of space. In the shelter, they do rhymes, perform to one another, imaginative play. [...] With the animals, learning and care and play run in parallel. Just life skills. Sharing, taking turns

Crucially, at Oldrow, adult practitioners take a step back: as Maura puts it, 'we're here to oversee and intervene [in problematic situations]'. Thus, Oldrow's specific 'take' on informal learning was to privilege peer-group learning among young people.

Zooming out in terms of spatial scale, Oldrow's approach to the micro-scale, inter-personal encounters in what Maura called the farm's 'different kinds of space' was inexorably linked to the positioning of the farm within its community, which was twofold. Firstly, in a pedagogical sense, the farm was

> a space to experience challenging behavior, deal with it, and talk about it. A space to just be, kind of between the school and the street. [...] It's more supervised [than the street] but not so regimented [as school] – you see that in the physical space, it's slightly ramshackle, paint peeling off, not like commercial playgrounds, and that's the point. The children are drawn to it and it's a space where they can work some of these things out on their own (Maura)

Like Banbuck, Oldrow was positioned as an 'in-between' space. Maura imagined Oldrow sitting as a *necessary* space somewhere between school and the street – where the combination of material spaces (play equipment, etcetera) and adult intervention (or lack thereof) embodied that sense of between-ness.

Secondly, this liminality *matters* because of the particular location of the farm within a deprived suburban community. Resonant with Ursula's depiction of Heathermount, Maura told me that the whole ethos of Oldrow was that 'it's just for the community'. She figured the farm as a necessary 'escape valve' for many young people:

> They come here just to be. If they're having a bad time at school. Or home. Sometimes it's quiet time. Sometimes, it's angry outbursts. Some children can't get to the countryside because they can't afford it. But it's important that we're nearby, they can come straight here. And because it's local, they can walk here, the parents get some respite too

Maura was persuaded, then, that the very *localness* of the farm – within walking distance – was one of its greatest facets. Significantly, she did not depict Oldrow as a kind of vital, 'natural' space, with innate therapeutic capabilities, just *because* it was a farm (compare, for instance, Louv, 2005, on the therapeutic properties of 'nature'). Rather, she placed the farm as *vital for* the community, because of the combination of material/social spaces within the farm, and its literal and figurative location within the community. If this seems like analytical hyperbole on my part, Maura – like Ursula – explained to me that Care Farms will likely have a greater role to play in (literally) propping up the life of disadvantaged communities:

> I think we're going to have to step up, I'm going to have to do the work that the Children's Centres did [State run centres, often located

in deprived communities] because their funding is at risk with the new Government. It is a burden that's going to fall disproportionately on this kind of place. Parents have come to expect provision [...] but now the money's being pulled back again, it's reinventing everyone's expectations. The parents have started to help – we've been asking them to provide money for flour, for biscuits, we now rely on that. And one woman, she sponsors our pig, basically keeps it alive. So you see *everyone* is increasingly relying on this kind of place. It is vital for community life, otherwise the community will die, I think

I have argued elsewhere that alternative education spaces do not only provide learning experiences that flow *from* everyday life, as per some common definitions of informal education (e.g., Falk et al., 2009). Rather, they also constitute learning spaces and communities that (re)imagine and support *life-itself* – from that of a pig to a whole community (Kraftl, 2013, Chapter 8). It may seem melodramatic to say this, but in my research at Care Farms and other alternative education spaces, many practitioners have voiced their concerns that under the UK Government's austerity measures, it would be incumbent upon them to fill gaps left by public service withdrawal. Whether this will be the case remains to be seen; this lack of certainty notwithstanding, the example of Oldrow Farm offers yet another, important, sense of the multiple ways in which Care Farms seek to connect with and constitute a place *for* their local communities, in and through informal learning.

Conclusion

This chapter aimed to examine the implications for concepts, practices and spaces of informal education when it takes place in alternative education settings. Taking the example of contemporary UK Care Farming, this chapter has outlined two such implications. These are neither all-encompassing, nor revolutionary for scholarly research on informal education. Yet they should provoke further research about the multiple confluences (and possible divergences) between informal and alternative education.

The first contribution has been to identify particular kinds of informal education that *do* take place within Care Farms. Most Care Farms privilege dialogue between learners and practitioners, seek to foster trusting relations, and base learning within everyday activities and concerns of young people. Yet Care Farms do not (quite) present the same kinds of settings as, for instance, the more familiar environments of the school or youth work (see Part III of this volume). I argued that Care Farms offer a more limited repertoire of experiences – a 'tool-kit' of spaces – from which young people choose, and which will be more relevant to some young people than others. As institutions in their own right, they have particular rules and regulations – from client safeguarding to codes of conduct. They are, I have argued, semi-formal spaces, which often pitch themselves somewhere *between* school, the street and home. This means that Care Farms – like other alternative education spaces – constantly negotiate a tension between providing informal learning experiences and pressures to formalise that learning. Ultimately, many Care Farms provide opportunities for informal learning that maybe multi-sensory, therapeutic, playful, peer-led and/or conversational. At the same time, they feel a responsibility to ensure that young people progress and, eventually, leave for further education, training or work.

The second contribution of this chapter has arguably been more important: to acknowledge the multiple styles in which Care Farms position themselves within their local communities. Informal educators are often acutely aware of how the micro-scale relationships between young people and informal educators may be 'scaled-up' to a consideration of wider socio-political relations (Cartwright, 2012). However, the examples in this chapter demonstrate that the up-scaling of education practices from the micro-spaces of the Care Farm to the *local*, community spaces that surround it are of utmost importance to the constitution of alternative education spaces. Indeed, the kinds of tactile, multi-sensuous, micro-scale inter-personal, informal education that they offer *inside* the farm gate are almost always inexorably related to careful attempts to position Care Farms with respect to those people and places *outside*. This is not the same process as the support of school-based learning at home – an issue that has attracted important research in the mainstream educational sector (Hartas, 2011; Holloway and Pimlott-Wilson, 2011). Rather, the chapter has cited multiple ways in which 'local' communities are both imagined and related – from viewing local families as (virtually) a customer base, to reducing stigma about the clients of a Care Farm, to acting as an open resource for a disadvantaged community, to being a vital part of community life-itself. At each Care Farm, the 'local' means something slightly different in terms of scale (arguably largest at Heathermount, and smallest at Oldrow). The local community is also conceived in relation to the kinds of learning that *may* happen – sometimes as a community of learners, and sometimes as a population who could become engaged should they require a resource.

There remains scope for considerable research to tease out in greater detail and in other settings the multiple imbrications of alternative and informal education. In addition, there remains a need to interrogate the experiences of learners themselves – both identifiable (young) 'clients' and the communities with which institutions like Care Farms engage. Most importantly, Care Farmers felt (in 2012) that they were under increasing pressure to take up what one practitioner called 'the burden' of public service withdrawal in countries like the United Kingdom. Thus, the relationships with local communities that are so vital to the constitution of the (informal) educative role of alternative learning spaces like Care Farms warrant ongoing, and serious, attention.

Note

1. The project adhered to strict ethical codes of conduct. All of the farms and individuals who took part wished to remain anonymous. For this reason, I have not named individual Care Farms, and have as far as possible removed identifying information (other than to indicate the region of the United Kingdom in which they are situated). Names of farms and individuals are pseudonyms.

References

B. Berget and B. Braastad (2008) 'Animal-assisted therapy with farm animals for persons with psychiatric disorders', *Annals Ist Super Sanita*, 47, 384–90.

L. Cameron (2006) 'Science, nature and hatred: "Finding out" at the malting house garden school, 1924–9', *Environment and Planning D: Society and space*, 24, 851–72.

I. Cartwright (2012) 'Informal education in compulsory schooling in the UK', in P. Kraftl, J. Horton and F. Tucker (eds) *Critical Geographies of Childhood and Youth* (Bristol: Policy Press).

J. Falk, J. Heimlich and S. Foutz (2009) *Free-choice Learning and the Environment* (Lanham, MD: AltaMira Press).

K. Ferguson and T. Seddon (2007) 'Decentred education: Suggestions for framing a socio-spatial research agenda', *Critical Studies in Education*, 48, 111–29.

M. Fielding and P. Moss (2011) *Radical Education and the Common School* (London: Routledge).

P. Freire (2008 [1974]) *Education for Critical Consciousness* (London: Continuum).

C. Hanson Thiem (2007) 'The spatial politics of educational privatization', in K. Gulson and C. Symes (eds) *Spatial Theories of Education* (London: Routledge).

D. Hartas (2011) 'Families' social backgrounds matter', *British Educational Research Journal*, 37, 893–914.

J. Hassink, M. Elings, M. Zweekhorst, N. van den Nieuwenhuizen and A. Smit (2010) 'Care farms in the Netherlands: Attractive empowerment-oriented and strengths-based practices in the community', *Health and Place*, 16, 423–30.

D. Haubenhofer, M. Elings, J. Hassink and R. Hone (2010) 'The development of green care in western European countries', *Explore*, 6, 106–11.

R. Hine, J. Peacock and J. Pretty (2008) 'Care farming in the UK', *Therapeutic Communities*, 29, 245–60.

S. Holloway and H. Pimlott-Wilson (2011) 'The politics of aspiration: Neo-liberal education policy, "low" parental aspirations and primary school Extended Services in disadvantaged communities', *Children's Geographies*, 9, 79–94.

T. Jeffs and M. Smith (2005) *Informal Education* (London: Educational Heretics Press).

S. Knight (2009) *Forest Schools and Outdoor Learning in the Early Years* (London: SAGE).

P. Kraftl (2006) 'Building an idea: The material construction of an ideal childhood', *Transactions of the Institute of British Geographers*, 31, 488–504.

P. Kraftl (2013) *Geographies of Alternative Education: Diverse learning spaces for children and young people* (Bristol: Policy Press).

P. Kraftl (2013) 'Towards geographies of alternative education: A case study of UK homeschooling families', *Transactions of the Institute of British Geographers*, 38, 436–450.

R. Louv (2005) *Last Child in the Woods* (Chapel Hill, NC: Algonquin Books).

D. Massey (2005) *For Space* (London: SAGE).

S. Mills (2013) '"An instruction in good citizenship": Scouting and the historical geographies of citizenship education', *Transactions of the Institute of British Geographers*, 38, 120–34.

A. Neuman and A. Aviram (2003) 'Homeschooling as a fundamental change in lifestyle', *Evaluation and Research in Education*, 17, 132–43.

I. Oberski (2011) 'Rudolf Steiner's philosophy of freedom as a basis for spiritual education?', *International Journal of Children's Spirituality*, 16, 5–17.

E. O'Brien (2009) 'Learning outdoors: The forest school approach', *Education 3–13*, 37, 45–60.

L. Richardson and M. Wolfe (2001) *Principles and Practices of Informal Education* (London: Routledge).

A. Sliwka (2008) 'The contribution of alternative education', Chapter 4 in *Innovating to Learn, Learning to Innovate*, OECD, available at: http://www.oecd-ilibrary.org/education/innovating-to-learn-learning-to-innovate_9789264047983-en;jsessionid=2iqj0etjq4gi7.epsilon, date accessed 8 June 2012.

P. Woods and G. Woods (2009) *Alternative Education for the 21st Century* (Basingstoke: Palgrave).

5
'A Powerful Educational Instrument': The Woodcraft Folk and Indoor/Outdoor 'Nature', 1925–75

Sarah Mills

Introduction

> The Woodcraft Folk... seeks to enlist the enthusiasm and energy of youth for the great task of our generation... it believes that any attempt to establish a new, world-wide economic order is dependent upon the training of youth in the science of our age and the deliberate cultivation of a world outlook in children and young people. To achieve this end the Folk seek to forge a *powerful educational instrument* which shall inculcate those habits of mind and habits of body necessary to bring man to devotion to world peace and a new world order.[1]

This quote from the declaration of the Woodcraft Folk in 1930 – five years after its inception by Leslie Paul – encapsulated its rationale as a new youth organisation, as well as cementing *education* at the heart of its motivations and methods. This chapter explores the pedagogical practices of the Woodcraft Folk in the United Kingdom across the first 50 years of the organisation (1925–75), as while still popular today, it is in these formative years that it sought to forge a 'powerful educational instrument' and developed its training programme. In doing so, this chapter illustrates how the Folk drew upon a number of spaces and practices of (informal) education to inculcate those 'habits of body and mind' expressed above. Specifically, this chapter considers how 'nature' and elements of folk culture and arts and craft – such as song and dance – were used as part of this project. While academics and popular imaginaries of youth organisations tend to focus on experiences of nature on camp, here I focus on the deeper, symbolic and performative place of nature in the Folk's indoor activities and wider ambitions.

There have been a number of historical studies about the explicit politics of the Woodcraft Folk, and in particular its links to the co-operative movement and Labour Party (Prynn, 1983; Davis, 2000). Here, rather than discuss its utopian visions for world peace and institutional engagements with left-wing politics, I want to highlight the embodied ways in which young people in the Folk were seen to need certain skills, attributes and training in order to travel on the 'road to citizenship via woodcraft'.[2] There is a wider conceptual point to make here in how British youth movements positioned children and young people as both citizens-in-the-making and 'young citizens' simultaneously, reflecting how young people continue to exist as children and young people in the here-and-now and as adults 'not-yet-become' (Evans, 2010). Elsewhere I have explored the explicit citizenship projects of British youth movements, notably the Scout Movement (Mills, 2013). In many ways, the Folk was established as the antithesis to scouting and its perceived middle-class and militaristic activities (Warren, 1986). These alternative roots lie in the short-lived and controversial Kibbo Kift Kindred established by ex-Scouter John Hargrave. The genealogical emergence of the Woodcraft Folk is not the focus of this chapter – but rather – how a training programme emerged within the Folk and the ways in which 'nature' was mobilised to envision and deliver informal education in 'the woodcraft way'. In doing so, this chapter contributes to emerging work on the geographies of alternative and informal education (Kraftl, 2013, this volume) as part of a wider disciplinary interest in the geographies of education and learning (Holloway and Jöns, 2012). It also makes a specific addition to literature on British youth movements within historical studies (Springhall, 1977) by highlighting how these learning spaces operate in far more contingent and 'messy' ways (see, e.g., Kraftl, 2013). Finally, in discussing the everyday and imaginative ways in which the Folk envisioned young people would be trained using 'nature', this chapter moves away from the primacy of the camp as the arena through which youth movements work (Cupers, 2008; see also Kyle, Chapter 2, and Bannister, Chapter 3, this volume).

Drawing on original archival material from the Youth Movement Archive, held at the London School of Economics, United Kingdom, the remainder of this chapter is structured in four sections. First, it gives a brief outline of the Woodcraft Folk's aims and wider philosophies as articulated by its founder Leslie Paul – himself aged just 19 when he established the organisation. Second, it introduces the 'evolutionary' justification for arts and crafts in the Folk and discusses the badge programme. The next section gives two illustrative examples of the performative element to the Woodcraft Folk's activities: song and dance. Finally, the chapter concludes by reflecting on the wider geographies of informal education in the Woodcraft Folk and argues for closer attention to the 'alternative' pedagogical practices of learning spaces in civil society.

The Woodcraft Folk and informal education

'Woodcraft' has its origins in the writings and activities of Ernest Thompson Seton (1860–1946) and his attempts to preserve the crafts, traditions and nature-lore of Indian tribes (see, e.g., Seton, 1906). He later became Chief Scout of the Boy Scouts of America (1910–15) and developed the term 'woodcraft' to advocate open-air life and engagements with nature (rather than crafting or carving wood). In Britain, Seton's woodcraft had many admirers, not least Robert Baden-Powell, who trialled an experimental scout camp in 1907 which eventually led to the massive growth of scouting worldwide (Proctor, 2002). After the First World War however, Scout Commissioner for Camping and Woodcraft John Hargrave left the movement and founded the Kibbo Kift Kindred based on woodcraft principles. Due to a largely autocratic leadership by Hargrave, several co-operative youth including 19-year-old Leslie Paul broke away from the Kindred and formed the Woodcraft Folk based on peace, equality and justice in 1924. The Woodcraft Folk were secular and co-educational, with Leslie Paul describing them as a 'democratic organisation of mainly young people who believe in (1) education for social change (2) the principles of the co-operative movement and (3) the abolition of war, racial hatred and prejudice'.[3] The national organisation was structured into local groups run by adult volunteers and internally structured into age-based sections, including elfins (7–10) and pioneers (10–16); these ages varied over time however and several different versions of names and age sections were used. In weekly meetings, adult volunteers delivered an educational programme (explored later in this chapter), with Paul (later 'Little Otter') describing woodcraft as the 'art and adventure of fending for oneself outdoors'.[4] To understand the Woodcraft Folk however, I argue that indoor spaces (and practices that crossed indoor/outdoor boundaries) were vitally important (see also Kyle, Chapter 2, this volume). The Folk is still active today with around 25,000 members (divided into woodchips [under 6], elfins [6–9], pioneers [10–12] venturers [13–15] and district fellows [16–20]), describing itself as a 'movement for children and young people... where children will grow in confidence, learn about the world and start to understand how to value our planet and each other' (Woodcraft Folk, 2013).

In their formative years – the focus of this chapter – the Folk expressed that they believed that children 'learnt by doing' and therefore instructed adult volunteers in groups across the United Kingdom to lead and encourage young people to 'have a go' at various skills and activities under the guise of woodcraft. In a pamphlet on the *History of the Woodcraft Folk* from the 1930s, the organisation stated:

> The Boy Scouts used a lukewarm version of his [Seton's] woodcraft. Now some version or other is the basis of the best new educational experiments. The strength of woodcraft lies in the psychology of its appeal to the youngster. All children... wait for opportunities to do things rather than reading of them or listening to lectures.[5]

The Folk therefore positioned themselves at the forefront of alternative and experimental educational techniques in the early twentieth century – as well as a real substitute to Baden-Powell's organisation. In theory, this child-led and active learning philosophy was premised on principles of informal education such as spontaneity, conversation, and that this 'learning' could take place in any setting (Richardson and Wolfe, 2001; Jeffs and Smith, 2005). However, one could argue that the Folk also drew on mechanisms used in schools (textbooks, repetition techniques) as well as other features of the Scout Movement (badges, ceremonies) that it was trying to distance itself from.

The place of woodcraft in the Woodcraft Folk and Native American imagery was central in its early iconography and emergent practices. Woodcraft Folk clothing was not 'uniform' (as in the Scout Movement or Boys' Brigade) but rather 'costume'. In the 1930s, the Folk elders stated 'although no ruling has been made the traditional colours of the Folk costume are green, brown or grey...the jerkin or dress should be decorated by hand as desired and the addition of a leather fringe to the jerkin makes it strikingly picturesque'.[6] In addition, several Folk Committee and Council members had Native American-based names. For example, at the end of the 1928 yearbook, it states 'with such a splendid report Silvertip moved that it be accepted, Orion seconded and all Folk agreed'.[7] These names were often taken to tokenistic extremes in later years; for example, in a glossary of folk terms from 1961, it lists the following roles on camp: 'Camp Chief, Master of Festival, Keeper of the Wood and Keeper of the Garbage' with the latter responsible for 'maintaining sanitation service at camp and for cleaning up after hikes, merrymoots etc'.[8] However, in the 1960s, terms such as 'pow-wows' were still being used, described as 'the only medium widely available to us by which we can pass on information about subjects which cannot be learned by practice alone'.[9] Overall, during the first 50 years of the Folk, woodcraft and Native American connections to 'open-air life' were popular: several charters stated that '[a]ll members of the Folk, young and old, must consider themselves members of a kindred of outdoor people'.[10] While the Folk envisioned themselves belonging to this wider – almost spiritual – 'kindred of outdoor people', here I want to focus on the *indoor* performances and practices used to emulate and invoke ideas of 'nature' as part of their informal education.

Inside/outside: Performing 'nature' and evolutionary arts and crafts

Rather than focusing on the campsite, with its obvious connections to notions of adventurous outdoor citizenship, idealised rural childhoods and fitness (Matless, 1998; Cupers, 2008), I use the remainder of this chapter to illustrate how nature was imagined, invoked and artificially created within meeting places through specific practices and performances. While a leaflet documenting the spaces of the Woodcraft Folk includes the campsite and 'silent places', it also depicts indoor spaces – club rooms and meeting halls – as 'fellowship meetings' where young people met locally each week (rather than an annual camp or international adventure).[11] This was, during wartime, an absolute necessity. As a 1940 report of the Woodcraft Folk states, 'some of our success in the face of such difficulties [war] may result from our dual work "indoors and outdoors". Often, where one is impossible or limited, the other side of group life can be developed and this contact maintained.'[12] The Folk therefore operated through both outdoor and crucially *indoor* spaces. Furthermore, it tried to position itself as a 'middle ground' through attempts to 'be neither aimless play centres nor dreary discussion circles', stressing that 'we must learn and apply the social value of education through many varied activities – education towards that real community citizenship of a New Society'.[13]

A crucial aspect of operating in this 'middle ground' and a unique feature of the Folk was the priority it gave to wider arts and craft activities. These were seen to directly illustrate the organisations' 'particular evolutionary philosophy' which 'we must examine, amplify and disseminate ... present it by all the resources of art and craft and the example of our lives to the world'.[14] There was therefore, for Folk authorities, something innate about the process of making something 'new' from material, from designing and performing a skill or production 'from scratch', that was seen to replicate the wider global processes and evolutionary development of humankind. As part of the Woodcraft Folk charter, young people were encouraged to declare 'it is our desire ... to develop ourselves ... by using the creative faculty both of our minds and our hands'.[15] Here, we can again see references to the mind/body dualism expressed in this chapter's opening quote in relation to habits of mind and habits of body. More broadly, this learning philosophy of using arts and crafts to emphasise the 'evolutionary' aspect of the world, I would argue, reflects an attempt by the Woodcraft Folk to envision and anticipate the future British nation and world (Anderson, 2010) and positions young people as the hope for an alternative utopian future based on principles of the organisation (Kraftl, 2008). Indeed, it is worth highlighting the much-broader historical relationship between informal education and utopia (Cartwright, 2012; Donnachie, Chapter 6, this volume) that both precedes and has been inspired by the work of Leslie Paul and the Woodcraft Folk (for more on a range of utopian thinkers and theories of informal education, see www.infed.org).

Having now discussed the general impetus and rationale behind utilising arts and craft activities within the Woodcraft Folk, I now want to turn to how they were integrated into the learning and training programme, specifically through tests and badges. As previously mentioned, badges were a feature used by the Folk that mimicked other youth organisations. These tactile rewards reflected achievement in a repeated programme of learning that measured a young person's ability and proficiency in a set series of tests. The following badges (italics) and required skills (in parenthesis) are a record of the tests passed by one ten-year-old Folk member – 'Wild Cat'[16] – based in a group in Northern England between 1948 and 1949:

> *Campers* (camp layout, sanitation, firelighting), *Supple Limb* (running, swimming, natural movement), *Hiker* (map reading, compass lore, hiking lore), *Backwoodsman* (weather lore, star lore, tree lore) *Lone Crafter* (silent tongue, sunburnt skin, lone hike), *Keen Eye* (trail laying, observation), *Craftsman* (group symbol craft, personal symbol craft), *Festival Craft* (produce mime/play, yarn spinner, folk ceremony), *Citizen* (local government, local industries, local Co-operative, local trade union), *World Citizen* (comradeship, governments, language, solidarity).[17]

This record card reveals the wider training programme that younger Woodcraft Folk members worked towards and the types of skills the organisation deemed necessary to its citizenship training programme. We can see that a traditional staple of camp knowledge, physical fitness and orientation skills were also combined with more mythical and experiential knowledge about nature (e.g., the skills of silent tongue, sunburnt skin and lone hike required for the *Lone Crafter* badge) as well as performative craft-based and amateur dramatic skills (e.g., producing a mime/play, spinning 'yarns' and folk ceremonies required for the *Festival Craft* badge). The specific learning practices here in relation to craft can be connected to wider regional geographies of craft and crafting, especially as local knowledge would have been vital to the training young people actually received from volunteers (see, e.g., Thomas and Jakob, 2012). The final two badges listed here on Wild Cat's record card – *Citizen* and *World Citizen* – also reflect the wider scale-based citizenship formations that the Woodcraft Folk and British youth movements used in their training schemes (Mills, 2013). All of these badges required an adult observer to judge and mark the competency and proficiency of individual Folk members before the presentation of a fabric badge – all of which usually took place in a regular indoor meeting space. In relation to craft, one promotional leaflet states how:

> We like learning exciting handicrafts, making toys and models, and painting pictures. We embroider banners, flags and badges, carve totem poles, and make belts and moccasins of leather. Sometimes we have exhibitions and films for the grown-ups to see what we do. So we train our bodies and minds for the service of the People and the fashioning of a New World.[18]

Overall then, indoor spaces were important sites of learning, training, practice, performance and celebration. In the next section, I illustrate this argument through two specific performances – singing and dancing – and their place within the Folk, in both indoor and outdoor spaces. Indeed, while songs and dances might have been performed at national camps or international trips, there was an emphasis on practising these performances within the comfortable and familiar spaces of meeting places. Furthermore, these songs and dances were utilised by the organisation to re-affirm the Woodcraft Folk's rationale, moral framework and connections with nature.

Singing (*repeat last line twice...*) and dancing (*this is repeated two or three times...*)

In declaring the Folk's rationale and activities, Leslie Paul often used the phrase 'we shall go singing to the fashioning of a new world'.[19] Notwithstanding obvious connections to folk music and folk culture here (Revill, 2000; 2005, explored later), the ways in which specific Woodcraft Folk songs were used to communicate messages to young people about the beliefs and values of the organisation is important to consider in the context of this chapter's wider argument. In addition to camp, where the Folk described that '...the stars look down out of the purple blanket of night and the woods echo with our Woodcraft yells and rhymes',[20] songs were also part of indoor meetings and regular activities. In the *Woodcraft Folk Song Book*, it states that its chosen songs represented 'the best of their kind and are eminently suitable for singing at campfires and indoor group meetings...they range from pure folk songs of many lands to relatively modern songs of fellowship and international understanding'.[21]

While Hayden Lorimer (2007) has examined recorded sounds and songs from archives, the Woodcraft Folk material held at the Youth Movement Archive does not hold recorded songs or performances. However, the place of songs and singing can be analysed through other material. Songbooks and lyric sheets still give an insight into the types of messages Woodcraft Folk songs conveyed; in particular here, I draw on a songbook printed for members of the Folk attending the World Youth Festival in Sophia, Bulgaria, in 1968 (and also included in the aforementioned *Woodcraft Folk Song Book* and other similar publications). These songs were incredibly self-affirming and drew most powerfully on distinctions between idealised rural landscapes and the (im)moral landscape of the city (on these debates in relation to childhood, see Jones, 1999; Philo, 1992). For example, in *City Folk Are Staring* the first and second verse state:

> The city folk are staring with wonder and surprise,
> At the Folk in bright green jerkins,
> They're asking many questions with civilised eyes,
> Of the Folk in the bright green jerkins.

> Hurrah for the pine trees, hurrah for the sun;
> We don't think much of the work you've done,
> Here's to the new trail we've just begun,
> Wearing the bright green jerkins.[22]

Here, with direct reference to their green costumes, this self-affirming dec-laration makes a clear distinction between urban and rural spaces in a celebration of nature and a new 'trail'. In other songs, references to nature directly relate to biological constructions of childhood as a phase of natural growth and development. Here, in the first and third verse of *Youth Song*, we read:

> Youth and maiden side by side,
> To the tramp of feet we're singing,
> To the world new hope we're bringing,
> Hope of life with us abide.
> (repeat last line twice).
> Bloom of birch and bursting spray,
> Mother nature gives us freely,
> Who have welcomed life so gleely,
> Youth will walk in light to-day.
> (repeat last line twice).[23]

As well as direct references to hope, and specifically childhood-hope (Kraftl, 2008), this song contains natural imagery echoed in the written creeds and laws recited by young people who joined the organisation. For example, part of the Elfin Creed in 1948 declared:

> I will grow strong and straight – like the pine; supple and limb – like the hare; keen of eye like the eagle. I will seek health from the greenwood, skill from crafts, and wisdom from those who will show me wisdom.[24]

As well as metaphors of growth and a further reference to craft skills, there is an active declaration here that young people will 'seek wisdom from those who will show me wisdom'. In one sense, this can be read as wishful thinking on the part of the adult volunteers here as the extent to which young people wholeheartedly embraced this creed (or conversely, mimic, forget, laugh or subvert it) is unknown and could form the basis for future research.

Overall, while the lyrics to Woodcraft Folk songs prepared for Sophia in 1968 have been analysed here, it is important to remember the contex-tual and performative dimensions of singing within the organisation. These songs would have been performed by young people at previous camps and festivals, but also practised in indoor meeting halls in preparation for this specific trip to Bulgaria and most likely on trains as part of the journey, before *eventually* at the 'outdoor' international festival of youth. In the diary of a teenage Woodcraft Folk member who attended a similar international camp to France in 1954, it was written that 'it was an uneventful journey apart from Johnson's (alias "Rover") constant flow of mirth and song'[25] and that overall 'we were easily the smallest delegation, but we gave a very good account of ourselves and participated fully (and often spontaneously) in the different shows'.[26] Indeed, these international events often had spontaneous singing indoors, outdoors and as part of the journey. Furthermore, there would have been a wider sharing and exchange of songs between young people from different nations that is important to note. There is therefore an explicit politics in performed 'sonic experiences', as suggested by George Revill (2000), and in particular I would argue that this is most powerful when transported from one nation (and youth organisation) to be shared and performed with members of other youth organisations. While Revill framed his argument in the context of English music between 1880 and 1940, I would echo his comments that 'musical sounds themselves . . . [helped] define the moral and social role of the citizen' (2000, p 610), and by extension here, the *young* citizen. There are wider connections between song, tradition, authenticity and working-class culture (see also Revill, 2005) that could be explored further here, as well as considerations of hope and utopia in recorded music (Anderson, 2002); however I have drawn upon this example to specifically highlight one way in which performing arts and crafts were used by the Folk as part of their informal education project.

Another performative feature of the Woodcraft Folk was its use of dance (for geographical analyses of dance in the context mobilities research and non-representational theory, see Cresswell, 2006; McCormack, 2008; Merriman, 2010). Popular dances in Woodcraft Folk ceremonies included 'peace' 'fire' and 'snapdragon', their very titles emphasising the rationale and natural imagery of the Folk through performed and embodied movement. In the instructions for the following two dances – 'social dance' and 'wolf' – we can see the careful prescriptive logics of time and space used to choreograph youthful bodies into imitations of animals:

Social Dance: For this dance, two circles are formed one inside the other. The inner and smaller circle moves 'with the sun' from right to left . . . Then they all stop, bend down like wolves squatting and give a long drawn out coyote howl; '*ki-yi-yi-yippy-yippy yi-yi-yi*' . . . This is repeated two or three times. . . . At a signal on the drum . . . conclude with inner and outer circles.

Wolf: The Wolf Dance may be performed solo, or by up to 12. Their bodies are bent forward . . . and they swing their heads from side to side like wolves. They circle the fire in centre of dance group. They give a long wolf howl . . . [and] chant the following standing: '*We are the grey brothers, we roam the prairies wide, no sign escapes our knowing; we hunt together – our strength is our unity . . . From dusk to dawn the grey brothers prowl.'*[27]

The clear animalistic character of these dances – with young Folk members transformed into roaming and prowling wolves – represents the close familial bond that was said to unite members of this youth organisation. However, as Merriman (2010) stresses in his writings on dance and mobility, rather than choreographed dance always being 'regulatory' or 'oppressive', the realities are more complex. Here, I would argue that the dances used in Woodcraft Folk meetings would have varied depending on the ways in which they were taught by adult volunteers and varying levels of enthusiasm for them. Clearly, in some cases they could have been highly regulated and constantly rehearsed; in other cases, more open and 'fun'. It is here where I want to make a wider argument about the need to explore local cultures of volunteering through oral histories with Folk members to understand how these dances (and other Folk activities) were understood, negotiated and experienced (on young people, agency and the limits of archives, see Gagen, 2001). Again though, we can see through the diary quoted in the previous section that dances were also shared and important parts of the Folk programme and social lives of young people. The teenage boy who attended an international youth camp in France in 1954 from his local Woodcraft Folk group describes the sharing of dances (as well as song):

> When the Germans had settled down we seized 3 girls and therefore, with our own, sole, English girl we had a full set for a couple of dances. We taught the [group name] two dances: discussion circle and the Cumberland Square Eight.[28]

Through the two brief examples in this chapter, it is clear that the practices of an arts and crafts programme within the Woodcraft Folk were performed not only at spectacular campfires but also on long train journeys and as part of indoor meetings. Towards the end of the period this chapter has focused on (1925–75), there is a sense in which these more artistic and creative pedagogical practices were becoming out dated or seen as less relevant. For example, in a re-statement of policy and recommendations in 1966, the Folk stated that 'there is evidence that the "craft" of the Woodcraft Folk has been replaced from one of the higher priorities on our list by a desire to meet the demands of children and youth in modern society'.[29] This perhaps hints that the post-war period, and the 1960s in particular, marked a turning point in a number of British youth movements who were struggling to find their place among emerging youth sub-cultures and 'modern' Britain (Gledhill, 2013). Overall, in these examples, we can see how 'nature' in the Folk was not only limited to camp but was a regular, sometimes subtle feature, evoked through creative performances that also took place indoors.

Conclusion

The more cultural and artistic pedagogical practices outlined in this chapter are perhaps hidden examples of how youth movement spaces operated and performed their training programmes. They are historically specific, and yet, some of these features remain in the Woodcraft Folk's contemporary formations: while the Native American names for committee positions are long gone, the role of modern music, song, dance and amateur dramatics remains part of Woodcraft Folk activities.

Overall, this chapter has highlighted how the Folk sought to forge a 'powerful educational instrument', but did so through often artistic and cultural practices *alongside* direct engagements with nature on camp. The 'educational instrument' of the Folk was, at other times, called an 'educational machine',[30] and this illuminates some wider social constructions of childhood that drew upon notions of production, growth and futurity in the twentieth century. Indeed, the contemporary 'generalising tendency to futurity', particularly in policy contexts, is nothing new (Katz, 2008; Evans and Honeyford, 2012). In many ways, British youth movements – including the Woodcraft Folk – used futurity as a way to justify their rationale, methods and pedagogical practices. There is therefore scope for further analyses of how the Woodcraft Folk's pedagogical practices intersected with direct political action and wider cultures of activism, volunteering and social movements. Indeed, as Stephen Sadlier (Chapter 7, this volume) highlights, teaching (in that case, at school) can shape and be shaped by cultures of protest and activism. As geographers more broadly have explored cultures and practices of activism in diverse contexts, including within the discipline itself (Pickerill and Chatterton, 2006; Brown and Pickerill, 2009), it is clear that the historical and contemporary connections between activism and spaces of informal education are worthy of much more attention.

Acknowledgements

I would like to extend my thanks to the Woodcraft Folk for copyright permission, as well as the staff at the London School of Economics Library and Archives.

Notes

1. London School of Economics/Youth Movement Archive/Woodcraft Folk (hereafter LSE/YMA/WF)/2/Report of the Commission on Folk Law to Althing, 1930, p.3, emphasis added).
2. LSE/YMA/WF/358/III/22/*Follow paths of progress*, Poster.
3. LSE/YMA/WF/10/105B/*Who are the Woodcraft Folk?* c.1930s–1970s.
4. LSE/YMA/WF/10/105B/*Who are the Woodcraft Folk?* c.1930s–1970s.
5. LSE/YMA/WF/11/125/*History of the Woodcraft Folk*, c.1935.

6. LSE/YMA/WF/10/95-6/*Who's for the Folk?*, Folk Pamphlet 2, c.1930.
7. LSE/YMA/WF/1/1/Yearbook, 1928.
8. LSE/YMA/WF/7/53A/Leaders Diploma Course, c.1961.
9. LSE/YMA/WF/7/53A/Leaders Diploma Course, c.1961.
10. LSE/YMA/WF/6/50/Charter of the Woodcraft Folk, 1949.
11. LSE/YMA/WF/10/105B/*On the Trail*, Pamphlet, c.1930s–1970s.
12. LSE/YMA/WF/1/3/Reports and Accounts for 1940.
13. LSE/YMA/WF/1/4A/Annual Report, 1947.
14. LSE/YMA/WF/1/1/Yearbook, 1928.
15. LSE/YMA/WF/10/95-6/Charter of the Folk, c.1930s.
16. 'Folk names' are used rather than children's real names due to ethical considerations.
17. LSE/YMA/WF/6/50/Record of Tests Passed, 1948–9.
18. LSE/YMA/WF/10/105B/*On the Trail*, Pamphlet, c.1930s–1970s.
19. LSE/YMA/WF/1/1/Yearbook, 1931–2.
20. LSE/YMA/WF/10/105B/*On the Trail*, Pamphlet, c.1930s–1970s.
21. LSE/YMA/WF/10/106/*The Woodcraft Folk Song Book*, London: Woodcraft Folk, p.1, c.1920s–1950s.
22. LSE/YMA/WF/191/9th World Youth Festival Sofia Song Sheet, 1968.
23. LSE/YMA/WF/191/9th World Youth Festival Sofia Song Sheet, 1968.
24. LSE/YMA/WF/6/50/Membership Card, 1948.
25. LSE/YMA/WF/185/Diary, The International Falcon Rally – France, 1954.
26. LSE/YMA/WF/185/Diary, The International Falcon Rally – France, 1954.
27. LSE/YMA/WF/219/Tribal Dances 1, no date.
28. LSE/YMA/WF/185/Diary, The International Falcon Rally – France, 1954.
29. LSE/YMA/WF/10/104/Re-statement of Policy and Recommendations, October 1966.
30. LSE/YMA/WF/1/3/Reports and Accounts, 1939.

References

B. Anderson (2002) 'A principle of hope: Recorded music, listening practices and the immanence of utopia', *Geografiska Annaler: Series B, Human Geography*, 84, 211–27.

B. Anderson (2010) 'Preemption, precaution, preparedness: Anticipatory action and future geographies', *Progress in Human Geography*, 34, 777–98.

G. Brown and J. Pickerill (2009) 'Space for emotion in the spaces of activism', *Emotion, Space and Society*, 2, 24–35.

I. Cartwright (2012) 'Informal education in compulsory schooling in the UK', in P. Kraftl, J. Horton and F. Tucker (eds) *Critical Geographies of Childhood and Youth: Contemporary policy and practice* (Bristol: Policy Press), 151–68.

T. Cresswell (2006) 'You cannot shake that shimmie here': Producing mobility on the dance floor, *Cultural Geographies*, 13, 55–77.

K. Cupers (2008) 'Governing through nature: Camps and youth movements in interwar Germany and the United States', *Cultural Geographies*, 15, 173–205.

M. Davis (2000) *Fashioning a New World: A history of the Woodcraft Folk* (Loughborough: Holyoake Books).

B. Evans (2010) 'Anticipating fatness: Childhood, affect and the pre-emptive "war on obesity" ', *Transactions of the Institute of British Geographers*, 35, 21–38.

B. Evans and E. J. Honeyford (2012) ' "Brighter futures, greener lives": Children and young people in UK sustainable development policy' in P. Kraftl, J. Horton and F. Tucker (eds) *Critical Geographies of Childhood and Youth: Contemporary policy and practice* (Bristol: Policy Press).

E. A. Gagen (2001) 'Too good to be true? Representing children's agency in the archives of playground reform', *Historical Geography*, 29, 53–64.

J. Gledhill (2013) 'White heat, guide blue: The girl guide movement in the 1960s', *Contemporary British History*, 27, 65–84.

S. L. Holloway and H. Jöns (2012) 'Geographies of education and learning', *Transactions of the Institute of British Geographers*, 37, 482–88.

T. Jeffs and M. K. Smith (2005) *Informal Education: Conversation, democracy and learning* (London: Education Now Publishing Co-operative).

O. Jones (1999) 'Tomboy tales: The rural, nature and the gender of childhood', *Gender, Place and Culture: A Journal of Feminist Geography*, 6, 117–36.

C. Katz (2008) 'Childhood as spectacle: Relays of anxiety and the reconfiguration of the child', *Cultural Geographies*, 15, 5–17.

P. Kraftl (2008) 'Young people, hope, and childhood-hope', *Space and Culture*, 11, 81–92.

P. Kraftl (2013) *Geographies of Alternative Education* (Bristol: Policy Press).

H. Lorimer (2007) 'Songs from before – shaping the conditions for appreciative listening' in E. A. Gagen, H. Lorimer and A. Vasudevan (eds) *Practising the Archive: Reflections on method and practice in historical geography* Historical Geography Research Series, 40.

D. Matless (1998) *Landscape and Englishness* (London: Reaktion Books Ltd).

D. McCormack (2008) 'Geographies for moving bodies: Thinking, dancing, spaces', *Geography Compass*, 2, 1822–36.

P. Merriman (2010) 'Architecture/dance: Choreographing and inhabiting spaces with Anna and Lawrence Halprin', *Cultural Geographies*, 17, 427–49.

S. Mills (2013) ' "An instruction in good citizenship": Scouting and the historical geographies of citizenship education', *Transactions of the Institute of British Geographers*, 38, 120–34.

C. Philo (1992) 'Neglected rural geographies: A review', *Journal of Rural Studies*, 8, 193–207.

J. Pickerill and P. Chatterton (2006) 'Notes towards autonomous geographies: Creation, resistance and self management as survival tactics', *Progress in Human Geography*, 30, 1–17.

T. Proctor (2002) *On My Honour: Guides and scouts in interwar Britain* (Philadelphia: American Philosophical Society).

D. Prynn (1983) 'The Woodcraft Folk and the labour movement 1925–70', *Journal of Contemporary History*, 18, 79–95.

G. Revill (2000) 'Music and the politics of sound: Nationalism, citizenship and auditory space', *Environment and Planning D: Society and space*, 18, 597–613.

G. Revill (2005) 'Vernacular culture and the place of folk music', *Social and Cultural Geography*, 6, 693–706.

L. D. Richardson and M. Wolfe (eds) (2001) *Principles and Practice of Informal Education* (London: Routledge).

E. Seton (1906) *The Birch Bark Roll of the Woodcraft Indians* (New York: Doubleday).

J. Springhall (1977) *Youth, Empire and Society: British youth movements 1883–1940* (Beckenham: Croom Helm).

N. J. Thomas and D. Jakob (2012) 'Situating craft guilds in the creative economy: Histories, politics and practices', Conference Paper at the Annual Meeting of the Association of American Geographers, New York, February 2012.

A. Warren (1986) 'Citizens of empire – Baden-Powell, scouts and guides and an imperial ideal 1900–1940' in J. Mackenzie (ed.) *Imperialism and Popular Culture* (Manchester: Manchester University Press).

Woodcraft Folk (2013) Woodcraft Folk Website, http://woodcraft.org.uk/ (homepage), date accessed 4 February 2013.

Part II

Negotiating In/formal Education Spaces

6

People, Places and Spaces: Education in Robert Owen's New Society

Ian Donnachie

> *The children and youth in this delightful colony are superior in point of conduct and character to all the children and youth I have ever seen. I shall not attempt to give a faithful description of the beautiful fruits of the social affections displayed in the young, innocent and fascinating countenances of these happy children.*
>
> Dr Henry Macnab (1819)

Introduction

During the later eighteenth and early nineteenth centuries popular education, formal and informal, developed slowly in various contexts, though with perennial debate about its purpose and content. Formal education expressed in the limited curricula of the time is readily identifiable, informal less so, but nevertheless much in evidence in this chapter. It is clear that Robert Owen (1771–1858), eschewing books for younger children, attached great importance to informal experiential learning and to play and other activities promoted by the great Pestalozzi. While acknowledging the activities of other practitioners, Andrew Bell (1752–1832) and Joseph Lancaster (1778–1838) among them, this contribution focuses on Owen's educational thinking and achievements central to his social reform agenda. It examines the significance of environment on his educational thought, the places, personalities and ideas which influenced his work in Britain and elsewhere, with special emphasis on teaching and the curriculum in the School for Children and in the Institute at New Lanark and briefly in other Owenite communities. A variety of spatial processes and themes can be identified, including the cultural and linguistic geography of mid-Wales, migration from Wales and from the Scottish Highlands, the economic and social geography of London, Stamford, Manchester and Glasgow, the location of New Lanark on a prime water power site, the relatively small, material scale of the institute and school relative to the community they served. Attention will thus be devoted to the geographical places and spaces where all of this happened and the role of New Lanark as a locus of social reform nationally and internationally. While essentially a historical case study, the chapter shows that Owen's ideas were in the vanguard of changes in approaches to childhood (and adult) education, hardly implemented generally until the twentieth century. Finally we will briefly assess how Owen's wider agenda underpins the interpretation of New Lanark as a World Heritage Site, promoting education, co-operation, environment and sustainability.

Historical analogies are always dangerous and while some present-day thinking about the role of education for the majority of children is relevant, during the later eighteenth and early nineteenth centuries the debate was more fundamental: should people in the lower echelons of society be educated beyond literacy and numeracy, and if so, to what purpose? Beyond religion, which could be seen as a form of social control, did education, whatever form it took, pose a threat to the existing order? So despite the many interesting developments described here, always in the background is the question about how much actually filtered down to any significant percentage of the working class?

The Scottish 'lad of parts', or clever boy (never at the time a girl), who was encouraged to do well and get to university, no doubt had many parallels elsewhere, but provision was generally far from universal and teaching poor (Anderson, 1995). However, an interesting feature of the industrialisation era was the growth of technical education, again both formal and informal. Noteworthy were the mechanics' institutes, which offered lectures and demonstrations targeted at artisans, as well as the numerous libraries established in mining or factory communities (Cooke, 2006). The informal lecture, as we shall see, was certainly prominent in Owen's curriculum.

The Age of Enlightenment, at least in Scotland, saw remarkable developments in the universities, providing a sound basis for further expansion during the nineteenth century. Growth was accompanied by a shift in the curricula towards the natural, physical and social sciences in contrast to classics and theology, which previously dominated university instruction in Scotland, and was to remain the norm in England until the establishment of the University of London (Anderson, 1995).

There was a parallel growth in schooling, in great variety and in a wide range of contexts. Most prominent were the grammar schools in England and Wales and the academies in the Scottish burghs, catering mainly for the needs of the growing middle class. There was a huge range of other schools, which like many of the academic institutions were organised informally by private individuals (though often supported by religious, charity or other organisations), teaching diverse subjects like navigation or surveying for boys and domestic economy for girls.

Owen's background and early career

Robert Owen (Figure 6.1) was a product of schooling in one mid-Welsh community, Newtown, Montgomeryshire, where the small-town setting, the rural environment of the Upper Severn valley and the Welsh culture all influenced his personal development, and ultimately educational thinking. Kin, class and language also had considerable impact on the personality and thinking of a highly precocious child. The skills Owen acquired in Newtown were essentially practical: reading, writing, simple accounts, shop work, potential social skills and, interestingly, monitorial duties at school, supervising younger pupils on behalf of the master. Owen read widely, supported by his teacher and a local vicar, who lent him books conveying enlightened messages. There were also interesting religious and linguistic influences. He was apparently highly religious and, while the family were Anglican, perhaps touched by evangelical Methodism. Much of his later writing was certainly millennial in tone and he also picked up typically Welsh oratorical skills, deployed to good effect promoting his ideas on public platforms. Beyond education, religion and language were certainly to become significant issues later in his life (on Owen see Harrison, 1969; Butt, 1971; ; Pollard and Salt, 1971; Donnachie, 2005; for Owen's works see Claeys, 1993, 2005).

Migration was a notable feature in Owen's early career. Leaving mid-Wales, apprenticeship and retail experience followed in geographical locations as diverse as Stamford, Lincolnshire, London and Manchester. All represented interesting contrasts of size, location and function, reflecting in different ways the economic and social turmoil of the period. Owen was also astute enough to learn how to deal with different classes of customer, deferring to his betters as seemed appropriate. Mentors were always critical, notably James McGuffog, a successful Scottish linen draper and leading citizen of Stamford, who showed him how employees could be treated with consideration.

Thereafter, Owen made rapid occupational shifts, ultimately managing cotton mills in Manchester and Scotland. En route he absorbed enlightened and reformist ideas garnered through membership of the Manchester Literary and Philosophical Society and of the town's Board of Health. He actually delivered several papers at the ML&PS about education, while the latter body was one of the first to address problems of urban industrialism, especially the condition of factory children. So Owen's activities in Manchester further reinforced his growing interest in childhood education (Donnachie, 2005).

New Lanark, 1785–1800: Community and philanthropy

Turning now to the main locus of this chapter, New Lanark in southern Scotland was established in 1785 by a prominent Scottish merchant, David Dale, philanthropic employer and Owen's future father-in-law. Though

Figure 6.1 Robert Owen, c. 1821, seen surrounded by iconic images of Owenism, including his essays on *A New View of Society* and the implements of spade husbandry, a fad of the time and an early example of efforts to promote environmental sustainability

typical of many factory communities, it was one of the largest of the early industrial era and uniquely located near the famous Falls of Clyde, the most spectacular and celebrated in the country. While the falls attracted growing numbers of (mainly) upper and middle-class tourists interested in romantic scenery, the mills also became objects of curiosity because large factories and the number of women and children employed were unusual (Donnachie and Hewitt, 2011). Some families were migrants from the Highlands, victims of the clearances, or the many children (500 or more), orphans rescued by Dale from the streets, parishes or orphanages in Edinburgh, Glasgow and other towns (see Nicolson and Donnachie, 2003 on the Highland migrants). New Lanark's founder, while anxious to see the best returns on his investment, was motivated by religion to provide homes and schooling for his youthful workers. As McLaren (2000) has shown, the education Dale provided was better than that of parochial schools – even including informal activities like singing, dancing and merry-making generally. Owen, arriving in 1800 as managing partner for a Manchester consortium, and having married Dale's eldest daughter, therefore had a useful legacy on which to build (McLaren, 2000).

Other educational reformers

In advance of Owen others of philanthropic dispositions (some religiously motivated) were concerned about the condition of children and their education. Both Bell and Lancaster were advocates of the monitorial system, what the French called *education mutual*, by which often large numbers of scholars could be taught by what amounted to rote learning.

Bell, though a Scot, was an Anglican clergyman, whose mission in India was primarily focused on running schools in Madras, where before 1792 he introduced a monitorial system. Returning to England in 1796 he tried without much success to promote his ideas, which he continued to do as a clergyman in both England and Scotland. Later, in 1811, he was persuaded by Anglicans and others to promote his system along religious lines. The National Society for the Education of the Poor was partly designed to counter the dissenting notions promoted by Lancaster and Owen. Like the latter, Bell visited von Fellenberg and Pestalozzi, whose methods generally eschewed anything resembling rote learning.

The greatest promoter of working-class education was the Quaker, Joseph Lancaster, who established his first school in 1798. He opened the Borough Road Free School in Southwark in 1801, soon developing a monitorial system based on ordered discipline and rewards in which older scholars, suitably trained, communicated knowledge to youngsters. Lanacaster published the first of several manuals, *Improvements in Education* (1803), which went through a number of editions, and in which he acknowledged his debt to Bell. He subsequently travelled widely promoting his system, invariably accompanied by young assistants who had served as monitors able to demonstrate the method and thus encouraging the establishment of more monitorial schools.

Given the constraints of travel and distance at the time, the geography and reach of this pedagogy, if limited in adoption, were surprisingly widespread, including Ireland and Scotland, to which Owen, already formulating his own ideas about education, invited Lancaster in 1812. Owen, flanked by professors from the university and by churchmen, chaired a dinner in Glasgow at which Lancaster explained his system, introducing one of his assistants to help demonstrate its key features. Owen's reply indicated his vision. With a rational education, he announced, 'all those in the lower walks of life, and the character of the whole community, will rise many degrees...and while none will suffer, all must be essentially benefited'. Further, those exposed to the system 'must learn the habits of obedience, order, regularity, industry' which were as important as learning to read, write and count, vital though these skills undoubtedly were. In an oblique reference to future plans he suggested the schools which 'contain the younger children in the day time, will likewise serve for evening and Sunday schools, at which times those who may be past the proper age for the first, and strangers who may come amongst us, may be instructed' (quoted in Donnachie, 2005, p.110).

Owen's early reforms at New Lanark

The year 1812 also saw crucial developments in Owen's thinking about how New Lanark, already subject to his workplace and community reforms, might become a template for education and regeneration nationally (Donnachie and Hewitt, 2011, pp.59–84). As a means of encouraging new partners sympathetic to his ideas he produced his *Statement Regarding the New Lanark Establishment*. Partly a business prospectus and partly a summary of what he visualised for further improvements at New Lanark, it described his early management of the community. It also articulated his aspirations for the future and gave some indication of the way his thoughts were developing, many of which fed through to his famous essays on *A New View of Society*. What briefly were his main proposals?

Owen said he wanted to increase the population, reduce expense, enhance domestic arrangements and improve character. This would be done by developing the facilities of the 'New Institution' (just built, but not yet fitted out), opening a village store, establishing communal cooking and dining facilities, providing a dance hall, school and lecture rooms (doubling as a church), and improving communications with the neighbourhood. He also proposed that in the dining room the 'immediate removal of the tables to the ceiling' for dancing and concerts was to be accomplished by means of hoists. This method of saving space was used elsewhere, notably in the schoolrooms, where the famous visual aids could be lifted off the floor to an appropriate height.

These proposals suggest that Owen was already thinking about social improvement driven by education and training. The communal arrangements for the supply of provisions and cooking, dining and leisure activities are extremely interesting and might well have had wider application. There was also a hint of this in the closing section of the *Statement*, where Owen suggested these benefits would, in any case, be extended to the wider community beyond the confines of New Lanark.

Moreover, by ensuring that the profits had been ploughed back into the business and by following enlightened management principles, he had created an establishment which was more like 'a national benevolent institution than a manufacturing works founded by an individual'.

A New view of society

Owen's famous essays on *A New View of Society* (1812–14, collected ed. 1816) stressed the importance of environment on 'character formation' and called for a national system of education (Claeys, 1993; Davis and O'Hagan, 2010). Briefly, the essays stated his opinion that education held the key to social progress and at the same time social renewal with strong moral undertones. This was exemplified in essays Two and Three by reference to New Lanark, apparently transformed by his presence and ideas, and then everything promoted in essay Four to a scheme of national, even international, regeneration.

Such theory as underpinned by these notions, as suggested, came from Owen's upbringing and experience, both much influenced by the environment and culture of rural mid-Wales and his numerous occupational shifts. Possibly he had read Rousseau in Manchester or at a later date when he became interested in education and the educational systems of Lancaster, Bell and others. He may also have had access to translations of further work by Pestalozzi, thanks to French officers billeted in Lanark, one (or more) of whom acted as a tutor to his children. Rousseau's *Emile* (1762 when an English edition also appeared) was concerned with education of the whole person for citizenship and life and also contained some specific advice about raising children. It was known to some educational reformers, though few of its recommendations were followed (on either side of the Channel).

Since defective characters could be reformed, as he had proved, Owen's ideas had immediate appeal to the elites, who felt threatened by potential disorder. Apparently within the gates of New Lanark there were no fears, no resort to the law, so Owen claimed. And despite rumours to the contrary not only was religion tolerated it was even promoted, possibly as another means of social control, though Owen was careful to avoid suggesting this. But there was much more in the essays beyond character formation and popular education, for they included extended discussions on factory conditions, particularly those of the numerous children employed in textile mills like his. However, most were much worse off than those at New Lanark.

The essays brought Owen instant fame as a reformer, since anyone with solutions to the dire economic and social problems at the end of the French Wars was likely to command attention and attract considerable publicity. Owen's extensive campaigns for factory, poor law and educational reforms followed on from *A New View of Society* and indeed the year of their publication as a single volume proved a monumental one in the development of infant and childhood education at New Lanark.

The Institute and School

Although workplace and community reforms continued apace the most radical innovations occurred in education (Browning, 1971; Donnachie, 2003; Davis and O'Hagan, 2010). Owen had begun 'to clear the foundation for the infant and other schools, to form the new character of the rising population' as early as 1809, and his *Statement* three years later described the planned 'New Institution' and its various functions. When New Lanark was advertised for sale in the *Glasgow Herald* of 24 December 1813, a building 145ft long by 45ft broad 'at present unoccupied' was described as having been 'planned to admit of an extensive Store Cellar, a Public Kitchen, Eating and Exercise Room, a School, Lecture Room and Church'. This became the Institute and was said by Owen to have been erected at a cost of £3,000. In 1814 the articles of the new reforming partnership included a school on Lancaster's system, a monitorial instructor, Alexander Burrage of Ipswich, being appointed soon after. Teaching aids would be provided by the British and Foreign School Society, the brain-child of Owen's partners, among others, and religious instruction was to be non-sectarian, with the Bible used only as a reading aid.

With Owen in effective control of the mills and village, the long-planned building entirely devoted to education could be fitted out at the cost of another £3,000. Another building which became Robert Owen's School for Children was described as a 'Public Kitchen' on a plan of 1809 but probably not built till later. When John Griscom (1771–1852), the American educational reformer, visited New Lanark in 1819, he noted that this building was 'nearly completed' and had been designed as 'a kitchen for the whole village'. At that point Owen thought this could save £4,000–5,000 a year, 'besides the superior training and improved habits it will produce', but it never became a reality. Subsequent descriptions suggest that Institute and School were virtually inter-changeable, though the former always housed the infant school. William Davidson, writing in 1828 after Owen had left, observed dancing taught in the school, which was also used for lectures in rooms still housing the 'historical maps and paintings' as well as a terrestrial globe 19ft in circumference (Figure 6.2).

The Institute for the Formation of Character was officially opened on New Year's Day 1816 (Figure 6.3). In a lengthy address, punctuated by a musical

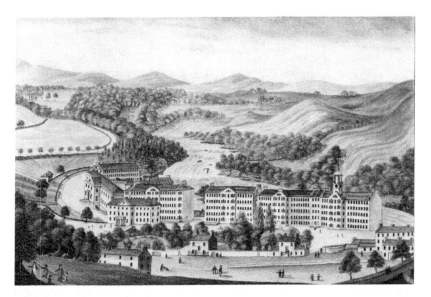

Figure 6.2 Water colour of New Lanark by John Winning, c. 1818, showing the mills in middle ground with the River Clyde beyond, Institute (left of centre with columns) and the School for Children to its left. Children can be seen in the playground in front of Institute and also walking down one of the many paths Owen laid out for recreational and educational purposes
Source: New Lanark Trust.

recital, Owen explained his educational philosophy to an audience of 1,200 villagers. 'The character of man is without a single exception, always formed for him', and saying that

> it must be evident to those who have been in the practice of observing children with attention, that much of good or evil is taught to or acquired by a child at a very early period of its life; that much of temper or disposition is correctly or incorrectly formed before he attains his second year; and that many durable impressions are made at the termination of the first 12 or even 6 months of his existence.

Owen probably got much of this from his own experience. But descriptions and critiques of Pestalozzi's methods began to appear in English c. 1805, which he may have read as he refined his ideas. In essence, his theory of character formation and general education involved the belief that social training ought to begin 'from the very moment a child can walk alone', which was close to Pestalozzi's thinking.

Owen's son, Robert Dale Owen (1801–77), recently returned from Philipp von Fellenberg's school in Switzerland, and writing in *An Outline of the System*

Figure 6.3 Dancing class at New Lanark watched by visitors, including many women, (early 1820s). The girls' dresses and uniforms for the boys were specially designed by Owen, who may well be one of the figures looking on in the right foreground. The walls are hung with some of the famous visual aids designed by Catherine Whitwell, a pioneer of visual education

of Education at New Lanark (1824) provided an excellent description of the layout:

> The principal school-room is fitted up with desks and forms on the Lancastrian plan, having a free passage down the centre of the room. It is surrounded, except at one end where a pulpit stands, with galleries, which are convenient when this room is used, as it frequently is, either as a lecture-room or place of worship.

> The other and smaller apartment on the second floor has the walls hung round with representations of the most striking zoological and mineralogical specimens, including quadrupeds, birds, fishes, reptiles, insects, shells, minerals etc. At one end there is a gallery, adapted for the purpose of an orchestra, and at the other end are hung very large representations of the two hemispheres; each separate country, as well as the various seas, islands etc. being differently coloured, but without any names attached to them. This room is used as a lecture- and ball-room, and it is here that the dancing and singing lessons are daily given. It is likewise occasionally used as a reading-room for some of the classes.

> The lower storey is divided into three apartments, of nearly equal dimensions, 12ft high, and supported by hollow iron pillars, serving at the same

time as conductors in winter for heated air, which issues through the floor of the upper storey, and by which means the whole building may, with care, be kept at any required temperature. It is in these three apartments that the younger classes are taught reading, natural history, and geography.

(quoted in Donnachie and Hewitt, 2011, pp.98–9)

Beyond the Institute and some time after 1816 the nearby school was fitted up the same way, the largest of the upper rooms (now restored to its Regency splendour) also having a musicians' gallery.

The infant school

While there was much that was innovative in the educational provision at New Lanark, the infant school, thought to be one of the first, was certainly remarkable. Children were admitted from the age of two, staying until they moved on to the school when four years old. Until well established Owen 'daily watched and superintended... knowing that if the foundation were not truly laid, it would be in vain to expect a satisfactory structure'. With his usual finesse in matters of human relations he evidently 'acquired the most sincere affections of all the children' and also won over the parents 'who were highly delighted with the improved conduct, extraordinary progress, and continually increasing happiness of their children'.

Owen initially chose 'two persons who had a great love for and unlimited patience with infants', James Buchanan, a Swedenborgian and former weaver, and Molly Young, a 17-year-old village girl. Buchanan, interestingly remained at New Lanark until c. 1819 when he moved to London, opening the city's first infant school at Brewer's Green, Westminster. He later inspired Samuel Wilderspin (1791–1866), who became a leading promoter of infant education.

His instructions to the staff forbade corporal punishment, children had to be treated kindly and encouraged to make each other happy. Reflecting Lancaster's monitoring system, the older children from 4 to 6 were to take special care of the younger ones. Much of this came indirectly from Pestalozzi, who also emphasised the importance of kindness and common sense in his teaching. It also echoed the philosophy of Jeremy Bentham, one of Owen's partners, regarding the greatest happiness of the greatest number. But by 'happy' did Owen really mean 'docile'?

A playground outside the Institute, said to be the first, was used in fine weather, where visitors observed children coming forward to be patted as Owen went round! Indeed, the school was run on the play principle, no child being forced in any way, not even to mid-morning rest, although 'when an infant felt inclined to sleep it should be quietly allowed to do so'. Emphasising the informality, infants played together, rarely had toys and few books, but relied on natural objects gathered on excursions to surrounding gardens, woods and fields – including small animals. In fact extensive use was made of the surrounding environment at all levels of schooling. Complementing this were paintings of flora and fauna, just a few of the numerous visual aids, found throughout the schools. Again the emphasis on observation and experience was borrowed from Pestalozzi.

In Owen's opinion the infants were completely unlike others of their age; indeed, he said, 'unlike the children of any class of society'. Griscom took a more pragmatic view, saying that 'this baby school is of great consequence to the establishment, for it enables mothers to shut up their houses in security, and to attend to their duties in the factory', without having to worry about their off-spring.

Curricula

Children from five to ten or 12 attended the main schools, either in daytime or in the evening. Among many reforms, Owen in 1816 reduced working hours and stopped employing children under 10, which had a dramatic impact on attendance. Evening sessions, attracting 350 before reform soon averaged 500. The classes for reading, writing and arithmetic adopted some of Lancaster's ideas, including the deployment of monitors passing on learning by rote, in a sense the factory system applied to education. For writing, copy-books were abandoned as soon as possible, and children encouraged to develop their own style. Arithmetic was first taught 'on the plan generally adopted at that time in Scotland', but soon Pestalozzi's system of mental arithmetic was introduced.

Alongside elementary studies, and forming one of the most notable features of Owen's system, was instruction by lecture, discussion and debate, on subjects such as geography, natural science, ancient and modern history, and civics, much favoured by Pestalozzi. Lectures in both day and evening schools would be attended by 40–50 children, though sometimes as many as 100 on occasion. Lectures were illustrated with maps, pictures and diagrams, aids shown on a contemporary print of one of the upper rooms in the Institute, and much favoured by Owen.

Outstanding in this respect were geography and history, which both had an important place in the curriculum at New Lanark. In what were clearly designed as public performances for visitors up to 150 children vied with each other in pointing out places on large wall-maps of the world, apparently with such degrees of competence that one of the country's leading admirals who, as Owen put it, 'had sailed round the world, (but) could not answer many of the questions which some of these children not 6 years old readily replied to, giving the places most correctly'. Field studies, as in the infant school, also played a part, with youngsters encouraged to go out into the woods and fields surrounding the village, through which Owen cut paths and walks, collecting specimens and making observations. Historical geographers have indicated that such activities were far from universal even a century or more later (Gruffudd, 1996; Ploszajska, 1996).

Geography also had strong moral undertones, for the children were often reminded that but for an accident of birth they might have been born into a different society with values totally unlike those of their own. They were taught to respect other people's ideas and way of life and never to be uncharitable or intolerant, suggesting that the subject was seen as part of Owen's citizenship agenda (McLaren, 2000).

History also relied heavily on visual aids as Robert Dale Owen describes:

> Seven large maps or tables, laid out on the principle of the Stream of Time, are hung round the spacious room. These being made of canvass, may be rolled up at pleasure. On the Streams, each of which is differently coloured, and represents a nation, are painted the principal events which occur in the history of those nations. Each century is closed by a horizontal line, drawn across the map. By means of these maps, the children are taught the outlines of Ancient and Modern History, with ease to themselves, and without being liable to confound different events, or different nations. On hearing of any two events, the child has but to recollect the situation on the tables of the paintings, by which those are represented, in order to be furnished at once with their chronological relation to each other. If the events are contemporary, he will instantly perceive it.
>
> (quoted in Donnachie and Hewitt, 2011, pp.104–5)

The history time-charts, as well as other visual aids, were the work of one of the teachers, Catherine Whitwell (born 1791), sister of the Owenite architect, Stedman Whitwell, who deserves recognition as a pioneer of both visual and inter-active methods, formal and informal. Whitwell was remarkably progressive for her time not only for her artistic skills but also in her pedagogy and curricula, part undoubtedly from Pestalozzi, part of her own devising. Apart from artistic skills she was well informed about natural sciences, author of a book on astronomy, first published in 1816. This takes the form of a dialogue between mother and daughter, possibly modelled on the format of Jane Marcet's *Conversations on Chemistry* (1806). Rumoured, like some other Owenites, to be an advocate of free-love, Whitwell was dismissed after Owen left New Lanark, but subsequently taught at Orbiston (1825–8), another Owenite community near modern day Motherwell.

An icon of reform

During 1815–5 New Lanark received thousands of visitors (including many women) from all over Britain, Ireland, Europe and the United States, among them major Enlightenment figures and reformers (Donnachie, 2004). What attracted most attention were the Institute and School, where beyond the innovative teaching more informal activities such as dancing, musical recitals and concerts could be observed. Dancing lessons were begun at two years of age and visitors were astonished to see how

> these children, standing up 70 couples at a time in the dancing room, and often surrounded by many strangers, would with the uttermost ease and natural grace go through all the dances of Europe, with so little direction from their master, that the strangers would be unconscious that there was a dancing-master in the room.

Dancing lessons were also given in the evening and Griscom saw 50 or 60 young people thus engaged. 'Owen', he noted, 'has discovered that dancing is one means of reforming vicious habits. He thinks it effects this by promoting cheerfulness and contentment, and thus diverting attention from things that are vile and degrading' (quoted in Donnachie, 2005, p.170).

The children were also taught to sing in harmony in choirs of 200 or more, performing settings of Scottish and other traditional songs, and at the close of the evening school all would gather in one room and sing a hymn. A recently discovered handbill (now in the National Library of Scotland) for a concert and ball to raise funds for a new school house in the nearby village of Nemphlar not only gives details of the songs and instrumental music by the village band and orchestra but also confirms Owen's interest in promoting education in the wider community.

One final feature must be mentioned. Both boys and girls were regularly drilled in the playground in front of the Institute or in the village streets 'with precision equal, as many officers stated, to some regiments of the line'. Contemporary accounts described these military exercises, accompanied by the band, though in the context of a militaristic age were probably less sinister than might have appeared. Owen, as with dancing, nevertheless expounded on their value in several of his writings.

Conclusion

What lessons can be learned from this case study of Owen's experiments?

Owen's curriculum, drawing to an extent on Pestalozzi, Von Fellenberg and Lancaster, was highly innovative, embracing subjects rarely taught at the time and deploying specially designed visual aids, natural history and environmental studies. The schools were open to boys and girls equally, adult evening classes replicated much of the day-time subject matter, and popular lectures, concerts and dances figured strongly. While our main interest is in children, Owen was unusual in the context of his time, showing awareness of adult and continuing education. This first meant offering the same curriculum in evening classes to those who had missed out on the basics earlier in life, and then more innovatively providing lectures to members of the community in a wide range of popular, if uplifting and utilitarian subjects. Whitwell was one of the lecturers and certainly continued to deliver evening lectures at Orbiston, where she was said to have made a dramatic impression on her audiences. By then, however, Owen had moved on to the United States where he played a leading role in another community at New Harmony in Indiana (on education there see McLaren, 1996; Donnachie, 2005). As the most recent re-assessment demonstrates, considerable controversy still surrounds his activities in and beyond New Lanark (Thompson and Williams, 2011).

New Lanark, a World Heritage Site since 2000, remains an icon for many of Robert Owen's ideas on education, citizenship, gender equality, welfare, co-operation, the environment and sustainability. All of these concerns underpin the interpretation for visitors and the extensive resources provided for children and their teachers both on line (see New Lanark website) and in hard copy. Children in school parties and family groups constitute a substantial proportion of visitors to New Lanark (as they also do at New Harmony). Indeed, more than a third of paying visitors (whether school parties or families with children) are children. Of non-paying visitors, children are likely to be a similar proportion. Children are exceptionally well catered for at New Lanark, especially in the reconstructed Regency school laid out on Lancastrian lines, with recreations of the famous visual aids, maps, a massive globe, historical time charts and other learning resources, some serious, but mostly fun as they were undoubtedly intended in Owen's time. The virtual host and moderator of the highly entertaining historical ride in the Visitors Centre and the presenter of the keynote film in Robert Owen's School for Children is Annie Macleod, a fictitious young mill worker of the period described in this chapter.

References

R. Anderson (1995) *Education and the Scottish People* (Oxford: Clarendon Press).

M. Browning (1971) 'Owen as an educator' in J. Butt (ed.) *Robert Owen: Prince of cotton spinners* (Newton Abbot: David & Charles).

J. Butt (ed.) (1971) *Robert Owen: Prince of cotton spinners* (Newton Abbot: David & Charles).

A. Cooke (2006) *From Popular Enlightenment to Lifelong Learning: A history of adult education in Scotland 1707–2005* (Leicester: National Institute of Adult and Continuing Education).

G. Claeys (ed.) (1993) *Selected Works of Robert Owen* (4 vols.) (London: William Pickering).

G. Claeys (ed.) (2005) *Owenite Socialism: Pamphlets and correspondence* (10 vols.) (London: Routledge).

R. A. Davis and F. O'Hagan (2010) *Continuum Library of Educational Thought: Robert Owen* (London: Continuum).

I. Donnachie (2003) 'Education in Robert Owen's new society: The New Lanark institute and schools', *The Encyclopaedia of Informal Education*, www.infed.org/thinkers/et-owen.htm.

I. Donnachie (2004) 'Historic tourism to New Lanark and the falls of clyde 1795–1830', *Journal of Tourism & Cultural Change*, 2, 145–62.

I. Donnachie (2005) *Robert Owen: Social visionary* (Edinburgh: Birlinn). New ed. 2011.

I. Donnachie and G. Hewitt (2011) *Historic New Lanark: The dale and owen industrial community since 1785* (Edinburgh: Edinburgh University Press).

P. Gruffudd (1996) 'The countryside as educator: Schools, rurality and citizenship in inter-war Wales', *Journal of Historical Geography*, 22, 412–23.

J. F. C. Harrison (1969) *Robert Owen and the Owenites in Britain and America* (London: Routledge).

D. McLaren (1996) 'Robert Owen, William Maclure and New Harmony', *History of Education*, 25, 223–33.

D. McLaren (2000) 'Education for citizenship and the new moral world of Robert Owen', *Scottish Educational Review*, 32, 107–16.

M. Nicolson and I. Donnachie (2003) 'The New Lanark highlanders: Migration, community and language 1785–c1850', *Family and Community History*, 6, 19–32.

T. Ploszajska (1996) 'Constructing the subject: Geographical models in English Schools, 1870–1944', *Journal of Historical Geography*, 22, 388–98.

S. Pollard and J. Salt (eds) (1971) *Robert Owen: Prophet of the poor* (London: Macmillan).

N. Thompson and C. Williams (eds) (2011) *Robert Owen and his legacy* (Cardiff: University of Wales Press).

Archive collections

Records of Owen and his educational activities are both extensive and widely scattered. The following are representative:

Glasgow City Archives (www.csglasgow.org/archives)

University of Glasgow Archive Services (www.glasgow.ac.uk/archives)

National Co-operative Archive, Manchester (www.archive.coop/)

University of Southern Indiana (www.usi.edu/library/archives.asp)

New Harmony, Indiana, Workingmens' Institute (www.workingmens inst.org)

New Lanark Trust (www.newlanark.org/searchroom)

North Lanarkshire Archives (www.northlanarkshire.gov.uk/archives)

The Robert Owen Memorial Museum, Newtown, Powys (www. robert-owen-museum.org.uk)

Scottish Archives Network (www.scan.org.uk)

Senate House Library, University of London.

7

The Tarpaulin and the Tablecloth: Cover and Non-Traditional Education in Traditional Spaces of Schooling

Stephen T. Sadlier

In late 2006, Andrea walked on the cobblestoned street when she met an elderly woman in an apron selling candy out of a palm reed basket. Like all her teacher colleagues, Andrea knew the Federal Preventative Police (PFP) would soon reach Oaxaca City and break up the protests that flourished after the local police had raided a teacher encampment in the Zócalo, the principal square downtown. Many protesters had abandoned the streets in fear, though the Sección 22, the local chapter of the Educators Union (SNTE) with affiliation in the CNTE dissidence, had not agreed to dissolve the manifestations just yet. Walking by, Andrea's gaze must have revealed her fear, for the candy vender approached handing prayer cards. Greeting Andrea she said, 'I bought these for you teachers, to keep you safe'. Five years later, Andrea would explain to me how many different sectors of society backed the teachers during that struggle, while the encounter with the vendor's prayer cards would bring tears to her eyes. Regardless, after the events of 2006, Andrea would never teach the same again. This chapter focuses on how Andrea and her colleague Osvaldo brought to their rural public school classrooms teaching practices derived from their experiences in street protests in Oaxaca City.

Teachers at the Plantón

Teaching, activism and eating all come up in this story, one which revolves around the well-publicised events of the 2006 Oaxacan teachers' movement (Martínez Vásquez, 2007; Osorno and Meyer, 2007; Denham and C.A.S.A. Collective, 2008). Riding one morning to attend a protest in Oaxaca City one summer day in 2010, I learned how my former student and career elementary school teacher, Lourdes, was unhappy about missing classes. It was almost four years since the police raids and teacher manifestations noted above. Oaxaca, like abutting Chiapas State renowned for the ski mask-wearing Zapatista autonomy activists, has a long history of grassroots activism whereby unionised public school teachers have mobilised around issues of salary, democratic authority and social justice (Yescas Martínez, and Zafra, 1985). Still, Lourdes indicated that her work primarily centred in schools rather than the streets and that her absence from school would incur parental contempt when she returned. Given that she wished to be teaching in the classroom, I listened curiously for ideas on how attendance at the Oaxaca City teacher protest encampments or *plantones*[1] mattered to Lourdes and her colleagues. The permanent *plantones* of the past used to encompass dances, but now there is nothing but administrative housekeeping there, Lourdes lamented. Getting to Oaxaca City, Lourdes parked several blocks west of Alameda Park and began to speak on the phone with a colleague. Outside, I observed the *plantón*, the blue sky of June overhead, the green canopy of *laureles de la India* trees and the blue-green vinyl tarpaulins. 'Okay', Lourdes, summoned me from my peering; 'we have to go back', pointing west towards where her union delegation had set up a roadblock. 'But first, let's eat', she suggested.

If Lourdes hesitantly left school for the protests at the *plantón*, Osvaldo and Andrea have described those spaces as socially effervescent, rife with pedagogies of care, concern and at times playfulness. To start, the 2006 protest spaces around Oaxaca City contended with violent repression at the hands of state forces that killed at least 23, disappeared 32 and injured 350 with impunity (Beas Torres, 2007, p.72). The popular response to this authoritarianism involved marches, performances, thousands of neighbourhood roadblocks and a petition to oust the Oaxacan governor, or, to Oaxacan popular radio presenter Berta Elena Muñoz, the '*Desgobernador*', a word that plays on 'non-governor' and the verb 'to misrule' (Comisión Civil Internacional de Observación por los Derechos Humanos, 2007, p.177). These were disturbing and creative months of repression and mobilisation during which Osvaldo felt an itch. At the marches, roadblocks and *plantón* activities, he met with Andrea and others at '*las mesas*', the public discussion tables that occurred around town to seek what Martínez Vásquez (2007, p.133) called 'dialog', 'democracy' and 'governability' in Oaxaca in light of state-sponsored violence. The disarray on the streets inspired Osvaldo, as he devised a plan to develop reading interest through the spoken word. Similarly, for Andrea, the beleaguered city in 2006 became a space where she intensified her commitment towards school-based inclusion for students with handicaps. She related to me how the importance of inclusion, regardless of (dis)ability, struck her in *las mesas* when she found herself clashing with parents who felt frustrated over classes cancelled for teacher protests. Andrea recognised the value of open arguments at *las mesas* and realised that such organised public encounters of difference were teachable in schools. But these *mesa* dialogs shut down suddenly, Andrea detailed, during the most trying period in October when protesters became aware of the encroaching PFP. At this moment in time, Andrea met the candy vender described above and graciously received the gesture of solidarity that the prayer cards represented.

Government and misrule

To show how Osvaldo and Andrea brought their teaching practices from the protest movement into the classroom, I offer two fabric metaphors, the 'tarpaulin' and the 'tablecloth'. These covering materials show how the two teachers conducted spaces that called for another kind of schooling. Valorising these spaces in educational geography terms might, following Holloway et al. (2010), broaden the zone of where teachers and researchers locate sites for non-formal educational practices. Yet at the same, as will become clear below, as unconventional as the tarpaulin and the tablecloth may be, they appear in 'traditional sites' (Holloway et al., 2010, p.595) of education related to school, planned parties at home and labour union gatherings. How the tarpaulin and the tablecloth unfold in spaces deemed traditional, however confounding this may seem, provides an opening for non-formal education and critical pedagogy which is the scope of this chapter.

To understand the uses of space I aim for here, I draw from the theory of government to show the tarpaulin and the tablecloth as politically viable projects for teachers (Dean, 2010, p.21). In Dean's words:

> Government as the 'conduct of conduct' entails the idea that the one governed is, at least in some rudimentary sense, an actor and therefore a locus of freedom. Government is an activity that shapes the field of action and thus, in this sense, attempts to shape freedom. However, while government gives shape to freedom, it is not constitutive of freedom. The governed are free in that they are actors, i.e. it is possible for them to act and to think in a variety of ways, and sometimes in ways not foreseen by authorities.

Government, here, suggests that attempts of the state to shape behaviours and to repress bodies rarely diminish one's ability to posit a different kind of power dynamic, even in spaces of repression and rule like the streets and the schools. Official practices of government may set out the parameters of how teachers counter them, that is, whether Andrea chooses to leave *las mesas* to avoid getting arrested. Still, authoritarianism cannot wholly prevent her from intersecting with Osvaldo, feeling the warmth of the candy vendor's gift or expressing to me how schools could become hothouses of democratic education given the existing despotism. In the end, the teachers are actors rather than targets, and as we see below, the misrule of the state lays the terrain for pedagogies that clamour for other conducts, namely, tarpaulin and the tablecloth modes of non-formal learning and socialisation for rural school communities.

In order to approach teaching as critical and political, I need to recognise how school-based teaching practices that strive for another kind of government rather than a wholesale shift in school practices and policies may ring as false consciousness or apolitical to those with more radical views of power and education. Schooling as an ideological practice to dissidents across Mexico in the CNTE caucus within the SNTE (CNTE, 2010) as well as in critical social theory and pedagogy in general (Freire, 1994) has long been associated with the maintenance of unequal power relations. That is, schools perpetuate the elements of culture and economics that keep the poor in poverty and the rich in privilege. And as such, critical pedagogies promote socially just education to overturn this, whereby teachers as 'transformative' (Giroux, 1988) intellectuals engage historically marginalised students, families and communities to become *aware of* and *transform* the mechanisms of injustice. Teachers in Oaxaca, however, work among students, families and colleagues who need little introduction into the stresses caused by, among other things, teargas canisters shot by the state police. The teachers I have observed who have faced police repression show awareness of the radical versions of critical pedagogies available to them, but instead they apply immediate and face-to-face interventions which may not lead to social change at all. In this regard, I suggest letting our gaze fall, as the governmentality of Dean (2010) suggests, on how teachers conduct themselves in unanticipated ways, even when within the more traditional sites of schooling and unionism. To approach these counterconducts as critical overtures for non-formal education, in the following pages I offer the tarpaulin and the tablecloth.

The Tarpaulin

Who is an activist in Oaxaca? One day in the spring of 2005 a mammoth shade-casting laurel de la India on the Oaxaca City Zócalo dropped to the ground, cut down to make space for a reconstruction project. In that Oaxacans are fond of their grand trees,[2] service workers and residents from around the Zócalo came out to the streets livid. Zócalo trees are particularly popular, providing shelter so deep into the sky that, standing below, the pedestrian can gaze at the blue and still feel protected from the sun. The term *bajo el laurel*, or below the laurel tree, has become code for open-air cultural events, dances, readings and social meetings in the shady spots around the Zócalo and nearby open spaces. One teacher would often suggest meeting *bajo el laurel* during my fieldwork. In addition to the fallen tree, public rage stemmed from the project's invoicing of building materials at as much as 100 times the market value (Sotelo Marbán, 2008, p.44) to 'beautify' and 'dignify' the Zócalo, which was already exalted as a UNESCO

World Heritage Site (Verástegui, 2010, p.291). Ire poured out from Zócalo pub workers and street vendors; with little formal link between them, they organised a 'vigilance committee' to monitor the construction and undertook public opinion surveys regarding the renovations. In the end, despite the support they generated, the renovations proceeded as planned and the tree activists were met with arrogance, threats and official explanations of tree blight. And then, another tree fell (Arrellanes, 2007, p.143). In all, by April, 2005, the protesters' attempt to halt the buzz saws and concrete mixers would presage the 2006 protests after the governor sent thousands of police officers to raid the teachers' *plantón*. And then later, when diverse participants came out to protest, a dynamic assembly of organisations and individuals called the People's Assembly of the *Pueblos* of Oaxaca (APPO) formed. The APPO would take great pains to be inclusive. The insertion of the word Pueblos, or Peoples, in the title, for example, referred to the multiplicity of Oaxacan worldviews represented within (Esteva, 2007, p.16). It would, however, face media smear campaigns calling it driven by dangerous ideologues (Bautista Martínez, 2008) even as it grew as a pluralistic assembly rather than a mission-driven organism (Martínez Vásquez, 2007; Osorno and Meyer, 2007; Sotelo Marbán, 2008). All of this is to suggest that Oaxacans have deep-rooted and actively negotiated ways of joining with others of differing perspectives. This becomes visible in times of conflict and is negotiated and taught on a daily basis among teachers and students, neighbours, colleagues and family members (Figure 7.1).

Around the time that the Zócalo trees fell in 2005, Osvaldo was convening at interdisciplinary reading workshop seminars at the National Pedagogical University (UPN) to address a problem of a different magnitude. These reading sessions ceased in May 2006 because the teachers' movement had taken full force and the business of in-service training seminars yielded to the protests. Osvaldo notes that the movement had developed in two phases, each central for his school-based reading project. First, the May and June 'trade union' struggle marked the beginning of the tussle; then he continued to reflect on the suspended UPN reading seminars. Later in the summer, the second part began with what he called 'intensified' disputes where the 'state' opposed 'civil society'. At this point, the teachers' movement turned into the wider social movement involving the APPO and many others outside of Sección 22 teachers. Osvaldo ended up at *las mesas* where anyone could gripe or propose solutions on how to bring Oaxaca back from the brink of a total state/civil society rift. During the dialogs, Osvaldo met parents annoyed with the teachers for missing classes for Sección 22 activities. Furthermore, during this second phase of the struggle, Osvaldo noted how distress among the activists had ruled the streets. In one event in the atrium of Carmen Alto church in downtown Oaxaca City, a group had organised a public cultural event with folk singer Lila Downs, actor-activist Ofelia Medina, the group Mujeres sin Miedo, or Fearless Women, and other performers. Osvaldo said

Figure 7.1 Oaxaca City, 15 February 2011, northwest of the Cathedral on Independencia Avenue. Earlier, a disturbance on the Zócalo, a block to the south, pitted teachers against the police, leaving street debris and a smoke plume from a police vehicle carrying riot fencing, torched by protesters. Rumours among the teachers ran that infiltrators had provoked the police, turning the peaceful protest into a violent one. Note the laurel de la India in Alameda Park (right)

that 'in Oaxaca we were living with fear' of police and paramilitary violence, so he found it inspiring listening to Fearless Women speak. Osvaldo detailed that the storyteller named Don Luis Cuentacuentos impressed him most of all the artists. Then, with his sights still on fomenting reading in his school, Osvaldo approached Don Luis to discuss how storytelling linked with reading. When Osvaldo indicated that his school was public rather than private, Don Luis added that he would be glad to come and tell stories for free. Months later, as this intensified conflict and mobilisation had dissolved and the teachers left Oaxaca City for their home communities, Osvaldo's collaboration with the storyteller set in motion a school-based reading project. So in the end, the pedagogies of the streets had made inroads into his classroom practices.

Eventually, Osvaldo's reading project expanded to include coordinated and more costly efforts like a multi-day book fair. For this, Osvaldo and his colleagues needed greater financial backing. While the public schools officially depend on the state educational bureaucracy through the Oaxaca office of public education, the IEEPO, in practice, Osvaldo and his colleagues would opt to accept funding from anyone who would help. They would oftentimes petition the IEEPO for support and never get a response; while in contrast, within 24 hours they would receive promises of help from a well-known Oaxaca City-based non-governmental organisation (NGO) with connections to the banking industry.[3] The teachers proceeded with their public school-based pedagogies by courting private and NGO sector assistance. With this aim, one day Osvaldo and three others from his school went to Oaxaca City to meet with a programme coordinator of the enterprise NGO. Sitting in the patio of a café, drinking orange-aid in the sundrenched late afternoon, the teachers thanked the coordinator for having funded a recent school trip to an archaeological site south of Oaxaca City. Then, one teacher tallied and handed over a stack of Mexican Peso bills, as the trip was partially subsidised by parental contribution. During the gathering, the coordinator greeted me with curious intent; with this opening I asked her how her organisation came to support school-based reading. Reading should be fun instead of an obligation, she insisted, though, even in her own schooling, reading the classics had always seemed a chore instead of a joy. The coordinator's project strove towards making students more autonomous readers, a matching goal to Osvaldo's. On this note, during the meeting, Osvaldo began to describe and sketch out a tree house he had envisioned for student reading. In all, conversing with the coordinator in Oaxaca City was a tactical choice so that Osvaldo and his colleagues could maintain relationships and sound out future funding projects like the tree house. The teachers would accept support from anyone who offered it, Osvaldo reiterated, but only if total pedagogical control remained in the hands of the teachers.[4] For the moment, this meant requesting support from the enterprise NGO, a business-friendly organism, which, though new as a stakeholder in fomenting quality education, follows a long tradition of business-sector activism in Oaxaca (Zafra, Hernández Díaz and Garza Zepeda, 2002). For this reason, NGO's are interested in thoughtful school-based projects run by self-starting teachers, a detail not lost on Osvaldo and his colleagues.

Still, no chance encounter with a storyteller during a protest or bankroll from an NGO could make a school-based reading project come to life. It would take one more step, the restoration of relationships with school parents, and from this, the construction of a tarpaulin over the school patio to hold reading events. To start, when Osvaldo and his colleagues returned from the city to the village school after missing nearly half a year of classes in 2006, the parents held a community-based 'general gathering'. One of the mothers felt that the teachers owed a debt to the community, saying: *Bueno maestros, ya se fueron a luchar, ahora queremos una educación de calidad*, or 'okay teachers, you had your fight; now we want quality education'. Through the school's advisory committee on pedagogy and technology, the teachers projected their version of what quality education might look like. And step by step, first by coming to consensus on the singular importance of reading for all academic disciplines and then by implementing a 'reading club', the teachers began to cultivate rapport in the community. Eventually, with the support of the parents' committee,[5] the teachers staged the annual book fair, a four-day festival to promote reading for pleasure and develop an appreciation of how oral stories influence written ones. The fair would include lullabies and informal conversations to promote camaraderie, or *compañerismo* (Trinidad Galván, 2001) to scaffold children's literacy, understood as the ability to accomplish social, academic and critique-oriented goals where reading and writing play a significant part (Gee, 2001). The book fair event would eventually enjoy parental support, thriving on in-kind sponsorship such as borrowing chairs from a chilli growers' collective and a Catholic Church, technical assistance offered by in-service trainers from the Centro de Maestros, an in-service training centre under the IEEPO as well as financial donations from local, national and international organisations, including a California-based NGO and a potluck fundraiser organised by a southern US-based teachers' group.

In 2010, I would observe the cultural, learning and social fun events of 4th annual book fair (see Figure 7.2). In one instance, I sat beneath the

Figure 7.2   22 June 2010. Foreground: Storytellers and teachers facilitate comic book production based on personal narratives for mothers and grandmothers at rural elementary school in the Central Valleys of Oaxaca State. The village brass band sitting in the background would throughout the day musically commemorate events and participant achievements when anyone, students included, called out 'a Diana please!'

tarpaulin which blocked the rays of the June sun. Among many student and adult public-speaking moments, the above-mentioned corporate NGO coordinator had issued kind opening words on reading. Then there was what they called a 'didactic' concert with a puppet master of ceremonies who introduced each song that folk ensemble. Other puppets would then discuss the different regions of Oaxaca where the songs came from, including the local food, plants and clothing. Then a storyteller took the podium who with gestures and different voices presented fables to which the students responded enthusiastically. During all this, children sat in the nave of the makeshift theatre with teachers, parents and community members off to the side. There, children would come to sit on the laps of the adults and ask for the autograph of the storyteller seated beside me. During the day, I would note how the parents and Osvaldo each laboured in tacit collaboration, which might seem unlikely given the conflictive relationship between them over the years. During recess, the male and female members of parents' committee cooked and served food to all of us adults seated at a long table. I joined in conversation with Centro de Maestros trainers who would lead workshops later on, and socially lubricated by tamales, scrambled eggs and *atole*, they seemed interested how all this interested me coming from the States. The tarpaulin, far enough above us so that we did not feel solar radiation off the plastic, loomed as a structural element of the whole event, keeping us shaded in our airy pavilion. I recall its shelter later in the day, too, as it lapped above in the faint wind bursts that often mark afternoons in the rainy season when it is not raining. The parents' committee had roped the tarpaulin onto tree limbs and building roves. In all this, they coordinated efforts and resources separate from yet alongside the teachers who focused more on the workshop aspects of the event.

The Tablecloth

After the visit to the 2010 *plantón* mentioned above, Lourdes and I ended up having lunch outside of town. What began as a table for two ended up for a group of eight as we kept bumping into other teachers. I would eventually meet Osvaldo there and learn about the book fair. Lourdes and two others commented that they needed to stop by the *plantón* to 'sign in', a practice undertaken so one's delegation avoids Sección 22 sanctions but which comprises of teachers signing in for others in collegial solidarity. As the three teachers left, two others invited me to spend the afternoon with them at a textile museum. In the evening, an even larger group would meet at the cinema. Being a teacher involved maintaining affective bonds with colleagues, former students and former teachers. Many of these relational lines were developed over food, drink and celebration. In light of this, I use *tablecloth* as a second metaphor to illustrate how Oaxacan teachers carry out their practice via food, love and celebration.

Like the tarpaulin providing cover for Osvaldo's reading project, the tablecloth mediated the post-2006 movement pedagogies for Andrea. Given that the streets for her were no longer viable as what she called 'democratic' spaces, the school needed to take on a greater role in fomenting democracy, especially for her students with handicaps who face the greatest exclusionary measures. For Andrea, if her students missed out on the abundance of school-based socialisation, they would lack social proficiency needed in harder times. Visually impaired students, she noted, especially depended on affinity group interaction to overcome the lack of informational input through sight. But there remains a tendency even among the more vocally radicalised instructors to withdraw students with disabilities from the mainstream, putting them, for example, in evening classes instead of the daytime ones. Andrea chose to interrogate this student tracking practice and secure more of what she repeatedly called democratic education. Sitting with Andrea and hearing her carefully chosen utterances between long pauses, I learned how she could not return to the pre-movement school norms. The time was right for democratic education.

Andrea exemplified what critical inclusion and democratic education meant for her after the experiences on the streets of Oaxaca City in 2006. Her story features her intervening on behalf of one student with multiple handicaps who remained marginalised in school. After 2006, she pushed for an assembly at the child's house where teachers, neighbours and extended family could converse with the student about what would bolster his quality of life in and out of school. The get-together involved a series of amusement activities, including tracing the student's body on construction paper and setting out tablecloths on card tables in the patio; laying tablecloths on the metallic folding tables, Andrea found out speaking with the boy's mother, signalled *fiesta*, a place where he could be himself. So Andrea made sure the tablecloths were out at this school and community event, given that the meeting needed to proceed in an egalitarian fashion akin to what she sought for in school. At this festive and strategic gathering, different people spoke up about how to advocate for the young person. Andrea was impressed at the sophistication of the comments of the individuals in the student's life which discerned his habits, needs and aptitudes. Though such an event tapped into a stream of active relationships, Andrea indicated that it took great organisational impetus on her part to coordinate it, festively situate it on tablecloths and thwart the tendency to cast off the student as un-teachable or better off with parents. For her, the school must remain accessible to all in order to instil the democratic process that the rule of force had clamped down on people on the streets in 2006. Andrea coordinated this gathering over tablecloths as a democratic teaching intervention, and on the tablecloths the people spoke with more openness and solidarity.

The tarpaulin and the tablecloth

The periodic violence on the Oaxacan streets and the practices of ableist exclusion make less for a radicalised version of pedagogy than for a politics of play, love and concern. As Andrea and Osvaldo met in the church atria and plazas around Oaxaca City for the dialogs at *las mesas* in 2006, Andrea also found herself conversing with parents who failed to grasp why the teachers left the classrooms for protests. Osvaldo confronted similar disquiet among school parents, suggesting that conflict is a principal part of assembling with others. In the end, Osvaldo established the reading project whereby the parents, those most frustrated with the teachers, willingly slung vinyl tarpaulins over the interior courtyard of the school to secure a shaded space for literacy and pleasure. Laying the tarpaulin did not signify parental acceptance of the teachers, for those relationships have remained tense over the years. Nonetheless, the parents and teachers beneath the tarpaulin found a shared aim in the assorted activities of the reading project. I use the tarpaulin descriptively and metaphorically to reveal how Osvaldo united teachers, state educational functionaries, venture philanthropists, as well as churches and international, regional and local NGOs, together in support of children's reading. The tarpaulin linked these actors in ways that ordinary school life would not. At times, the tarpaulin covered the purposeful assembly across ideological and institutional divides without seeking harmony or agreement. Osvaldo drew in enterprise NGO coordinators and IEEPO teacher educators; checks exchanged hands; cameras flashed; orators orated. But Osvaldo remained firm that the teachers controlled the pedagogical track beneath the tarpaulin.

In addition to covering the reading gathering, the tarpaulin provided teachers with pedagogical refuge. Specifically, the conducts of teaching have been conducted – on the one hand by the official push linking education as human capital development to poverty reduction (Giugale, 2001) – and on the other by the Sección 22's promotion of teaching for critical consciousness and emancipation (SEDES 22, 2009). Osvaldo and his colleagues, though serving as state agents and dissident unionists, have avoided entrenchment within these two loci; by intimating quality education through communality, they operated with relative freedom beneath the tarpaulin. Similar to how ethnographer Kirsten Norget (2007, p.72) marvelled at how at Oaxacan funerals ardent adversaries mingle, when a community gathers around the support of children, common ground may be easier to build. The tarpaulin, which includes actors of diverse political strands, provided shelter for teaching in desired ways. This strategic position of working with adversaries runs deep in Mexican dissident union politics, notably how teachers across Mexico in the CNTE and in Oaxaca in the Sección 22 never fully detached from the mainstream SNTE or how in protests Oaxacan teachers would denounce the IEEPO while keeping friendships with teachers who had offices there. Still, for teachers, their version of quality and community beneath the tarpaulin might worry the official scripts for quality; by bringing people together in their canopied events, the teachers resumed their institutional roles in their rural school after the 2006 conflicts, taking greater license to shift the school-based practices towards discovery, joy for reading and renewed horizontal relationships. The politics of the tarpaulin, by gathering people together in school under the egis of promoting reading, further recalls the politics of inner city Mumbai observed by Appadurai (2002) whereby activists would accept aid from any organisation provided it came without coercion to support a given political party. This emergent pedagogical space of the tarpaulin represents a conduct of schooling counter to learning-as-human-capital or learning-as-emancipatory favoured by State and the Sección 22, respectively.

If the tarpaulin received anyone who wished to come inside to participate, the tablecloth situated relationships of mutual care. The conditions of poverty and violence in Oaxaca are not abating, and the recent modernising reforms driven by economistic notions of quality and professionalisation have equated education with test score results (SEP/SNTE, 2008). Andrea returned to her school in late 2006 with invigorated resolve for inclusive and democratic schooling. She often opined that humanising participation among individuals on the streets and in schools would serve as a stabiliser, for being with others helps teachers and students endure conditions of severity with a modicum of joy and humanity. For Andrea, the school needs to teach social solidarity. She had found herself on the streets of Oaxaca City when *las mesas* had shut down as rumours circulated of the arrival of the PFP. There she met the candy vendor who had bought prayer cards for the teachers, a contribution which, given the inhumanity of the beatings and incarcerations, touched Andrea. Such cohesion is teachable, and the school becomes the preeminent site to secure more democratic social practices when the streets where union activities take place remain at risk of police occupation.[6] So if the schools are essential, inclusion becomes vital. Thus, she set up a meeting on behalf of her student who was cast aside by teachers and administrators as unteachable. Andrea approached the intervention via a party, a gathering over tablecloths. 'Tablecloth', she would later email me, serves as a 'symbol of welcome, a special distinction offered to the other person, and at the same time, a way to say that you and I are the same'.

Spacing out criticality and non-formality

In terms of spatiality, the tarpaulin and the tablecloth link to the human body with practices of caring for others, ally and adversary alike. This is to say that these are spaces of schooling-based 'intercorporeality' (Simonsen, 2007, p.172). As the body can conduct itself in and outside of institutions, the practice of the tarpaulin and the tablecloth need not unfold in what is ordinarily deemed unofficial or non-formal given how these can come up anywhere a person finds retreat and conviviality. Indeed, occurring within schools and other formal spaces, the social gatherings presented here may enjoy a measure of freedom unavailable when teachers stand alone. We see this with the *bajo el laurel* events and political activities occurring on the Zócalo below the shady *laureles de la India*; we see this in the *plantones* and roadblocks where teachers would stand together to stop traffic; we see this at *las mesas* in churches where physical proximity to others abated the fear of impending violence. Indeed, organising and learning alone or in detachable groups is less appealing. When the shade trees fell, people gathered in indignation before the police. When the teachers faced the incoming PFP, a street vendor handed out prayer cards. The tarpaulin and the tablecloth, as I present them here, unfurl and unfold as an intentional pedagogical strategy of togetherness. This depends on traditional spaces like schools and parties involving educational officials rather than *interstitial* (Holloway et al., 2010) or *autonomous* (Pickerill and Chatterton, 2006) locales for learning.

Still, the play and solidarity of tarpaulin and the tablecloth, with corporate and state support, may not work for many versions of critical pedagogy. Indeed, if the uniting ideological adversaries and the expressions of mutual care become *political*, then have we expanded the domain of the political so far as to dilute it? Following the work of Osvaldo and Andrea, the misrule of the state led to fertile soil for the emergence of critical, school-based projects. Conflict inspired diverse groups with different aims to protest in 2006; a different kind of politics became possible within the normative parameters of schooling thereafter. Rather than on idealist or utopian views of empowerment or school improvement, the critical project of the tarpaulin and the tablecloth rests squarely on actual responses to bad governance and misrule. Practices like love and concern, instead of depoliticised, infuse into a strategy for teaching and learning in a slightly freer and more human manner. In this the school remains key for two reasons. First, with public protest criminalised, it remains a mainstay of learning how to live in the world outside. Second, the school, under the aegis of helping students progress, also provides a relatively police-free refuge for teachers and students to engage in another kind of political project.

Notes

1. Encampments were deployed in the Mexico City Zócalo during the 1958–9 labour struggles (Loyo, 1985) while the plantones, as Oaxacan protest practices, appeared after 1979 (Yescas Martínez and Zafra, 1985).
2. Trees have inspired tourism and activism in Oaxaca. The *sabino* tree in El Tule outside of Oaxaca City is locally venerated as the oldest tree in the world. Oaxacan public intellectual Gustavo Esteva related how a chain store had illegally felled trees to break ground on public land. Activists successfully halted the project upon

discovering no groundwater study had been submitted. Still, trees would take a century to grow back, Esteva lamented.

3. 'Venture philanthropy' NGOs (Lipman, 2011, p.100) across Mexico intent on reducing '*rezago educativo*' or educational backwardness, to develop 'human capital', have recently become primary stakeholders in education with fomenting interest in reading as a major strategy.

4. The Sección 22 supports the public character of education and opposes private incursions, so accepting funding from pro-business NGOs bent put the reading project outside the realm of the union-sanctioned pedagogies and might have incurred the ire of union militants in their delegation.

5. In 418 of 570 Oaxacan municipalities, residents are legally bound to undertake non-monetary public welfare assignments. Serving on the parents' committee is one such role. So, even as parents' committee members may come to pick up their children, their presence at school is an extension of formal town politics.

6. The police rarely enter school grounds. 'We'd run them out', assured a graduate of an all-women's normal school when asked if police were welcome on campus.

References

A. Appadurai (2002) 'Deep democracy: Urban Governmentality and the horizon of politics', *Public Culture*, 14, 21–47.

A. A. Arrellanes (2007) 'Un Zócalo Destruido, Pueblo Enfurecido', *Cuadernos Sur*, 11, 139–48.

E. Bautista Martínez (2008) 'Oaxaca: La Construcción Mediática del Vandalismo y la Normalidad', *El Cotidiano*, 23, 37–44.

C. Beas Torres (2007) 'Batalla por Oaxaca' In *La Batalla por Oaxaca* (Oaxaca, Mexico: Ediciones Yope Power).

CNTE (2010) *Resolutivos, IV Congreso Nacional de Educación Alternativa*, 28–30 Mayo (Mexico City, Mexico).

Comisión Civil Internacional de Observación por los Derechos Humanos (2007) 'Entrevista a la Doctora Berta Elena Muñoz' In *La Batalla por Oaxaca* (Oaxaca, Mexico: Ediciones Yope Power).

M. Dean (2010) *Governmentality: Power and rule in modern society* (Los Angeles: SAGE).

D. Denham and C. A. S. A. Collective (2008) *Teaching Rebellion: Stories from the grassroots mobilization in Oaxaca* (Oakland, CA: PM Press).

G. Esteva (2007) 'La Otra Campaña, la APPO y la Izquierda: Revindicar una Alternativa', *Cuadernos Sur*, 11, 7–37.

P. Freire (1994) *Pedagogy of the oppressed: New revised 20th anniversary edition* (New York: Continuum).

J. P. Gee (2001) 'What is literacy?' In P. Shannon (ed.) *Becoming Political, too: New readings and writings on the politics of literacy education* (Portsmouth, NH: Heinemann).

H. A. Giroux (1988) *Teachers as Intellectuals: Toward a critical pedagogy of learning* (Granby, Mass: Bergin & Garvey).

M. Giugale (2001) 'Synthesis'. In M. Giugale, O. Lafourcade, and V. H. Nguyen (eds) *Mexico, a Comprehensive Development Agenda for the New Era* (Washington, D.C.: The World Bank).

S. Holloway, P. Hubbard, H. Jo¨ns and H. Pimlott-Wilson (2010) 'Geographies of education and the significance of children, youth and families', *Progress in Human Geography*, 34, 583–600.

P. Lipman (2011) *The New Political Economy of Urban Education: Neoliberalism, race, and the right to the city* (New York: Routledge).

B. E. Loyo (1985) *La Casa del Pueblo y el Maestro Rural Mexicano: Antología* (Mexico City: SEP, Subsecretaría de Cultura, Dirección General de Publicaciones).

V. R. Martínez Vásquez (2007) *Autoritarismo, Movimiento Popular y Crisis Política: Oaxaca 2006* (Oaxaca, Mexico: UABJO).

K. Norget (2007) 'The drama of death: Popular religion and performing the good death in Oaxaca' In A. Gálvez (ed.) *Performing Religion in the Americas: Media, politics and devotional practices of the twenty-first century* (New York: Seagull Books).

D. E. Osorno and L. Meyer (2007) *Oaxaca Sitiada: La Primera Insurrección del Siglo XXI* (Mexico City: Random House Mondadori).

J. Pickerill and P. Chatterton (2006) 'Notes towards autonomous geographies: Creation, resistance and self-management as survival tactics', *Progress in Human Geography*, 30, 730–46.

SEDES 22 (2009) *Talleres Estatales de Educación Alternativa: TEEA 2009–2010*. (Oaxaca, Oaxaca, Mexico).

SEP/SNTE. (2008) *Alianza por la Calidad de la Educación entre el Gobierno Federal y los Maestros de México Representados por el Sindicato Nacional de Trabajadores de la Educación*. Mayo 15 (Mexico City, Mexico), http://alianza.sep.gob.mx/pdf/Alianza_por_la_Calidad_de_la_Educacion.pdf, date accessed 1 February 2011.

K. Simonsen (2007) 'Practice, spatiality and embodied emotions: An outline of a geography of practice', *Human Affairs*, 17, 168–81.

J. Sotelo Marbán (2008) *Oaxaca: Insurgencia Civil y Terrorismo de Estado* (Mexico City: Era).

R. Trinidad Galván (2001) 'Portraits of Mujeres Desjuiciadas: Womanist pedagogies of the everyday, the mundane and the ordinary', *International Journal of Qualitative Studies in Education (QSE)*, 14, 603–21.

F. Verástegui (2010) 'Oaxaca: Árboles y Resistencia Civil' In I. Yescas Martínez and C. Sánchez Islas (eds) *Oaxaca 2010: Voces de la Transición* (Oaxaca, Mexico: Carteles Editores).

I. Yescas Martínez and G. Zafra (1985) *La Insurgencia Magisterial en Oaxaca 1980* (Oaxaca, Mexico: IISUABJO).

G. Zafra, J. Hernández Díaz and M. Garza Zepeda (2002) *Organización Popular y Oposición Empresarial: Manifestaciones de la Acción Colectiva en Oaxaca* (Mexico City: Plaza y Valdés Editores).

8
Limiting Spaces of Informal Learning among Street Children in Perú

Dena Aufseeser

Education has long been presented as one of the main paths to both national and human development, and is increasingly embraced by a wide range of actors such as the World Bank, Save the Children and local non-governmental organisations as a key element of poverty reduction. Yet, education is almost exclusively defined as formal schooling, neglecting alternative spaces in which many children learn. This chapter explores the learning experiences of street children, or those young people who work in informal jobs in the city streets of Lima and Cusco, Perú, in the context of increased formalisation of education. I argue that following supposedly universal models of childhood serve to devalue certain spaces of learning, as well as whole groups of children themselves. In direct contrast to arguments promoted by international development organisations, school is not the only space in which learning takes place. Yet, false assumptions about where and how children learn may actually limit the ability of some children to succeed in school, as well as hinder their learning opportunities in other spaces. In particular, in the context of anti-child labour campaigns, which are organised on the basis of the incompatibility of work and education, the amount of learning that occurs through street work is increasingly limited.

This chapter first examines the ways in which work may actually be a site of development and learning among Andean children, drawing particular attention to the importance of space and social context. However, an emphasis on formal education through the school system, combined with the devaluation of street work, has negatively affected some children's experiences of working. The chapter then considers a second educational space which has received much less attention from scholars and practitioners alike. Even more than the actual labour in which children engage, much of which does in fact take place under exploitative conditions, Perú's Child Workers' Movement, the oldest movement of child workers in Latin America, itself arguably serves as an important space of learning, development and identity formation.

By analysing such examples, this chapter responds to Holloway et al.'s (2010) call to examine how beliefs about 'normal' childhoods serve to structure educational experiences. In particular, I argue that assumptions that education means formal schooling actively devalue other spaces of learning and exclude those children trying to balance both work and school. Of the few geographers that have begun to look at informal learning, they often examine informal learning within the same school spaces and institutions (Cartwright, 2012; for exceptions, see Kraftl, in press). In focusing on spaces of informal learning outside of the classroom, this chapter addresses such a gap. This chapter also responds to a need to move the subjects of education into the foreground (see Holloway et al., 2010; Kraftl, 2013) and adds to a growing number of studies examining children's learning experiences in the global south (see Ansell, 2004; Punch, 2004; Jeffrey et al., 2008) and critical analyses of the role of work in young people's lives (Liebel, 2003; Bourdillon, 2006; Bromley and Mackie, 2009).

Methodology and research context

This chapter employs a child-centred research approach, placing an emphasis on including children's own opinions and interpretations of the different spaces of learning in their lives, rather than simply making assumptions about what is best for young people (see Liebel, 2003; Aitken et al., 2006). It is based on over 150 interviews, informal conversations and participatory observation carried out over the course of 2009 and 2010 with government officials, educators and NGO staff, and child workers between the ages of 7 and 18 in Lima and Cusco. I focus on children who work in public spaces such as plazas, markets, streets and buses, and include both children who return home to family at night and children who are now sleeping in the streets, hostels or abandoned buildings. All the children worked in the informal economy, engaging in jobs such as selling candy or snacks, shining shoes, performing on buses, and renting cell phones, among others.

Child policies within Perú have been significantly influenced by global discourses of childhood and are intricately connected to narratives of international development. In 1990, the Peruvian government ratified the United Nations Convention on the Rights of the Child (CRC). In doing so, it committed to provide all children with access to education, as well as to protect them from economic exploitation. And in the past two decades, school enrolment rates, especially in primary schools, have increased significantly (INEI, 2009). However, an exclusive focus on enrolment rates fails to reflect actual attendance rates, as well as the poor quality of many Peruvian schools. The same year that the Peruvian government ratified the CRC, President Alberto Fujimori introduced an extreme version of neoliberal economic policies, eliminating food subsidies, privatising government enterprises and reducing public expenditures (Green, 1998; Hays-Mitchell, 2002). Despite more recent economic growth, investment in education remains low, at less than 3 per cent of GDP (UNESCO, 2011). The lack of financial commitment to education is reflected in the poor quality of the Peruvian education system. Only 20 per cent of second-graders pass basic proficiency examinations in reading and one in ten achieves basic proficiency in mathematics (NAPA, 2011). Despite the experiences of children in Peruvian schools, as well as studies arguing that education in the global north itself is in flux (Thiem, 2009), international development organisations continue to promote schooling as a means for poverty reduction and economic growth (see OECD, 2010).

Reinforcing the incompatibility of education and work

The CRC has arguably done much to draw attention to children's rights issues. However, critics argue that it presents as universal Western middle-class experiences of childhood as a time of innocence, play and school and overlooks childhood as socially constructed, linked to specific geographical spaces and time periods (Ruddick, 2003; Valentine, 2004; Liebel, 2006). This comes across most clearly in attitudes regarding learning and work. International children's rights organisations frequently present learning and work in direct opposition to each other. However, many children in Perú are actually working in order to pay their school matriculation fees, and for required uniforms and school supplies. In fact, within Perú, children are more likely to *both* attend school and work at the same time than they are to just work (Ray, 2002; Ersado, 2004). Further, many parents actually believe that work is an important space of learning. While Western frameworks isolate children in separate institutions, in Andean culture, learning, play and work are highly integrated activities (Bolin, 2006). Independent learning through experience and observation is highly encouraged, in direct contrast to forms of learning often promoted in school (Bolin, 2006; Invernizzi, 2008). Children begin helping in the fields, with housework, or to care for younger siblings as soon as they are able. Through such tasks, they actively learn to become members of Andean society, contributing to the development of themselves, their families, and their country. Yet, by regulating children along supposedly universal understanding of childhood, such beliefs are disregarded.

Out-of-place in the classroom

School itself does not always provide a productive and safe site of learning for all children. In this study, the majority of children trying to juggle both work and school received little special attention to help them manage both. Some children explained that they often felt out of place or ostracised in school because of their poverty or their need to work. One youth who had since dropped out of school reflected on his experiences when he had attended: 'I felt sad in school. I saw kids with food. My mom worked washing clothes. She only gave me 20 cents. I could only buy gum. My clothing was worse' (personal interview, 2010).

Beyond inequalities among peers within the classroom, the school curriculum itself is often disconnected from the context of children's lives. Many teachers still utilise old-fashioned teaching methods of rote memorisation with physical punishment or verbal humiliation for those children who do not learn well or conform to the school environment. Delegates of Perú's child workers movement explained, '[s]chools are designed for kids who don't work. Kids do math with speed and precision in work but then can't do it in school. It's the same with communication' (MANTHOC, 2002, p. 12). Working children also reported being denied entry into the class if they arrived late or with dirty hands. Once they had missed too much school, they were either forced to drop out or to repeat the year, further limiting their ability to learn through formal means.[1] And in direct contrast to beliefs that schools are much safer than the streets, some children, especially those in Cusco, emphasised that the secondary schools were dangerous, with a lot of fighting and some incidents of sexual abuse (personal interviews, 2010). Thus, assumptions that children are better off in school than other learning environments both neglect the context in which such schooling takes place and ignore the power and politics that are an important part of schooling (Ansell, 2005; Jeffrey et al., 2008).

Learning through work?

In fact, learning through work may offer children more positive social identities than they acquire in school. Cartwright (2012) suggests that informal learning can help improve young people's self-esteem and social skills. Children in this study frequently reported feeling 'proud' of their ability to help their family and emphasised that through work, they learned responsibility. Sixteen-year-old Nancy explained that she did not just work to earn money but also to learn to be responsible: 'I like working. I started working to help my parents but then I kept working. I started selling books on buses. I liked it. It made me feel useful' (personal interview, 2010). Similarly, 8-year-old Elmer explained how work provided him with various learning opportunities: '[y]ou need to learn how to sell to tourists, what things you should say to make them buy more. And I learned how to make the right change quickly, and how many (Peruvian) soles equal a dollar.... When I sell, I also get to play soccer with my friends.'

Elmer's comments also speak to the importance of social context when considering work as a space of learning. It is not just the actual tasks in which children engage that may provide them with learning opportunities. Rather, work may also provide children with a positive space for social development, and access to peers and adult contacts that they may not have otherwise

(Dyson, 2008). For example, in the case of an 11-year-old girl who sells finger puppets in Cusco's main plaza, she said that she felt 'cold and lonely' sitting at home at night, waiting for her mother to arrive. Instead, she liked to be in the plaza selling where she could not only earn money for food and to pay her school fees but also could walk around, talk to people and play with her friends (personal interview, 2010). Such comments necessitate recognition of the actual alternative spaces in which children sometimes spend time (in this case an empty cold house, which itself most likely offers few opportunities for learning), rather than idealised ones.

However, young people's ability to learn from work depends highly on the space and context in which they are working, even within Peru. Although perhaps obvious, this variety is often overlooked in social and development policy. Without dismissing the exploitation that occurs in Cusco, I suggest that working in Cusco's main plaza may actually facilitate more opportunities for social mobility than some children find in school. Youth have even been able to use the language skills and familiarity with tourists that they acquire in the informal economy to obtain more stable jobs working in restaurants in the area. This was the case with Julio, who originally learned to interact with tourists through his work shining shoes, applying the skills he had learned to obtain a much coveted restaurant position. Such opportunities are especially important considering the inability of many youth to access post-secondary schooling. By working at an early age, street children gained skills that other students were paying to acquire in certificate programmes in tourism.

In contrast, in Lima, street children's work has fewer tangible benefits, reaffirming the role of spatiality in children's learning experiences. Some children did report learning communication skills, how to make sales and become quicker with basic math, all of which may potentially serve them in the future. The majority of other skills, however, were directly relevant to their current occupations, such as where to buy shoe polish or window cleaners. However, none of the children with whom I worked wanted to continue jobs such as shining shoes in the future, making such specific forms of knowledge only useful for their current occupation. While children acquire knowledge that helps them survive on a day-to-day basis, and may even learn some beneficial longer-term traits, such as responsibility, the majority of behaviours they learn are not highly valued by the rest of society.

Learning the 'wrong' things

Through their street work, young people learned to better navigate the city and easily move between various neighbourhoods and spaces within Lima and Cusco, respectively, knowledge that proved helpful for children's working strategies. However, familiarity with streets and public spaces often served to further marginalise certain children. In fact, it is the very acknowledgement that children may learn from street work that is a cause of concern for some practitioners. One street educator explained, '[w]hen children start working in the streets, they get to know older youth who rob and use drugs. They may feel pressure to engage in such behaviors, and slowly start distancing themselves from their homes and their work' (personal interview, 2010). Such fears are not entirely unfounded. During conversations about what they had learned through their work, some children specifically mentioned learning to rob in groups or how to sniff glue. Yet, even when children do learn skills that are at least partially beneficial, such as how to set up businesses, defend themselves from police, or safely navigate crowded street areas, skills that may help them survive in the informal urban economy, they are increasingly marginalised by their links to the streets.

Views of the street as a morally polluting environment (Invernizzi, 2008) have intensified in recent years, and are arguably linked to the spread of dominant images of childhood as a protected life phase, as well as changing urban economic and social conditions. More generally, I suggest that the potential of work to serve as a learning opportunity is severely hindered by socioeconomic shifts that have pushed children into vulnerable working positions and the campaigns that work to further stigmatise that work. Many children in this study worked in exploitative or stressful conditions under which little beneficial learning takes place. International organisations enforce children's feelings of inadequacy by excluding them from categories of 'normal' childhoods. Green (1998, p.48) suggests that 'working children are seen as a schizophrenic barbarism: as children they are not real workers, and as workers they are not real children'. Children themselves then reject their own experiences of childhood. Instead of taking pride in the initiative or responsibility they demonstrated from working, attributes that would be valued as part of *adult* neoliberal subjectivity, work is primarily a negative experience in their lives. I suggest that this goes beyond the actual conditions of work and instead is linked to the fact that children are increasingly being asked to deny their identities as workers.

While the actual conditions of work may not have changed, children's *experience* of work has ironically worsened because of anti-child labour campaigns. Thus, their ability to learn and take pride in their work is hindered by the bombardment of messages that they should not be working, and that parents who allow their children to work are not 'proper' or 'good' parents. Those children who were still attending school implored me not to tell their peers that they also worked, especially when they worked in informal street jobs. The idea that they were doing something shameful had been internalised. A 13-year-old explained, 'I felt embarrassed selling candy. I never go on buses... They look at you... I don't know. It makes me feel bad. I don't want the other kids to know' (personal interview, 2010). Thus, even when children are engaging in the same types of activities as in the past, the value associated with the learning from such work has been decreasing, indicating the ways in which narrow interpretations of children's rights can negatively combine with neoliberal economic policy to further marginalise children.

The ability of educators to reach children outside of the classroom is also increasingly limited by anti-child labour legislation, a trend that is exacerbated by the tendency of NGOs and the Peruvian government to rely on international sources to fund many of their social services (personal interviews, 2010). In fact, Educators of the Street, a national programme that used to provide outreach to street children, has seen significant budget cuts in recent years (Vasquez, 2007), and its Lima-based office now actually requires that children stop working in order to participate,[2] thus excluding those children who nonetheless need to keep working from potentially supportive benefits. Yet, for children who have primarily experienced feelings of failure and alienation in spaces such as schools, education programmes that take place in the streets may feel safer. The alternative ways in which many street educators define learning also indicate very different goals, with potentially positive consequences for addressing marginalisation and inequality. The director of an outreach programme working with street children explained that street educators aim to make children feel visible, listened to and heard (personal interview, 2010).

> Learning does not just include literacy and mathematics. Especially with street children, it is important to teach them they have value as people ....to help them leave behind aggression and feel loved. We teach them solidarity, tolerance...about their rights. Most importantly, we teach them to be social subjects, that they are protagonists in their own lives.

This emphasis on active participation is in direct contrast to the methodologies employed by most state-run schools in Perú. Yet, more stringent programme requirements limit children's ability to access such programmes.

Programmes that used to focus on helping children learn in alternative spaces also increasingly try to avoid any language associated with 'work'. This came out clearly in conversations with the director of Ecological Kids, a municipal programme in Lima that provides adolescents with a stipend in exchange for gardening and other urban improvement projects. Despite being listed as a work-capacitation programme on the city's web site, the director placed a big emphasis on stressing that it was not a work programme.[3] The director explained, '[w]e aren't a work training programme. We are a learning programme. We do not pay children. We provide stipends'. Yet, avoiding language associated with work limits the programme's ability to help youth take pride in their identities as workers and active contributors to their families, and thus does not fully address their marginalisation.[4]

Other programmes, such as those that prepare young people to work in bakeries and carpentry workshops, have faced similar pressure to limit their accessibility to youth over the age of 18, meaning that formal educational outreach beyond the classroom is increasingly limited. In such regards, assumptions about where and how children learn, and in this case, the incompatibility between work and school, ironically exclude working children from academic support programmes or alternative learning programmes, and ultimately hinder their actual ability to succeed or learn from *either* the school environment or the work environment.

The child workers' movement as a site of learning

Yet, some programmes continue to work to foster more positive identities among Perú's young working population. Perú's child workers movement, officially called the Movement for Adolescent and Child Workers, Children of Christian Workers (MANTHOC), began in 1977, long before the ratification of the UN's CRC.[5] It formed to help young people defend themselves from exploitation. In contrast to arguments put forth by the International Labour Organisation, which is also against exploitation, MANTHOC argues for the right of children to work in conditions of dignity, actively challenging the idea that all work is bad, while trying to create spaces of empowerment and participation. Groups of children and adolescents meet in 27 different locations throughout Peru, gathering to discuss problems that arise from working conditions, and to learn about their rights and the history of labour within Peru. MANTHOC also organises a school for working children, and runs various skills building workshops, and an after-school support programme and technical-vocational programmes in Lima.[6]

While MANTHOC has ultimately made limited progress in its attempts to address exploitative working conditions, I suggest that in and of itself, the movement actually serves as a primary space of learning, teaching children to take pride in themselves and develop political consciousness. In such regards, it provides an alternative form of citizenship building than that promoted by schools (see Staeheli and Hammett, 2010; Pykett, 2012). In contrast to more static conceptions of citizenship, Invernizzi and Williams (2008) point out that citizenship also relates to children's active learning through valuing their role, defining their rights and common interests as they emerge from everyday lives, promoting their rights and negotiating solutions and policies with authorities. They argue that there is a need to link learning and empowerment, rather than separating the two. Thus, in contrast to arguments that youth are increasingly apathetic and politically disengaged (O'Toole, 2003), in the case of the child workers' movement, children actively organise and mobilise on their own behalf, expressing an interest in politics and laws both that directly and indirectly concern them.

Each neighbourhood base elects delegates to represent them at regional, national and even occasional international conferences, as well as workshops and events organised by MNNATSOP, a larger umbrella organisation for working children's groups within Peru. Such conferences are led by the young people themselves, although adult collaborators help organise and train delegates. As the delegates attend meetings and discuss inequalities with their peers, children learn to connect their everyday lives to regional, national and even international political processes (Philo and Smith, 2003). The children who participated in MANTHOC were much more aware of their rights than were other street children (personal interviews, 2010). They played an active role interpreting what they thought various Conventions, legal codes, and national plans meant, and should mean, rather than simply leaving interpretations to adults (field notes, 2010; also see Liebel, 2003), and learned important critical thinking skills that they can apply to other areas of their lives.

In contrast to the marginalisation that child workers often feel in school because of their work, the movement directly aims to combat the negative effects of anti-child labour campaigns on children's identities. Instead of feeling shame, it teaches children to take pride in their identity as child workers. A 13-year-old delegate explained,

> [t]hrough the movement, I learned to value what I do to support myself and my family ... Being part of the movement has helped my self-esteem. I have better relationships with my parents. We have much better communication and they respect my opinions. I have learned to defend myself with words and can accept my errors.
>
> (Personal interview, 2009)

The experience of being a delegate provides young people with skills that can benefit them in other areas of their lives, and gives them the confidence to believe in themselves. A 16-year-old MANTHOC delegate explained,

> [n]ow I have experience that will help me in my professional life and in school. I want to be someone in life. I want to be a scientist. If I only work, I can't improve. But if I only study, I don't know what real work is. Both are important for human life. Both form you and help you on a personal level.
>
> (Personal interview, 2009)

Although the child workers' movement may not play a big role in reshaping economic conditions, it helps young people develop the ability to articulate themselves and the confidence to speak to those in power. In this sense, MANTHOC not only offers an alternative space of learning but also may specifically address marginalisation and social inequality in ways that state schools do not.

Conclusion

Despite its strength as a potential learning space, the child workers movement currently only reaches a very small percentage of the more than two million working children and adolescents in Perú (INEI, 2009). Increased international pressure and anti-child labour legislation have also limited its ability to outreach working street populations. Although both the international community and the Peruvian government emphasise the importance of education, continued assumptions that in the case of young people, work and learning are incompatible ironically further marginalise those children who nonetheless continue working. In order to better reach a larger segment of young people, there is a need for greater flexibility and acknowledgement that learning can take place in multiple spaces. Many Peruvian children themselves place a high value on schooling, and recognise the potential role that formal education can play in social advancement. Yet, at the same time, it is often their very work that allows them to attend school in the first place, as well as acquire other skills that help their social, intellectual and career development. Consistent attacks on child labour, as well as a lack of acknowledgement that many young people both work and study arguably limits their success in either space. Thus, rather than advocating for *either* schooling or work, if organisations were given more space to develop some of the connections between formal and informal spaces of learning, those young people trying to balance both work and school may have more chances of acquiring the skills they need to be successful in their present and future lives.

Notes

1. While young people in this study reported that work limited their ability to participate in group projects or complete homework, and often resulted in them arriving tired to class, it also specifically provided them with the income to pay school matriculation fees in the first place (personal interviews, 2010), complicating the argument about the relationship between work and schooling.
2. Because of limited funding, the Lima-based office of Educators of the Street partnered with the municipality of Lima, and some internationally funded NGOs, which required that that the programme emphasise an anti-child labour component. Thus, the one national programme for working children now requires that such children deny their identity as such in order to participate.
3. In fact, my initial attempts to contact him for interviews were denied because I had asked the municipality if they had any programmes for working children and adolescents.

4. While the programme initially targeted street children working in the informal economy, it increasingly focuses on those young people who are living with their families and attending school. Recent programme requirements, such as a need to be studying at least four hours a day, have worked to exclude many of the street children who could most benefit from a work-training programme.

5. Yet, it now uses the CRC, as well as Peru's code for children and adolescents, as a tool to gain support for the right to work, in direct opposition to minimum age laws and other campaigns against child labour.

6. Children in some bases have themselves taken initiative to start various community service programmes in their neighbourhoods.

References

S. Aitken, S. Estrada, J. Jennings and L. Aguirre (2006) 'Reproducing life and labor: Global processes and working children in Tijuana, Mexico', *Childhood*, 13, 365–87.

N. Ansell (2004) 'Secondary schooling and rural youth transitions in Lesotho and Zimbabwe', *Youth and Society*, 36, 183–202.

N. Ansell (2005) *Children, Youth and Development* (New York: Routledge).

I. Bolin (2006) *Growing up in a Culture of Respect: Childrearing in highland Peru* (Texas: University of Texas Press).

M. Bourdillon (2006) 'Children and work: A review of current literature and debates,' *Development and Change*, 37, 1201–26.

R. Bromley and P. Mackie (2009) 'Child experiences as street traders in Peru: Contributing to a reappraisal for working children,' *Children's Geographies*, 7, 141–58.

I. Cartwright (2012) 'Informal education in compulsory schooling in the UK: Humanising moments, Utopian spaces?' in P. Kraftl, J. Horton and F. Tucker (eds) *Critical Geographies of Childhood and Youth* (Bristol, UK: Policy Press).

J. Dyson (2008) 'Harvesting identities: Youth, work, and gender in the Indian Himalayas', *Annals of the Association of American Geographers*, 98, 160–79.

L. Ersado (2004) 'Child labor and schooling decisions in urban and rural areas: Comparative evidence from Nepal, Perú and Zimbabwe', *World Development*, 33, 455–80.

D. Green (1998) *Hidden Lives: Voices of children in Latin America and the Caribbean* (London: Cassell).

M. Hays-Mitchell (2002) 'Resisting austerity: A gendered perspective on neo-liberal restructuring in Peru', *Gender and Development*, 10, 71–81.

S. L. Holloway, P. Hubbard, H. Jöns and H. Pimlott-Wilson (2010) 'Geographies of education and the significance of children, youth and families', *Progress in Human Geography*, 34, 583–600.

Instituto Nacional de Estadistica e Informatica (INEI) (2009) *Peru: Niños, Niñas y Adolescentesque Trabajan, 1993–2008* (Lima: INEI).

A. Invernizzi (2008) 'Everyday lives of working children and notions of citizenship' in A. Invernizzi and J. Williams (eds) *Children and Citizenship* (London: Sage).

A. Invernizzi and J. Williams (eds) (2008) *Children and Citizenship* (London: Sage).

C. Jeffrey, P. Jeffrey, and R. Jeffrey (2008) *Degrees without Freedom? Education, masculinities and unemployment in North India* (Stanford, CA: Stanford University Press).

P. Kraftl (2013) 'Towards geographies of "alternative" education: A case study of UK home schooling families', *Transactions of the Institute of British Geographers*, 436–450.

M. Liebel (2003) 'Working children as social subjects: The contribution of working children's organizations to social transformations', *Childhood*, 10, 265–85.

M. Liebel (2006) *MalabaristasdelSiglo XXI* (Lima, Peru: IFEJANT).

MANTHOC (2002) *Propuesta Pedagogicadesde los Niños, Niñas y AdolescentesTrabajadores* (Lima: MANTHOC).

NAPA (2011, April 20) 'Y La Educacion.Que?: Evaluacion de Estudiantes 2011', *NAPA*, http://napa.com.pe/2011/04/20/y-la-educacion-%C2%BFque-evaluacion-de-estudiantes-2011/

OECD (2010) *The High Cost of Low-Educational Performance: The long-run economic impact of improving PISA outcomes* (Paris: OECD).

T. O'Toole (2003) 'Engaging with young people's conceptions of the political', *Children's Geographies*, 1, 71–90.

C. Philo and F. Smith (2003) 'Guest editorial: Political geographies of children and young people', *Space and Polity*, 7, 99–115.

S. Punch (2004) 'The impact of primary education on school-to-work transitions for young people in rural Bolivia', *Youth and Society*, 36, 163–82.

J. Pykett (2012) 'Making "youth publics" and "neuro-citizens": Critical geographies of contemporary education practice in the UK' in P. Kraftl, J. Horton and F. Tucker (eds) *Critical Geographies of Childhood and Youth* (Bristol, UK: Policy Press).

R. Ray (2002) 'Child labor, child schooling, and their interaction with adult labor: Empirical evidence for Perú and Pakistan', *The World Bank Economic Review*, 14, 347–67.

S. Ruddick (2003) 'The politics of aging: Globalization and the restructuring of youth and childhood', *Antipode*, 35, 345–62.

L. A. Staeheli and D. Hammett (2010) 'Educating the new national citizen: Education, political subjectivity and divided societies', *Citizenship Studies*, 14, 667–80.

C. Thiem (2009) 'Thinking through education: The geographies of contemporary educational restructuring', *Progress in Human Geography*, 33, 154–73.

UNESCO (2011) *UIS Statistics in Brief*, http://stats.uis.unesco.org/unesco/TableViewer/document.aspx?ReportId=289&IF_Language=eng&BR_Country=6040&BR_Region=40520

G. Valentine (2004) *Public Space and the Culture of Childhood* (Aldershot: Ashgate).

E. Vasquez (2007) *Niños no Visiblespara el Estado* (Lima: Universidad del Pacifico).

9
Learning How to Behave in School: A Study of the Experiences of Children and Young People with Socio-emotional Differences

Sophie Bowlby, Jennifer Lea and Louise Holt

Introduction

This chapter discusses the ways in which children in school learn behaviours that are deemed to be acceptable within the school environment. It focuses on the experience of students who are defined by teachers as having 'Behavioural, Emotional and Social Difficulties' (BESD)[1] in one primary school and one secondary school in the same English Local Authority (LA).

All schools have both formally defined and informal norms of behaviour within the school environment. The ability to enact certain forms of behaviour – such as listening to the teacher, concentrating on a task, being quiet – is widely believed to affect a pupil's ability to learn – and indeed, there is evidence that it does do so (Gutman and Vorhaus, 2012). Moreover, it is considered that the 'bad' behaviour of some pupils affects the ability of others to learn. Thus, in an environment such as the United Kingdom in which schools' academic 'standards' are central to their survival, pupils' behaviour is believed to be of great importance to the schools' overall academic performance (reflected in a plethora of Government guidance on behaviour policies in schools and in the widespread use of the term 'Behaviour for Learning' in schools' policies on behaviour[2]). An important element of behaviour concerns relationships with other pupils and with teachers. Thus, schools also focus on the social skills of relating to others, resolving disagreements and conflicts with others, making friends and showing concern for the well-being of other people. Many schools have statements about the school as a 'society' or 'community' which emphasise the priority given to harmonious social relationships among members of the school. Hence, finding ways to ensure that children adhere to particular norms of behaviour during the school day is an important preoccupation of educators.

Schools try to inculcate particular forms of behaviour through a mixture of explicit rules, discipline, rewards and exhortation; through informal social pressure; and also, in some schools, the explicit teaching of such skills as containing anger, dealing with conflict and exploring feelings. In this chapter we focus on the interrelations between formal learning of behavioural norms and informal education and learning. We define formal education as situations in which the knowledges and skills to be learned are made explicit and the roles of learner and teacher are formally defined – typically in the classroom. Informal education, by contrast, occurs through informal social exchanges where the learning goals are not made explicit to the learner. However, formal and informal education are not clearly separated. For example, informal learning can be part of classroom social relationships and informal relationships can be managed by teachers to achieve particular learning goals. Here we examine how the methods adopted in two particular schools impact upon children who are designated as having BESD. In the following sections we discuss the nature of BESD and the concepts that underpin our study. We next briefly describe the methods used in the empirical study we have carried out before discussing our findings. We finish with a brief conclusion.

Defining BESD

In the United Kingdom children with BESD are defined as having a Special Education Need or SEN[3] because their behaviour presents a barrier to their learning. In England, in 2009, children with BESD made up 22.8 per cent of all students with statements of SEN and those with SEN at School Action Plus[4] (14.3 per cent and 26 per cent of each individual category respectively) (DCSF, 2009), but the proportion varies markedly from school to school as does the proportion categorised as experiencing SEN. SEN diagnoses relate to physical and/or mental conditions which affect children's ability to learn in the normal classroom environment – for example, they may have such conditions as mobility, hearing or speech impairments, be on the autistic spectrum or have Down's syndrome. Most of these conditions have more or less clear criteria for their diagnosis and they are conditions which pertain beyond the school gates. However, the identification of BESD is *not* linked to a clear set of criteria or clinically identifiable psychological condition – rather it is a term used to describe children who are, within the school, 'withdrawn and isolated, disruptive or disturbing, hyperactive and lacking concentration, [with] immature social skills, presenting challenging behaviour arising from other complex special needs' (DCSF 2008a, paragraph 49). This description covers a very wide gamut of behaviour and depends on the subjective judgement of teachers and other staff. For example, the decision as to whether they have 'immature social skills' will depend on teachers' ideas about appropriate social skills and social behaviour in school for pupils of a given age. Commentators have noted that such judgements are influenced by classed, gendered and racialised expectations about 'normal' social behaviour. Thus the behaviour of some children diagnosed with BESD may be considered 'acceptable' for children of a particular gender, race or class among adults from a similar social background outside school but may be unacceptable within the school environment. In particular, commentators have remarked that working-class boys, boys of African Caribbean heritage and Traveller children of Irish heritage are more likely to be categorised as having BESD than other children (Lindsay et al., 2006; DCSF, 2009; Youdell, 2011).

Many authors would agree with Thomas' (2005, p.77) suggestion that use of the term EBD is a 'confused collation of notions...which, nevertheless share one feature: the attribution of behaviour problems to the disposition of the child and his or her personal circumstances' (see also Youdell, 2006, 2011; Runswick-Cole, 2011). Importantly, the problem is seen to reside in the child and her or his 'background'. Moreover, most such children are seen as capable, in principle, of being taught 'how to behave' given appropriate teaching of emotional and social skills at school. However, it is easy for many adults in schools to see them as 'irredeemable' because the influence of 'their background' is too strong to be erased. In this case teachers and staff may feel that the influence of such students within the school must be contained or removed in order to prevent them from adversely affecting other students (Youdell, 2011). Moreover, judgement of the adequacy of social skills has moral and ethical overtones – students who behave in a socially unacceptable way can become seen by teachers as unworthy, 'bad' or 'not willing to change', a set of teacher attitudes that can become self-fulfilling.

In order to challenge the idea that the 'problem' lies primarily within the mind, emotions and body of the child, Holt (2010) uses the term 'Socio-Emotional *Differences*' to describe those categorised as having Behavioural, Emotional and Social *Difficulties*. The term *differences* rather than *difficulties* is a strategic attempt to express that the differences are located at least as much in socially constructed, and socially and spatially specific, expectations of behaviour and emotional competence as within the young people. The diagnosis of BESD is specifically located within the institutionalised set of practices that are involved in SEN diagnoses and government and school responses to such diagnoses. They cannot be understood as objective and uncontentious 'facts' about particular children and young people.

Norms, friendship and embodied social capital

The existence of norms of acceptable social behaviour which pertain within the school gates is central to the categorisation of children with BESD. Norms are established and maintained within groups both by formal sanctions and rewards and by informal, sometimes beyond-conscious reactions. These communicate to members of the group which forms of behaviour are acceptable or unacceptable. In schools, teachers and other staff are empowered to set formal sanctions and rewards, but teachers, other staff and children will also communicate norms informally. The existence of group norms creates the possibility that those who do not adhere to the norms are perceived not only as 'other' but negatively 'other'. Thus, it is not simply that particular behaviours are seen as unacceptable, but that those displaying these behaviours become socially unacceptable and excluded. Children and young people categorised as having BESD are therefore at risk of being socially excluded within school – that is, seen by staff and other children and young people as 'bad', undesirable as friends, and excluded from taking part in many informal social activities within the school.

Butler (1997, 2004) argues that humans subconsciously subject themselves to normalisation because human beings' existence and identity is defined in relation to others. We suggest that there is an emotional investment in such identification which is central to the maintenance of group norms and group members' ways-of-being that are expressed in Bourdieu's notion of habitus (Bourdieu, 1990; Holt et al., forthcoming). Humans' desire to be accepted and their participation in a particular group will result in their adoption of both conscious and beyond-conscious bodily and mental habits that are characteristic of that group. Such a 'habitus' involves the members of the group acquiring embodied social capital (Holt, 2008) which may affect positively or negatively their ability to take part in particular social practices and so influence the types of embodied social capital they continue to acquire.

Norms are not fixed – they are changeable and often fuzzily defined – and some are more open to modification than others. While those who behave differently may be denigrated and socially excluded, a group also may modify its norms in response to such differences, enlarging the range of social behaviours considered acceptable and allowing those who behave differently to become socially included. Thus norms are open to change through the reactions and innovations of individuals in interaction with one another (Holt et al., 2012). Children and young people designated as having BESD are, by definition, not adhering to the norms of social behaviour considered acceptable within the school – at least as defined by school staff, within the context of expectations placed on the school by the broader education institution. However, it is possible that social interactions between children labelled as having BESD, other children and school staff will lead to acceptance within the school of some behaviours previously considered unacceptable.

Acceptance within a group and participation in the activities of that group is important to the ability to make friends within the group. Children and young people seen as 'unacceptable' in the school environment may find it difficult to make friends – perhaps because they are kept physically away from interaction with potential friends and/or because many of their peers also see them as 'unacceptable'. Friendship is a relationship that is not given or fixed by virtue of being in a particular family, as are kin relationships.

It is not socially prescribed by virtue of having particular social characteristics. Rather it seems to those who are friends that it is a *chosen* relationship which can be revoked if desired (Spencer and Pahl, 2006). Nevertheless, friendships are most commonly made between people of similar social status and backgrounds (Bunnell et al., 2012). Friendships not only provide companionship in activities but they often lead to supportive and caring relationships between friends and provide a source of identity and self-esteem (Bowlby, 2011). For children and young people they are an important indicator of social acceptance by a person or people beyond the family.

In this chapter we examine how school staff try to modify the social behaviour of pupils designated as having BESD or severe behavioural problems and 'teach' them how to make and keep friendship. We also examine whether there is evidence that the norms of acceptable behaviour within school are changed in any way to render such children more socially acceptable. Such questions relate to the move that has taken place over the last 18 years towards 'inclusive education'. Some see this primarily as a move to 'include' children with a variety of disabilities in mainstream education through 'assistance' targeted at the individual child. However, this approach to inclusion has been criticised as absorbing 'difficulties that arise in education for a wide variety of reasons within the frame of individual defect' (Ainscow et al., 2006, p.17). A broader approach to inclusion focuses not only on disabilities but on the 'barriers to learning and participation that arise in education as a result of the way boys and girls, or children from different class and ethnic groups, are treated within and outside schools' (Ainscow et al., 2006, p.17). At present, however, policies and practices in schools are constrained within the first, narrower approach to inclusion. In this chapter we are concerned with the effects of this type of approach on the ways that children designated as having BESD and similar behavioural problems learn about relationships and practices of friendship within school. We focus on relationships and friendships because we argue that for children and young people in school having friends and feeling accepted by other children and young people as well as by adults in the school is vital to their participation in other aspects of school, including formal learning. As we will show it is also seen as of central importance by teachers and school staff.

The study

This chapter draws upon data from a larger study of children and young people's relationships within school. The broader research project focuses upon the inclusion and exclusion of children and young people with and without disabilities and explores their relationships within the school space in the context of their relationships in home and leisure spaces. It examines how students identified as having particular disabilities were socially valued within school.

The study took place in three LAs within southern England which had differing policies towards inclusion. In each LA three schools were studied – one primary, one secondary and one special school. The schools had a variety of specialist facilities, socio-economic composition and academic performance. Data from the Pupil Level Annual Schools Census (PLASC) and national census have been analysed to contextualise the case studies.

The discussion in this chapter is based on research in a primary and secondary school within one LA which we have selected because it encouraged schools to focus on the significance of social relationships and social/emotional norms more strongly than the other two LAs. The two schools both draw pupils from areas of deprivation. Primrose School – the primary school – has 37.3 per cent of its pupils entitled to Free School Meals[5] (compared with 19.2 per cent nationally in 2011 (DfE, 2011)) and 33.5 per cent of its pupils labelled as having SEN; of those 30.3 per cent had BESD as their primary SEN category. Sorrel School[6] – the secondary school – has 16.5 per cent on Free School Meals (compared with 15.9 per cent nationally in 2011), 26.6 per cent of pupils with a SEN diagnosis and of those, 15.0 per cent are recorded to have BESD as their primary SEN category.

In each school in-depth observation of children's and adult's interactions in a range of spaces (classrooms, corridors, assemblies, playgrounds, school trips, breakfast, lunch and after school clubs) were made over a period of at least 30 days. These observations were recorded in a research diary. Children and young people were told of the observation. In addition, about 12 children or young people in each school took part in semi-participatory research designed to enable them to tell us about their friendships, everyday interactions and activities with others in and out of school. We also carried out semi-structured interviews around themes of friendship, inclusion and special educational needs with parents of participants; key actors within each school such as the SENCo,[7] Teaching Assistants, After School Club staff; local actors (e.g., staff from the LEA, local charities and providers of services and leisure activities for young people with disabilities); and national actors (e.g., staff from national charities and interest groups).

In this chapter we explore the nature and impact of interventions to modify the behaviour of children with BESD, drawing mainly on the interviews with adults and our in-depth observations. In subsequent analyses we will analyse in more depth the ways in which young people talked about adults' interventions and their own friendships and activities.

Learning to behave

School practices

The LA in which the two schools discussed are located used to send many children with SEN to special schools, often outside the LA. Recently this policy has changed and the LA now tries to educate the majority of children with SEN in mainstream schools. The LA runs a Behaviour Service for children with SEN and has a close relationship with an active NGO which works with parents of children with disabilities. It also organises regular meetings between SENCos from clusters of schools where ideas can be exchanged and new initiatives discussed. It provides considerable support and training to all adults (not only teachers) involved with children with SEN and encourages Teaching Assistants (TAs) to structure and plan interventions on their own. This was the only LA among the three we studied where this level of support was given. An annual conference, where academics and experts talk about specific issues pertinent within the LA, is organised by the SEN team. The professional focus on and interest in the significance of social relationships, friendships and social/emotional norms distinguished this LA from the other two that we studied and this approach permeated the approach taken within the two schools.

Primrose has adopted a 'whole school' approach to promoting social and emotional well-being and good behaviour. That is, practices concerned with these issues are available to all pupils in the school. The school employs an Inclusion Mentor whose role is to work with children who have particular behavioural problems. The school also employs Learning Support Mentors, TAs and Individual Needs Assistants (INAs) who give tailored help to individual children with differences. Specific practices aimed at supporting 'good' behaviour were the provision of a room staffed by an adult (most often the Inclusion Mentor) where children could go if they were not able to conform to the demands of classroom behaviour ('the Refuge'[8]); a drop-in Breakfast club and drop-in Lunchtime Library club where pupils were supervised; a system where children could put their name down to talk over a problem later in the day with a staff member; the promise of 'Special Time'[9] – a session on Fridays when children could chose to spend time on a range of leisure activities – those who behaved badly would lose 'Special Time'; in addition the school ran a nurture group (which was not available to all children and thus an exception to the whole school policy). Recently the needs of a couple of children from the same class had dominated the activities of the Inclusion Mentor.

At Sorrel the school had special units in three separate areas for learning support, supporting transition and for inclusion. Alongside a learning support area (where pupils received help with literacy and numeracy), there were two 'transition learning groups' teaching young people needing support in moving from Primary into Secondary school. These took place in two classrooms with dedicated teachers and teaching assistants. The classrooms were organised like a primary classroom with shared tables. Pupils also went to some mainstream classes with the aim of them eventually attending mainstream classes full time. The inclusion unit supported young people throughout the rest of the school who were considered to have behavioural difficulties, and also dealt with punishment for pupils who had temporarily been excluded from school. In addition, the inclusion unit ran 'circle of friends' groups to help isolated young people make friends with peers so that they would feel more socially comfortable in the school, and arranged small group trips (for those seen to be at risk of exclusion) for sporting, musical or art activities outside school to build confidence and team work. An important aspect of the school's approach to teaching about social relationships was the use of approaches derived from restorative justice involving mediation between young people and between teachers and young people involved in disputes with one another (see Lea et al. (forthcoming) for a more detailed discussion of the role of the restorative justice approach in another school that we observed).

The amount of time the children and young people spent unsupervised and away from direct adult influence affected the role that adults had in mediating friendships and social relationships, and was strikingly different at the primary and secondary school. At Primrose almost all the time is supervised directly or indirectly by adults – by the playground supervisors before and after school and during break, in the lunch clubs, in small group working, in the classroom (by teachers, TAs and INAs). Some children who were particularly prone to involvement in disputes with their peers had closer supervision – sometimes one-to-one – so that individual adults had a very large influence on them. This adult supervision can be seen as a mixture of formal and informal education in which adults have some formal control over and responsibility for children's behaviour but with variable levels of informality in child–adult relationships and explicitness over behavioural norms. In Sorrel the majority of students were less closely supervised during break and lunchtime. The special units (learning support and inclusion) were not open at lunchtime. However, the students in the transition classrooms were able to attend a lunchtime and break club in their classrooms (children from the wider school were not allowed to attend) where there was close scrutiny similar to that in the primary school (Figure 9.1).

Teaching emotional skills

One of the things that framed these school practices and adult interventions was the 'Social & Emotional Aspects of Learning' (SEAL) programme that was promoted under the Labour Government (DfES, 2005) and derives from Goleman's work in the United States on 'Emotional Intelligence' (Goleman, 1996). This is based on the principle of teaching children and young people emotional and behavioural skills designed to allow them to understand and control difficult emotions and bodily reactions and resolve disagreements between themselves and others.

The premise of SEAL is that emotional skills can be and should be taught as part of the explicit formal curriculum. These ideas permeated both schools and were especially evident at Primrose where ideas from SEAL had been

Figure 9.1   Primary-style classroom in Sorrel: A place for formal and informal learning about how to behave in secondary school

promoted throughout the school. However, these ideas did not derive solely from SEAL – as the teacher in change of its implementation said:

> we spend so much of our school time dealing with children with huge emotional issues that what SEAL did was give us a bit of structure to do it within [...][10] I think we were already doing a lot of the talk but it gives you a framework.

An important element of SEAL at Primrose is the use of 'circle time' to talk about managing emotions and behaviour. Observing circle times it seemed that the children who have most difficulties with emotions and behaviour also find joining in the lesson most problematic, For example, in one circle time observed one child will not join the circle and is eventually taken out, another leaves the circle and when he returns is disruptive and evidently not listening. The teacher suggests that those who stay in the room are 'still listening to all of it and they still know what you've been talking about [...] I think they're accessing it in some way'. We are less confident of this. Importantly, the ideas and practices promoted in circle time were echoed both in other formal lessons and informal interactions between children and staff.

SEAL is no longer promoted by the DfE but the principles are still used by many schools. It has attracted criticisms, which claim SEAL was established without clear evidence to support this type of intervention, and indeed that there is no convincing evidence that SEAL and similar programmes are effective. SEAL has been seen as part of a wider tendency to turn 'children's emotional life and their friendships into a problem to be solved' (Craig, 2007, p.60); to promote anxiety in children about emotional competence; and encouraging children to accept rather that challenge social norms (Furedi, 2004; Craig, 2007; Ecclestone and Hayes, 2008; DCSF, 2008b; Humphrey et al., 2010; Watson et al., 2012). In contrast to the other two LAs in which research was done, this LA did problematise this realm of life, offering counselling in schools, using psychology-based tools such as sociograms to map friendships, and SEAL. While this LA had recognised the significance of social and emotional lives to learning, the critiques of SEAL were not debated, and an uncritical acceptance of the value of such interventions has the potential to be problematic.[11]

Modelling norms

In both schools there was an explicit belief in the significance of staff and children 'modelling' appropriate behaviour in non-classroom school contexts – an idea that owes much to theories of Vygotsky. For example, in Primrose the Breakfast Club co-ordinator described the value of informal interaction with the children in the following terms:

> we have got those challenging children who come to breakfast club, um, but you want them to be there in a way because they can see that there are certain behaviours that aren't acceptable not just at mealtimes but in general but actually you sit down together and you have breakfast and you've got these good manners, um, and just sort of the sharing of each other's bit of life as well

Inclusion Mentors, Learning Mentors and TAs can be important in forging links between the local society of parents and friends in which the child is embedded and the world of school. Many of them come from the local area and are

> parents that have gone into schools you know, because their kids have gone to school and they've become the dinner lady and then the teaching assistant and they're just, you know, they're just so good at their job, really, really good (LA Learning Mentor Co-ordinator)

At Sorrel local context is less significant since pupils come from all over the urban area. At Primrose it means that some adult 'models' of appropriate behaviour come from a familiar social background – as in the case of the Breakfast Club co-ordinator quoted above. It provides staff with insight into the home situation of the children and helps establish good relations with parents.

It was also evident that staff managed children's social contacts on an everyday basis – sometimes to facilitate them being with others who might be a 'good' influence, sometimes to limit their contact with those who might be a 'bad' influence. This was particularly evident at Primrose, where the opportunities for such management were greater than at Sorrel because of the high levels of adult supervision.

Making friends

At both schools there were explicit interventions to help children who lacked friends to make and keep them. Helping with friendships was seen as important not simply to reduce intra-school conflict and for the welfare of the individual but because staff considered that friendships are important to learning:

> If you're excluded from friendships it massively impedes their learning [...] you actually want them talking and working together, and if you're not included in that then, you know, your learning just stops. (Teacher/Personal, Social & Health Education (PSHE) co-ordinator, Primrose)

Inappropriate friendships or lack of friendships were seen as particularly important to the school experience of children and young people with behaviour problems:

> those children that are the ones that are heavy on resources, that staff find hardest to manage [...] the ones that don't make progress, which are all these kind of EBSDs, school action, school action plus pupils, they're, it's all about friendships, and there are so many of them struggle with their friendships (SENCo, Sorrel)

In both schools children who were seen to be excluded or isolated were taken out of class to work as a group on some non-curriculum activity with children:

> who we think will help them make friends, so good role models, or children who are quite quiet but confident and we have been able to help them by having [...] the learning mentors, work with very small groups for quite a long period. (Teacher/PSHE co-ordinator, Primrose)

The discussion in one 'circle of friends' group at Sorrel that we observed aimed to make the young people reflect on their everyday experiences, set and meet their own targets for activities, build self-esteem by recognising their achievements outside and inside school and to think about family relationships and friendships. The group interactions could also be seen as providing a template for social interaction with friends. For example the rules for the group's conduct were 'Respect each other; What's said in the room stays in the room; Listen to each other; Always be nice to each other'. Students told us in interviews that they were aware that the purpose of the group was to help them with social interactions.

Both schools also used approaches based on restorative justice to help students deal with conflicts between each other or conflicts with staff. At Sorrel a new member of staff with experience in restorative justice had recently been appointed to develop this work which was being strongly supported within the school. He described the approach as follows:

> It's a great opportunity for me to sit down with a young person who is in here, you know, say for verbally abusing the teacher [...] say to them, well OK, what happened, and what were you thinking about at the time, and how do you feel about things now, and what do we need to, what do you think needs to be done to put things right?[...] and then we'll bring the teacher down, put the teacher and the young person together and let then kind of resolve the conflict between them, with a bit of help from us, you know. (Manager of Inclusion Unit)

At Primrose similar methods were used although explicit use of restorative justice was only just being introduced. Sally and Tracy, who are involved in the incident described below, are both labelled as having BESD.

> ...went up to the community room with Mrs X, Sally, Tracy and Lea[12] They had had a breaktime altercation when they were playing tag and each had the opportunity to speak and tell what happened. This really did go round in huge circles in that one would say and then another would disagree, or really talk at cross purposes. At one point Sally said she had had enough and walked out. After 2–3 minutes she came back in (the others had carried on talking without her) and they apologised in the end. Lea said she might not play with Sally any more because she always storms off [...] After we went back downstairs I asked Lea and Tracy if it had been useful talking to Mrs X – Tracy said yes and Lea said that it was OK – she would talk to Sally but wouldn't be her friend. (Research Diary, Primrose)

The similarity in approach at the two schools stems, in part, from the SENCo meetings arranged by the LA.

In both cases the staff interventions try to promote both understanding of and empathy with the experience of others and the ability to make restitution – even if this is simply an apology. This emphasis on empathy and understanding is characteristic of restorative justice.

Conclusion

In these two schools staff put enormous effort into developing the ability of children with BESD and behavioural problems to behave more acceptably and to help them make friends. Stress is put upon the individual child learning to control their behaviour, to become self-reflexive, to develop empathy with others and to build their self-esteem through both formal learning, semi-formal interventions in behaviour and informal, 'hidden' management of social relationships. Staff provide opportunities for children to make 'desirable' friends and limit contact with 'undesirable' friends. It was clear from our observations and interviews that the children and young people generally appreciated these efforts.

The interventions did help many of the children and young people we observed with their friendships, although some remained somewhat isolated. The dominant intent, and effect, of these interventions was to move these children's norms of behaviour towards the mainstream. There was little encouragement for children, young people or staff to question the norms of sociality that pervaded the schools. However, the use of the techniques of restorative justice does involve an obligation for others – staff and children – to listen to the experiences of children with BESD and hence provides an opportunity for some small shifts in the types of behaviour that are deemed socially acceptable.

Informal learning of norms and behaviours is an inevitable part of school social life. The trials and tribulations of friendships are central to such informal learning but it is important to recognise that they can be destructive of self-esteem and independence as well as promoting them; thus adult interventions are necessary. Schools have always sought to regulate and influence informal learning, but critical analysis of informal education is necessary if it is to promote a more inclusive educational experience for all. Practices designed to improve the social inclusion of children and young people with behavioural differences must include informal education to promote more inclusive norms rather than only encouraging them to conform to dominant behaviours. This will benefit both the long-term welfare of these children and young people and improve their formal learning.

Despite the broadly positive reaction of the children and young people we talked with to about the types of help they were given, we do consider that there is a danger of over-emphasising individual emotional deficit resulting from the focus on social and emotional issues promoted by the LA and evident in the two school we studied. However, challenging the individual deficit model by changing teaching methods to further expand the inclusivity of the school would be extremely difficult in an educational climate which prioritises achievements in public exams. Tackling the processes producing the social inequalities that are acknowledged to be closely linked to diagnoses of SEN and, in particular, BESD requires national political commitment that is, at present, lacking.

Notes

1. The terms 'Social, Emotional and Behavioural Difficulties' (SEBD), 'Emotional, Social and Behavioural Difficulties' (ESBD) or 'Emotional and Behavioural Difficulties' (EBD) are also used to describe such Children.
2. E.g., 'Behaviour for Learning policy' at Cherwell School http://www.cherwell. oxon.sch.uk/content/index.php?page=201for
3. A child is labelled as having a Special Educational Need (SEN) if they have difficulties in learning that require special educational provision beyond that provided to the majority of pupils. 'School Action' involves extra help being given to a child labelled as having SEN by teachers within the school; When teachers and the SENCo are also given advice about a child's education by outside specialists the child is designated as receiving 'School Action Plus'; a Statement of Special Needs is intended for children with more severe problems and sets out the specific extra help that the Child should receive.
4. A child that the school identifies as having Special Educational Needs will be given extra help with their education from school resources – this level of help is designated as 'School Action'. 'School Action Plus' means that the school will also involve external support services in the child's education.
5. In England children whose parents are on one of a range of benefits are entitled to Free School Meals (DfE, 2012). The proportion of children on FSM is commonly used as an indicator of deprivation among pupils' families.
6. These school names are pseudonyms.
7. The SENCo is the member of staff who has responsibility for coordinating the special educational needs provision within a school.
8. Not the real name for this room.
9. Not the real name for this time.
10. The symbols [...] within a quote indicates that some of the quote has been omitted.
11. Having said this, while SEAL was a prominent feature of the teaching at Primrose it was not strongly in evidence at Sorrel. In this it was similar to many secondary schools in which – perhaps because of the demands of the exam curriculum, or a lack of belief in the programme on the part of teachers, or a lack of resources – the programme has been given only lukewarm support (Humphrey et al., 2010).
12. Pseudonyms.

References

M. Ainscow, T. Booth and A. Dyson (2006) *Improving Schools, Developing Inclusion* (London and New York: Routledge).

P. Bourdieu (1990) *The Logic of Practice* (Cambridge: Polity Press in association with Oxford: Blackwell Publishers).

S. Bowlby (2011) 'Friendship, co-presence and care: Neglected spaces', *Social and Cultural Geography*, 12, 605–22.

T. Bunnell, S. Yea, L. Peake, T. Skelton and M. Smith (2012) 'Geographies of friendships', *Progress in Human Geography*, 36, 490–507.

J. Butler (1997) *The Psychic Life of Power: Theories in subjection* (Stanford, USA: Stanford University Press).

J. Butler (2004) *Undoing Gender* (London and New York: Routledge).

C. Craig (2007) *The Potential Dangers of a Systematic, Explicit Approach to Teaching Social and Emotional Skills (SEAL)* (Glasgow: Centre for Confidence and Wellbeing).

Department for Children, Schools and Families, DCSF (2008a) *The Education of Children and Young People with Behavioural, Emotional and Social Difficulties as a Special Educational Need* (London: DCSF).

Department for Children, Schools and Families, DCSF (2008b) *Primary Social and Emotional Aspects of Learning (SEAL): Evaluation of small group work*, carried out by N. Humphrey, A. Kalambouka, J. Bolton, A. Lendrum, M. Wiglesworth, C. Lennie and P. Farrell. Research report DCSF-RR064.

Department for Children, Schools and Families, DCSF (2009) *Children with Special Educational Needs 2009: An analysis*, https://www.education.gov.uk/publications/eOrderingDownload/DCSF-00949-2009.pdf (accessed 29/11/12)

Department for Education (2011) *DfE: Schools, pupils and their characteristics*, January 2011, http://www.education.gov.uk/rsgateway/DB/SFR/s001012/index.shtml (accessed 18/12/12)

Department for Education (2012) *Free School Meals Eligibility Criteria*, http://www.education.gov.uk/schools/pupilsupport/pastoralcare/a00202841/fsmcriteria (accessed 18/12/12)

Department for Education and Skills (2005) *Excellence and Enjoyment: Social and emotional aspects of learning*, DfES 1378–2005, https://www.education.gov.uk/publications/eOrderingDownload/SEAL%20Guidance%202005.pdf (accessed 10/4/13)

K. Ecclestone and D. Hayes (2008) *The Dangerous Rise of Therapeutic Education* (London: Routledge).

F. Furedi (2004) 'Reflections on the medicalisation of social experience', *British Journal of Guidance and Counselling*, 32, 413–5.

D. Goleman (1996) *Emotional Intelligence: Why it can matter more than IQ* (London: Bloomsbury Publishing).

L. Gutman and J. Vorhaus (2012) *The Impact of Pupil Behaviour and Wellbeing on Educational Outcomes*, Department for Education, Research Report DFE-RR253, https://www.education.gov.uk/publications/eOrderingDownload/DFE-RR253.pdf (accessed 7/12/12).

L. Holt (2008) 'Embodied social capital and geographic perspectives: Performing the habitus', *Progress in Human Geography*, 32, 2, 227–46.

L. Holt (2010) 'Young people with socio-emotional differences: Theorising disability and destabilising socio-emotional norms', in V. Chouinard, R. Wilton, and E. Hall (eds) *Towards Enabling Geographies: 'Disabled' bodies and minds in society and space* (Farnham: Ashgate).

L. Holt, J. Lea and S. Bowlby (2012) 'Special units for young people on the autistic spectrum in mainstream schools: Sites of normalisation, abnormalisation, inclusion, and exclusion', *Environment and Planning*, 44, 2191–206.

L. Holt, J. Lea and S. Bowlby (2013) 'Emotions and the habitus: Young people with socio-emotional differences (re)producing social, emotional and cultural capital in family and leisure space-times', *Emotion, Space and Society*, 9, 33–41.

N. Humphrey, A. Lendrum and M. Wigelswort (2010) *Social and Emotional Aspects of Searning (SEAL) Programme in Secondary Schools: National evaluation*, Department for Education, DFE-RR049, https://www.education.gov.uk/publications/standard/publicationDetail/Page1/DFE-RR049 (accessed 7 December 2012).

J. Lea, L. Holt and S. Bowlby (2012) *Keeping Everybody In? The use of restorative approaches to justice in the inclusion of young people with behavioural, emotional and social difficulties*. Working Paper 1 (copy available from authors).

G. Lindsay, S. Pather and S. Strand (2006) *Special Educational Needs and Ethnicity: Issues of over- and under-representation*, Department for Education and Skills (University of Warwick: Research Report 757).

K. Runswick-Cole (2011) 'Time to end the bias towards inclusive education?' *British Journal of Special Education*, 38, 112–9.

L. Spencer and R. Pahl (2006) *Rethinking Friendship: Hidden solidarities today* (Princeton, NJ and Oxford: Princeton University Press).

G. Thomas (2005) 'What do we mean by EBD?' in P. Clough, P. Garner, J. Pardeck and F. Yuen (eds) *Handbook of Emotional & Behavioural Difficulties* (London: Sage).

D. Watson, C. Emery, P. Bayliss, with M. Boushel and K. McInnes (2012) *Children's Social and Emotional Wellbeing in Schools: A critical perspective* (Bristol: The Policy Press).

D. Youdell (2006) *Impossible Bodies, Impossible Selves: Exclusions and student subjectivities* (Dordrecht: Springer).

D. Youdell (2011) *School Trouble: Identity, power and politics in education* (Abingdon: Routledge).

10
Education, Technology and the Disruptive Innovations Challenging the Formal/Informal Education Divide

Kate Edwards

Introducing the formal/informal educational divide

In a recent speech by Michael Gove, Secretary of State for Education in the United Kingdom, he noted:

> One of the greatest changes can be seen in the lives of children and young people, who are at ease with the world of technology and who communicate, socialise and participate online effortlessly...children are increasingly embracing technology at a younger age...yet the classrooms of today don't reflect these changes. Indeed, many of our classrooms would be very recognisable to someone from a century ago. While there has been significant investment in technology in education, it has certainly not transformed the way that education is delivered.

This chapter takes up this challenge to technology and seeks to contribute to debates on geographies of informal education. It does so by exploring the potential of digital technologies to create collaborations between formal and informal educational practices rich with the potential to transform the way that education is delivered. Notably, it looks at one example of digital technology in practice, the development and piloting of the Always Learning Gateway (ALG) by Pearson Education working in a collaborative partnership with five UK secondary schools. In doing so it explores the emergence, development and disruptive potential offered by digital technologies to create a hybrid of formal and informal educational practices.

The chapter is divided into a further three parts. The next section presents a case for why digital technologies disrupt the boundaries between formal education and informal learning practices and explores the utility of the concepts of hybridity and 'thirdspace' to enhance our understanding of the collaborative potential of these two domains. This is followed by a brief outline of the background to the Always Learning Gateway project; some of the key findings of the project as articulated by the students on the pilot and an exploration of the inferences that can be made. The chapter concludes by highlighting to the tensions that emerge from this hybrid pedagogical practice and sets out directions for further research.

Disrupting the formal/informal education divide

Although seemingly self-evident terms, the variety of interpretations of formal and informal educational practices contained within this book are testament to the fact that they are terms often described and interpreted in a variety of different ways. My interpretation of the two terms is informed by the work of Livingstone (2006), who describes them as referring to the degree of directive control of learning. Reflecting this understanding, in this chapter, formal education is understood as being characterised by a pedagogic approach defined by dominant teacher control and the delivery of the formal national curriculum. At the other end of the spectrum, more informal approaches to pedagogy are dominated by self-directed, learner control and seek to develop skills and competencies that extend beyond the traditionally taught and examined curriculum. Unlike other definitions of formal and informal learning, I do not seek to further dichotomise the terms by considering formal and informal learning as marked by social and spatial differentiation, with formal learning only taking place within the spatially fixed institution of a school delivered by a teacher and informal learning taking place elsewhere socially and spatially within the community. This is a result of an increasing need to consider the emergence of what I characterise here as 'non-formal' approaches to learning. These are hybrid, pedagogic approaches that utilise digital technology to disrupt the formal/informal learning divide, delivering a learning experience that is both 'formal' and 'informal'.

Digital technologies, disruptive innovations and non-formal pedagogy

Research undertaken by the Centre for Evaluation and Monitoring, Durham University, evaluating the impact of classroom interventions on educational outcomes, states that 'there is evidence across age groups and for most areas of the curriculum over the last 40 years or so that the impact [of technology on learning] is relatively robust' (Higgins et al., 2011, p.17). In their evaluation they calculated that technology had the potential to have an effect size of 0.35 on learner outcomes or the equivalent of +4 months of learning. This is not in what John Hattie (2009, p.19) calls the 'zone of desired effects' which is from 0.4 upwards. However, Higgins et al. (2011) added the caveat to their assessment that the key problem with evaluating impact on outcomes in this area was a result of 'the increasing pace of technological change and that research often evaluated yesterday's technology rather than today's'. Equally, they noted that the real impact of technology is dependent not on the technology but on how it is used (2011, p.17).

Silberman-Keller (2006) argues that any given pedagogy creates and reflects a narrative about the role of educators, learners and teaching and learning processes. Equally, all forms of pedagogy are characterised by understandings and uses of space and time. Digital technologies, and the changing use of space and time they enable, disrupt established relationships between formal education and informal learning. In doing so, they provide us with what Singh (2003) describes as a 'blended learning model' that can combine various delivery modes. These might include blending off-line learning and online learning; blending self-paced and live, collaborative learning; blending structured and unstructured learning; blending custom content with off the shelf content; blending learning, practice and performance support. What makes the non-formal pedagogy enabled by digital technology such an important critical case to explore is the emergence of early evidence 'that blended learning not only offers more choices but also is more effective' (Singh, 2003, p.51). The perceived potential of technology-enhanced approaches to improve outcomes is in the possibility they offer to rework hierarchies and reconfigure learning relationships. This positions them as playing an integral role blurring the boundaries between formal and informal learning a practice, creating a 'thirdspace' that it is both timely and necessary to explore further.

Journeys through 'thirdspace'

The concept of 'thirdspace' was first developed by Homi Bhabha as a metaphor for the space in which cultures met. In his usage of the term it is a space in which colonial authority is challenged and hybrid identities created. The concept draws on wider work in postcolonial studies (Said, 1978; Bhabha, 1990) and feminist studies (Spivak, 1996) and has been further developed in fields such as geography (Soja, 1996), but it has only recently gained recognition within education particularly within the emerging area of education technology.

As part of this newly emerging field of research, Green and Hannon (2007) have proposed that digital technologies can be seen as pedagogical tools enabling the creation of a third space between formal and informal contexts. In their work, exploring the impact of web 2.0 tools and how young people are integrating these online opportunities into their lives, they describe the online world as a terrain 'where young people can create portfolios of digital media, engage in peer teaching and develop their confidence and voice'. Specifically, they maintain that the use of online tools is ingrained into the lives of young people, 'through their engagement with media sites and online games' (2007, p.7).

Significantly, Green and Hannon (2007, p.23) note, however, that while the development of more innovative approaches to learning is paramount, if we are to continue to engage students in learning, the idea that students can be taught to use these digital tools 'in any traditional sense with a teachers standing at the front of a classroom is disputable'.

This begs the question, how might digital technologies practically be used in the classroom? And, in exploring their usage, how might the idea of hybridity or 'thirdspace' further enhance our understanding of the relationship between digital technologies and formal and informal learning practices? Despite the fact that there continue to be debates over the meaning of 'thirdspace', at its core is a rejection of binaries and a recognition of the need to contest and re-negotiate boundaries. This makes it a relevant theoretical development to use to enhance our understanding of the potential impact of digital technologies might have on the relationship between formal and informal approaches to learning.

The remainder of this chapter focuses on examining the research findings from a pilot involving five secondary schools in England. This is used as a critical case study to explore the collaboration between formal education and informal learning that is enabled by digital technology. The concept of 'thirdspace' is applied, therefore, as a lens through which it is possible to explore student perceptions of the addition of the virtual space into the real world of the classroom and the learning outcomes it supported. Particular attention is paid to exploring how the non-formal pedagogy the adoption of this form of intervention can promote disrupts the boundaries between formal/informal learning creating hybrid identities and challenging traditional patterns of authority.

Always learning in 'thirdspace'?

The Always Learning Gateway is an online, student-facing, technology-enhanced curriculum supporting six of the subjects making up the English Baccalaureate (English, mathematics, science, geography, history, French) at Key Stage 3. It is radical in that it calls for a shift in classroom practices towards more student centric approach to pedagogy. This is because the curriculum content, assessments and resources can, if desired, be accessed more independently by students anytime, anywhere via the internet. This is a result of them being woven together using a student focused learning narrative. The gateway is being developed by Pearson in the United Kingdom as part of a wider suite of school improvement tools and services that focus on adopting an evidence-based approach to put the learner, and learner outcomes, at the centre.

The intended role of the Always Learning Gateway in school improvement is in its potential to support a schools capacity to adjust to the challenges posed by twenty-first-century learning, work and life by supporting teachers to harness technology as a means of improving student outcomes.

In some contexts, the term 'school improvement' is used to denote reform of the formal curriculum in the service of neoliberal political economies and future subjects. As Priestley and Humes (2010, p.358) note, however, the curriculum is a contested space in which conflicting views of the social function of schooling are expressed. In this instance, while the curriculum content of the gateway is to be aligned with the proposed changes taking place within the National Curriculum, its scope and focus go well beyond the curriculum specified by the Department for Education in England. The team developing the gateway are committed to developing an approach to teaching and learning whose essential focus is on the improvement of a wider range of student outcomes, to support success and well-being in both learning and life, than the formal curriculum alone, while also focusing on improving the effectiveness of an institution to support improvement of those outcomes. Hopkins et al.'s (1994, p.3) definition of school improvement captures this when they note that school improvement is

> a distinct approach to educational change that enhances student outcomes as well as strengthening the school's capacity for managing change. In this sense school improvement is about raising student achievement through focusing on the teaching and learning processes and the conditions that support it. It is about strategies for improving the school's capacity for providing quality education in times of change, rather than blindly accepting the edicts of centralized policies and striving to implement these directives uncritically.

Set against this backdrop, and reflecting this conception of school improvement, the outcomes of teaching and learning the gateway is seeking to address are: raising student engagement, enjoyment, achievement and attainment across six of the core curriculum subjects (English, mathematics, science, geography, history, French) and developing skills such as independence, leadership, resilience, critical thinking, problem solving, creativity and communication. It is, therefore, being designed to be a distinct approach to educational change focused on teaching and learning with the aim of enhancing a range of student outcomes that extend beyond the confines of the National Curriculum.

Education, technology and school improvement

Only limited research has been undertaken exploring the impact of technological initiatives on school improvement in the United Kingdom. Reports by Becta (Crook et al., 2010) are examples of evidence available in this field.

Established examples of successful digital initiatives that share similar origins to the Always Learning Gateway approach, and have worked well in other contexts and countries, include the Learning Portal utilised by the Kunskapsskolan school chain in Sweden and the Learning Algorithm behind the School of One initiative in the United States. More recently still we have seen the massive growth in popularity of the Khan Academy, the popularity of schools such as High Tech High in the United States and the incursion of other global media and digital organisations such as News Corp, Apple and Google into the arena of digital approaches to learning.

Despite the far-reaching implications of these innovations, there has also been little research, to date, exploring the role of technological innovations of this kind in the space of the classroom and the impact they have on pedagogy, teacher effectiveness and learner outcomes. Notable exceptions to this are the 2011 evaluation by the Research and Policy Study Group of New York City's Department of Education of the impact on learner outcomes of the pilot of the School of One initiative and the OECD report *Connected Minds* (2012). Nor has much attention been given to how links can be made between industry, research and practice to realise the potential of digital education to transform outcomes for learners. The approach taken to develop the Always Learning Gateway by Pearson and the research findings reported in this chapter partially fill these gaps.

My role in this project was to lead the research programme for the Pearson school improvement team. During the initial phases of this project we were specifically concerned with testing a number of different versions of the user interface and exploring how, why and in what ways teachers and students adopted the resource. During the later phases the emphasis shifted to linking the knowledge and best practice from research with the design, development and ongoing evaluation of the gateway. We formed a close, collaborative partnership with five schools and were supported with additional input from a small team of researchers at Oxford University led by Professor Pam Sammons a world leading expert in teacher and school effectiveness. The schools participated in an iterative process of specification gathering, technical development, user testing, data collection (quantitative and qualitative), with all findings fed back into the development and design process. This meant we were able to prioritise a bottom-up rather than top-down approach to change putting students, teachers and academic research at the core of the design process and viewing teachers, leaders and researchers as what Fullan (1991), Hopkins et al. (1994) and MacBeath (1999) describe as agents of innovation and change.

The composite result was a desire to strengthen the connections between schools, research and the development of technological innovations to help students to make progress with their learning. The findings of the pilot shed as much light onto the enormous benefit that can come from collaborative partnerships of this kind between industry, schools and research institutes as they did on the development of the gateway itself. This theme will be returned to in the conclusion.

The Always Learning Gateway pilot

The 2011–2 pilot fell into two key phases. Phase one was a flexible, agile research and development phase the focus of which was to deliver a 'beta' level product to schools for students and teachers to test out, provide feedback and contribute input about how to shape and further refine it. This took place between September 2011 and February 2012. Phase 2 took place between May and July 2012 after the Always Learning Gateway had undergone a period of re-development and design. A mixed methods approach was used to collect data involving questionnaires, focus-groups, depth-interviews, teacher action research and student research projects. The purpose and value of this method of research design was to explore key research questions from a number of different stakeholder perspectives. Despite what Leitch et al. (2007) call the twists and turns of working with students as co-researchers the research evidence cited in this chapter was gathered by and from students between May and July 2012 in the variety of research roles they undertook. These included acting as research advisors via focus groups, data gatherers via their project work and co-interpreters of data via participation in a student conference about the impact of the ALG on their approaches to learning. Focus groups with students were recorded, transcribed and analysed inductively through description, classification and interconnection based on a quasi-grounded theory approach (Kitchen and Tate, 2000).

In each participating school, formal agreements to participate in the research project by the schools were followed by individual, collaborative agreements and informed consent by both students and each ALG classroom teacher whose students' experiences of learning were the main focus of the study. In total the study consulted 700 students in classrooms across six curriculum subject areas engaging over 70 students in focus groups and 35 students as co-researchers actively contributing to the research process. Parallel research programmes took place with teachers and leaders. The findings from this research are beyond the scope of the chapter.

In this second phase of the pilot teachers were given freedom about how to integrate the use of the ALG into their teaching practice. The research findings indicated that teachers adopted a range of pedagogic practices. Some teachers integrated the ALG into their existing pedagogy, utilising it as a front of class resource or selecting resources from the learning units to supplement their existing schemes of work. Other teachers went on a transformative journey with the ALG. Across the pilot teachers were seen to adopt at least two other different pedagogic approaches. These ranged from using the ALG for specifics interventions when they wanted to support targeted, independent use of the gateway by students for specific purposes, to allowing students to undertake self-guided learning over the course of a half term. In the latter example, the relationship between the teacher and students underwent, with differing degrees of effectiveness, changes in terms of resource, pedagogy and classroom culture.

An examination of student-centred components of the research highlights at-least two different zones of boundary crossing between formal and informal learning that were facilitated by the virtual, 'thirdspace' created by the introduction of the Always Learning Gateway into the teaching and learning dynamic. The first is a zone relating to learner self-identities this is explored in terms of student explanations of how established identities were disrupted via a process of 'trying on' and developing newly emergent hybrid identities. The second is a zone relating to teacher practice. This is described as a disruption operating at the scale of the class due to the way the use of technology challenged traditional boundaries between the powerful [teacher] and the less powerful [student].

Disrupting student identities

Two of the core opportunities offered by the ALG flagged by students were the range of materials it contained and that the activities encourage students to work with and learn from others. The learning resources contained exercises and activities not just via text, but using a range of audio-visual media. These could be done as a whole class, in groups, in pairs or individually. Its potential lay in its capacity to support the creation of new learner identities and learning opportunities in a variety of non-formal sites and settings.

What does your student 'id' say?

What attracted students to using the ALG was that it enabled them to personalise their approach to learning and begin to express and monitor the development of their individual learner identities and those of others:

> there are just so many activities, like group work and projects and stuff and you can choose how you go about learning.

> Girl, year 7

The capacity to choose different pathways to access the learning material was highlighted by one student who said:

> My teacher often likes to start with a power point when we are using the ALG. He puts that up on the interactive board before we start ... this outlines which resources you need to use by the end of the lesson and you are then allowed to do them in whatever sequence you like, but you need to have done them by the end of the lesson. For me I think it's good to be given a bit of freedom with it [the ALG] so you can play about with

it and approach what you are learning about in your own way rather than in the same way as everyone else.

Boy, year 7

This indicated some students could, and did, blend linear and non-sequential routes according to their interests. This independent learning process was akin to approaches to learning traditionally undertaken outside the formal learning environment. They liked that that they could gain knowledge as tasks demanded rather than always from a teacher before they undertook an aspect of learning:

the online library – the 'Knowledge Centre' – I think that helps us most because it's quite interactive and you can find out things to help you without needing to ask a teacher.

Girl, year 8

Gaining knowledge as tasks demanded helped them assert their independence too. Others saw that learning and demonstrating understanding and skills in groups (rather than working alone) made them more independent too.

we have our own computer, but we work in pairs or groups on things and work things out together.

Girl, year 7

The issue and meaning of independence was a key theme to which students returned often. One student noted that:

independence is about knowing that some of the topics you are learning about you need to be taught by the teacher as a class, but it's also about knowing you can learn by working with a partner, even working with a partner you can still work independently from a teacher.

Girl, year 8

This recognition that formal, transmissive education, where the teacher transmits and students receive was just one mode of delivery and more informal, experiential learning, where meaning is made and shared through experience with others, was as valuable was significant.

One student reflected they were now not so bored in class:

it's [using the ALG] better than learning in the classroom when the teacher gives long speeches. I just listen and get bored then, but when you do individual work its better cos you can work at your own pace without nobody having to make a long speech

Girl, year 9

Students did not all have the same experience of what working independently might mean. One student described it as:

someone who works on their own and doesn't really need that much help from teachers and different things, she gets on with it and doesn't really ask that many questions, doesn't have group discussions with people to get help and things like that.

Girl, year 9

Having the independence to choose how to go about learning, particularly in terms of accommodating different paces of learning, was seen as a real bonus of working using online resources:

you can go at your own pace, so if someone else is just rushing off you can take your time over the questions.

Boy, year 7

The ability to work more independently also highlighted differences in learner identities too. Students noted that:

the fast people in the class you can now see are like really fast and they just move when they need to as the teacher can help them to choose what they want to do next.

Girl, year 9

If independence and difference were two emerging aspects of learner identities that emerged, resilience was a third.

it's [the ALG] like, built my confidence a bit because we work in groups more now and I can go on it and look at things again on my own at home too.

Girl, year 7

This point was explored further by another girl who explained that the meaning of the word resilient:

it's about finding different ways to get some more information when you don't know the answer

Girl, year 9

The fact that they could assess themselves on the progress they were making contributed to this. One student noted:

> the 'Test Myself' thing helped me the most 'cause normally you can do all this work in a lesson, but then you don't know if you've remembered it and the 'Test Myself' means you can see if you can actually remember it and if you get it wrong it lets you try again so it helps you to think about where you are going wrong.
>
> Boy, year 7

A fourth emerging identity was associated with a growing awareness in the process of learning how to learn. This was a result of the ALG providing tools to support students to reflect on how the new approach to learning was impacting on how they were learning how to learn. This included access to a journal where they could reflect on their learning journey.

In focus groups students were keen to articulate the effect they thought they ALG was having on their approach to learning. One noted that the flexible way of accessing the site could be of particular help in another subject he was not using the ALG in:

> I'd like to use it in history because if you forgot some of the facts or something, instead of having to go and find your teacher in the day you could just go on it at home and go onto an activity and try and maybe find it out for yourself.
>
> Boy, year 7

When asked if they would like to carry on using the Always Learning Gateway beyond the pilot some students again flagged up the effect the approach could have to their engagement in learning:

> I would like to continue using the ALG in subjects that I don't like very much ... cause it can almost help me over come that, make me stick with it when I find if boring.
>
> Boy, year 7

For some students the act of being able to access a whole programme of learning for themselves online, at their own pace, had the potential, to produce an 'effect' (Thrift and Dewsbury, 2000) on their learning. Thrift and Dewsbury's interpretation of the meaning of 'effect' is useful here. The examples illustrate that if students were to be able to use this approach to learning and sustain these new identities over time, they envisaged these new subjectivities may 'spill over' in an iterative manner to produce new selves with the potential to support or blend with how they approached learning in other sites and settings.

Despite being able to verbalise learning developments in focus groups, students found writing about this independently more challenging:

> the Learning Journey gives you a chance to tell your teacher what you know about what you're doing and how confident you are, or not, because the teacher doesn't tell us what to write I just don't know where to start.

Girl, year 7

While having the opportunity to reflect on their learning was valuable some students thought it was not as useful as it could be because:

> I was expecting the teacher to come and see us and ask us how we're doing, but you just type it and then nothing comes back from the teacher.

Girl, year 7

The focus group discussions outlined above highlighted how the introduction of the ALG had hybrid, non-formal student identities to be asserted. Central to Bhabha's third space thesis is the notion that identity is produced through (in)between spaces which provide 'the terrain for elaborating strategies of selfhood – singular or communal – that initiate new signs of identity, and innovative sites of collaboration, and contestation' (Bhabha, 1994, p.1). The evidence explored here suggest that students using the ALG can be likened to groups (in)between, 'neither One nor the Other, but something else besides, in-between' (Bhabha, 1994, p.224): that is, set between the freedom and autonomy of being able to learn in a more independent way and the often 'learned' dependence many had on certain aspects of formal, teacher-directed forms of learning.

While Joyce et al. maintain that significant growth requires discomfort, and learner dependencies needed to be challenged if we are to improve student learning, they are clear that a critical part of a teachers task in learning to use a new teaching strategy has to do with helping learners acquire the skills necessary to relate to that new approach (2008, p.395). Students, therefore, were quite right to place strong emphasis on the significant and ongoing role they saw for teachers to monitor progress and provide feedback when non-formal, technology enhanced pedagogic approaches were adopted.

Trying 'id' on

While there were notable positive's that students saw in the introduction of the ALG:

> when you are on the computer, most people are engaged, most people are quiet; focusing.

> Girl, year 9

In nearly all the focus groups students believed using technology was causing marked changes in some other aspects of student identity and behaviour.

One boy described how when they were supposed to be using the ALG in fact:

> Some people end up like going on You Tube and things ... because I mean it's quite distracting when you use computers because there is lots of other stuff that you can go and look at so people sometimes mess around and abuse the computers and stuff.

> Boy, year 7

The need for self-awareness and self-regulation were key issues when using the ALG. But, in the 'thirdspace' created by the ALG, where roles and responsibilities were shifting both for teachers and for students, self-awareness and self-regulation were not always existing learner habits for all students.

> I think we all go a bit hyper and then we don't get as much done' and 'it can get quite out of hand, because people go on the internet and start screaming.

> Girl, year 9

Students were self-reflective about this issue though:

> when you use the laptop at school you're like 'Yeah, yeah laptop' and it's really exciting and then you get home you're just like, Oh, it's a laptop, it's just a laptop. Because you are on your own with it, it doesn't make you so hyper.

> Boy, year 7

This additional vignette illustrates that despite the transformative potential offered by the ALG, not all of the new learner identities that students experimented with or 'tried on' were illustrative of positive learner identities. For some students the use of technology was not associated with structured approaches to learning and instead formed the basis of their social life and prompted different learner behaviours moving outside the defined content of the gateway to rhizomatically explore the virtual world they had access to according to wider interests. For others, the use of 'technology' in the classroom was something that was 'out-of-place'. Its presence was used as an excuse to transgress school boundaries as the use of technology was considered as being associated with what Madge et al. (2009) describe as activities like socialising and talking to friends, and other acts of behaviour that were contrary to those expected of a formal learning environments, rather than for actually doing work.

In Learning for Life Hargreaves (2004) argued that pedagogy should at its best be about what teachers do that not only helps students to learn, but actively strengthens their capacity to learn. As the ALG was predominantly being used as a resource in class the role of the teacher in determining who, what, when, where and how the resource was used was paramount. Evidence from the student research indicated that some, but not all teachers adopted modes of using the ALG that had the potential to create new student learner identities characterised by learning in more independent, resilient and collaborative ways. These are what Guy Claxton calls positive learning dispositions (2007, p.115). That students of a range of different levels of attainment were able to recognise and articulate changes taking place in their approach to learning was an indication that using technology to adopt a more non-formal approach to teaching and learning had the potential to create new learner identities defined by these positive learner dispositions. However, the different ways teachers chose to introduce and use the ALG contributed to the creation of a dynamic zone of tension, 'discontinuity' and 'disjuncture' an 'interstitial space' (Bhabha, 1994, p.219) where students tried out both positive and negative learner dispositions. Of key importance in understanding this was their ongoing participation in the research process as a means of expressing their changing understandings of their own identities as learners, openly discussing the role they understood and expected both teachers and learners to play.

Disrupting class

To further understand how hierarchies were being reworked in the classroom students were asked to describe the teaching methods and practices different teachers adopted using the Always Learning Gateway. The focus group discussions illustrated how the use of technology in the classroom appeared to transform the class into a 'performative, liminal space' (Madge and O'Connor, 2005) in which students and teachers 'tried out' not only different identities, but different roles too. This was not necessarily due to the use of technology alone. Rather, as Higgins et al. (2011) note, it was in its capacity to support a different approach to teaching and learning that disrupts traditional classroom hierarchies and shifts the role of the teacher from being a formal 'sage on the stage' to being more of an informal 'guide on the side'.

Describing the new role of the teacher in the classroom, one of the boys said:

> he's always walking around helping us and like, if we finish early, I mean, one time I'd done some more of the exercises at home, so I finished before everyone else, so he just told me to move on to the next topic and then 'Test Myself' to see how much I had understood. So it works well that way having your own access whenever you want and being able to move at your own pace.
>
> Boy, year 7

What students particularly liked about this changed classroom dynamic was that:

> he'll [the teacher] quite often come over and have a conversation with us and go through part of it. It's better than on the interactive whiteboard because he's going through where you are specifically on your computer.
>
> Boy, year 7

What made all the difference to these interactions was that they were not predetermined as many formal learning encounters were thought to be. Instead, they were tailored to when, where and with whom the teacher was engaging:

> he hasn't got anything scripted for the whole class he's like, right, how do you find this and then I'll say it, he'll explain it and I'll find out more and then I become clearer about it.
>
> Boy, year 7

Christensen et al. (2008, p.101) note that the use of digital technologies can enable teachers to teach less monolithically and function more as one-to-one tutors. Students specifically noted the degree of personalisation it enabled. As one student said:

> For me, my teacher has become a lot more into my learning... he's like, he's always willing to talk.
>
> Boy, year 7

At the other end of the spectrum though was the view that the non-formal, guide on the side approach:

> can make some teachers a bit... lazy
>
> Boy, year 7

Lack of the use of direct teaching by some teachers was one of the reasons cited for this:

> he'll just walk around for about five minutes and then he'll sit down for the whole lesson.

> Boy, year 7

Despite students describing some examples of ineffective teaching practices being used students believed that there were still benefits for them from having less formal engagement with the teacher and cited that

> in some ways that's good because we are learning independently

but then they went on to say:

> that's [sitting down] not really what the teacher is meant to be doing.

> Boy, year 7

This situation was compounded for some other students who observed that the adoption of a non-formal pedagogy meant that some teachers:

> don't really seem to plan any more or directly teach and structure a lesson.

> Boy, year 7

What students cited as being key was the need for teachers to support how they could personalise their learning by providing differentiated learning opportunities. This was because:

> you need them to understand what you're doing and that so they can help you.

> Boy, year 7

Even though the ALG contained materials pitched at three different levels, one student noted that:

> they [teachers] need to go through the ALG before they use it in class to know what it's like and set people different stuff on it for different levels.

> Girl, year 7

Ko and Sammons (2012) highlight that there is a time and a place for direct teaching regardless of whether you are pursuing more a constructivist, or non-formal, approach to learning. They draw on the work of Rowe (2006) who maintains that both formal, direct approaches and non-formal more constructivist approaches have merit in their own right. This is provided that the students have the basic knowledge and skills (best provided by direct instruction) before engagement in 'rich' constructivist learning activities. The problem arises when constructivist learning activities precede explicit teaching or replace it with the assumption that students have adequate knowledge and skills to effectively engage with the constructivist learning activities designed to generate new learning (2006, p.14).

Higgins et al. (2011, p.17) note that

> overall studies consistently find that ICT is associated with better learn-ing, however there is considerable variation in impact. The gains are usually moderate and it is certainly the case that it is more important to think about the way the technology is used which is important rather than the technology itself.

They added that on the whole it is additional training and support which is likely to make the difference on how well the technology is used. As the findings from the focus groups illustrate this was also the case on the ALG pilot. The roles that teachers chose to adopt were as impor-tant to the success of the pilot as the new identities students themselves developed.

Research on teacher training has repeatedly uncovered a 'discomfort' fac-tor as teachers acquire new repertoires (Joyce and Showers, 2002). On the pilot, the discomfort experienced in using digital technology to adopt a more non-formal pedagogical approach was three fold. It was partially expe-rienced because students were being exposed to new strategies and needed to learn complimentary skills and adopt new roles so that they could maximise the learning gains from them; it was in part because the teachers needed to adapt other well-ingrained skills and roles in order to use the new strate-gies and it was in part because the teachers appeared to students to be less confident with the new roles and strategy than they were with their older repertoires.

This blurring of the duality between the role of the powerful (all know-ing) teacher and role of the less powerful student was not always an easy transition to make. As one student put it:

> my teacher, he's not very electrical if you know what I mean, he's quite old fashioned so he doesn't know much about the computers. We often need to help him.

Boy, year 7

Students cited other examples of shifting roles changing the dynamics of the classroom. One of these was the viewing the ALG as playing the role of an additional teacher.

One student noted:

> what's good is that the ALG it gives you tips and things that help you so it's almost like having another teacher, just one that doesn't speak' and 'if we're stuck we can ask him [the teacher].

Boy, year 7

The ALG could be used to enable students to learn not just from the teacher, but from other students too.

> I think it works well when some smarter children work with some non smart children to help them. I don't think all people should work individually because pair work can help you too.

Boy, year 7

In some classes opportunities to learn from other students were taken further:

> when I've finished my teacher asks me to go round and help other students. I like this, it's better than sitting there with nothing to do

Girl, year 7

In a contrasting scenario a student at a school with significant numbers of mid year admissions explained:

> being able to see what the class had learned before I arrived meant I was able to catch up with them when I was at home.

Girl, year 9

At the same school, where students often spoke English as an additional language, they commented that in some ways using the ALG provided opportunities for them to access teacher from another country.

> it's great, I copy the text from ALG and put it into Google translate. It's helped me to learn history (and English) so much faster.

Girl, year 9

Role reversals sometimes involved a switch between the teacher and student with the student becoming the teacher of the teacher, on other occasions the student became the teacher to other students, or alternative sources of authority emerged within the classroom or beyond. Or, as one girl who had used the ALG at home to go beyond what had been asked of her, using the ALG was like being given access to a more effective teacher:

> I'd gone on to look at some more of the history resources and my teacher wasn't very happy I'd moved ahead of the class onto another topic, and when I explained this to him didn't know what to do next

Girl, year 7

In their examination of how technology can disrupt the traditional roles adopted in the classroom Christensen et al. (2008, p.92) note that one-to-one tutors are largely limited to the wealthy and for the privileged few. The fact that some students saw the ALG as offering access to opportunities to learn for longer periods of time, from more than one teacher indicated the value they saw in gaining support from more than one source of authority, customising when and how they learned to their own learning needs. The ALG also was seen by some students as acting as a symbolic space providing tools and opportunities for cultures to meet. Rather than being disenfranchised as a result of their limited English language skills some students were able to access multiple sources of authority enabling them to supplement their learning by finding ways to 'speak' and learn that would not normally be available to them.

Contestations of roles and identities in the manner outlined above can be likened to what Bhabha (1994) described as the symbolic staining of places by the hybrid acts. The acts described above contributed to a blurring of the prescribed duality of the powerful (teacher) and the less powerful (student). The introduction of the ALG destablised entrenched hierarchies between teachers and students enabling traditional social conventions of the classroom to be contested, such as the teacher as 'the sage on the stage' positioning them sometimes as 'the guide on the side'. The examples cited above highlight a complex politics about learning. On the one hand, this was choreographed and conducted by sets of deeply invested and widely shared (adult) values and evidence about who could and should directs the process of teaching and learning. On the other hand, it was representative of attempts to challenge and usurp those roles and relationships both by students and by the connections they were able to make with new sources of authority that were enabled as a result technology.

Disruptions in third space

By focusing on the everyday experiences of students using the Always Learning Gateway it is clear that there is considerable strength in the use of 'thirdspace' as a metaphorical concept that can challenge the duality of formal and informal approaches to learning and the roles and identities of students within them. Indeed, the examples cited here illustrate how accessing virtual, 'thirdspaces' is a lived, rather than simply analytic concept reworking hierarchies, changing social divisions, creating new possibilities and opportunities for learning.

The observed changes taking place in the classrooms adopting the Always Learning Gateway indicate that technologies like this are already showing evidence of their potential to enable students to take more ownership over their learning, to piece together their own identities as learners, to try out new identities (by adopting more independent approaches to learning), to develop more resilient approaches to learning and stand apart, if only temporarily, from the more formal, dependent approaches to learning that dominate much of the educational landscape. The findings also indicate they have the potential to disrupt the role of the teacher as the sole voice of authority in the classroom and blur the duality of powerful teacher and less powerful student. The key point to note though is that these changes are not about the technology; they are about the behaviour shift in terms of teacher and student roles and identities that they can help to foster.

Findings such as these indicate that positioning formal and informal learning at opposite ends of the educational spectrum simply turns them into another of what Barber et al. (2012) call the 'false dichotomies' by which education is frequently defined. The challenge lies in further exploring why these false polarities still perpetuate and examining ways to break down the duality. We need to find ways both practical and theoretical of blending and blurring the boundaries between them while still remembering the importance of critically evaluating the boundaries and tensions that continue to exist within these spaces of practice for these are spaces in which geography still matters.

This research project highlights that significant work remains to be done if we are to explore these emerging themes in more detail. Further longitudinal examinations are needed to explore the impact of such technologies not only on engagement and enjoyment but also on student achievement and attainment. As part of this work there needs to be further examination of student identities and subjectivities, particularly those associated with the (often false) perceptions of students as 'digital natives'. Research undertaken for the pilot study indicated a significant proportion of students (c.50 per cent) lacked the skills to confidently use technology. On a different, but related theme it is both timely and necessary to interrogate further the production and contestation of teacher identities, subjectivities and pedagogies in relation to the use of technology to support teaching and learning and in doing so examine in more detail the continuing professional development needs that are required to support the integration of more digital approaches to teaching and learning. Finally, work also needs to be done to explore the potential innovative and creative benefits for learning which might emerge from the creation of collaborative partnerships between industry, schools and research to develop digital resources.

The fears with which this chapter started, that educational practices were failing to be transformed by technology, were again flagged in a recent report, exploring the proof, promise and potential of digital education (2012). In the introduction, Lukin et al. (2012) echoed the sentiment of the speech by Michael Gove with which this chapter started when they stated that: 'in the last five years UK schools have spent more than £1 billion on digital technology. From interactive whiteboards to tablets, there is more digital technology in schools than ever before. But so far there has been little evidence of substantial success in improving educational outcomes' (Lukin et al., 2012, p.1).

Despite concerns that something continues to be going wrong within digital education the findings of Lukin et al.'s research resonated with those of the research and development pilot project for the Always Learning Gateway. They found that future is not as bleak as some might presume. While the OECD (2012, p.11) maintain that a lack of empirical evidence means that the jury is still out on the potential of technology to radically transform teaching and learning in formal education, both Lukin et al. and the research presented here highlight a newly emerging picture. This is one defined by emerging *proof* of technology supporting effective learning, emerging technologies that show *promise* of impact and exciting 'non-formal' teaching and learning *practice* that highlights a clear role for technology in terms of bridging the formal/informal learning divide.

Acknowledgements

I would like to thank the students, teachers and leaders from the five secondary schools involved in the pilot for all their interest, enthusiasm and engagement in the research components of the project. I would also like to acknowledge the invaluable contribution made to the evaluation of different aspects of the pilot data set by Professor Pam Sammons, Susila Davies and Nina Hood, Department of Education, University of Oxford. All interpretations (or shortcomings to the argument) are the authors own. A final thanks go to Mark Gosling for his efforts to capture the student experiences in the classroom on film.

References

M. Barber, K. Donnelly and S. Rizvi (2012) *Oceans of Innovation: The Atlantic, the Pacific, global leadership and the future of education* (London: IPPR).

H. Bhabha (1990) 'The third space', in J. Rutherford (ed.) *Identify, Community, Culture and Difference* (London: Lawrence & Wishart).

H. Bhabha (1994) *The Location of Culture* (London: Routledge).

C. M. Christensen, M. B. Horn and C. W. Johnson (2008) *Disrupting Class: How disruptive innovation will change the way the world learns* (New York: McGraw-Hill).

G. Claxton (2007) 'Expanding young people's capacity to learn', *British Journal of Educational Studies*, 55, 115–34.

C. Crook, C. Harrison, L. Farrington-Flint, C. Tomás and J. Underwood (2010) *The Impact of Technology: Value added classroom practice* (Coventry: Becta).

M. G. Fullan (1991) *The New Meaning of Educational Change* (London: Cassell).

H. Green and C. Hannon (2007) *Their Space: Education for a digital generation* (London: Demos).

D. H. Hargreaves (2004) *Learning for Life: The foundations of lifelong learning* (Bristol: Policy Press).

J. Hattie (2009) *Visible Learning* (London: Routledge).

S. Higgins, D. Kokotsaki and R. Coe (2011) *Toolkit of Strategies to Improve Learning: summary for schools spending the pupil premium* (London: The Sutton Trust).

D. Hopkins, M. Ainscow and M. West (1994) *School Improvement in an Era of Change* (London: Cassell).

B. Joyce and B. Showers (2002) *Student Achievement Through Staff Development* 3rd edition (Alexandria, VA: ASCD).

B. R. Joyce, M. Weil and E. Calhoun (2008) *Models of Teaching* 8th Edition (Boston: Allyn and Baron).

R. Kitchen and N. J. Tate (2000) *Conducting Research into Human Geography* (Prentice Hall: Harlow).

J. Ko and P. Sammons (2012) *Effective Teaching: A review of research* (Reading: CfBT).

R. Leitch, J. Gardnera, S. Mitchella, L. Lundya, O. Odenaa, D. Galanoulia and P. Clough (2007) 'Consulting pupils in assessment for learning classrooms: The twists and turns of working with students as co-researchers', *Educational Action Research*, 15, 459–78.

D. W. Livingstone (2006) 'Informal Learning: Conceptual distinctions and preliminary findings', in Z Bekerman, N. C. Burbules and D. Silberman-Keller (eds) *Learning in Places the Informal Education Reader* (New York: Peter Lang Publishing).

R. Lukin, B. Bligh, A. Manches, S. Ainsworth, C. Crook and R. Noss (2012) *Decoding Learning: The proof, promise and potential of digital education* (London: Nesta).

J. MacBeath (1999) *Schools must Speak for Themselves: The case for school self-evaluation* (London: Routledge).

C. Madge, J. Meek, J. Wellens and T. Hooley (2009) 'Facebook, social integration and informal learning at University: "It is more for socialising and talking to friends about work that for actually doing work"', *Learning, Media and Technology*, 34, 141–51.

C. Madge and H. O'Connor (2005) 'Mothers in the making? Exploring liminality in cyber/space', *Transactions of the Institute of British Geographers*, 30, 83–97.

OECD (2012) *Connected Minds: Technology and today's learners*. Centre for Educational Research and Innovation (Paris: OECD).

M. Priestley and W. Humes (2010) The development of Scotland's Curriculum for Excellence: Amnesia and déjà vu, *Oxford review of Education*, 36, 345–61.

K. Rowe (2006) *Effective Teaching and Learning Strategies for Students with and without Learning Difficulties: Constructivism as a legitimate theory of learning and teaching?* (Victoria, Australia: ACER).

E. Said (1978) *Orientalism: Western Conceptions of the Orient* (Penguin).

D. Silberman-Keller (2006) in Z. Bekerman, N. C. Burbules and D. Silberman-Keller (eds) *Learning in Places the Informal Education Reader* (New York: Peter Lang Publishing).

H. Singh (2003) 'Effective blended learning programmes', *Educational Technology*, 43, 51–4.

E. Soja (1996) *Thirdspace: Journeys to Los Angeles and other real and imagined places* (Malden, MA: Blackwell).

G. Spivak (1996) *The Spivak Reader* (London: Routledge).

N. Thrift and J. D. Dewsbury (2000) 'Dead geographies – and how to make them live', *Environment and Planning D: Society and Space*, 18, 411–31.

Part III
Youth Work Spaces

11
Rehearsal Spaces as Children's Spaces? Considering the Place of Non-formal Music Education

Luke Dickens and Douglas Lonie

Introduction

This chapter contributes to research on the geographies of informal education through a focus on a model of non-formal music education advanced by the work of the National Foundation for Youth Music (Youth Music), a charity working with children and young people in England. Significantly, while this model differs from formal music education in its concern for musical learning beyond the school curriculum (generally considered as *formal* music education), it also differs from many of the current theoretical descriptions of informal education, which tend to focus on unstructured activity occurring in and around formal contexts of school or work (Coffield, 2000; Bekerman et al., 2005), or *ad hoc* ways in everyday life (Richardson and Wolfe, 2001). Despite being implemented within highly organised national and regional infrastructures by a range of third, public and private sector partners, and impacting on the lives of many thousands of children and young people each year in England alone (Lonie and Dickens, 2011), the role of such non-formal educational provision is yet to be fully taken into account within a renewed interest in the geographies of childhood, learning and education (Hanson Thiem, 2009; Holloway et al., 2010).

In this chapter we provide a detailed examination of non-formal music education through the distinct spatiality of the music rehearsal studio, using two illustrative case studies: the 'Community Recording Studio' in Nottingham, and a mobile 'rehearsal studio' project run by the Cornwall Youth Music Action Zone (CYMAZ). Both spaces were initiated under a pilot scheme to establish 14 music rehearsal spaces across England, funded by the Department for Culture, Media and Sport (DCMS) in 2009.[1] Taking a detailed look at these contexts, we aim to build on our conceptual positioning of non-formal music education (Lonie and Dickens, 2013), especially in relation to the importance of working with children experiencing 'challenging circumstances'[2] or living in areas of multiple deprivation, and our arguments on the distinct importance of supported creative learning in community settings (Dickens and Lonie, 2013).

Specifically, we consider these dynamics as they are experienced, practiced and understood by the children and young people participating in such contexts. By bringing non-formal music education into view through the perspectives of those children and young people actually using rehearsal spaces, a rather different sense of musical learning emerges alongside the discourses attached to the rationale for this project by its key policy advocates (which centred on the reduction of social costs through arts interventions, and the economic logic of 'regeneration' achieved through nurturing 'innovation' and 'creativity'). In particular, while participating young people concurred that the rehearsal spaces were an important and valuable policy intervention, they expressed this in terms of the opportunities such provision presented them: to learn music in a collective and informal mode that they felt was unavailable to them through music making in school contexts or elsewhere in their everyday lives. Our analysis therefore explores evidence of the ways such rehearsal spaces might exemplify the kinds of participatory, creative and ethically focused 'children's spaces' advocated for by scholars of education (Hart, 1992, 2008; Moss and Petrie, 1997, 2002; Jans, 2004; Percy-Smith and Thomas, 2009; Percy-Smith, 2010).

The place of non-formal music education

While we note a good deal of diversity and interchangeability in the literature on 'formal', 'informal' and 'non-formal' education (McGivney, 1999; Colley et al., 2002), we would nonetheless argue that non-formal education has some important distinctions. Despite occurring beyond the auspices of formal education, non-formal education is equally characterised by structured institutional delivery mechanisms and infrastructures, and thus also differs somewhat from informal learning occurring in everyday contexts. In the United Kingdom, recent non-formal education provision has been funded by considerable investments in community-level delivery settings, workforce development and semi-formalised accreditation and recognition pathways, organised at a national scale and by a broad range of third sector and public–private partnerships (e.g., see Lonie and Dickens, 2011). In this regard it appears closer to the kinds of 'alternative' educational spaces and provision discussed by Kraftl (Chapter 4, this volume).

Non-formal education also appears pedagogically distinct both from the formal and informal thus far conceived. While having many parallels with informal learning, non-formal education differs on the key point of intentionality, where the learner consciously and explicitly opts to participate in a sustained learning experience. Yet in this regard it also differs from formal education for an emphasis on learning through the tacit development of skills and experiences, rather than formal assessment and accreditation. Non-formal education further differs from formal education for its emphasis on the collective rather than the individual, aligned closely with Lave and Wenger's (1991) notion of 'legitimate peripheral participation' that recognises the mutual necessity of belonging to a group to learn effectively, while learning shared practices is taken as central to establishing a sense of belonging.

Moreover, while some have viewed the non-formal being defined by adult and continuing education or in workplaces (Eraut, 2000), we would argue that there is an important role for the non-formal education of children and young people, particularly those experiencing 'challenging circumstances' or excluded from formal educational contexts. In this, despite the distinctions outlined, non-formal pedagogical relationships most closely align with the informal or 'natural' learning styles of certain mentoring practices of youth work (Philip and Hendry, 1996; Philip, 2000; Deane et al., 2011).

In many ways, the above sets out an idealised and simplistic definition, and points to the importance of the detailed examination taking place within this volume. There are also potential threats in the ways the structured provision of non-formal education might blur the distinction between formal/informal learning, or take the form of class-based social engineering (Colley, 2003), and thus advocacy for such provision, particularly as it expanded under both the New Labour and current Coalition governments in the United Kingdom, deserves further critical examination. As such, while we want to focus on a neglected but significant mode of educational provision, we take Colley et al.'s point that 'the most significant issue is not the boundaries between these types of learning, but the inter-relationships between dimensions of formality/informality, in particular situations' (Colley et al., 2002, no page; see also Miller, 2005; Cartwright, 2012). Indeed, following Folkestad (2006), our work elsewhere has shown how music education opportunities encompass both formal and informal dimensions, but with non-formal music education being defined by an explicit oscillation between such modes (Lonie and Dickens, in press; see also Hargreaves et al., 2003; Saunders and Welch, 2012). We also agree with the important context specificity of any such distinctions (Kraftl, 2013), and thus seek to examine non-formal education as it occurs in the particular spaces set aside for such activity, whether dedicated spaces, or achieved by re-purposing existing facilities (for a detailed study of the cultural politics of non-formal music making with young people in such contexts, see Dickens and Lonie, 2013).

Rehearsal spaces as 'children's spaces'?

This chapter considers non-formal music education in the context of the music rehearsal space, drawing on empirical research with examples from a wider DCMS pilot scheme. Outlining the aims of this scheme the Secretary of State for Culture, Media and Sport at the time explained:

> We are focusing our efforts on areas of deprivation – both urban and rural – where there may be few other facilities for young people. These fully-equipped spaces will make a big difference for young people who are looking for somewhere to practice, spend time and find an outlet for their creative skills.
>
> (Rt. Hon. Andy Burnham MP, in UK Music, 2009)

The project followed the then government's wider belief in the role of such supported arts interventions as a tool for tackling social problems, such as anti-social behaviour or family breakdown, while stimulating wider processes of community development and urban regeneration.[3] While it falls beyond the scope of this chapter to unpack these aims further, it is important to appreciate how the creation of such rehearsal spaces presented a chance to critically examine the place of non-formal music education in more detail. Given these dimensions as set out above, this chapter asks whether such spaces represent a further layer of instrumental policy development in the governance of young people's lives, or whether, as Moss and Petrie (2002) called for over a decade ago, they represent the creation of 'social spaces *for* childhood, as part of life, not just preparation for life' (Moss and Petrie, 2002, p.123, original emphasis) with all that this might imply for their learning within such contexts. Such a question is drawn into sharper relief with how dated such 'joined-up', 'non-formal' provision might now appear in an age of crisis and austerity (where funding for similar provision has been widely cut back).[4]

In part, this question attempts to understand how such contexts are comprised beyond the physical provision of buildings and music equipment; that 'the provision of physical *hardware* must be complemented with the cultivation of a creative *heartware* – spaces sensitively customized for the arts and accompanying policy mindsets that appreciate the arts for their intrinsic rather than economic value' (Chang and Lee, 2003, p.139 original emphasis). The intended use of the spaces for music rehearsal rather than musical performance seems pivotal here, since 'rehearsals assemble the elements of a musical event, offering an experimental space where sounds are put together and taken apart, played with, argued over' (Wood et al., 2007, p.874). Thus Moss and Petrie's observation that 'Where children set the agenda, play is a central activity' (2002, p.131) suggests that the making of music in such contexts can be an important end in itself.

This question also draws upon a growing interest in the wider settings of music making – physically, but also socially, culturally and politically – and in 'using music to bridge the gap between individuals and communities, to creating a space for common *musicking* and sharing of artistic and human values' (Ruud, 2004, pp.11–12, original emphasis). This work has a distinct social change agenda and seeks to place an emphasis on collective outcomes based on the recognition that

> [m]usic is not designed for privacy or containment – it naturally reverberates, permeates, goes through boundaries and walls. And in doing so it calls to others, attracts, gathers, connects people together. It creates community.
>
> (Stige et al., 2010, p.16)

Here then the question concerns the extent to which the rehearsal spaces might serve as children's spaces for the ways they operate 'as environments provided through the agency of public policy for collectivities of children [and] settings where young people meet each other as individuals and where they form a social group' (Moss and Petrie, 2002, pp.107–8). In this light, the aim of community building is assessed for the ways the rehearsal spaces might enable a distinct 'community of practice' to emerge (Lave and Wenger, 1991; Wenger, 1999), one centred on the participatory and publically shared interests of young musicians (Deane et al., 2011).

Preliminary findings from the Rehearsal Spaces pilot scheme

Two sites were selected from the 14 spaces awarded funding from the DCMS Rehearsal Spaces Scheme (four of which had existing relationships with Youth Music when approached to take part in the study). The participating sites encompassed both urban and rural aspects of the scheme, and worked with quite different young people and musical genres, as may be expected when considering the implications of local culture(s) on personal, social and musical identities. Nonetheless, the comparison of different spaces, communities of practice and modes of engagement provides a useful insight into the factors contributing to the effects of non-formal education within such spaces. These case studies are not intended to be representative, but illustrative of some of the themes in the practice and experience of non-formal music education.

The first case study, the 'Community Recording Studio', had been located in the Russell Youth Centre in the St Ann's area of Nottingham for nearly 20 years. Trevor Rose, hip hop musician and youth worker was a key figure within the Centre. The project worked with many young people facing the effects of multiple deprivation, and who generally engaged with the Centre when other avenues to education, employment, training, and recreational opportunities were unavailable. Daily professionally led music sessions specifically targeted young people in challenging circumstances and those referred by agencies such as Youth Offending Teams and local schools. Funding through the DCMS Rehearsal Spaces Scheme secured and sound-proofed additional space to rehearse, and allowed the Centre to purchase a range of musical instruments, PA equipment and computers. The Centre was further funded by Youth Music to deliver workshops in music production, mixing and recording as well as live performance opportunities.

The second case study was a county-wide mobile resource based in East and Mid Cornwall. In addition to dedicated venue at a youth centre called 'The House' in St. Austell, this resource was in effect a range of musical equipment delivered to suitable locations across rural Cornwall in the back of a van by a specialist music leader, Giles Wooley, to ensure a wide-reach to isolated, rural communities. The project was managed by CYMAZ (Cornwall Youth Music Action Zone) with Cornwall Council (Creative Services), and intended 'to build sustainable community development models' across Cornwall based on this partnership model.[5] Two such mobile kits were paid for by the DCMS funding and music leader time was paid for through the Youth Music grant.

Given that the DCMS Rehearsal Spaces were intended ultimately for use by young people, it was felt appropriate that this research took both conceptual and methodological steps to place young people at its centre. Two focus groups with young people were conducted at each site and observations of four music sessions were used to establish how participating young musicians valued and experienced a dedicated place for learning, creating and experimenting with music. In Nottingham, interviewees were all boys, predominantly black or mixed-race and aged between 14 and 19 ($n = 11$), while in Cornwall the interviewees were all white, an even mix of boys and girls, and aged between 12 and 15 ($n = 8$). The focus groups were constituted by those who volunteered to participate, and were approached by asking the young people to discuss the range of practices they undertake while using these spaces (Hitchings, 2012), and the ways they understood and imagined the role of rehearsal spaces overall. While the role of adults was clearly significant in terms of the pedagogical relationships that developed, and in the administration of funding and maintenance of the spaces, it was felt important that this role was discussed indirectly here through the perspectives of young people.

Non-formal learning in non-formal settings

Learning to be a musician

Across both sites the participating young people described how the approach of the practitioners and the way they were encouraged to engage with each other, with the equipment, and with the space, focused on making music and learning to be a musician, as much as on the acquisition of specific musical skills. While the rehearsal spaces were clearly seen as a place to hone musical skills across specific instruments and styles, the broader skills required to engage with the rehearsal space were noted as particularly rewarding by the young people in both Nottingham and Cornwall.

Nottingham:

NP1: I'm just glad that [the rehearsal space] is here. So long as it's here.
NP2: Yeah well definitely. I mean, what do I know about all this stuff? I would never have known what to do with any of this, d'you know what I mean.
NP1: [...] Now I can set up all of this. I can set up a mic. I can plug speakers into the amps, and the mixing desks. Before I didn't know nothing, I didn't even know how to switch on a Mac. Imagine that! [...] Before this room was built, [...] we weren't giggin. So this is a learning curve really. We're learning in here. Y'get me? When we're gonna do a live performance, we're learning how we're gonna sound through these [points at PA speakers].

Cornwall:

CP1: before if you gave me a microphone and a lead I wouldn't know where to begin.
CP2: Yeah, like the first week we came here we spent like an hour just setting up the amps and just learning how to do it. But now we're like...
CP1: Yeah but now we can do it in like 10 minutes [...] before I came here, music was just, kind of, a subject at school. Now because we've been shown how to use a mixing desk and recording equipment and amps and how to set them up, it's become more like... I don't know... but it's just become a lot better [...] It goes a lot further than just sitting in a class room.

The accounts of the young people here illustrate how in order to use the space as an authentic and able musician they had to learn how to use rehearsal and recording equipment. In both contexts young people were observed arriving in the space, before unpacking and setting up equipment independently as an apparently routine part of their music sessions. They described this as a clear learning outcome that extended their musical identity (towards the identity of being a musician), at the same time as extending their learning identity (towards being a person of increased knowledge). There was a clear recognition that skills had been acquired, but also that this process was necessary in obtaining the identity of 'able' musician, rather than 'certified' musician. This tacit, self-directed learning of skills beyond directly musical ones indicated the substantive difference of what was being learned in the rehearsal space from what was felt to be learned in the classroom. Ultimately, these were technical skills being developed but were nonetheless understood by the young learners to be part of a holistic, embodied musical identity rather than as a subject oriented skill set.

A place to practice

The importance of the rehearsal space as a place to practice, experiment and create was repeatedly described by participants. Participants in both settings described how they felt comfortable with creative risk in a way they might not in other places, and how the rehearsal spaces provided opportunities to explore their musicality that were not available in the formal learning spaces in their lives. This was also linked to the participants' perceived sense of ownership and control over the spaces, meaning they were free to direct how the learning would take place and the parameters of their own and their peers' creativity.

Cornwall:

> CP3: Its better 'cos in school you're like one big group, here it's one tiny group like five of you. In school it's like 'play these five notes'. That's all they say. And they don't even like tell you the notes.
>
> CP1: Yeah. Like it's quite hard to improvise at school, but here you can play whatever you like, and you can do what you really want to do. And they give you an instrument at school and you have to play it. You can't do anything else apart from play that.

Nottingham:

> NP3: school is kind of compulsory. So certain people won't put as much effort in. But people choose to come here. [...] I come here every day, like Monday to Friday. Cos really, I ain't got a job or nothing, so this is something for me to do other than standing about on the streets doing whatever... people enjoy coming here. It gives them something to do, it motivates them to do something.
>
> NP1: Yeah, I think there is a very big difference between doing music at school and coming here. Because at school it's just one of the subjects. Like three quarters of the people there they don't want to take it serious. But here, there is a lot of dedicated people around you, that's the main difference, people are serious.

These accounts echo the findings presented above in relation to the development of musicianship over and above the acquisition of pre-defined or directed musical outcomes. The spaces are described as places to play, to explore the ways that participants can learn to be musicians, and experiment with sounds and with identities. Again, the young participants themselves demarcated the spaces (and the practices therein) as providing opportunities that are *other than* school, and for musicians aiming to achieve something musically that was unlikely to be supported within formal learning structures. There was recognition of the different practices, opportunities and structures that exist in these places that fostered creativity in a less directive

Figure 11.1 Trevor offers the mic to one of the young participants in a turn-taking cycle of group 'freestyling'

way than in formal settings. Similarly, there was a notion of exclusivity and self-selection regarding ownership of the settings that also seemed counter to experiences of formal learning spaces.

Musical guidance

In both contexts the music practitioners and youth workers were observed taking steps to ensure all young people were given opportunities to join in with group music making at an early stage. As young people arrived at the sessions, or passed in to rooms where rehearsals were taking place, the practitioners were quick to offer a microphone, widen a circle of chairs, or step aside and brief someone on what the rest of the group were doing (see Figure 11.1). In one instance, a young boy arrived at his first ever session with the group in Cornwall, whereby Giles immediately showed him a few basic hand positions on the bottom strings of a guitar (an instrument he had never played but wanted to learn) and had him playing along with the rest of the group as they practiced their own composition; all within a few short minutes and without the group losing focus (see Figure 11.2).

The participants in Cornwall discussed how Giles engaged in pedagogical practices intended to be inclusive and supportive. They described how his aim was to drive creativity rather than prescriptive skill based learning outcomes. The participants thus concentrated on the development of ideas, and

Figure 11.2 Giles explains a rhythm to a new participant to enable them to play along with a group composition 'the surf song'

how progress was made through collaboration between Giles and themselves rather than in a more directive relationship from the former:

> CP2: He is a good music teacher because he listens to everyone and I think he brings out creative talent in everyone to be honest.
>
> CP4: Yeah, because if you don't get it or can't think of an idea he'll help you and show you how to do it.
>
> CP2: Yeah, and you can develop your own ideas and add them in. And Giles will give us ideas too, and stuff. And he'll just make sure everyone is involved and that no one is left out.

In Nottingham, the main practitioner was also described as a guide rather than an instructor. The participants spoke of Trevor first and foremost as a musician they respected, but also of how he set a quality benchmark that tacitly guided the direction of their music making. The participants described how his approach to progression was realistic but aspirational at the same time. As with the Cornwall site, the relationship was described in mutual and equitable terms rather than predominantly hierarchical:

> NP1: we actually want to take this somewhere, we actually want to go somewhere in music. So we're really using this as ... Trevor is like a stepping stone ... Y'get me. He's not trying to pave out our careers for us, we've got to find out ourselves innit. But here is like where you start [...]

I think for that most people want to get out of here, not in that way, but in a way that we have learned something. [...] obviously [Trevor] can't push the door for you, he shows us where the door is, you know. What we need to be able to do to get through.

This musical guidance was partly what made these education spaces 'non-formal' rather than 'informal'. Generally, the practitioners were described as guiding and shaping delivery rather than coercing or dictating what can, or should be learned and how. While it was implied that the practitioners had an idea of which learning outcomes might be achieved in a session (see Saunders and Welch, 2012), the participants themselves saw this instruction as open, equal, and subject to change based on their own creative impulses and inclinations. In this way, participants took ownership of their own musical development and output, while at the same time recognising the impact and influence of a respected musician and practitioner on-hand to guide and support the process.

Community, communication and collaborative music making

While community development was one of the explicit aims of the rehearsal spaces scheme, it was not clear how this may occur across such diverse settings. In both Cornwall and Nottingham there were two ways the participants described their experiences as fostering a sense of community, in ways that were both musically and contextually driven. Instructive here was asking the participants how they got on as a group:

Cornwall:

CP4: Really well.

CP1: Yeah it's been quite good. 'Cos, like before, I didn't really know [T] before, I knew of him but I didn't hardly know him if you see what I mean. And now we're like quite good friends.

CP2: Yeah, like over six weeks we've bonded. [G & L laugh] Yeah, we have actually bonded as a group! And we all listen to each other...

CP1: Yeah, and that's helped us. That's really helped us improve our music.

CP4: Yeah it's all done by a group decision. We're doing it. And if we don't like it we can easily change something.

CP2: Yeah, so if someone comes up with an idea, then we'll try it, and if it's not quite right then at least we've tried it.

Nottingham:

NP4: we can relate to what each other's doing and we know each other, so I can bounce off him like when we're doing a tune, we can go bar for bar and it will go together.

NP5: Yeah, like before. We all know [P], but like the type of music I do, back in the day when I first met him, he'd make like a hip hop beat but he add something else in, d'you know what I mean. Some rock or something, a little something else. So before coming here I didn't explore different genres and that. But coming here has helped me expand.

NP4: Yeah, we explore a lot of different things. So many people, like, everyone in here will know their own type of music. It's not like 'ah 'cos he likes that music, I'll like that music'. It's not like that. Everyone says what they like, and when it comes together it's a better sound.

These extracts demonstrate how music was being used as an alternative form of communication from the regular discourses that exist between these young people. Due to the rehearsal space being explicitly understood as a site of low-risk creative exploration, the usual musical knowledge of the participants was gradually challenged in a collegiate way by their peers. Both social and musical knowledge was exchanged with the result of strengthened relationships and, according to their own understanding, an increase in the quality of their musical outputs.

The extracts presented thus far indicate that the rehearsal space can be defined through shared ownership and respectful guidance, where musical experimentation is encouraged by peers and practitioners, and a community of practice might emerge, where difference is acknowledged but in no way perceived as a barrier to the common goal of quality musicianship and musicality.

The notion of common musical aims and pursuits extended even further in Nottingham, where participants described how the space had developed a family atmosphere that broke down social barriers all too prevalent in other spaces regularly occupied by the young people. The mutual respect developed between the young people and fostered by Trevor allowed the participants to see past the musical goals associated with the rehearsal space and into their everyday lives beyond it:

NP6: I knew this brother here [pointing round room]. But I didn't know him, I didn't know him, I didn't know him [...] I didn't even know Trev until my dad introduced me. And now, I'm gonna know them for the rest of my life. I'd probably guarantee that.

NP5: Yeah, we're staying together.

NP7: Yeah, we're like family, it's like a different family in here.

NP1: because of this place, we can all come together, d'you know what I mean. It makes something positive. [...] And do you know what it is, it's the inter-racial mixing thing as well, think about it. Obviously, everybody knows right now that there's a lot of things going on with this racial thing, whether we like it or not. But in here everybody looks past that, it's not, you know... who cares!

The understanding that musical collaboration, mutual respect and the acceptance of difference were regularly prioritised in these spaces was significant for these young people who understood that this was not something experienced in other aspects of their lives. The way that 'this racial thing' was understood as existing externally but not internally indicates an alternative cultural discourse being fostered and experienced through the accepted practices within the rehearsal space. The values being adopted were described as distinctive from other spaces and places in the young people's lives and were closely tied to the creative and musical identities of the young people over and above class, ethnic or other identities. The definition of the rehearsal space as egalitarian, both by the young people occupying the space and the practitioner, allowed for an alternative community to be constructed and maintained.

Aspiration and issues of multiple deprivation

Participants openly discussed funding issues and how facilities were offered and maintained within their localities, and there was a general sense that the opportunities encapsulated in the rehearsal spaces could be time limited and were dependant on some kind of funding structure. This was related to young people's own positioning of access to resources on a personal and group level. It was felt that the positive developmental opportunities being experienced could easily end with more negative consequences both for young people themselves and their communities, if not sustained.

Nottingham:

> NP7: Nobody's got any money to go into studios like this. No one's got anything.
>
> Trevor: Yeah, when we first started we had no funding, nothing.
>
> NP8: We're living in a deprived area.
>
> NP7: And to be fair, if we didn't have the studio, I don't know what all of us would be doing right now. We'd probably be on the street corner and probably just be causing a bit of trouble. I mean, what else are kids our age doing round here?

Cornwall:

> CP2: it doesn't cost anything which is a really good opportunity. Because if it did, you'd probably get two or three people. But we get, like, eight a week normally.

Significantly, the notion that this type of activity was merely an instrumental *distraction* from more negative anti-social behaviours was not supported by the accounts of the participants. The developmental outcomes (musical and other than musical) have been described at length in the sections above.

In Nottingham, however, some participants spoke directly about how the rehearsal spaces project provided an essential resource and that their lives would be considerably more challenging without access to the space:

NP9: Well, I've been comin' for a couple of months. I used to go to college with a guy who comes here, though he doesn't come here that often any more. [Boy Name]. And he introduced me. I was on the phone to him and I was like, 'I'm feeling useless, I've got nothing to do'. I was on the dole, and he was like 'come down, you'll really enjoy it'.

NP6: [...] Some people have their own instruments, but for me personally, I just don't have the money to buy a mic, d'you know what I mean, and a desk so I can record at home. I'd never have the money to do all that. D'you know what I mean. Even if I wanted to buy a piano I can't buy one.

NP10: We've just got pens. That's my instrument! [laughter]

NP6: I come here and play the piano. Even if I'm just sitting here playing the piano, you can't do that anywhere.

These extracts indicate the participants' understandings of access to resources and dedicated spaces are essential components of the project, and that the creative exploration, musical and personal development discussed above simply would not occur otherwise. The participants described how their creative and musical identities would be stifled without access to this subsidised resource, which carries far greater meaning in their lives than much of the formal experiences of music education they may have previously accessed. Participants also perceived that their attendance and participation had an effect beyond the rehearsal space and their musical development. Particularly in Nottingham the participants described how the rehearsal spaces facilitated a development in self-confidence, self-efficacy and intrinsic motivation:

NP8: It's not just music that the studio helps. It's all aspects of life. It helps, it just helps.

NP10: I can't talk as someone whose been here a long time. But personally, if I came here when I was a bit older, it helps with the confidence, like speaking to the people that you wouldn't even approach.

NP11: Yeah like even with getting a job and stuff. You can see people's confidence as soon as they get here. Like the first day you get here your confidence just goes up and up.

The participants described a realistic and pragmatic route ahead. As the pedagogical model outlined above (i.e., the opportunity for young people themselves to direct the space, its uses and its values) would support, the young people eloquently identified the ways their experiences in the rehearsal spaces had influenced them, and the changes they can see in themselves and their peers. The participants described how the opportunity to be creative while also supported and challenged, in a low-risk space that was easy to access and sustained on egalitarian, non-hierarchical principles, had increased their confidence and self-determination. Some ambition was musical, but the participants also described extra-musical routes and opportunities they might explore. However, the notion that direct involvement in the space should remain was writ large throughout the accounts, indicating that the sustainability of positive change may well be dependent on the sustainability of the space itself.

Conclusion

In this chapter we have addressed the need and value of looking at non-formal contexts when thinking holistically about the purposes of education, and of the ways children and young people are able to learn for themselves. We have set out the central tenets of the non-formal music education advanced by funding from the National Foundation for Youth Music as a distinct, emerging and important area of practice, and one that has much to offer current debates on educational restructuring. The illustrative case studies presented here demonstrate some of the core dynamics of this model in relation to the thematic aims of the Rehearsal Spaces pilot scheme, and draw a close focus on the creation of the kinds of contexts and spaces *for* children, as advocated by educational scholars concerned by a tendency in current educational provision for 'primarily technical and disciplinary undertakings, concerned with regulation, surveillance and normalization, [which are] instrumental in rationality and purpose' (Moss and Petrie, 2002, p.2).

In both Nottingham and Cornwall, findings suggest some clear achievements in the aim to use the scheme to nurture musical creativity, providing groups of young people with the hardware *and* 'heartware' (Chang and Lee, 2003) necessary to intentionally explore and create their own forms of music making. Moreover, adults in these contexts appeared to act as 'meaning makers rather than "truth" finders and appliers' (Moss and Petrie, 2002, p.112), using their own experiences as musicians to undertake roles as 'natural' mentors who guide rather than instruct young people in their own musical development. It was also clear that the rehearsal spaces were valued by the young people who use them for the ways they were 'other than school': they were free to choose how they participated, and defined their own sense of ownership and belonging within such learning contexts.

In Nottingham in particular, the testimony of those attending the Community Studio suggests that such provision had been key to young people's increased engagement and participation in the creative practices of music making, and therefore in a wider cycle of the intrinsic development of inter-personal skills and sense of belonging. Thus on the intention to develop community through the Rehearsal Spaces, findings discussed here suggest how musical processes are intrinsically community processes, forming distinct communities of practice (Lave and Wenger, 1991) through the ways music making is undertaken as a profoundly collective activity rather than centred on individual outputs or achievements. The forging of new friendships in these creative contexts were strong examples of what Moss and Petrie suggest as a particularly valuable 'way in which children enter and become active in the wider community, outside the family, co-constructing with other children their own cultural forms [...] and increasing their sphere of social agency' (2002, p.104).

In terms of addressing local deprivation through the provision of Rehearsal Spaces, the case studies clearly enabled those young people who would otherwise not have the resources to pursue their own forms of musicality to do so, and there was some evidence to show how this could be linked to the personal and psycho-social outcomes outlined above. However, young people in both Cornwall and Nottingham also recognised that such provision was part of a funding structure and therefore may be temporally dependent on the commitment from government and third-sector agencies to sustain it in the longer-term. Moreover, there remains some way to go before such spaces might serve as the kinds of 'hubs' and 'talent bases' that the DCMS had originally hoped, and it is an open question whether this aim can be reconciled with the intrinsic merits of creating spaces for musical experimentation and participation under conditions that are owned and defined by young people themselves.

The case studies examined here have some significant differences in terms of local need and culture, and the particularities of participants' class, gender and ethnicity, but overall they were broadly similar in terms of their shared aims and intentions, and the pedagogical approaches of the music practitioners involved. Ultimately, we believe these similarities outweigh such differences for the ways they are suggestive of the wider role played by non-formal education, and the value of such contexts for young people who are often educationally excluded through a complex range of circumstances over which they have little control. We would argue for the on-going study of the ways such spaces, and the relational practices within them, might constitute the participatory, ethical and organic foundations of the kinds of 'children's spaces' advocated for by Moss and Petrie (2002), and hope that the important role of such non-formal provision continues to feature within the comprehensive assessment of a rapidly restructuring educational landscape.

Notes

1. Following recommendations made by the Live Music Forum in 2009, 14 spaces were identified across the United Kingdom, and allocated funding from

a total budget of £500,000: Liverpool, Cornwall (includes mobile facility), Manchester, Washington, Hastings, Coventry, Nottingham, Birmingham (two spaces), Rotherham, Bristol (two spaces), North and West Norfolk (includes mobile facility).

2. The National Foundation for Youth Music defines 'challenging circumstances' as 'those who are often marginalised by society, may be vulnerable or hard to reach, or have fewer opportunities than other young people their age'.

3. From personal correspondence between the project lead at the DCMS and the authors (April 2010).

4. The intention was to work with a range of public, private and third-sector partners including Youth Music, music and technologies sector Skills Council, Arts Council England, British Underground, Music Development Agencies, Connexions, those from the music industry, community radio and Local Authorities.

5. This partnership also included The House (St. Austell), Youth Cornwall, the Draceana Community Centre (Falmouth) and Livewire Youth Music Project (Saltash).

References

Z. Bekerman, N. C. Burbules, and D. Silberman-Keller (2005) *Learning in Places: The informal education reader* (New York, NY: Peter Lang).

I. Cartwright (2012) 'Informal education in compulsory schooling in the UK: Humanising moments, Utopian spaces?' in P. Kraftl, J. Horton and F. Tucker (eds) *Critical Geographies of Childhood and Youth: Contemporary policy and practice* (Bristol: Policy Press).

T. Chang and W. Lee (2003) 'Renaissance city Singapore: A study of arts spaces', *Area*, 35, 128–41.

F. Coffield (2000) *The Necessity of Informal Learning* (Bristol: Policy Press).

H. Colley (2003) *Mentoring for Social Inclusion: A critical approach to nurturing successful mentoring relations* (London: Routledge).

H. Colley, P. Hodkinson and J. Malcolm (2002) 'Non-formal learning: Mapping the conceptual terrain. A consultation report', *INFED and Learning and Skills Development Agency*, http://www.infed.org/archives/e-texts/colley_informal_learning.htm (accessed 25 January 2011).

K. Deane, R. Hunter and P. Mullen (2011) *Move On Up: An evaluation of youth music mentors* (London: The National Foundation for Youth Music).

L. Dickens and D. Lonie (2013) 'Rap, rhythm and recognition: Lyrical practices and the politics of voice on a community music project for young people experiencing challenging circumstances', *Emotion, Space and Society*, 9, 59–71.

M. Eraut (2000) 'Non-formal learning, implicit learning and tacit knowledge', in F. Coffield (ed.) *The Necessity of Informal Learning* (Bristol: Polity Press).

G. Folkestad (2006) 'Formal and informal learning situations or practices vs formal and informal ways of learning', *British Journal of Music Education*, 23, 135–45.

C. Hanson Thiem (2009) 'Thinking through education: The geographies of contemporary educational restructuring', *Progress in Human Geography*, 33, 154–73.

D. Hargreaves, N. Marshall and A. North (2003) 'Music education in the twenty-first century: A sycholgical perspective', *British Journal of Music Education*, 20, 147–63.

R. Hart (1992) *Children's Participation: From tokenism to citizenship* (Florence: UNICEF International Child Development Centre).

R. Hart (2008) 'Stepping back from "the ladder": Reflections on a model of participatory work with children' in A. Reid, B. Jensen, J. Nikel and V. Simovska (eds) *Participation and Learning: Perspectives on education and the environment, health and sustainability* (Dordrecht: Springer).

R. Hitchings (2012) 'People can talk about their practices', *Area*, 44, 61–7.

S. L. Holloway, P. Hubbard, H. Jöns and H. Pimlott-Wilson (2010) 'Geographies of education and the significance of children, youth and families', *Progress in Human Geography*, 34, 583–600.

M. Jans (2004) 'Children as citizens: Towards a contemporary notion of child participation', *Childhood*, 11, 27–44.

P. Kraftl (2013) 'Towards geographies of alternative education: A case study of UK homeschooling families' *Transactions of the Institute of British Geographers*, 38, 436–450.

P. Kraftl (forthcoming 2013) *Geographies of Alternative Education: Diverse learning spaces for children and young people* (Bristol: Policy Press).

J. Lave and E. Wenger (1991) *Situated Learning: Legitimate peripheral participation* (Cambridge: Cambridge University Press).

D. Lonie and L. Dickens (2011) *Youth Music Outcomes and Impact Report 2010–2011* (London: The National Foundation for Youth Music).

D. Lonie and L. Dickens (in press) 'Better musicians or better people? The aim and function of non-formal music education with children and young people in "challenging circumstances"', *Research Studies in Music Education*.

V. McGivney (1999) *Informal Learning in the Community: A trigger for change and development* (Leeds: National Institute of Adult Continuing Education).

T. Miller (2005) 'Across the great divide: Creating partnerships in education' *INFED*, http://www.infed.org/biblio/partnerships_in_education.htm (accessed 25 January 2011).

P. Moss and P. Petrie (1997) *Children's Services: Time for a new approach – A discussion paper* (London: Institute of Education, University of London).

P. Moss and P. Petrie (2002) *From Children's Services to Children's Spaces: Public policy, children and childhood* (London: Routledge).

B. Percy-Smith (2010) 'Councils, consultations and community: Rethinking the spaces for children and young people's participation', *Children's Geographies*, 8, 107–22.

B. Percy-Smith and N. Thomas (eds) (2009) 'A handbook of children's participation: Perspectives from theory and practice' (London: Routledge).

K. Philip (2000) 'Mentoring: pitfalls and potential for young people', *Youth and Policy*, 67, 1–15.

K. Philip and L. B. Hendry (1996) 'Young people and mentoring: Towards a typology?' *Journal of Adolescence*, 19, 189–201.

L. Richardson and M. Wolfe (2001) *Principles and Practice of Informal Education: Learning Through Life* (London: Routledge).

E. Ruud (2004) 'Foreword: Reclaiming music' in M. Pavlicevic and G. Ansdell (eds) *Community Music Therapy* (London: Jessica Kingsley).

J. Saunders and G. Welch (2012) *Communities of Music Education* (London: Youth Music/iMerc, Institute of Education).

B. Stige, G. Ansdell, C. Elefant and M. Pavlicevic (2010) *Where Music Helps: Community music therapy in action and reflection* (Farnham: Ashgate).

UK Music (2009) UK music launches groundbreaking music rehearsal space initiative in Liverpool, http://www.ukmusic.org/education/112-uk-music-launches-groundbreaking-music-rehearsal-space-initiative-in-liverpool (accessed 23 August 2009).

E. Wenger (1999) *Communities of Practice: Learning, meaning, and identity* (Cambridge: Cambridge University Press).

N. Wood, M. Duffy and S. J. Smith (2007) 'The art of doing (geographies of) music', *Environment and Planning D: Society and space*, 25, 867–89.

12
Managing the Spaces of Freedom: Mid-twentieth-Century Youth Work

Simon Bradford

Introduction

This chapter considers aspects of English youth work (as a mode of informal education) roughly between 1940 and 1960. This period marks the beginning of an incipient professionalisation conditional upon youth workers' attempts to manage youth cultural and social transitions. As educational spaces existing beyond school (Stimson, 1948), urban and rural youth clubs and organisations were sites constructed by youth workers to encourage young people to develop their capacities for responsible citizenship. Youth organisations were, as now, 'spaces of power' (Newman, 2012, p.61) in which youth workers aimed to produce particular educational outcomes.

Before the Second World War, youth work existed largely outside the contours of the state forming a heterogeneous network of organisations (church-based, secular, military and voluntary) working with young people mainly in their leisure time (Kyle, Chapter 2, Mills, Chapter 5, this volume). Residual elements of youth work's nineteenth-century voluntary ethos with its commitment to eliciting young people's identifications with religious, nationalist, military or class-based ideologies continued into and beyond the years of the Second World War (Springhall, 1977). Political powers acknowledged youth workers' capacity to contribute to the maintenance of social and cultural orders, reflected in state support that established a Youth Service in England and Wales in 1939 (Bradford, 2007b). Youth work subsequently became caught in an expanding 'governmentality' (Bradford, 2004; Dean, 2010), a political rationale in which policies, organisations and agents are co-opted into the regulation of populations, communities and cultural spaces. Above all, this form of twentieth-century (essentially neo-liberal) political rule has consistently relied upon the individual as active citizen, a '... social being whose powers and obligations (are) articulated in the language of social responsibilities and collective solidarities' (Miller and

Rose, 2008, p.48). Reflecting this, youth workers have consistently sought to create a compact between individual desire and shared identifications.

This chapter considers how youth workers articulated informal educational spaces (youth clubs, for example), the embodied identities of young people and incipient neo-liberal discourses of choice and personal responsibility in the formation of young citizens. The chapter suggests that although these matters had particular salience in wartime (Bradford, 2007a, p.298), they designate a continuity that resonates in contemporary social policy.

Shaping transitions: The service of youth

Modern and pre-modern societies have understood youth as a cultural landscape through which individuals pass towards notional adulthood. Cultural transitions often entail periods of separation, *liminality*, in which the status of those in transition is socially, temporally and spatially ambiguous. The concept of liminality designates transitions from one cultural or social standing to another and constitutes a preparation for reincorporation into the social mainstream in a new social status (Turner, 1975, p.232). Importantly, liminality is always *spatialised* and archetypal liminal zones are readily identifiable: shorelines, marshlands, airports, stations, doors and bridges all assume the in-between-ness of liminality. Youth organisations and clubs are, of course, exemplary liminal spaces. Such spaces are invariably subject to cultural regulation as those within them exude both power and danger. Liminars' (young people, for example) power derives from their imputed capacity for change, disorder or renewal and they are considered dangerous because they are somehow culturally 'placeless', '... transition is neither one state nor the next, it is undefinable' (Douglas, 1966, pp.117–9).

During the interwar years, broad cultural shifts generated recurrent anxieties about young people's complex transitions, in effect fears about liminality. Changing labour market characteristics and expanding markets for goods and services aimed at increasingly economically independent young people encouraged new practices of generation and gender-specific consumption and an incipient youth culture emerged during the 1930s (Tinkler, 1995; Todd, 2005; Fowler, 2008). War exacerbated anxieties about the effect of youth culture on transition (Morgan, 1939) and the management of youth leisure spaces assumed increasing significance. The 'Service of Youth' was established in 1939 to systematically manage young people's leisure (Board of Education, 1939). The new Service became linked to a centralised system of compulsory youth registration, organised jointly by the BoE and the Ministry of Labour and National Service. This audit of youth (as both national asset and potential social problem) sought to formalise young people's deployment in war service by *encouraging* them to take up non-compulsory leisure activities (Board of Education, 1941a, 1942, 1942a). Carefully managed, youthful energy, spirit and enthusiasm were resources with potential for war service but, if wasted, could be a source of disorder. Registration provided the opportunity for systematic intervention in working-class space and lifestyles so that the '... the apparent aimlessness of the way in which young people spend their leisure...' (Board of Education and Scottish Education Department, 1943, p.16) could be supplanted by approved forms of recreation. Registration raised the important question of training for youth workers. S. H. Wood, Principal Assistant Secretary in the BoE, advised, '... we are... pressing (youth) to join services which are inadequately equipped with leaders and at the same time are doing nothing about the equipment of leaders' (Wood, 1942). Between 1942 and 1947, one year training courses for youth work were established in five English and Welsh universities, tacitly supported by the Board of Education (BoE) and later by the McNair Report on training for teachers and youth workers (Board of Education, 1944).

During the early 1940s, various policy claims were made for the Youth Service managing young people considered to be outside of the apparently weakening regulative boundaries of domestic, educational and employment spaces.

The Service's three main purposes would contribute to the resolution of problematic transitions. First, it responded to youth crime (Board of Education, 1939; Board of Education and Home Office, 1941, p.3), exacerbated by 'war disturbance'. Second, it aimed to improve young people's mental and physical condition through organised and approved leisure opportunities. Physical health and fitness were not private matters and the healthy and compliant body, defined in terms of physique, sexuality, productivity and fighting capacity, was a commodity to be mobilised as '... an act of service to the country...' (Board of Education, 1940, para.8). Third, the Service helped young people to engage in war-specific 'service' to their communities through informal citizenship education and individual acts of service. These aims resonated powerfully with liberal democratic principles in which personal responsibility and informed decision-making were central motifs. The idea of service was especially valorised in wartime and the new Youth Service aimed at institutionalising mutuality, '... service *by* youth as well as service *for* youth' (Board of Education and Home Office, 1941, p.8, original emphases), although tensions existed over whether participation should be compulsory. Compulsion was never imposed but young people's voluntary involvement aimed to ensure successful transition through liminal space towards a citizenship able to exercise responsible and discriminating choice. The binary distinction between the '... gangster spirit... found in the pitch-and-toss and gambling clubs which are a feature of Sunday afternoons in the waste lands of our cities...' (Brew, 1943, p.47) and the wholesome activities and identifications with the youth club, '... a little commonwealth having its place in a democracy... which professes to voice an answer of Democracy to Fascism' (Edwards-Rees, 1943, p.84), neatly draws out the Youth Service's aspirations.

Bodies (and minds) as manageable spaces

Youth workers often divided young people according to age and gender, marking out separate spaces where young people could participate in organised and approved activities. In effect, they categorised young people as different and socially distinct, enhancing their professional capacity to intervene in the apparently universal spaces of transitional experience (Bernstein, 2000, pp.5–7). The 'sagging' and 'stooping' bodies of working-class young people (Brew, 1943, pp.185–6) were the constituent elements of the *body of youth* and, as now, offered sites for informal educational intervention. Importantly, the youthful body is a body in transition – a changing and liminal body that is neither child nor adult, but represents the *future* social body. Youth workers were charged by the state with managing the transformation of youthful bodies, and minds, into an appropriately socialised adult body.

The body occupies both discursive and material space. Its corporeality is socially inscribed, the '... social body constrains the way the physical body is perceived' (Douglas, 1996, p.72). Bodies (as both individual and collective entities) are never more significant than in the context of 'total war'. Wartime threats to the spatial status of the social body (through attack, border incursion, invasion or annexation, for example) are invariably projected onto the physical body whose surveillance and discipline becomes increasingly important. Indeed, the prosecution of successful military and civilian activity relies on the managed physical condition of those contributing to the war effort. Social order, the maintenance of the *collectivity* of the physical body in productive and willing form, is crucial. Youth workers were constituent elements in a strategy to enhance morale by regulating young people's personal conduct, controlling the potential and actuality of transgression and encouraging 'Better Citizenship' (Edwards-Rees, 1943, p.28). The physical discipline of the body was central, as was the imposition of '... emotional and rational discipline ... whereby you achieve freedom and fit yourself to carry its responsibilities....' (Brew, 1943, p.194). Existing transitional spaces of home, neighbourhood, school and work were assumed to be deficient and youth clubs and organisations constituted important informal spaces where young people could be helped to 'achieve freedom'. Properly managed, leisure space could compensate for wider inadequacies. Youth workers aimed at normalising and correcting three embodied aspects of transitional experience.

Bodies of delinquency

A joint BoE and Home Office circular suggested that the 'large' increase in juvenile crime in the early war years represented '... only a small proportion of the number of boys and girls...' (Board of Education and Home Office, 1941, p. 3; Home Office, 1947, pp.7–8). Central government anticipated that youth crime would become more widespread with '... opportunities given for easy looting, especially in the blackout...' (Board of Education and Home Office, 1941, p.4). Delinquency existed at the intersection of gender, poor discipline and social deprivation, involving an assumed minority of under-regulated and poorly socialised young men. Convictions for crimes committed by young women in the early war years were few in absolute terms, but increased proportionately more than those committed by young men (Ferguson and Fitzgerald, 1954, p.21). The Youth Advisory Council had no doubt of the culpability of problematic spaces of working-class domestic life. The '...main causes of juvenile delinquency...are to be found in the broken home, the unhappy home and the home where, for one reason or another, [young people] are deprived of affection and wise guidance' (Board of Education, 1943, p.6). The home was thus constituted as hazardous space as '...thousands of young people have to live in surroundings which make it almost impossible for them to grow into decent citizens' (Board of Education, 1943, p.6).

The demands and opportunities created by the wartime economy resurrected an older problem of 'boy labour' that designated young men engaged in casualised and unregulated work outside of structured labour market transitions (Hendrick, 1990, p.9). This aspect of the wartime youth labour market was understood as morally and socially dangerous and its effects on young men needed careful management partially through informal educational intervention. 'Boys going out to work are faced with new temptations and at this age the provision of leisure activities becomes very important...unexpected pocket money has brought new temptations' (Board of Education and Home Office, 1941, p.4) and '...high wages have undeniably been the cause of delinquency...the only real remedy is a greater sense of responsibility in the young people themselves' (Board of Education, 1943, p.9). Young men's inability to make good leisure choices rendered them subject to irresistible temptation. They were considered vulnerable and potentially dangerous because of being beyond the positive influence of adults (signalling the problem of absent fathers), and coming from an '...unsatisfactory environment...they are generally the most difficult to persuade to join youth organisations and participate in organised activities' (Board of Education and Home Office, 1941, p.8).

These dangers drew youth workers into the attempt to cultivate these young people's bodies and in so doing to enhance their capacity to discriminate between 'good' and 'unwholesome' uses of leisure. This entailed their participation in formally regulated leisure spaces in which youth workers could invoke particular identifications with the club as a *place* with an enduring existence that '...is worthwhile not to destroy' (Paneth, 1944, p.120). Implicit in such aspirations is the desire to control or contain elements of 'wild' population. Containment included the attempt to render youthful bodies healthy and fit, an ambition that involved young people in active work on their own bodies.

Fit bodies

In wartime policy discourses of youth work, young people's bodies were always somehow '...in deficit, unfinished or at risk' (Evans and Davies, 2004, p.215), important factors in youth work's spatialised educational interventions. Indeed, 1940s health interventions on young people's bodies in informal educational spaces anticipate contemporary health concerns and policy focus, for example, on young people and obesity (Evans, 2010; Evans et al., 2011). Physical fitness in the 1940s (as now) was not just a matter of personal choice as the healthy body could be mobilised in the collective service of the nation. The high profile of physical activities and the involvement of the War Office in providing instructors for youth work indicate the importance accorded to disciplining young people's bodies through games, drill, training, dancing, athletics, boxing or camping (Board of Education, 1940a, p.2). In addition to developing physique, group activities also instilled a sense of collective responsibility, rendering these bodies potentially productive in the context of war. Indeed, bodies become useful capital only when effectively caught in a system of subjection, but especially when the individual young person takes personal responsibility for health matters. The simple, routine and ritualised activities offered to young people were conceived to emphasise consensus, and they immersed young people in the dominant expressive order of their youth organisations (Bernstein, 1975, p.55), assuming a symbolic significance in the broader attempt to integrate youth as an active component of the population at war.

The BoE asserted that physical recreation '...help(s) to create physical and mental alertness, self-reliance, endurance and determination, and thus contribute to the development of character and the balanced individual...It constitutes an essential factor in the attainment of positive health...' (Board of Education, 1940, p.2). The preoccupation with bodily fitness assumed a distinctly classed orientation and working-class bodies were the primary source of anxiety and the target of youth worker intervention. The evidently precarious spaces of working-class home life provided the rationale, as

> ...working boys and girls still grow up in oppressive houses where gravy-paint, gas-jets and stuffiness predominate, where baths are difficult to come by, and where the standard of personal hygiene is low. The tastes and the standards of these boys and girls are not yet set, and on the whole they are prepared to try new ideas.
>
> (Jephcott, 1942, p.165)

Working-class neighbourhoods were similarly problematic. Whether decaying areas that could no longer support '...any successful social life' or new housing estates, the fear was that '...the slum that stunts the body has merely been exchanged for the slum that stunts the mind' (Brew, 1943, p.215). 'Indigenous' working-class leisure activities were construed as culturally problematic. In 1939, Morgan asked what had been done

> ...to train the innate desires of boys and girls for the exercise of bodily power and skill? Have we any right to expect a breed of young men and women preferring active bodily recreation to the negative passivity of the cinema and the pin-table, of watching football or having a flutter on the dogs or the football pools.
>
> (Morgan, 1939, p.198)

Such evidently worthless popular activities were characterised by their underlying *passivity*, making no contribution to *active* notions of health and fitness or to the war effort.

The supposed destructive consequences of passivity and hedonism for national culture, the family and individual identity surfaced recurrently in youth work texts of the time. The '...constant picture-going and dancing, when carried to excess, are fundamentally sterile ways of recreation...There is nothing that is creative here, nothing that puts any responsibility on young people or makes any demands on them as members of society' (Jephcott, 1942, pp.124–5). Rather than being spaces in which freedom could be properly exercised and enhanced, the cinemas and dance halls were no more than places of injurious gratification. Pleasure was a complex and ambiguous state and commodity that could have either beneficial or morally corrosive consequences, dependent on how it was managed. Insofar as it resonated with governmental and pedagogical aspirations (e.g., the wholesome pleasure of organised youth activities which developed health, fitness, character and responsibility) it was a valuable means of attracting young people to participate in legitimate activities and it had a productive function. Youth organisations were charged with pedagogising pleasure, and ensuring its incorporation into informal strategies designed to secure young people's successful negotiation of treacherous leisure landscapes.

Sexual bodies

Underlying concerns about the moral perils of 'boy labour', dance halls and cinemas, in wartime Britain young people's (hetero)sexuality was a compelling symbol of the condition of the social order. Its potential as a gendered source of disorder, and even chaos, generated wide anxiety. Jephcott expressed these fears in a combined bio-psychologistic and social discourse that explained young people's vulnerability. There was, she suggested, a need for intervention to counterbalance the negative influences of unregulated leisure spaces in which the '...syncopated music...the lowered lights, and the excitement of all the new contacts mean that for many young adolescents, the sex instinct is being over-stimulated at precisely the age when this should be avoided....' (Jephcott, 1942, p.125). In the attempt to preserve the integrity of sexual boundaries and categories (chastity, for example), youth work (like schooling) was, historically, gender-specific (see Spence, Chapter 13, this volume), and youth organisations and clubs were spatially and temporally segregated, reflecting wider class- and gender-based concerns about youth and sexuality. However, evidence suggests that some youth workers challenged rigid divisions between young men and young women (Jephcott, 1942, p.166; Brew, 1943, p.56).

In the 1940s, as now, these informal education spaces offered scope for the management of youth sexualities, and youth workers were enjoined to intervene in young people's understandings of sexual conduct as well as in supervising the development of sometimes idealised sexual identities. For example, BoE Staff Inspector C. A. Richardson reported to a BoE committee considering youth worker training in 1941 that youth workers should establish spaces in their organisations for young people to have '...thoroughgoing debates and (better) informal discussions...I am aware that such "freedom" is regarded as having "dangers", but I believe that in the long run, the dangers of repression and restriction (always ineffective) are far greater' (Richardson, 1941, p.1). Richardson seemed to have an intuitive notion of the nature of liberal democracy and was clear that the problem of sexuality crystallised the liberal-democratic predicament of bounded freedom. Importantly, he also recognised the spatial and temporal context of youth sexualities (Brown et al., 2007, p.2) and the capacity for informal educational intervention in these. Thus, youth workers sought to ensure that young people understood themselves as sexualised beings while illuminating the proper boundaries to sexual conduct.

The sexualised, gendered youthful body was, itself, a space upon and around which a 'special urgency' had arisen. Disquiet existed over young women's alleged promiscuity as 'young girls in considerable numbers are the victims of indiscriminate associations, with an increased incidence among them of venereal disease' (Board of Education, 1943a, p.4; Hall, 2001, p.131). Such infection was a powerful metaphor for the pollution of the individual and collective body and a signal that youth (especially young women's) sexuality should be carefully scrutinised. Anxieties about pollution of sacred boundaries by an assumed working-class promiscuity was reflected in implicit fears that the ordered social body was in danger from unbounded ego *within* as well as from external threat (Martin, 1981, p.139). The BoE issued guidelines on how youth workers might intervene in regulating working-class young people's 'impulse and emotion' (Board of Education, 1943a, p.4). However, consistent with broader liberal practices, youth workers encouraged young people to develop their own capacity for self-regulation, through discussion and reflection on sex as part of a process in which pedagogic practices were designed to encourage the formation of a 'responsible self'. Sexuality is no given state and is produced in discourse and practice. Youth workers were required to deploy sexuality and to regulate the youthful desire that animated it. Their work assimilated a broad strategy of power aimed at demarcating appropriate sexual conduct and preventing transgression, giving discourse on sexuality '... an analytical, visible, and permanent reality: it was implanted in bodies, slipped in beneath modes of conduct...' (Foucault, 1979, p.44). As such, and as in Richardson's account above, sexuality becomes a potentially powerful pedagogical tool in the informal spaces of youth work. The BoE showed how one youth organisation sought to shape the sexual identities of young women.

'The following testimony from a girls' organisation is perhaps worth noting. 'A really good woman doctor, preferably married, youngish, with a modern approach, and modern clothes is the most successful. The girls trust the doctor and welcome her counsel as a married woman, and she looks the sort of woman they would like to be'.

(Board of Education, 1943a, p.18)

The idealised gender and class identity modelled by the woman doctor becomes the pedagogic text in which regulative discourse (defining appropriate conduct) is embedded in an overall instructional framework that leads to the acquisition of specific knowledge and skill (Bernstein, 2000, p.13). The resultant cultural capital is to be acquired by young working-class women who transform themselves in the light of the pedagogic exemplar. This is not simply a matter of providing the *right* information and instruction, but of encouraging young people to carefully work on self in the spaces of reflexive responsibilisation. Such intervention exemplifies an informal educational approach that articulates discourse, bodies and spaces in the attempt to shape young people's sense of their own capacity to exercise freedom. This approach resonates in contemporary policy discourses of citizenship, choice and responsibility.

Conclusions: From wartime austerity to mass youth culture

The Second World War exacerbated the sense that working-class youth transitions required more careful regulation than hitherto, and youth work was deployed as a form of wartime population management. Youth workers achieved some recognition that contributed to a discourse of developing professionalism embodied, particularly, in the provision of university courses for youth workers between 1942 and 1947, through which about 300 students passed. However, youth work's professional project achieved limited success during the late 1940s and 1950s. The immediate crisis of war provided justification and support for the training of youth workers, but the momentum for professional development weakened as wartime conditions changed. The politics of the post-war budget, a political commitment to increasing school places and expanding technical education through the early 1950s, the ambiguity of youth work as a distinct occupation and professional career, a reluctance by the state to over-govern in the light of a strong discourse of English voluntarism, as well as conscription's importance as a surrogate youth service constrained expansion of youth work and youth worker training (Bradford, 2007a). This changed during the 1950s with the emergence of post-war mass youth culture in Britain, accompanied by acute moral panic. In 1958, the Minister of Education appointed the Countess Albemarle to chair a committee to report on the state of the Youth Service in England and Wales as it had '... suffered in morale and public esteem ...' (Ministry of Education, 1960, p.5). The Committee's report carefully mapped the genesis and contours of the 'youth problem' and recommended a *professionalised* youth service targeting young people and, as in the 1940s, exploiting the spaces of informal education.

Reading the policy and professionalisation literature of wartime and postwar youth work, one gains a profound sense of how material and discursive spaces were articulated by youth workers in the management of youth transitions. A constant binary relation between the hazardous spaces of transition in which young people's proper development was threatened and those in which appropriate adult sensibility could be secured and enhanced underlies this literature. Working-class young people's liminal status rendered them problematic and the private and public spaces of working-class home and family, the neighbourhood, the school and the labour market were, it seemed, unable to support successful transitions in a wartime (and subsequently modernising) economy. Youth organisations became spaces of power that framed the bodies of young people in discourses of pleasure, sexuality, health and compliance. They were, thus, implicated in broader governmental strategies that sought to regulate youth through the careful management of leisure time and space. This chapter has suggested the extent to which the histories and geographies of youth work and informal education have been continuously entwined. Indeed, youth work has become largely synonymous with informal education, defined spatially and temporally. Although the focus in this chapter has been principally on the 1940s, the underlying substance of this account forms a continuing narrative in contemporary policy and practice discourse.

Youth work (and by implication, informal education) sought to uphold the values of choice and responsibility (especially in contrast to wartime threats from totalitarianism), encouraging young people to practice 'self government'. In that sense, its subtle exercise of social control should be understood as embodying a complex form of power, both enabling and productive as youth workers sought to open up material and discursive spaces in which young people could be encouraged to exercise freedom as responsible citizens of a liberal democracy. It is their work in managing the often ambiguous and contradictory zones of freedom that distinguishes youth workers from other occupations concerned with children and young people. Their partially successful sequestration of the informal leisure spaces and places of youth work (streets, clubs and centres of different kinds), contributed to the professional potential of youth workers during the war and in the early years of the welfare state. This was enhanced by their claims to be able to maximise young people's sense of social obligation through augmenting their capacity to exercise responsible choice. In the mid-twentieth century (as now) the conviction was powerfully held that freedom could not be left to the individual, but was contingent upon a '... well regulated and "responsibilised" liberty' (Barry et al., 1996, p.8). The informal spaces and places of youth work, especially in the form of the *club* but sometimes the street or the school, were construed as settings where youth's capacity for responsible agency could be enhanced through such regulated liberty. Youth workers sought to achieve this in the intersection of discursive and material spaces where ideas of popular democracy articulated the pedagogies of youth work spaces with the bodies of young people.

References

A. Barry, T. Osborne and N. Rose (eds) (1996) *Foucault and Political Reason: Liberalism, neo-liberalism and rationalities of government* (London: UCL Press).

B. Bernstein (1975) *Class, Codes and Control, Volume 3, Towards a Theory of Educational Transmissions*, 2nd Edition (London: Routledge and Kegan Paul).

B. Bernstein (2000) *Pedagogy, Symbolic Control and Identity: Theory, research and critique* (Oxford: Rowman & Littlefield Publishers Ltd).

Board of Education (1939) *The Service of Youth*, Circular 1486 (London: HMSO).

Board of Education (1940) *Youth, Physical Recreation, and Service*, Circular 1529 (London: HMSO).

Board of Education (1941a) *Registration of Youth*, Circular 1577 (London: HMSO).

Board of Education (1942) *Registration of Girls*, Circular 1585 (London: HMSO).

Board of Education (1942a) *Registration of Young persons Aged 16*, Circular 1600 (London: HMSO).

Board of Education (1943) *The Youth Service After the War, A Report of the Youth Advisory Council appointed by the President of the Board of Education in 1942 to advise him on questions relating to the Youth Service in England* (London: HMSO).

Board of Education (1943a) *Sex Education in Schools and Youth Organisations*, Educational Pamphlet No.119 (London, HMSO).

Board of Education (1943b) *Registration of Young Persons Aged 16*, Circular 1635 (London: HMSO).

Board of Education (1944) *Teachers and Youth Leaders. Report of the committee appointed by the president of the board of education to consider the supply, recruitment and training of teachers and youth leaders* (London: HMSO).

Board of Education and Home Office (1941) *Juvenile Offences* (London: HMSO).

Board of Education and Scottish Education Department (1942a) *Training and Service for Girls* (London, HMSO).

Board of Education and Scottish Education Department (1943) *Youth Registration in 1942, Presented by the President of the Board of Education and the Secretary of State for Scotland to Parliament by Command of His Majesty* (London, HMSO).

S. Bradford (2004) 'Management of growing up', in J. Roche, S. Tucker, R. Thomson and R. Flynn (eds)*Youth in Society* 2nd edition (London: Sage Publications).

S. Bradford (2007a) 'The "good youth leader": Constructions of professionalism in English youth work, 1939–45', *Ethics and Social Welfare*, 1, 293–309.

S. Bradford (2007b) 'Practices, policies and professionals: Emerging discourses of expertise in English youth work 1939–1951', *Youth and Policy*, 97/98, 13–28.

J. Brew (1943) *In the Service of Youth, A practical manual of work among adolescents* (London: Faber and Faber Ltd).

G. Brown, K. Browne and J. Lim. (2007) 'Introduction or why have a book on geographies of sexualities?' in K. Browne, J. Lim and G. Brown (eds) *Geographies of Sexualities: Theory, practices and politics* (Farnham: Ashgate Publishing Limited).

M. Dean (2010) *Governmentality: Power and rule in modern society* 2nd edition (London: Sage Publications).

M. Douglas (1966) *Purity and Danger: An analysis of concept of pollution and taboo* (London: Routledge and Kegan Paul).

M. Douglas (1996) *Natural Symbols: Explorations in cosmology* (London: Routledge).

D. Edwards-Rees (1943) *The Service of Youth Book* (Wallington: The Religious Education Press Ltd).

B. Evans (2010) 'Anticipating fatness: Childhood, affect and the pre-emptive "war on obesity"' *Transactions of the Institute of British Geographers*, 35, 21–38.

B. Evans, R. Colls and K. Hörschelmann (2011) '"Change4Life for your kids": Embodied collectives and public health pedagogy', *Sport, Education and Society*, 16, 323–41.

J. Evans and B. Davies (2004) 'Endnote: The embodiment of consciousness, Bernstein, health and schooling', in J. Evans, B. Davies and J. Wright (eds) *Body Knowledge and Control, Studies in the Sociology of Physical Education and Health* (London: Routledge).

S. Ferguson and H. Fitzgerald (1954) *Studies in the Social Services* (London: HMSO and Longmans Green and Company).

M. Foucault (1979) *The History of Sexuality, Volume 1, An introduction* (London: Allen Lane).

D. Fowler (2008) *Youth Culture in Modern Britain, c. 1920–1970* (Basingstoke: Palgrave Macmillan).

L. A. Hall (2001) 'Venereal diseases and society in Britain, from the contagious diseases acts to the national health service' in R. Davidson and L. A. Hall (eds) *Sex, Sin and Suffering* (London: Routledge).

H. Hendrick (1990) *Images, of Youth: Age, class and the male youth problem, 1880–1920* (Oxford: Clarendon Press).

Home Office (1947) *Criminal Statistics, England and Wales, 1939–1945. Summary of statistics relating to crime and criminal proceedings for the years 1939–1945* Cmd. 7227 (London: HMSO).

P. Jephcott (1942) *Girls Growing Up* (London: Faber and Faber).

B. Martin (1981) *A Sociology of Contemporary Cultural Change* (Oxford: Basil Blackwell).

P. Miller and N. Rose (2008) *Governing the Present: Administering economic, social and personal life* (Cambridge: Polity Press).

Ministry of Education (1960) *The Youth Service in England and Wales,* Report of the Committee Appointed by the Minister of Education in November 1958 (London: HMSO).

A. E. Morgan (1939) *The Needs of Youth, A Report Made to King George's Jubilee Trust Fund* (London: Oxford University Press).

J. Newman (2012) *Working the Spaces of Power: Activism, neoliberalism and gendered labour* (London: Bloomsbury Academic).

M. Paneth (1944) *Branch Street: A sociological study* (London, George Allen and Unwin).

C. Richardson (1941) *Sex Education in the Training of Youth Leaders, Informal youth training committee report, Paper No.14*, October 11th, PRO ED 124/16.

J. Springhall (1977) *Youth, Empire and Society* (London: Croom Helm).

C. Stimson (1948) *Education after School* (London: Routledge and Kegan Paul).

P. Tinkler (1995) *Constructing Girlhood: Popular magazines for girls growing up in England, 1920–1950* (London: Taylor and Francis).

S. Todd (2005) *Young Women, Work and Family in England 1918–1950* (Oxford: Oxford University Press).

V. Turner (1975) *Dramas, Fields and Metaphors: Symbolic action in human society* (Ithaca, NY: Cornell University Press).

S. H. Wood (1942) Internal memorandum to the secretary of the board of education, 25 February 1942, PRO ED 124/16.

13
Feminism and Informal Education in Youth Work with Girls and Young Women, 1975–85

Jean Spence

Background

In the mid 1970s, a set of distinctive feminist practices were deployed by women youth workers to address gender inequality within the British Youth Service. In the wake of the publication of the Albemarle Report (Ministry of Education, 1960), the statutory service, particularly in England and Wales, had expanded significantly, supplementing and working in partnership with the voluntary sector. The focus of Albemarle was upon developmental or 'social' education with young people defined in terms of opportunities for 'association, training and challenge'. Among other innovations, Albemarle precipitated a youth club building programme (Robertson, 2009), encouraged the development of 'experimental' approaches to young people who did not readily access clubs, and instituted a National Training College for youth leaders whose methods of experiential learning, group work and personal development came to exert an important influence on the social educational discourse of youth work practice (Davies and Gibson, 1967; Bradford, 2011).

Even though the Albemarle Report stressed that it was not advocating a Service which would merely react to delinquency, as Bradford argues in the previous chapter, the Committee was established in the context of 'acute moral panic about youth'. The preoccupations of the time included the post-war 'bulge' in the birth rate, the growth of an assertive (and sometimes aggressive) working-class white male 'Teddy Boy' youth culture, racial conflict and the abolition of National Service. The distinctive 'teenage' youth cultures which emerged during the 1950s were distinctively masculine and working class, reflecting the traditional gendered stereotypes of working-class life. They were underpinned by the new securities associated with conditions of full employment, the safety-net of the welfare state and an emergent market targeted to stimulate teenage consumerism, each of which was predicated upon the assumption of distinctive gender roles, and female dependence. Albemarle stressed that its recommendations were designed particularly to meet the social and developmental needs of non-academic young people and in so doing set the scene for the expanding Youth Service to be not only focused upon working-class youth but particularly upon young men.

As was argued within academic work focused upon youth subcultures during the 1970s, especially that associated with the Centre for Contemporary Cultural Studies (CCCS) at Birmingham University (set up by Richard Hoggart who had co-written the Albemarle Report), post-war youth cultures tended to reproduce and re-inscribe young people within inherited social relationships of class, gender and race (e.g., CCCS, 1975; Willis, 1977; McRobbie, 1991). Within these youth cultures (and in the empirical studies associated with them), young women were relatively invisible, making appearances as appendages to young men, as lesser-paid satellites in male worlds, presumed to lack a sub culture of their own (McRobbie and Garber, 1975). This reflected the realities of youth clubs – where some of the research had been undertaken – in which working-class masculine subcultures were the centre of attention.

The post-Albemarle expansion of the Youth Service was predicated upon a situation which was already marked by specific conditions of gender inequality than can be traced structurally to the years following the First World War. The interwar period had been marked by a 'modernisation' of youth work provided by the voluntary sector, which favoured mixed sex provision. While boys' clubs generally refused to mix, girls' clubs had incrementally changed their composition to include boys, and as a consequence had suffered a decline in female membership (Macalister Brew, 1957; Butterfield and Spence, 2009). When the state entered the field at the outbreak of the Second World War, there was already an assumption of mixed-sex provision.

One of the consequences of mixing was a narrowing of the terms of reference for working with girls, which, as Bradford's discussion indicates, began to focus more narrowly on the management of their sexuality to the detriment of the broader educational agenda which had characterised the girls' clubs of the previous era. Albemarle noted that 'fewer girls than boys are members of youth organizations', stating that 'much more thought will need to be given to their specific needs' (Ministry of Education, 1960, para. 57). However, while the Albemarle Report pursued the ideal of an open, universal, social educational service, attention to the 'specific needs' of girls and young women is indicative of their secondary status in conceptualising the work. Traditional gender roles and inequalities had been reinforced in the post-war years and attention to young women related primarily to the nature of their relationships with young men. In that relationship, responsibility for control of teenage sexuality was female. Meanwhile, the professionalising process which accelerated after Albemarle reflected the gender inequalities of the labour market, providing opportunities which were predominantly accessed by male youth workers reinforcing the conditions of the youth club as a predominantly male space dominated by male agendas (Sawbridge and Spence, 1991). It is no accident that Ray Gosling's (1961) account of an experimental club in Leicester is entitled *Lady Albemarle's Boys*.

Later, in view of rising immigration, inter-racial conflict and the racial bias of youth work practice, the Hunt Report, *Immigrants and the Youth Service* (DES, 1967) acknowledged the predominance of white youth and suggested the necessity for greater integration, but this too was perceived primarily in terms of 'raced' young men: nowhere was gender a shaping concern. By 1969, the Fairbairn-Milson Report, *Youth and Community Work in the 1970s*, acknowledged that 'the Youth Service has not proved to be conspicuously successful since Albemarle in meeting the needs of girls and preparing them for their changed role in society' (DES, 1969, para.82).

Youth work had developed a heavy emphasis towards the interests of working-class young men that was related to their problematic presence in public places in their leisure time. Masculine youth work, since its inception in the nineteenth century, was primarily concerned with the question of controlling male energies associated with delinquency, and social education in these terms meant promoting self-discipline and building 'character' (Eager, 1953; Butters and Newell, 1978) towards the 'respectability' of an appropriate adult male ideal of citizenship. In working towards these aims, and bearing in mind the voluntary nature of participation, the agenda was heavily skewed towards providing programmes for association, training and challenge which would be attractive to boys, relying heavily upon male leisure interests, including physical activities, team games and competition, supplemented by opportunities for learning work-related skills, such as the ever-popular joinery. In this climate, work with girls and young women was understood as 'specialist', subservient to male constructions of the nature of youth work, and conceived educationally with reference to traditional adult female roles in the family.

Masculine domination of space, time and perspective drove girls out, or to the margins of youth buildings and programmes where they were viewed through a masculine lens. A report of the London Federation of Boys' Clubs noted, for example, that a sixteen-year-old girl 'may already be thinking about marriage', and that as such, 'her club desires are often primarily social, or the means of finding a boyfriend' (quoted in Davies, 1999, p.95). Any provision made especially for girls and young women tended to be conceived in the realm of conventional femininity – of fashion, beauty, sexual health and hygiene, and the domestic arts. Hanmer observed in 1964, '... girls do not receive the same financial support as boys. In a sense girls are being told "behave like boys and money for programme and staff is available"', but even had they wanted to, there was little incentive for girls to 'behave like boys', and 20 years later, research undertaken for NAYC indicated significant bias in funding towards male-only organisations and masculine youth work (Smith, 1984).

However, by the early 1970s, the still expanding and professionalising youth service was recruiting and training a new cohort of workers, many of whom were influenced by the radicalism of student and community politics. Increasing numbers of recruits to full-time work were women who had been able to take advantage of expanding educational opportunities and grants for mature students. Gender inequality was becoming a burning issue in higher education and in the arena community action from where many female community and youth work students were recruited. When women from such backgrounds encountered male-dominated youth provision, they drew upon their experiences of student and community politics to address the situation.

Against standard and complacent attitudes in youth work that considered 'the problem of girls' to lie in the nature of (hetero-sexualised) girlhood itself, feminist workers, themselves experiencing the frustrations of working in male-dominated settings, pointed to structural bias, arguing that the problem was not 'of girls' but of the institutionalisation of sexist ideas and practices. Their aim was thus to change those structures and the ideas inscribed within them not only for the benefit of young women but also for themselves as workers. Drawing upon the example of single-sex organisation within the women's movement, their first priority was to secure single-sex space in which girls could feel comfortable and safe, and in which female youth workers could develop alternative perspectives and practices. The intention was to provide an environment in which girls might be perceived as fully human, rather than as relative to boys, of only minority interest and in which a female perspective might gain some influence within the profession.

Feminist youth work was established through what became known as the 'Girls' Work Movement'. In feminist practices, the social educational agenda which was understood as primarily concerned with questions of socialisation and learning in an informal context was extended into what now would be understood as informal education. The themes of association, training and challenge were mobilised for a distinctively politicised agenda which prioritised the needs and interests of girls and women, with particular reference to the distorting impact of gender inequality upon female personal and social development using methods which stimulated critical questioning of received understanding. Feminist youth work adopted educational methods which were grounded in everyday lives and experiences, pursuing on that basis a democratised practice. The intention of the feminist informal education approach in youth work was ultimately to struggle for social and political justice to achieve 'human flourishing' (Smith, 1994, p.3).

The issues and concerns of the Girls' Work movement were documented and communicated mainly in an outpouring of project, conference and research reports and the widely circulated *Working with Girls Newsletter* (WWGN) produced between January 1981 and March 1987 by the Girls Work Unit of the National Association of Youth Clubs (NAYC). A few related publications tended to follow from the practice texts appearing throughout the 1980s and into the 1990s. They included the NAYC book *Coming in from the Margins* (Carpenter and Young, 1986), which dealt with the range of practice in work with girls and young women, articles in *Feminist Review* which focused upon the attitudes of girls towards lesbianism (Nava, 1982) and a chapter on 'Gender Race and Power' in a general collection on the subject of racism (Parmar, 1988).

My own work began in the environment of higher education in a feminism making its appearance in the social sciences in the early 1970s. When I was employed as a youth worker in 1976, there were already stirrings of feminist organisation within the profession, and in that year a group of feminist youth workers was meeting regularly in the women's centre in Earlham Street in London. Like others, I was able to develop my own practice, theory and research in work with girls and young women partly through the availability of resources for women's consciousness-raising and action emerging in the general Women's Movement, and partly through the emergent network of groups, conferences and informal support networks which stimulated a creative and dynamic environment for challenging received wisdom about youth work supported by the central co-ordination of the Girls' Work Unit.

This chapter is inevitably informed not only by the documentary evidence produced during the period in question but also by my own experiences during that time and subsequently in continuing conversations with colleagues and through understanding which emerges from teaching and research in the professional context (Spence, 1988, 1996, 2010; Batsleer, 2013). This chapter considers the issues confronted by feminist youth workers and the framework in which they pursued their feminist understanding using single-sex space, the community context and the educational methods associated with Paulo Freire. It draws attention to the tensions which resulted in the decline of the movement and suggests that educational feminism is now entering a new phase.

Single-sex space

Feminist youth workers from the mid-1970s highlighted the marginalisation of girls and young women in youth work as a serious problem, suggesting that 'for too long youth clubs have tended to be boys clubs with girls in them' (WWGN 1, 1981, p.12). They argued that the masculine 'atmosphere' in youth work settings created conditions in which girls and women participated only in male terms. It became almost a cliché to associate pool tables and football with the physical domination of youth centre activities by boys. Female toilets and coffee bar areas were often the primary 'female' spaces. So common was the pattern of unequal gender access that pool tables for boys and toilets for girls became tropes in the feminist narrative. Thus women who initiated feminist work with girls in Northern Ireland remembered that

> ... there wasn't many youth centres in those days but we went into community centres knowing that you had to get the girls out of the toilets and get them participating ....
>
> (Morgan and McArdle, 2009, p.222)
>
> ... the first thing you would encounter would've been the pool table for instance ... then you'd talk to the young women about the **long walk from the door** to where the café area was ... (pp.226–7)

In masculine activities, physicality and the public display of skill were primary. Girls watched from the sidelines, chatted among themselves in the coffee bars or created disruption in the entrance hallways and in the female toilets, caught in what Hudson (1984) argued was a contradictory discourse between femininity and adolescence – dependent and passive females on the one hand and troublesome youth on the other. The embodiment of the youth presence and the practices associated with that presence was, as Bradford argues, distinctively gendered.

The atmosphere encountered by women who wished to work with girls was frequently intimidating and negative. The following description relates to a youth unemployment scheme:

> The boys were sexist and abusive, they dominated the atmosphere physically eg. lining the corridor during breaks, and even in their absence, graffiti was everywhere! Some of the young women were withdrawn and quiet in their presence, bored and fed up, and felt unable to use the common room which became the boys' space. The boys' attitude and behaviour towards the girls ranged from rating them sexually to actual assault; an Asian girl was burned with a cigarette, a West Indian girl had paint poured on her coat.
>
> (WWGN 4, 1981, p.5)

This description, which highlights the combined sexism and racism endured by some young women, contrasts sharply with the ways in which women workers in the WWGN variously describe the atmosphere of female-only work as 'non-intimidating', 'non-threatening', 'relaxed', 'supportive', 'sympathetic' and 'encouraging' (e.g., WWGN 2, 1981, pp.9, 14; WWGN, 3, p.14). The priority for female-only space was related to the need to provide a welcoming, comfortable and safe environment. The goal was to achieve a sort of privacy in the otherwise public arena of youth clubs for the development of female-defined programmes. At the outset, such development was perceived only in gendered terms, spaces for nurturing 'sisterhood', defined against male domination, which meant that other inequalities and biases in local provision – such as the domination of white young people – were largely unremarked. Priorities included the engagement of young women in the full range of existing options in the mixed-sex setting, and the possibility of exploring new, female-centred activity that might be offered under the social educational remit of the youth service. Feminist workers sought to create for girls 'opportunity to sample a wide range of experiences normally available to boys... to try out and develop new skills without fear of criticism and ridicule from boys and... a chance to discuss issues which girls find embarrassing in the presence of boys' (WWGN 9, 1982, p.16).

The ideal of single-sex space was generally presented in modest terms, and without reference to sectional differences between girls and women, using careful language expressed within the prevailing social educational discourses of youth work. To justify feminist interventions in 'acceptable' terms, the argument usually focused on the claims of the youth service to be 'open' for all young people, pointed to the low numbers of young women participating and suggested that a way to redress the situation might be to offer single-sex space in order to improve female confidence: '[b]riefly, girls need to gain confidence in themselves and... cannot do so... in a mixed situation' (WWGN 1, 1981, p.5; see also Spence, 1996). Where single-sex space was achieved the evidence of its benefits was incontrovertible, successfully demonstrating that the 'problem of girls' in terms of their levels of participation could be solved by small-scale, practical adjustments to provision. Girls and young women participated and enjoyed opportunities to take part in single-sex activities such as conferences, outdoor activities, regional and local Girls' Days and female-only group work sessions within prevailing social educational terms of reference.

Nevertheless, the argument for female-only space was contentious and the struggle to secure such space a continuous drain on the energies of feminist youth workers. Even the basic question of equality of access challenged existing rites of gendered behaviour. As Nava argued, one way in which gender inequalities were reproduced involved boys policing the behaviour of girls in public spaces such as youth clubs: '[i]n this culture outside the home, girls are observers of boys' activity and boys are observers and *guardians* of girls' passivity' (1984, p.12). The question was therefore not just one of physical differentiation of place and power over material space but of relational power within the spaces inhabited by young people. In the youth work environment, identified appropriately by Bradford (Chapter 12, this volume) as 'exemplary liminal spaces', young people were working out transitions to an adulthood that was received as unequally sexed, classed and raced. To challenge the reproduction of unequal social relations was a fundamental

204 Youth Work Spaces

threat to the maintenance of such relations, dangerous to the status quo and with consequences that might be much more wide-ranging than immediately apparent in the youth work setting. That boys themselves sensed a significant threat to their control was evident in their insistent determination to disrupt and invade female-only events and activities. That male youth workers sensed a similar threat was evidenced in at best in their lack of co-operation, and at worst in their active hostility. Faltering attempts from mainly socialist male colleagues were made to develop 'anti-sexist' work with boys (e.g., Taylor, 1984), but these never received widespread support.

Mainly, boys and young men adopted whatever tactics they could to divert and subvert female-only youth work. My personal experience, especially in attempting to introduce female-centred sex-education, in setting up girls' groups, and in organising Girls' Days, included boys attempting to climb through windows, banging at doors and setting off fireworks in the vicinity of girls' activities. Sometimes disruptive behaviour was dangerous. The following had racist as well as sexist connotations that illustrate the necessity of understanding the youth club within its wider community setting.

> White lads, for the first 7 or 8 months drifted along just to see what was happening ... and gave us the usual sort of trouble like trying to get in and swearing at whoever was on the door. For quite a long time it was nothing that wasn't within our control ... [w]ithin the last 6 months there's been quite a lot of violence in the area which has hit the newspapers ... the lads have been coming down to the club in increasing numbers ...; it's reached 25–40 ... They're there before the girls or the workers arrive and they're fairly determined, as they say, to close down the night or certainly to turn it into another mixed night ... sometimes they're coming down with weapons. Sharpening sticks, accumulating boulders and various other things. Other times its mainly insults and mild assaults ... like pushing and shoving and then on two or three of the worst evenings they've actually done things like try to knock down the doors with 10 feet long poles, smashing windows and generally being pretty frightening and intimidating to girls and women workers. We've boulders, slabs of concrete and sticks thrown at us. Our cars have been scratched up. All our energy is having to go at the moment towards dealing with the boys, which is exactly what they want.
>
> (WWGN 13, 1983, p.10)

In the face of varying degrees of hostility, women workers generally argued that their male colleagues should support them by undertaking anti-sexist educational work with the boys while girls' work was in progress, but this was seldom forthcoming in practice. In the case above, the women wrote, 'the male youth leader has been questioning the way we work ...' (p.11). Indeed, male colleagues themselves sometimes engaged in behaviour designed to subvert female control of space. For example:

> I had to wait until the male worker turned up with the keys to open the office and the cupboards. I told him he was the man with the keys, with the power. I won the battle. I haven't the front door keys, but the office and the cupboard.

> I opened the cupboard and there was nothing there! After I'd got the keys!

> ... He said, 'I decided to have a change-around'.
>
> (Quoted in Spence, 1996, p.51)

Partly born of defensiveness in the face of persistent opposition and partly because they were keen that their work should be recognised as legitimate and mainstream, feminist workers consistently attempted to present their case through prevailing youth work priorities and language. They situated themselves squarely within the accepted framework of a service which promoted universal and equal access offering social educational opportunities for all young people. However, what was unavoidable from the perspective of feminism, which made feminist youth work disruptive and its educational methods more challenging, was the specific argument for gender equality. In pursuing this aim, even within the standard discourse of youth work, feminist practitioners inevitably and necessarily disturbed existing gendered boundaries and the relations of power that those boundaries encased.

For example, in terms of 'association', girls and women wishing to meet without a male presence upset assumed social relations of power and control. If girls and young women sought 'training' based on their own identification of their needs (e.g., for classes in self-defence), this highlighted the fact that all was not well in gendered social relationships. Meanwhile, seeking opportunities for 'challenge' might simply mean fully participating in activities programmes – playing football, riding motor bikes, learning joinery or asking for time on the pool table, and this was a direct threat to male domination of space and resources. All such activity conformed to the social educational terms of reference of youth work to use its facilities to promote the constructive use of leisure and enhance personal confidence and skill. However, it also challenged received roles and relationships, not only within the youth work setting, but with reference to the world beyond. The physical redistribution of resources away from boys and men could not but be experienced by them as an absolute loss, compounded by loss of control over female behaviour. Single-sex work not only developed the confidence of girls and women but provoked them to behave more assertively, with consequences for the experiences of power in the mixed sex setting.

The single-sex approach of feminist youth work actively enhanced the analytic and cognitive skills of young women which were otherwise inhibited by restricted opportunities for exploring physical space (Katz, 1993, cited in Pearce, 1996, p.4). The following case suggests the incremental development of feminist educational practice in this regard:

> Initially I spent a long time sitting with groups of girls chatting to them; I encouraged them to try to odd game of pool or snooker with me so that I could attempt to diffuse the derision which this met. I tried to encourage other staff to see that the girls' passivity was not a sign of contentment... Finally, when I had won some of the girls' trust, I took them away from the mixed setting to some girls only evenings and to three days of girls' activities.

> Taking the girls out of the club into the single sex setting developed the work enormously. The girls returned from this with renewed confidence, making demands, and wanting to experience different activities, such as weight lifting which had previously been the boys' domain.
>
> (WWGN 13, 1983, p.13)

Feminist-inspired activity, dialogue and discussion gave meaning and direction to new experiences and changing behaviour, stimulating female agency in ways that raised much wider questions about accepted social roles and relationships. The 'benign' social educational 'repertoire' of mainstream youth work was invariably politicised in ways which suggested the pursuit of a 'radical paradigm', an informal educational perspective which could not but be threatening to vested and conservative interests (Butters and Newell, 1977). As Jeffs and Smith have suggested, 'education that seeks to foster democracy and vision is inherently risky' (Jeffs and Smith, 1999, p.114).

The inherent radicalism of feminist youth work to some extent derived from and coalesced easily with the political education and activism which had emerged within the related profession of community work. Moreover, the second spatial dimension of feminist youth work, which located female lives in the private as well as the public arena, meant that feminist youth workers were particularly open to contextualising their work in the framework of 'community'.

Privatised lives

In feminist thinking, the sexual division of labour was a key to situating the lives of women and girls in public and private spaces. The secondary role of women in the labour market and the association of female identity with domestic, personal and emotional labour dulled the career aspirations of young women, encouraged their dependence upon young men and limited their potential for autonomous development. There was ambiguity about female 'leisure' time, because unlike waged employment, domestic responsibilities had no clear demarcation into work/not work. This was echoed in the gendered divisions of public and private space: institutions associated with matters of work and leisure were predominantly masculine in nature, while those associated with welfare, childcare and domesticity were predominantly feminine. Thus a detached youth worker in London quoted in a 1981 ILEA report said, '[m]any girls were only to be seen on their way home from school, on errands to the shops, in laundrettes or minding younger siblings' (cited in Nava, 1984, p.12), and a female youth worker operating in an area of high youth unemployment in North East England in 1982 noted:

> It seems that it is mainly boys who have little to do all day; unemployed girls are given tasks to do in the home, so the majority of Coffee Bar users were male. Indeed, when I was appointed in 1981, there were only two female users.
>
> (WWGN 13, 1982, p.16)

Such observations were supported by academic research. In 1980, McRobbie drew attention to the invisibility of young women in studies of youth subcultures, suggesting that '[i]t has always been on the street that most subcultural activity takes place ... [but] ... the street remains in some ways taboo for women' (quoted in McRobbie, 1991, p.29). Over 15 years later, despite greater acceptance of the idea of gender equality, Pearce (1996) suggested that young women's orientation remained primarily towards family homes and shops.

Understanding this orientation implied the necessity of engaging with young women with reference to their privatised social lives. The injunction to 'start where they are at' repeated ubiquitously within youth work as the foundation for social educational processes meant working with girls and with their identities inside *and* outside youth clubs, connecting with family and neighbourhood networks as well as with leisure-based peer and friendship youth groups, affirming what was positive about that, as well as acknowledging its limits. This presented its own problems, particularly with reference to inequalities associated with cultural and religious differences. For example, at the conference of Feminist Women Youth Workers held in Nottingham in 1981 after the inner city disturbances of that year, Black women workers expressed dismay at what they perceived to be the racist interpretation of the proposed public response of the conference to the 'uprising'. Later, Parmar accused 'White' feminist workers of 'pathologising' Asian families in their work with Asian young women. In questioning the 'universal' category of youth, feminist workers, workers themselves, operating within other structures of inequality and power, were often guilty of adopting stereotypes and failing to recognise bias in their own practice. The universalising concept of 'sisterhood' was as problematic as an undifferentiated concept of youth, and this was particularly evident in the community context, beyond the narrow concerns of space and time in youth clubs, and was ultimately to contribute to the demise of a 'movement'-based feminist practice.

More positively, positioning themselves beyond youth club walls situated female youth workers in the arena of neighbourhood community work and activism. The dovetailing of feminist youth work with feminist community work was encouraged and facilitated by policy and organisational development during the 1970s, increasingly bringing youth work, community work and adult education services into close alignment (DES, 1969; Youth Council for Northern Ireland, 1973; HMSO, 1975). Local education authorities re-organised and renamed their services to become 'youth and community' or 'community education' services, while professional training increasingly presented community education and youth work as one profession.

Community development work was in itself often a stimulant to local female activism, encouraging public action around domestic and neighbourhood 'issues'. Sometimes it was community rather than youth work that sponsored work with girls and young women. For instance, the first Glasgow Girls' Day was organised as a result of Scottish Women in Community Work Conference in Dundee in 1981 (WWGN 9, 1982, p.16). My own employment as a neighbourhood youth worker in Sunderland with 'responsibility for girls' emerged from Urban Aid-funded community work in the area, and the expressed desire of local women that something should be made available for their daughters (SNYP, 1979).

In neighbourhood-based community and youth work, 'private' matters such as housing, schooling, welfare benefits, racist intimidation and safety on the streets were the subject of learning which translated into collective, political issues. As political matters they were overlaid with questions of power, fairness, justice and equality, and thus linked positively with the concerns of a range of social movements reacting to oppression and structural inequality. Inevitably, community workers were allied with and helped stimulate participation in socialist and trade union organisations, anti-racist campaigns and groups, women's groups, lesbian and gay organisations and organisations working to end disability discrimination (Batsleer, 2013; Mayo, 1977, 1982).

The subjects addressed by community work, feminism and the Girls Work Movement were often indistinguishable. For example, violence against women and children was a crucial feminist theme that translated into active support for women through community-based funding and methods for women's refuges: the workers and managers of refuges were (as they still are) often qualified community and youth workers. Male violence was perceived by feminist youth workers in terms of assumptions about domination that included 'the daily invasions of our space' (WWGN 6, p.11), a concern as relevant to young women as to adults. In this regard, feminist youth work made a significant contribution to breaking silences around the sexual abuse of children (e.g., WWGN 8, 1982, p.7). Such issues affected female workers too and the personal, which was political, was also professional. Thus female-centred work in the community context implied a dissolution of age and status differentials in favour of identification with the conditions of being female – in favour indeed, of the notion of 'sisterhood'. Notably, at the annual feminist women youth worker conferences organised through NAYC's Girls' Work Unit, the favourite song at the Saturday social was 'We Are Family', as performed by Sister Sledge (Edwards and Rogers, 1978).

Community-based political activism resonated directly with the feminist slogan that 'the personal is political'. It was also intrinsically about informal education – about learning together on the basis of common experience and through processes of collective, democratic organisation and action. The methods used to encourage local participation in community activism, involved using informal educational approaches which in many regards could slip seamlessly into the consciousness raising and organisational approaches associated with the women's liberation movement.

Feminist education in youth work

The social and informal educational approaches of youth and community work overlapped in a complex interweaving during the 1970s and 1980s. Within youth work, social educational methods offered new peer-group experiences to young people, access to activities and one-to-one help and encouragement for personal development and programmes and processes through which to learn the social and practical skills associated with mature and active adult citizenship. After Albemarle, there was a growing emphasis upon group work (Klein, 1956, 1961; Goetchius and Tash, 1967; Tash, 1967; Button, 1971, 1974) and upon the 'non-directive' and 'non-judgemental' approaches (Batten, 1962, 1967, 1970; Lovell, 2009) which were favoured in the professional education of community and youth workers. The informal educational methods used in the community context of practice included group work and non-directive methods, but crucially, learning was located in the identities and experiences of participants. The focus was upon reflection rather than information, upon process rather than outcome, and the intention was towards democratic participation of young people in the here and now of youth work. This found direct parallels in the methods of awareness-raising and self-development associated with the feminist consciousness-raising group.

Feminist consciousness-raising, which took place in single-sex women's groups, was grounded in a belief in the commonality of the female experience of oppression. Each member was assumed to be of equal worth and her contribution to be of equal value – every experience counted. Groups were intentionally leaderless. Meetings proceeded through dialogue about experience and offered the space in which women could name their experiences and reflect upon them in a non-judgemental and encouraging and questioning environment. The primary aim was to break the silences associated with powerlessness, to identify the source of powerlessness in social structures and relationships and thereby to encourage female agency and organisation for change.

The ideal of consciousness-raising was integral to the approach adopted by feminist youth workers, but it was not a perfect fit. Firstly, the presence of paid workers implied inequality of responsibility and power between workers and young women. Secondly, the stress in feminist youth work upon working within the discourses of social education emphasised developmental rather than explicitly political learning and elided the problem of difference, not only of identity, but also of ideas about what constituted 'responsible adulthood' and citizenship as the goal of social educational practices. Many workers maintained the social educational language of 'confidence building' as their primary goal in work with girls to emphasis their underlying goodwill and to avoid the charge of 'feminism' (Spence, 1996). The feminist language of consciousness-raising was too easily perceived as threatening in the professional arena, as alienating in working-class communities, and as a hindrance to the creation of alliances with female workers who did not identify as 'feminists', and colleagues who prioritised other interests such as class and race.

To some extent, the divisive feminist language of consciousness-raising was replaced by that of radical education around which a range of sectional interests could find common ground. In particular, the educational theories of Paulo Freire as expounded in 'Pedagogy of the Oppressed' (1970) and 'Cultural Action for Freedom' (1972) were being widely adopted as representative of the approach and sympathies of progressive professional practice in the community and youth work field. Freire's analysis began with an acknowledgement of structural inequality, included the purposes of 'liberation' but at the same time acknowledged a role for the professional educator. The pedagogical principles which it embraced allowed for practitioners to organise in a way that was understood as politically 'neutral' with reference to party allegiances, and to move beyond the limits of the traditional Marxism of class-based analysis into questions relating to the personal experience of oppression. Freire's methods centred the processes of participation and of breaking silences and 'naming' the world on the basis of commonalities of experience. Politicisation was inherent in the act of naming as much as in anything associated with overt political campaigning or in organising around political 'issues'; it was in the act of naming that the group concerned could develop the means of taking independent political action. This was particularly appropriate to the community-based educator whose professional role was to *facilitate* rather than to indoctrinate, and it was especially useful for those wishing to move beyond the discourses of class into other cross-cutting arenas of inequality.

Freire's educational 'practice of freedom' resonated directly with the intentions of justice-based youth work interventions, including those inspired by feminism and anti-racism, enabling the practices of consciousness-raising to be legitimated in predominantly educational rather than political terms. Politicisation was an effect of education, not a purpose of intervention. The difference between Freire's framework for the development of literacy and 'conscientisation' among South American peasants and the feminist practice of consciousness-raising was only in the focus upon particular structures of power. For feminists, it was gender inequality which silenced women and refused to legitimate their understanding. For feminists, naming the world meant doing so on the basis of a distinctively female experience, and inevitably this brought the issue back to the question of the conditions in which such naming could be achieved. The struggle inevitably remained focused upon the possibilities for working in a female-only setting.

While the adoption of Freire's theoretical insights allowed for cross-sectional agreement about informal educational methods, it did not allow for the consequences of separate organisation around the range of identities associated with oppression. The identity-based approach was inherently fissiparous, and the cracks and fractures were to prove lethal to the movement for working with girls and young women in a climate of reaction. As the 1980s progressed, declining resources and an increasing problem-orientated approach to young people began to exacerbate already existing problems of coherence and collaboration in practice. Meanwhile, a determination by a centralising government to separate youth work from community work significantly weakened the community location of informal educational practice in feminist youth work. The consequence was a collapse of 'movement' approaches, a silencing of feminist language and a retreat into silos of 'difference' for many committed, progressive youth workers.

Conclusion

Because it was inspired by the Women's Liberation Movement and as such associated with other radical and left-wing movements, including black power, youth and student radicalism, gay rights, disability rights and class-based activism, feminism was from the outset perceived to be both politically disruptive and socially transgressive. Moreover, its alliances lay with those other movements as much as with the professional traditions within youth work. The ideas and practices of feminist youth work, when systematically deployed, challenged prevailing organisational relationships, systems of decision-making, accepted practice goals and, implicitly, the terms of reference for social education as the principle practice of youth work. Unsurprisingly, and whatever its achievements in encouraging and educating young women, feminism was never, and perhaps could never be, fully integrated into prevailing mainstream practice. As an explicitly political philosophy with an agenda involving a critique of power and inequality, feminist youth work provoked antagonism from those wedded to the emergent, fragile professionalism of the statutory youth service. Internally, feminism was also fragile. The defensive use of dominant liberal discourses associated with social education to pursue its case constrained its potential for radical change to structures and processes and also hindered the development of a cohesive feminist youth work philosophy that could identify, analyse and transcend its prevailing contradictions and limitations. Its focus upon personal identities and oppressions struggled to move beyond the dualisms of male–female/white–black/heterosexual–lesbian/able-bodied–disabled, which were then set against each other creating fault lines that fragmented when new voices such as those of Black women emerged to challenge the dominance of white women, and as cuts in public spending forced a retreat into conservativism and a silencing of 'liberation movement' and identity politics in general towards the end of the 1980s.

It is ironic that in early 1987, shortly after publishing *Coming in from the Margins*, about work with girls (Carpenter and Young, 1986), and less than four years after granting 'permanent' funding to such work, the NAYC unceremoniously closed the Girls' Work Unit (WWGN 15, 1983; WWGN Campaign Issue, March 1987). The closure of the Unit presaged a relentless decline in the autonomy of feminist-inspired youth work. Single-sex work with girls and young women was increasingly either absorbed into mainstream organisations under terms which did not admit the politicised pedagogies of feminism or cut entirely from youth service provision.

The decline of the Girls' Work Movement accelerated during the 1990s, mirroring an overall decline in youth work founded on the principles of social and informal education with voluntarily participating young people. Structural changes in youth work since the 1990s have ensured that there can be no return to the conditions in which the Girls' Work Movement flourished.

Historical analysis of the rise and decline of feminist youth work in the decade between 1975 and 1985 reveals dynamic tensions, which on the one hand propelled the feminist project into exciting and creative practices which exemplified the best that youth work might achieve, and on the other hand were the source of division and ultimately contributed to its destruction. Further research focusing upon female workers and young women who participated in feminist youth work during the significant decade would enable the impact to be objectively evaluated.

Contemporary research might also usefully gather evidence about the survival of a feminist ideal of youth work practice into the twenty-first century, and against the overall decline in informal educational opportunities in the statutory and large voluntary organisational setting. Feminist youth workers might have retreated into 'silos', but many retained and even developed their informal networks from these situations, across community as well as youth work, and across sectional interests. Others fought to establish themselves in positions of influence – particularly in higher education and in setting the terms of reference for professional standards, education and training. That there are signs of a new movement of independent feminist activism emerging within the informal educational discourses and practices associated with youth work is interesting in these terms. The focus is different now, concentrating upon the self-direction and participation of young women outside traditional organisational frameworks of youth work, but it is mobilising cross-generational alliances, and using the surviving informal networks of feminist practitioners, educators and researchers to enrich its understanding. Voluntary action accessing different funding sources such as those available for the arts, for heritage and for youth participation have provided the bedrock for informal education in a wider range of settings (Batsleer, 2013). Meanwhile, electronic systems of communication are facilitating the leadership of young women themselves in creating a more 'liquid' approach to politicised, but youth work-inspired feminist activity such as that demonstrated by Feminist Webs (http://www.feministwebs.com/). It is not clear how far such approaches have transcended the difficulties of inequalities of power between women, but the approach is certainly more inclusive and better informed than that of the original Girls' Work Movement. It is in these new conditions, using new institutional spaces, mobilising communication technologies and with different perceptions of space and place, that any contemporary informal educational approach to young women, whether or not it is defined as feminist youth work, must find its location.

References

J. Batsleer (2013) *Youth Working with Girls and Women in Community Settings: A feminist perspective* (Farnham: Ashgate).

T. Batten (1962) *Training for Community Development: A critical study of method* (Oxford: Oxford University Press).

T. Batten (1967) (with the collaboration of Madge Batten) *The Non-directive Approach in Group and Community Work* (Oxford: Oxford University Press).

T. Batten (1970) (with the collaboration of Madge Batten) *The Human Factor in Youth Work* (Oxford: Oxford University Press).

S. Bradford (2011) 'Anomalous Identities, youth work amidst "trashy daydreams" and "monstrous nighmares" ' in R. Gilchrist, T. Hodgson, T. Jeffs, J. Spence, N. Stanton and J. Walker (eds) *Reflecting on the Past: Essays in the history of youth and community work* (Lyme Regis: Russell House Publishing).

M. Butterfield and J. Spence (2009) 'The transition from girls clubs to girls clubs and mixed clubs: UK Youth, 1934–1944' in R. Gilchrist, T. Jeffs, J. Spence, and J. Walker (eds) *Essays in the History of Youth and Community Work: Discovering the past* (Lyme Regis: Russell House Publishing).

S. Butters and S. Newell (1978) *Realities of Training: A review of the training of adults who volunteer to work with young people in the youth & community service* (Leicester: National Youth Bureau).

L. Button (1971) *Discovery and Experience: A new approach to training, group work, and teaching* (London: Oxford University Press).

L. Button (1974) *Developmental Group Work with Adolescents* (London: University of London Press).

V. Carpenter and K. Young (1986) *Coming in From the Margins: Youth work with girls and young women* (Leicester: NAYC).

CCCS (1975) 'Resistance through rituals', *Cultural Studies* 7/8 (University of Birmingham: Centre for Contemporary Cultural Studies).

B. Davies (1999) *From Voluntarism to Welfare State. A history of the youth service in England volume 1: 1939–1979* (Leicester: Youth Work Press).

B. Davies and A. Gibson (1967) *The Social Education of the Adolescent* (London: University of London Press).

DES (1967) *Immigrants and the Youth Service* (Hunt Report) (London: HMSO).

DES (1969) *Youth and Community Work in the 1970s* (Fairbairn Milson Report) (London: HMSO).

W. Eager (1953) *Making Men: Being a history of boys' clubs and related movements in Great Britain* (London: University of London Press).

B. Edwards and N Rogers (1978) *We are Family*, Recorded by Sister Sledge for Atlantic Records, Warner Music International.

P. Freire (1970) *Pedagogy of the Oppressed* (New York: Herder and Herder).

P. Freire (1972) *Cultural Action for Freedom* (Harmondsworth: Penguin).

G. Goetchius and M. Tash (1967) *Working with Unattached Youth: Problem, approach, method,* (London: Routledge and Kegan Paul).

R. Gosling (1961) *Lady Albemarle's Boys* (London: Fabian Society).

J. Hanmer (1964) *Girls at Leisure* (London: London Union of Youth Clubs/London YWCA).

HMSO (1975) *Adult Education: The challenge of change* (Alexander Report) (Edinburgh: HMSO).

B. Hudson (1984) 'Femininity and Adolescence' in A. McRobbie and M. Nava (eds) *Gender and Generation* (London: MacMillan).

T. Jeffs and M. Smith (1999) *Informal Education: Conversation, democracy and learning* (Ticknall: Education Now Publishing).

J. Klein (1956) *The Study of Groups* (London: Routledge and Kegan Paul).

J. Klein (1961) *Working with Groups: The social psychology of discussion and decision* (London: Hutchinson).

G. Lovell (2009) 'T.R. Batten's life and work' in R. Gilchrist, T. Hodgson, T. Jeffs, J. Spence, N. Stanton, and J. Walker (eds) *Reflecting on the Past: Essays in the history of youth and community work* (Lyme Regis: Russell House Publishing).

J. Macalister Brew (1957) *Youth and Youth Groups* (London: Faber and Faber).

M. Mayo (1977) *Women in the Community* (London: Routledge and Kegan Paul).

M. Mayo (1982) 'Community action programmes in the early eighties', *Critical Social Policy*, 1, 25–40.

A. McRobbie (1991) *Feminism and Youth Culture: From Jackie to just seventeen* (London: Macmillan).

A. McRobbie and J. Garber (1975) 'Girls and subcultures: An exploration', in CCCS (eds) 'resistance through rituals', *Cultural Studies* 7/8 (University of Birmingham: Centre for Contemporary Cultural Studies).

Ministry of Education (1960) *The Youth Service in England and Wales* (Albemarle Report) (London: HMSO).

~~S. Morgan and E. McArdle (2009)~~ 'Long walk from the door: A history of work with girls and young women in Northern Ireland from 1969', in R. Gilchrist, T. Hodgson, T. Jeffs, J. Spence, N. Stanton, and J. Walker (eds) *Reflecting on the Past: Essays in the history of youth and community work* (Lyme Regis: Russell House Publishing).

M. Nava (1982) ' "Everybody's views were just broadened" A girls project and some responses to Lesbianism', *Feminist Review*, 10, 37–60.

M. Nava (1984) 'Youth service provision, social order and the question of girls', in A. McRobbie and M. Nava (eds) *Gender and Generation* (London: MacMillan).

P. Parmar (1988) 'Gender, race and power: The challenge to youth work practice', in P. Cohen and H.S. Bains (eds) *Multi-Racist Britain* (Basingstoke, Macmillan).

J. Pearce (1996) 'Urban youth cultures: Gender and spatial forms', *Youth and Policy*, 52, 1–11.

S. Robertson (2009) 'Withywood youth club', in R. Gilchrist, T. Hodgson, T. Jeffs, J. Spence, N. Stanton and J. Walker (eds) *Reflecting on the Past: Essays in the history of youth and community work* (Lyme Regis: Russell House Publishing).

M. Sawbridge and J. Spence (1991) *The Dominance of the Male Agenda in Community and Youth Work* (Durham University).

M. Smith (1994) *Local Education: Community, conversation, praxis* (Buckingham: Open University Press).

N. Smith (1984) *Youth Service Provision for Girls and Young Women* (Leicester, NAYC).

SNYP (1979) *Annual Report of Southwick Neighbourhood Youth Project*, Sunderland.

J. Spence (1988) 'Youth work and gender' in T. Jeffs and M. Smith (eds) *Young People, Inequality and Youth Work* (Basingstoke, Macmillan).

J. Spence (1996) 'Feminism in work with girls and women', *Youth and Policy*, 52, 38–53.

J. Spence (2010) 'Collecting women's lives: The challenging of feminism in UK youth work in the 1970s and 1980s', *Women's History Review*, 19, 159–76.

M. Tash (1967) *Supervision in Youth Work* (London: London Council of Social Service).

T. Taylor (1984) 'Anti-sexist work with young males', *Youth and Policy*, 9, 8–16.

P. Willis (1977) *Learning to Labour* (Farnborough: Saxon House).

WWGN (1981–1987) *Working With Girls Newsletter*. Nos. 1–37 (Leicester: NAYC Girls' Work Unit).

Youth Council for Northern Ireland (1973) *Recreation and Youth Service (NI) Act* (Youth Council for Northern Ireland).

14
After School: The Disruptive Work of Informal Education

Richard Davies

Introduction

The relationship between school teaching and youth work has, in the United Kingdom at least, always been close. School teachers trained before 1988 are deemed to be 'professionally qualified', and in the past many part-time and volunteer youth workers were teachers during the day. School buildings offered physical sites for youth clubs by offering either flexible (dual use) spaces *or* distinctive 'youth wings' (see DES, 1969). For a range of political and occupational reasons this interrelationship waned in the later part of the 1980s and youth work became increasingly separated physically and philosophically from school teaching (Booton, 1980). For very different reasons the last decade has seen a rise again of youth work in schools, but this time delivered by professional workers with a distinctive background in 'youth work', and usually as junior partners in the school space. Such 'co-located working' has been seen in education, health and elsewhere in the UK public sector as a positive response to a range of difficulties from child abuse to the need to increase examination scores. In England[1] this has been articulated as 'teams around the child' and in the Every Child Matters legislation (HM Treasury, 2003). The core commitment to multi-professional working in this area has been recently reaffirmed by the coalition government's 'Positive for Youth' agenda (see DfE, 2012). In Scotland the 'Curriculum for excellence' provides a similar umbrella strategy for education, including schools and community learning for young people.[2] The literature on co-located/multi-agency working has seen it as uncomfortable for both youth workers and teachers (see, e.g., on multi-agency working Carlisle et al., 2006; Farrell et al., 2008; or on the values tensions for youth workers, see Jeffs and Banks, 2010).

This chapter is an exercise in practical philosophy. After qualifying as a Science teacher, I spent 20 years as a youth worker within the Church of England, a privileged position offering the opportunity for a range of partnerships with local primary and secondary schools. I worked both as a youth worker and, at times, as a part-time teacher in mainstream schools and pupil referral units for those removed from mainstream schooling. As an academic tutor and practice supervisor I have worked over the last decade or so with many students on placements in schools and their mentors. This chapter is shaped not so much by the specificities of those conversations, but the discourse(s) that emerge – discourses which reflect youth workers' and teachers' struggles to understand the place of youth work in schools. There are many ways in which this can be framed and this chapter seeks to understand those discourses framed by the *material* arrangements for contemporary co-located working, especially in the context of 'the school' and the relationships between teachers and youth workers. The school provides an interesting case study for this type of analysis and the restriction to two professional groups is an attempt to simplify the account given. While teachers and youth workers are both 'education professionals' with professional qualification frameworks in place, they have generally conceived of their tasks, and acted, differently. Whereas other professional groups in a school are primarily there to support young people's achievement of academic qualifications, youth work is co-located in the school because it is recognised that there are other educational needs to be met. The claim in this chapter is that for a number of reasons youth work *disrupts* the school in several ways, some explicitly recognised and others tacitly so. The school is, furthermore, an interesting case study of co-location, in that while a number of professional groups work within its geographic confines, it is marked spatially by its role in formal education, and predominantly managed by those progressing from teaching roles. Unlike children's centres and more multi-purpose community assets, which were often designed to support a number of professional groups and composed as 'neutral spaces', the school is stamped with formal education's conception of the world, people and what are deemed 'valuable activities'. The school is a place with different meanings to different groups, and it is this interface between 'materiality' and 'meaning', what social geographers have referred to as 'place', that is the focus of this chapter.

Specifically, I want to focus on three geographically rich aspects of the school. Firstly, teachers and youth workers construe differently the nature and function of the school's physical boundary. For teachers the boundary demarks the edge of their fruitful and meaningful activity, the primary purpose of which is to enable to students to be transported 'portal to portal' to college, another bounded, formal, educational institution. For youth workers the school is a context for enabling relationships with young people that transcend that boundary, and they focus on developing educational activities which enable the young people to have meaningful lives beyond the school gates. Secondly, the school is spacially segmented, primarily in terms of the formal curricula, with youth workers either marginalised in out-buildings, youth wings or using classroom space when not required for more 'legitimate' activities. Not only is the space segmented along formal educative lines, into classrooms and laboratories, but these spaces reflect the status and power of the academic disciplines themselves. Thirdly, and related to the above two points, school teachers tend to focus on the cognitive over the embodied nature of human existence (see Hirst, 1974; Hung and Stables, 2011). The body is to be disciplined into quiescence and the mind into activitism. Youth work on the other hand seeks a more holistic engagement of body[3] and mind. Much youth work begins with a view of young people as embodied with particular perspectives on the world, and particular approaches to agency within their world. Young people's cultural, physical, intellectual, social, spiritual locations are not only a given but are to be embraced in educative work with them.

In drawing these points together, I conclude that differing conceptions of the school's materiality generates tensions between different professional groups, especially school teachers and youth workers. What is at stake is not inter-professional rivalry, but the *disruption* that legitimate conceptualisations of youth work, expressed within the school-space, creates. The implications of this analysis are both a need to consider whether this disruption can be creatively accommodated within school-space and whether it is in either professional groups', or young people's interests.

Space and the 'sensemaking' of place

Before moving on to consider, and defend these particular aspects of the school, I need to develop a background to the relationship between the material aspects of the school and the ways in which individual professionals act. In particular, I give attention to three assumptions built into the structure of this chapter, that physical environments influence and inform agents actions within those environments, the same features influence agents in different ways and that meaning is attached to these features, in part, as a result of the particular professional formation.

The first assumption can be interpreted in two ways. Firstly, we might be making a relatively straightforward claim that the physical structure of our environment restricts what is possible, and suggests ways of acting. For example, in a 400-seat tiered lecture hall it is difficult to introduce group work activities; the straight rows, height differential between adjacent rows and the difficulty of turning around in the seats, all militate against such an activity. It is not that such activity is impossible, but teacher and students need to be committed to such an activity to 'get it off the ground'. Such a lecture hall is best seen as a 'theatre', where the lecturer lectures, interspersed by setting quick individual consolidation activities, asking and taking questions, and perhaps running a 'twitterfall'. The students think as individuals, perhaps with the odd comment or note to a neighbour. The physical setting does not completely dictate but places restrictions on what is possible.

On the other hand, secondly, we might mean that certain spaces generate in the mind of the agent, which limit their conceptions of what is possible. In the above example, the semiotics of ~~the lecture hall struc-~~ ture the agents' engagement in that space, encouraging students to simply hear and write notes and tutors to *perform* their notes. Thus, giving rise to the common 'definition' of a lecture as 'the process by which the tutor's notes become the student's notes without necessarily going through the brain of either'. This limitation on thought and action reflects the concerns of many of the post-hegelians of both the left and right (e.g., Dewey, 1938; Freire, 2007). For them, our language and our 'perception of the possible' limit what in fact becomes possible, and it is the overcoming of these limitations that forms the core function of education. What is not sufficiently reflected in these accounts is the role of the physical environment (as opposed to oppressive relationships as in the case of Freire). Nevertheless, Weick (1995) as a social psychologist draws attention to the process of 'sensemaking' in organisations. In what follows I shall seek to outline Weick's account, yet without offering a defence, since this is beyond the remit of this chapter. Weick seeks both to draw together a plethora of previous research in the field and present a coherent account of 'sensemaking' as a critical aspect of agents' activities within organisations; the brevity of my review necessarily macerates the coherence of Weick's own account.

Weick claims that there are seven, interrelated properties of 'sensemaking'; these are:

- Grounded in identity construction
- Retrospective
- Enactive of sensible environments
- Social
- Ongoing
- Focused on and by extracted cues
- Driven by plausibility rather than accuracy

(see Weick, 1995, p 17)

These seven properties are chosen, he claims, because they are

> mentioned often in the literature on sensemaking; they have practical implications, ... each is a self-contained set of research questions which relate to the other six; each incorporates action and context; ... all seven can be represented crudely as a sequence.

(ibid., pp.17–18)

For Weick there are two 'shaping' aspects to sensemaking. Firstly, the process of sensemaking is *identity forming*. As I engage with my environment I am (slowly) transformed and 'become'. Secondly, the sense that is made, and the actions that result, shape the environment for the future:

> They act, and in doing so create the materials that become the constraints and opportunities they face. (ibid., p.31)

The kinds of sensemaking that Weick has in mind are 'in the moment', rather than the result of reflective practices. As such individuals depend on schema, the faster the need to make sense of the environment the more we depend on such schema. Mental schemas seek to routinise day-to-day life in order to give me time to act. As such individual agents tend to show a concern with values, 'clarity on values clarifies what is important in the elapsed experience' (ibid., p.28), and read 'past indeterminacy [in ways] that favours order and oversimplification...' (ibid., p.29).

Experiences are perceived as instances of general types stripped of their complexity. Weick draws attention to 'framing and cueing'. Quoting William James, he claims:

> [There are]...two great point of reasoning...first, an extracted character [cue] is taken as equivalent to the entire datum from which it comes...[second] thus taken suggests a certain consequence more obviously than it was suggested by the total datum as it originally came.
> (ibid., p.50)

Thus, in day-to-day activities individual agents tend to operate on the basis of mental schemas that draw on a codified, and hence simplified, repository of previous experiences. These schemas are sensitive to particular cues from the environment which tend to direct the agents' actions. In acting, the agents both create, in part, the environment for their further sensemaking and actions, and have their identity modified.

I have, however briefly, summarised Weick's basic position in relation to agents and their meaning making relationship to the environment. Weick notes that this process is a social not simply an individual process. For my purposes, however, I need to go further and make some plausible argument that professional formation[4] and membership of a particular professional group is significant. That is that members of that professional group are more likely to make similar meanings from similar situations. Given the shaping of identity within particular environment, Weick's claim is clearly that one's regular practices transform who one is; one is not only a teacher or youth work but overtime becomes one shaped by the routine activity of 'teaching' or 'youth work'. There would seem to be two versions of the argument. There is a strong version, claiming that our discourses and mental states are shaped by our professional formation and experience, and a weaker version, that those discourses shape connotations of key concepts. The weaker version will suffice, though my anecdotal sense is that these professional ways of seeing the world are more deeply embedded.

From Wittgenstein one might make a general claim that in order to be intelligible to each other we need, at the most general level, to share a common language and 'form of life'. If we both speak English then I can make sense of your claims about unicorns and voices in the wall (though only by designating you as mentally unwell if you think these are 'real'), however, I cannot understand what it is like to be a bat, even if that bat were rational and communicative (see Nagel, 1979). The issue is not simply that bats do not speak English, but that the form of life of a bat is so completely different from the distinctively human form of life that we would be unintelligible to each other. Nagel writes:

> It is often possible to take up a point of view other than one's own, so the comprehension of such facts is not limited to one's own case. There is a sense in which phenomenological facts are perfectly objective: one person can know or say of another what the quality of the other's experience is. They are subjective, however, in the sense that even this objective ascription of experience is possible only for someone sufficiently similar to the object of ascription to be able to adopt his point of view – to understand the ascription in the first person as well as in the third, so to speak. **The more different from oneself the other experiencer is, the less success one can expect with this enterprise**.
>
> (Nagel, 1979, pp.325–6, emphasis added)

Hacker (2002) critiques Nagel's general position in relation to consciousness per se, arguing against any coherent account of 'qualia', and stating that there is no phenomenological aspect of an experience as such, but the attitude of the one who experiences. He writes '[t]he experiences differ in so far as their objects differ' (Hacker, 2002). I need, however, something significantly less than a general defence of 'qualia'. Hacker's account would accept that one can be said to have an experience of X such that one *sees* X in a particular way. What I need is that *similarity* in terms of one's socio-cultural and linguistic viewpoint is indicative of the way one sees a particular object. This is a legitimate claim, both on Nagel's account and (I think) on Hacker's account.

One can read this not in terms of mental states as such, but of discourse and this may well be the most fruitful. For Foucault (1972, p.49), discourses '... systematically form of the objects of which we speak'. Thus in different discourses the same concept acquires different connotations. So it is possible to engage in two related discourses about the physical structures of the school and yet use words whose secondary meanings are different. This weakest form of the argument holds that professional formation is in part about achieving fluidity in profession-specific discourses, and these discourses shape ones views. The stronger form of the argument, based on Nagel, is that these discourses and professional practices shape not only language but mental states; one sees the world in particular profession-specific ways.

The question arises as to why professional formation is highlighted as opposed to ethnicity or faith, both of which may be, and probably are, significant in terms of closeness of 'point of view'. This is, of course, irresolvable at the philosophical level; the best that one can do is note that different sets of beliefs and practices provide overlapping influences on individuals. Teaching, one's subject discipline, faith position, and so on all provide potentially significant influences on what one experiences in relation to external objects. MacIntyre notes, however, the tendency for individuals to 'compartmentalize' their meaning making depending on the environment within which they are working (see MacIntyre, 2006, pp.196ff). Within a school context both teachers and youth workers will, if MacIntyre is correct about the psychology, tend 'unconsciously' to prioritise professional ways of making sense of the world. This is reinforced by teachers' own talk of 'acting like a teacher in school'.

The social geography of the school

There is a strange 'artificialness' in the modern school, constructed to reflect a single set of activities, and structured to enable 'inmates' to remain inside all day. In this it shares similarities with other totalising institutions such as prisons and military camps. There may of course be any number of other similarities, as Foucault (1975) noted in passing. My claim here is not that such similarities mean that schools are prisons or military camps, in the same way that prison cells and swimming pools having walls does not make them similar. It is rather the meaning we ascribe to these features which is important and the fact that the institution disciplines and controls (see Fielding, 2000; Collins and Coleman, 2008[5]). My concern here is with three features of the school, two are clearly physical: the boundary and the segmentation of the school, and the third more relational, the conception of the person (though I want to claim a conception which is emerges in a particular place). There may be, of course, other geographically rich concepts which could have been deployed, for example differing conceptions of space and time (see for example, Massey, 2005; Davies, 2012a). However, I think it a plausible that these three concepts, boundaries, segmentation and embodiment, are of particular importance.

Recent years have seen an increasing formalisation of the border around the school, both in terms of physical and metaphorical boundaries. Physically, the border dominates the landscape of many schools, and dictates the movement of 'inmates' and visitors alike, especially the restriction of movement via crossing points. Let me illustrate[6] the points by considering two schools in the East Midlands. The first has a trinity of fences around the school buildings. The first, a 2 metre high metal fence is topped with hoops and rounded tips, it surrounds the main school grounds, including the playing field; inside this a second fence, 3 metres high, metal and spiked, surrounds the school buildings, a narrow concrete path around the school and the teachers' car park. A third fence protects the teachers' car park. There is only one entrance through the second fence. The second example is a school with a 3½ metre high metal fence with a spiked top which surrounds the entire school grounds. The main building has only two entrances, one enables access to the playing field (which is inside the fence), and the other is the only access to 'the outside'. In both examples, the entrance is staffed and passage is only possible (for staff, students, and visitors) by a request to office staff situated behind a toughened glass window.

It might be argued that this structure of fences are a response to the increasing violence seen in and around schools, and perhaps if these schools were prone to being sites of violence this might explain the fences, but they are not. The first enjoys a suburban location, and student body to match. There may of course be the fear of violence, that is its phobic manifestation, but the fencing is not a proportionate response to the actual level of threat. The second is located in a small village, and had seen no significant increases of violence from when it was relocated from other, less imposing premises, some three years ago. The physical boundary, however, reflects other meanings; the boundary as 'border' sets the school apart from its surroundings. By this I mean that a boundary simply marks the extent of something, and perhaps offers some restrictions on the ability of individuals to 'step over' the boundary. As Jones (2009) points out we should see the boundary not as a thing in itself, but as concerned with what it bounds. A border differentiates one area from another that is significantly different. The archetypical border is between two distinct countries in which, although there are continuities, we recognise that the legal-political context is radically disrupted at, and by, the border itself.

The second feature of the school is its internal segmentation. There are clear differences in the ways that primary/elementary schools and secondary/high schools are segmented. My concern in this chapter is with youth work, and, at least in the United Kingdom, this means a focus on the Secondary/High School. I will describe my local secondary school as an example of the emerging architecture of the school. Clarke School was completely re-built some three years ago as part of a significant state investment in school buildings. There is one 'air-lock' entrance requiring admission by reception staff. One enters a large vaulted, glass domed space, three stories high with trees and other flora. It is used as a dining hall at lunch time, but is a 'transition space' during the rest of the day. To the north and east of this vaulted hall run corridors at two levels each dedicated to a particular curricula area, which include classrooms, teacher resource areas and curriculum specific staff rooms. To the south-east lie the library, private study spaces for students, and the main staff room. The academic corridors and library are jointed together by a range of open staircase and balconies. The sports hall and youth wing are to west and are entered by a small single door. During the school day the vaulted hall is the only way to move from one academic area to another; a journey undertaken by students, but rarely, because they remain in their subject area *(in both senses of the term)*, by teaching staff.

I want to draw attention to two aspects of this use of space. The first is the primary segmentation into academic subject areas (in both sense of the word), and the second is the clear separation of the academic subject areas from sports and youth work. Given that I usually see the school from the perspective of the youth wing, it is a particular view, and different from teachers within the school. It is not just the segmentation of space, but the location from which such space is perceived.

Finally, I now want to consider the influence of different 'framing of persons'. Hirst (1974) retains a significant influence on teachers' thinking and practice. For Hirst, education is based 'on the nature of knowledge itself' and his central concern was with the 'activity of the mind' (Hirst, 1974, p.30). Thus, teachers, while thinking as teachers, tend to see young people through a lens of 'the cognitive'. Further, given that we make others intelligible in the same way that I make myself intelligible, teachers see themselves through a cognitive lens, and the focus in the classroom on cognitive engagement. It is here that their status and power lies. This differs from youth work perspective which focuses on the embodied person, not just the cognitive. This focus on the cognitive not only characterises typical schooling practice, but foregrounds a particular conception of the developmental process of education. Youth workers foreground other conceptions.

At the heart of the youth work project are two critical themes. The first is that individual young people come together for a range of purposes which relate to their personal, social, emotional and spiritual development. In fact this list is itself a changing feast, both temporally and interculturally. What is at stake are core beliefs about what it means to be a 'human person'. This is spelt out in different ways in different comprehensive doctrines and the institutions that sustain them, for example, in secular youth work, humanist youth work, Christian youth work, Muslim youth work (see Davies, 2013a). The second theme is that education is concerned with living life well in general, not with a specific aspect of life. These points obviously link in that differing comprehensive doctrines articulate different (or no) *telos* for human persons (that is what is entailed by living life well). Education is not, on this reading of youth work, a good in itself, but only an instrumental good in relation to its ability to improve the ability of young people to live the good life (see Davies, 2003, 2013b).

Making sense of the school

Legitimate informal education disrupts. It does so in a number of ways, not least in the ways teachers and youth workers conceptualise the space they co-inhabit. The argument so far can be summarised as follows. Firstly, I have argued that one's professional identity significantly influences the meanings one attaches to the geography of one's workplace. Secondly, that school boundaries, segmentation and different conceptions of persons are salient in understanding the actions of schoolteachers and youth workers. I have given some account of the kinds of differences that in practice do occur, but there is little empirical research on this matter, rather a general professional unease, within youth work especially, of the relationship between school teaching and youth work. This is often seen as resulting from their differencing 'philosophy of education' or ideological conceptions of social justice. Yet my own experience of both teachers and youth workers is that they rarely have such a well developed account of their philosophy of education. At best they have some sense of core values and principles gleaned from their initial training, a process which inducted them into their future profession.

A response, from a UK perspective, to the argument so far might well take the form that of course schools are concerned primarily with formal education and its outcomes. Historically, this is so and it reflected in the very geography of the school. The school has been seen differently in other countries and educational systems, and at times there have been inklings of change in the United Kingdom (I think of the Community Colleges movement in the late 1970s). Recent government policy, since 1997, has once again placed the school at the centre of a range of community activities and as such brought into question the ubiquitous impact of schooling on the space provided by school buildings.

This shift in relation to young people has been premised on three reasons. The first is that schools provide a site for the broad education of young people and that this is significant not only for the young people, but for schooling itself. The second related reason is that other educators and welfare providers can contribute to an improvement in formal educational outcomes, especially for those deemed at risk of failure. So youth workers can be drafted in to support students as a whole and those at risk of becoming NEET (not in educational, employment or training) in particular. The third is a social need to provide 'wrap around care' on the school site, including breakfast, lunchtime and after school clubs as well as activities during the school holidays. The growing recognition is that schooling is not the only activity of the school, even in relation to formal educational outcomes. Youth workers (among other professionals) and youth work have become integral to the activity of them school (I have given a more theoretical account of this in Davies, 2003).

Given this shift, the question emerges as to whether, and in what ways, the geography of the school needs to be changed in order to reduce the negative effects of disruption, improve partnership working between teachers and youth workers and, consequently, enhance the broader educational experience of young people. I want to conclude by offering two practical responses to the analysis presented: the need for professionals to problematise the 'givenness' of their physical work environment, and emerging from this, the possibility of re-imagining that physical structure.

The school's boundaries, segmentation and the implicit conceptions of young people that underpin their task need to be foregrounded and excavated. The tension that I have articulated in different views of the boundary is not easily resolvable, for example Kumar's (1997) discussion of higher education makes much of the need for students to withdraw from the world and hence for a strong boundary between the educational institution and the outside world. Bauman (1997), in the same volume, is less convinced (see Davies, 2012b for a discussion). The question here is not how to resolve the issue, as there may be good reasons for different professionals holding their views, but understanding the difference. The same may be said of the internal segmentation of the school, as reflective of the activity of one professional group and obstructive to another. Foregrounding these conceptions allows for debate to occur, and differences understood. More fruitfully it enables different professional groups to learn from each other and perhaps see new possibilities. It is plausible that what emerges are new ways of physically structuring the school as a space for effective multi-professional activity and offer a more holistic and complete educational experience for all young people. This is a move beyond a policy of *simply co-locating* teachers and youth workers because both professions add something to young people's education. It is a move from different professionals *using* the same space, towards the co-creation of a shared space which transforms the educational experience of young people. In England, at least, the trajectory of educational policy seems to be undermining such a move. The advantage of devolution is that the futures of Scottish, and to some extent Welsh, schools seem more optimistic.

Notes

1. Youth work is a devolved aspect of government activity since 1998. It has been managed differently in the four jurisdictions of the United Kingdom, and is increasing divergent.
2. By this I mean 'youth work', though the term is not used in Scotland where Community Development and Community Learning have retained a power no longer evident in England.
3. I do not here imply that 'holistic' is necessarily good.
4. It is worth noting that by 'professional formation' I mean more than professionals-in-training ought to have supervised practice in an appropriate institution (e.g., a

school) as it has become to be seen in government policy (for example in relation to the development of the QTLS, see Institute for Learning, 2008)). Formation entails the changing of personal dispositions and common frameworks for perceiving and judging work-related activities.

5. I am not convinced, pace Fielding, and Collins and Coleman, that the focus ought to be the power of adults, but rather the power of the institution and its impact on *all* those within.

6. I emphasise that the use of examples is merely to illustrate the argument rather than to provide empirical support for the claims made.

References

Z. Bauman (1997) 'Universities: Old, new and different', in A. Smith and F. Webster (eds) *The Postmodern University? Contested visions of higher education in society* (Buckingham: Society for Research into Higher Education and Open University Press).

F. Booton (1980) 'Deschooling the youth service', in F. Booton and A. Dearling (eds) *The 1980's and Beyond* (Leicester: National Youth Bureau).

K. Carlisle, T. Gallagher, R. Kilpatrick and H. Daniels (2006) *Competition or Collaboration? A critique of multi agency working in Northern Ireland to meet the needs of young people at risk of exclusion from mainstream schooling*, paper presented at the British Association for International and Comparative Education Conference (Leeds, Education-line).

D. Collins and T. Coleman (2008) 'Social geographies of education: Looking within, and beyond, school boundaries', *Geography Compass*, 2, 281–99.

R. Davies (2003) *Education, Virtues and the Good life: The ability of schools to inform and motivate students' moral behavior* (Unpublished doctoral dissertation). Oxford University, Oxford.

R. Davies (2012a) 'Places to go, things to do and people to see: Space and activity in English youth work policy', in P. Kraftl, J. Horton and F. Tucker (eds) *Critical Geographies of Childhood and Youth: Contemporary policy and practice* (Bristol: Policy Press).

R. Davies (2012b) 'Liquefied or blended: A university for the 21st century', *The Gateway Papers*, 2, 1–8.

R. Davies (2013a) 'Youth work, 'protest' and a common language: Towards a framework for reasoned debate', *Youth and Policy*, 110, 52–65.

R. Davies (2013b) 'After Higgins and Dunne: Imagining school teaching as a multi-practice activity', *Journal of Philosophy of Education*, 47, 475–490.

DES (1969) *Youth and Community Work in the 70s. Proposals by the youth service development council* (The 'Fairbairn-Milson Report') (London: HMSO).

J. Dewey (1938) *Experience and Education* (New York: Kappa Delta Pi).

DfE (2012) *Positive for Youth: A new approach to cross-government policy for young people aged 13 to 19* (London: TSO).

P. Farrell, K. Kerr and N. Mearns (2008) ' "Swing, swing together": Multi-agency work in the new children's services', in C. Chapman and H. Gunter (eds) *Radical Reforms: Perspectives on an era of educational change* (London: Routledge).

S. Fielding (2000) 'Walk on the left: Children's geographies and the primary school', in S. L. Holloway and G. Valentine (eds) *Children's Geographies: Playing, living, learning* (London: Routledge).

M. Foucault (1972) *The Archaeology of Knowledge and Discourse on Language* (New York: Pantheon).

M. Foucault (1975) *Discipline and Punish: The birth of the prison* (New York: Random House).

P. Freire (2007) *Pedagogy of the Oppressed* (New York: Continuum).

P. M. S. Hacker (2002) 'Is there anything it is like to be a bat?' *Philosophy*, 77, 157–74.

P. Hirst (1974) 'Liberal education and the nature of knowledge', in *Knowledge and the Curriculum* (London: Routledge and Kegan Paul).

HM Treasury (2003) *Every Child Matters Green Paper* (London: TSO).

R. Hung and A. Stables (2011) 'Lost in space? Located in place: Geo-phenomenological exploration and school', *Educational Philosophy and Theory*, 43, 193–203.

Institute for Learning (2008) *Professional Formation* (London: IfL).

T. Jeffs, and S. Banks (2010) 'Youth workers as controllers', in S. Banks (ed.) *Ethical Issues in Youth Work* (2nd ed) (London: Routledge).

R. Jones (2009) 'Categories, borders, and boundaries', *Progress in Human Geography*, 33, 174–89.

K. Kumar (1997) 'The need for place', in A. Smith and F. Webster (eds) *The Postmodern University? Contested visions of higher education in society* (Buckingham: Society for Research into Higher Education and Open University Press).

A. MacIntyre (2006) 'Social structures and their threats to moral agency', in *Ethics and Politics: Selected essays vol. 2* (Cambridge: Cambridge University Press).

D. Massey (2005) *For Space* (London: Sage).

T. Nagel (1979) 'What is it like to be a bat?' in *Mortal Questions* (Cambridge: Cambridge University Press).

K. Weick (1995) *Sensemaking in Organisations* (Thousand Oaks, CA: Sage).

Part IV
Youth-Led Spaces

15
Catalysing Cultural Change: Youth-led Cultural Development as Informal Education

Shanene Ditton

Introduction

There is a growing body of literature critiquing the capacity of formal education systems to support the construction of young cultural leaders. Notably, studies in geography have shown that informal learning can equip young people to articulate and construct their own sense of cultural identity (e.g., Skelton and Valentine, 1998; Holloway and Valentine, 2000). Sociologists, educationalists, cultural theorists and other youth researchers have examined the cultural dimensions of informal education and the importance of devices such as 'play' (Miles et al., 2002; Baker, 2007; Bloustien and Peters, 2011). Much of this analysis chalks up informal arts and creative learning spaces as alternatives to mainstream schooling, arguing for recognition of other informal modes of development outside the heavily predicated educational sphere. Advocating for a youth-directed approach, recent work has focused on youth-centric modes of informal learning (Rodo-de-Zarate and Baylina, Chapter 16, this volume). This chapter's argument sits squarely within cultural geographies of informal education, as it seeks to bridge issues of cultural politics and identities, which are inextricably connected to complex geographies. Building on the existing literature, the aim of this chapter is to theoretically frame youth-led cultural development and to explore the potential of this informal learning to catalyse cultural change.

Cultural identities, dialogics and youth-led cultural development

Bennett (2010) states that the study of culture is of integral importance to youth studies. Insisting on the significance of culture as requalified by the 'cultural turn of the early 1990s', Bennett maintains that studying the cultural dimensions of young people's lives can help us to understand how youth as 'social actors play an active role in shaping their sociocultural environments' (2010, p.28). Following this thread, White and Wyn note that 'it is almost impossible to understand the decisions made by young people and the actions they take without understanding how they see themselves' (2004, p.185). Adding pragmatic weight to this argument, Miles et al. state that

> young people perceive youth cultural contexts they are involved in as the most important aspects of their everyday lives. Young people's lifestyles represent an important way of establishing their own social spaces and a sense of belonging. (2002, p.17)

Miles et al. in their engaging book *Communities of Youth – Cultural Practice and Informal Learning* present a convincing case for youth-led performing arts as vehicles of informal learning. In their book, Miles et al. (2002) present three case studies of a comparative European Union study that shows how previously marginalised youth were able to gain valuable informal skills, such as self-confidence, motivation and biographicity, in order to construct empowered cultural identities. According to Jensen and Arnett, 'forming a cultural identity involves making choices about the cultures with which one identifies' (2012, p.474). Youth-led cultural development, then, is a vital part of young people's lives as they develop a sense of cultural identity.

Drawing from UNESCO's definition of cultural development from the *Our Creative Diversity* paper (WCCD, 1996), and in line with Gibson's (2001) definition, we can come to understand cultural development to have two functions here: firstly to facilitate cultural diversity and enable youth to articulate their own cultural identities; and secondly, to 'promote cross-sectoral partnerships as tools for the encouragement of sustainable cultural activity' (Gibson, 2001, p.122). Youth-led cultural development is therefore understood in this context as cultural development activity run by youth for youth. The ways in which youth-led cultural development has been conceptualised are varied and include such ideas as 'play'.

Bloustien and Peters (2011) acknowledge the 'seriousness of play' in their research on Australian marginalised youth (p.44), with play being crucial to young people's development and identity construction:

> ... [a]ll aspects of play and fantasy constituted their self-making ... These were the essential ingredients in reflexivity, experimentation and risk-taking as they explored the boundaries of their gendered class and ethnically based sense of personhood through their musical practices. (2011, p.44)

By drawing on various playful sensibilities, youth are able to negotiate complex projects of self, using music, art, writing and other cultural practices.

In line with this idea of play, Baker's work (2007) on young people and community radio explores how alternative learning spaces enable young people to creatively construct their own cultural identities through music. Baker notes that

> Guerrilla Radio enabled young people to locate themselves more fully in the social and cultural fabric of the City of Playford and neighboring Council areas. It served as a means for Northern Region youth jointly to recognize their strengths and needs and to develop their own sense of creativity and cultural meaning. (2007)

Baker notes how this kind of alternative learning functioned as a space for inclusive dialogue as it enabled primarily marginalised young people to express themselves in a safe, encouraging environment, placing themselves 'within dominant societal discourses... from which they had previously felt disenfranchised and disconnected' (2007). As a kind of informal learning and cultural development, this example of community radio could be seen as the articulation of a 'cultural voice' as it enabled marginalised youth to resist their oppression in alternative spaces.

Singh points to Paulo Freire's concept of the 'cultural voice' (Friere, 1972) as a kind of 'process of conscious-awakening' (Singh, 2007, p.38) in response to oppressive and disempowering representations. In his seminal work *The Pedagogy of the Oppressed*, Freire champions a way in which people might articulate agency in the construction of their identity. Freire (1972) argues that the cultural voice is catalysed when people 'perceive the reality of their oppression not as closed world from which there is no exit, but as a limiting situation they can transform' (1972, pp.25–6). Although Friere uses the term 'cultural voice' in a specific developing world context, Singh argues (2010, p.13), as I do, that the term can indeed be extended to include other developed social environments.

Friere notes that, 'it is only when the oppressed find the oppressor out and become involved in the organised struggle for their liberation that they begin to believe in themselves' (1972, p.40). Discussing dialogic theory as a way of navigating the delicate relationship between teacher and student, Friere states:

> A revolutionary leadership must accordingly practice co-intentional education. Teachers and students (leadership and people), co-intent on reality, are both Subjects, not only in the task of unveiling that reality, and thereby coming to know it critically, but in the task of re-creating that knowledge. (1972, p.44)

So according to Friere, for youth to engage in serious cultural development, dialogic action needs to occur. In the remainder of this chapter, I will present an analysis of youth led cultural development as informal education on Australia's Gold Coast.

Methods

This research was conducted using mixed methods: large focus groups with up to 40 participants, small focus groups with up to six participants, one-on-one interviews with young people (aged 21–5) and adults who work with youth. Throughout this remainder of this chapter, Gold Coast youth narratives will be deconstructed alongside theoretical analysis and empirical research on youth-led cultural development. This will be grounded using practical examples of the Gold Coast Youth Committee with youth aged 12–25 (2003–05) alongside current youth-led cultural initiatives.

Young people and the commodified city

Australia's Gold Coast is a commodified city, a packaged destination sold to the world. Propelled by place competition in the context of globalisation, the Gold Coast has adopted homogenous urban branding and place promotion strategies that inevitably shape its cultural identity. This strong branding and place identity frames the Gold Coast as primarily a hedonistic leisure destination, and this image is perpetuated in national and international discourses, impacting negatively on young people's cultural identities.

Gold Coast youth are culturally stigmatised, framed as being creatively deficient. This negative branding is constructed through hyperbolic narratives, policies and media discourses that depict youth as empty vessels to be filled, rather than agents of cultural change. Youth on the Gold Coast are described as deviant, violent, lacking creative agency and largely problematic for society. These narratives feed into the Gold Coast's broader identity as the nation's coastal playground and cultural wasteland. But in between the cheap headlines many Gold Coast young people are actually engaged in youth-led cultural change, working tirelessly to break away from the yolk of their stereotype. Until recent times, their plight has been largely occluded by the commodification of the city.

The Surfers Paradise imagination

As you drive the M1 Pacific Highway south from Brisbane to the Gold Coast, there is a large reflective green road sign marked 'Surfers Paradise' fastened onto the Hope Island Road overpass. Visitors might be mistaken, due to the lack of clues otherwise, to think that Surfers Paradise is the main part of the Gold Coast, or worse, that it's the whole thing. Tourists will recognise this beacon immediately as the address to their luxury beachfront accommodation (though it's not all luxury), and most likely they will know of Surfers before they hear its city's name.

Surfers Paradise, affectionately known by locals as 'Surface Parasites', is the tourist glitter strip, extending an invitation to play 24/7 with its well-oiled beaches and strip clubs. In glossy magazines, tourists will have seen the sparkling beaches, sand lined with high-rises; they'll have read the crime stats in the paper. They'll have paid in advance for surfing lessons and a 'world pass' to the theme parks. They'll have consumed the Gold Coast before they even arrive. Such is the way it is designed: the Gold Coast reproduces itself.

The Gold Coast is the sixth largest city in Australia with half a million people peppered along 57 kilometres of coastline in South-East Queensland. To the south lies the border of New South Wales, and to the north sits the Gold Coast's big sister city, Brisbane, which is an hour away by car. With a population of over 500,000 residents, the Gold Coast boasts a modest size by any small city standards, but it is in fact a city that is not a city at all. The Gold Coast doesn't feel like a city and in fact most people don't believe it is a city. People don't live *in* the Gold Coast: they live *on* it. This is indicative of the Gold Coast's transient nature and it's branding in tourism and development as a space of leisure and mass consumption.

'Famous for fun' (Tourism Queensland, 2012), the Gold Coast has consistently drawn the holiday card with its 'sun and surf' and natural assets (Stimson and Minnery, 1998, p.194). From its colonial genesis as a timber-felling region in the 1840s, through to its twenty-first century guise as a cosmopolitan 'tourist mecca', the Gold Coast has sold itself as a leisure destination (Stimson and Minnery, 1998, p.194; see Figure 15.1). 'Contributing almost one dollar in every five generated within the city', tourism continues to drive the economy (GCCC, 2013). Iconic images of bathing-capped youth splashing in the sea with bikini-clad ladies are etched into the nation's psyche. These cheeky, sexualised, utopic depictions continue to lure an annual crowd of about 10 million people to the city (GCCC, 2013).

These representations construct the Gold Coast as the quintessential ephemeral city, a place that continually forgets its own history. Much like New York in the early days, the Gold Coast has always had a love affair with 'new beginnings' instead of 'origins', with homogenous mass culture, instead of authenticity (see Zukin, 2010). Wise notes, 'perpetually replacing itself, the Gold Coast seems to ignore history, to play out its (by now) clichéd role as a paradigmatically postmodern city, dipping into multiple "semblences" taken from other cities to produce its next version of itself' (2012, p.101). This perpetual development and transience paints locals as pseudo-residents, as people who are continually on holiday. Tanya, a young graphic designer talks about the impermanence of the city: 'The thing that frustrates me most [...] is that everything that we have – like, in our lifetimes, that

Figure 15.1 'Miami'
Source: Dean Oakley.

has been iconic on the Gold Coast – keep[s] getting bulldozed' (20 October 2010).

As well as being conceptually difficult to pin down, the Gold Coast is geographically everted. It's is an 'exopolis', to borrow Edward Soja's (1996) term; it's an 'inside out' heterogeneous city where multiple narratives play out: it's decentred and missing the traditional 'downtown' or city hub, and lacking the concentric, centre-focused, formations of more traditional cities. Because there is no city centre and no comprehensive online hub for the city, access to local cultural information and resources is challenging. Although such resources and opportunities do exist, they are largely invisible. Ken, who is a young theatre maker, conveys his frustration with the lack of connectivity between artists and community, and the difficulties faced trying to access cultural information on the Gold Coast:

> I've always found it really hard to find out about all these little [...] the unfortunate thing is, for some reason, and I don't know if it's my fault, or what but [...] But I don't seem to find out about [an event] until after it's been on or the night of. [...] Like, so there seems to be all these little underground groups doing this really cool great young fresh stuff, but fuck me if I can ever hear about it. And I don't hear about it.
>
> (Ken, 24 May 2011)

Ken expresses sentiments that many of the participants in my study echo. His dissatisfaction with current communication processes is reflected in terms of his own personal disappointment with his ability to network and communicate effectively:

And I don't know if that means I'm not looking in the right places or talking to the right sort of people, but I think that's probably maybe something that a lot of us from north to south on the coast, we're all letting ourselves down is that we're not touching bases with all these little pockets of people that are kind of interested in the same sorts of things. And how do we make those connections? Because we all seem so distant [. . .] but we're fighting for the same kind of thing.

(Ken, 24 May 2011)

Ken's problems are echoed by many of the participants in this study, and they reflect the geographical challenges mentioned above. But they are also reproduced through the Gold Coast's narratives. The fact remains that the voices of young people on the Gold Coast are rarely magnified.

In media and policy young people are promoted as deviant, and this is driven by larger narratives of the Gold Coast as harbouring a deadly underbelly of crime. Hailed as the 'Crime Capital of Australia' by national media (Smail, 2011), the Gold Coast's underbelly is embellished in local and international imaginations, smeared with scandal and sleaze. Despite not actually living up to this title, the Gold Coast loves to pretend it's tougher than its big sisters Sydney or Melbourne. The maintenance of the Gold Coast's hedonistic, criminal and leisure identities propels a discourse of youth as problematic for society.

Gold Coast youth as a problem

Baker, Bennett and Wise note that 'all around the Gold Coast the notion of youth as "problem" looms large' (2012, p.17). This framing of youth as a problem is not new in youth studies, dating back to the post-Second World War era (Skelton and Valentine, 1998, p.10). Henderson et al. (2007) note that 'youth violence and crime occupies a large space in the public imagination and policy agenda'. In their comprehensive biographical study of youth transitions, Henderson et al. suggest that 'in the United Kingdom, the perception is that youth delinquency levels are rising and that the morals of young people are in some way eroding' (2007, p.59). Gill Jones notes that 'Even when young people are just "hanging about" and doing very little, the rest of "society" seems to come down on them like a ton of bricks' (Jones, 2009, p.31). In the case of the Gold Coast, 'moral panics' (Cohen, 2002) about youth are constructed primarily through narratives of place, which feed into and are shaped significantly by signature local youth events such as 'Schoolies'.

Baker et al. acknowledge the 'stereotype of youth' as inextricably linked to 'Schoolies Week', where displays of violence and substance abuse are prevalent among school leavers during their final year vacation (Baker et al., 2012, p.17). For two weeks of each year, graduated students flock to the touristic heart of the Gold Coast, which inevitably morphs into a chemical playground. During Schoolies Week, Surfers Paradise is less known for its surf, and more for its inebriated youth and wild nightlife. This discourse paints Gold Coast youth as deviant and tarnishes their image with violence, sleaze and excessive chemical abuse, even though many Gold Coast youth do not engage with Schoolies or the idea of it. Rather, Schoolies attracts a certain type of demographic *to* the Gold Coast.

In contradistinction to these media discourses, research has shown that Gold Coast youth reject their stereotype. According to Lloyd, Harrington, Hibbins, Boag and Cuthill (2005) Gold Coast youth live structured existences similar in many ways to other Australian youth. Lloyd et al.'s study concluded that 'despite the images perpetuated by the media and tourism operators, life on the Gold Coast does not, for young people, live up to its mythical status' (Lloyd et al., 2005, pp.25–6). In the following, I argue that in line with this finding, young people's cultural identities are also inconsistent with their representation as culturally deficient. I will present a case study of one Gold Coast youth-led cultural development initiative that enabled young people to construct their cultural identities and articulate their cultural voice.

WAVE: GC speak up!

In 2001, the Australian Government in partnership with the Dusseldorp Skills Forum, acknowledged the need for more processes to support young people (Kellock, 2005). The Gold Coast was federally funded for a period of three years to produce one of six Youth Commitments in regional Australia from 2003–05 (Kellock, 2005). Although the Gold Coast already had a functioning Junior Council, which groomed high achievers for leadership, the Youth Commitment was set up to support a broader range of young people's needs in a coordinated way. Matthews and Limb (2003) acknowledge the limits of youth councils in the UK context, calling for more imaginative participatory means for young people outside 'adult political structures' (p.190). In the case of the Gold Coast, the Youth Commitment and subsequent Youth Committee enabled creative opportunities for young people to articulate their cultural identities in ways that were more meaningful for them.

While the aims of these Youth Commitments were predominantly career-focused and particularly aimed at 'at-risk' students, some of the outcomes were culturally significant. Jack, who was integrally involved in delivering the initiative, explains that the Gold Coast Youth Commitment was much more than just about encouraging youth networks: it was about impacting policy and enabling youth to articulate their youth cultures. Jack states that it '[...] was one way of getting community partnerships, and hopefully in the long term th[ey] would be the loud speakers for the community going back up the line. To say well, this is what we think should be happening [...]' (23 August 2011).

So it was essentially a process of youth-led cultural development, creating space for a youth cultural voice. In the three-year term of the Youth Commitment, one of the most significant outcomes was the creation of the Gold Coast Youth Committee and subsequent production of a local youth-driven zine called *WAVE: GC Speak Up!* Although the actual Youth Commitment consisted of adults who built community partnerships, the zine was one strategy in particular that was youth-led and involved a core group of young people (12–25) leading the project.

WAVE: GC Speak Up! Consisted of a group called the Gold Coast Youth Committee who worked alongside the Youth Commitment. Jack, who was a program leader, discusses his role of mentor in this process, rather than as a teacher. Implicit in his idea of mentorship is a dialogic relationship:

> We set up – as part of youth week – we set up a little organizing committee. And we tried to sort of mentor – our role was really just to mentor them. Not to be judgmental in that sense. But unfortunately a lot of mentoring becomes that, you know. And that sort of is not mentoring anymore, it's teaching. So we were pretty – I was pretty conscious of the role that we should play.
>
> (23 August 2011)

As stated in the zine, The Gold Coast Youth Committee was 'a team of dynamic and enthusiastic Gold Coast Youth dedicated to putting initiatives into action on the coast' (Gold Coast Youth Committee, 2005, p.11). Further,

> Members of the Gold Coast Youth Committee [could] get involved in organizing youth events on the Coast; creating initiatives for youth; representing the Gold Coast at a State Level; supporting youth arts on the Coast; accessing grants for yourself or a project; [and] the Gold Coast Youth zine.
>
> (Gold Coast Youth Committee, 2005, p.11)

Contents of the zine were varied: local gig guides; advertisements for local youth opportunities; articles pertaining to youth issues; 'where to get help' pages for youth problems, such as eating disorders or legal help; music reviews; 'must try pick-up lines'; 'where to get info about stuff' pages; 'what to do with $10 in one day' articles; as well as a range of other useful information for young people. Here it is worth mentioning a couple of the zine's functions that are particularly relevant to the cultural challenges facing youth on the Gold Coast today.

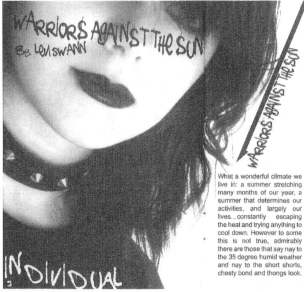

WARRIORS AGAINST THE SUN
By Len Swann

WARRIORS AGAINST THE SUN

INDIVIDUAL

What a wonderful climate we live in: a summer stretching many months of our year, a summer that determines our activities, and largely our lives...constantly escaping the heat and trying anything to cool down. However to some this is not true, admirably there are those that say nay to the 35 degree humid weather and nay to the short shorts, chesty bond and thongs look.

Rather they rebel against the summer and in opposition to its extreme heat what else is there to do but...wear black. I know for me and I'm sure a lot of others out there, the mere thought of wearing an entire 'get-up' of black clothes makes me sweat, let alone sporting an outfit comprised of a number of layers and even a trench coat. This rebellion against the sun is quite noticeable in Brisbane, and as I've heard is equally apparent in other areas of Australia. So if you are walking down the street wearing your T-shirt, shorts and thongs thinking "oh man, it is crazy hot today", think about those warriors against the sun and spare a thought for their crusade...

Just one additional note, although this is a satirical article, I think it touches on an awesome aspect of our society...that is individuality, and the freedom to express ourselves, clearly no matter what nature (or anything else) throws at us we wont let that impede our individuality.

Figure 15.2 'Warriors Against the Sun'
Source: Gold Coast Youth Commitment

Firstly, the zine was an important cultural resource; it enabled access to cultural information that youth were previously unable to access and it largely functioned as a community bulletin board. Because of the aforementioned urban dispersal and challenging network conditions, the Gold Coast (still) lacks spaces – both online and offline – where young people can go to find out information about local events. So in a sense, the zine popularised this critical youth community bulletin board with information about how to engage in these cultural youth networks with the purpose of distributing it to young people. In this simple way, the zine worked towards bridging holes in young people's cultural networks.

Secondly, the zine provided an empowering creative outlet for its designers to articulate and express their cultural identities. *WAVE: GC Speak Up!* was a space for young people to 'speak up' about their youth culture. It was a place where young people could tell their own valid stories, in contrast to the newspaper headlines. In a study involving interviews with young girls, Schilt discovered that zine-making 'can encourage girls to be more critical consumers of cultural products and lead them to feel more empowered to express their own ideas and opinions' (2003, p.79). Similarly, *Wave: GC Speak Up!* enabled young Gold Coast creatives to express themselves and become cultural producers through articulating their youth cultures. For instance, at the end of one article titled 'Warriors Against the Sun' (see Figure 15.2), a young person writes:

> Just one additional note, although this is a satirical article, I think it touches on an awesome aspect of our society...that is individuality, and the freedom to express ourselves, clearly no matter what nature (or anything else) throws at us we won't let that impede our individuality. (2003, p.4)

Despite its apparent outcomes, the zine was unfortunately short-lived, with just three editions from 2005–6. Sadly, the Gold Coast Youth Commitment was not able to convince state government to continue funding it after the federal government dropped it. Since this time however, there have been numerous attempts to fill its place.

Recent youth-led cultural initiatives

Since the collapse of the Gold Coast Youth Committee, there have been various other youth-led projects aiming to respond to the challenging cultural geographies of the Gold Coast. While none of these exclusively pick up where the Youth Commitment left off, they all have various roles to play in the providing crucial cultural development infrastructure for young people. While there are many I could detail here, I will briefly note a couple of important initiatives. One young participant I interviewed, Matt, created a popular blog to facilitate a space for artists to promote their work online. Matt explains his reason for creating the blog:

> The main thing I want to do for the Gold Coast is to link all of these people together because they don't talk to each other enough. And I want to do it with our blog and use our blog as a pathway between them. Because even with the Gold Coast City Council website, I go on there and I'm like, I'm confused already.
>
> (2 May 2011)

Matt clearly identified the aforementioned disconnect in local cultural networks and he acted on this by collaborating with other local youth, extending this interstate. The blog, which has mushroomed to include artists Australia-wide, has given many locals and interstate artists a platform to showcase their work.

Perhaps a more tangible example of youth-led cultural development can be found at rabbit + cocoon, the Gold Coast's creative precinct. The artist-run precinct operates fourteen warehouses, facilitates studio and event space as well as happenings such as Youth Week for young people. In a sense, perhaps this initiative has come the closest to filling the gap left by the

Gold Coast Youth Commitment. The precinct offers a number of cultural experiences and opportunities to young people to participate in, including a radio station, monthly creative markets and specific youth cultural events. The precinct is largely operated by young adults and young people, facilitating a community space for youth to create their own initiatives in. Since it began operation in 2010, rabbit + cocoon has become a kind of hub for young people to articulate their cultural voice.

Conclusion

In this chapter I have documented the significance of youth-led cultural development as informal education on the Gold Coast. I have highlighted the impact that youth-led cultural activity has on the construction of youth's cultural identities, and I have further argued that these modes of informal learning can actually create cultural change in society. Through youth-led cultural development initiatives we can begin to see an emerging cultural voice on the Gold Coast, one that is desperate to be heard. If the city is to truly see radical cultural change, local policies, media and youth initiatives need to amplify this cultural voice and acknowledge youth as valued contributors to the city. If more young people are encouraged to lead, we might well see youth impacting policies more explicitly, reinforcing positive youth cultural identities.

References

S. Baker (2007) 'Young people and community radio in the northern region of Adelaide, South Australia', *Popular Music and Society*, December, 30, 575–90.
S. Baker, A. Bennett and P. Wise (2012) 'Living "the strip": Negotiating neighbourhood, community and identities on Australia's gold coast', in C. Richardson and H. Scott-Myhre (eds) *Habitus of the Hood* (Bristol, UK: Intellect).
A. Bennett (2010) 'The continuing importance of the "cultural" in the study of youth', *Youth Studies Australia*, 30, 27–33.
G. Bloustien and M. Peters (2011) *Youth, Music and Creative Cultures: Playing for life* (Basingstoke: Palgrave Macmillan).
S. Cohen (2002) 'Moral panics as cultural panics: Introduction to the third edition', in *Folk Devils and Moral Panics: The creation of the mods and rockers* (London: Routledge).
P. Friere (1972) *Pedagogy of the Oppressed* (London: Penguin Books).
L. Gibson (2001) *The Uses of Art: Constructing Australian identities* (Queensland: University of Queensland Press).
Gold Coast City Council (GCCC) (2013) 'Tourism industry', http://www.goldcoast.qld.gov.au/business/tourism-industry-588.html (accessed 21 March 2013).
Gold Coast Youth Committee (2005) *GC Wave: Speak up!*, 1st edn, zine.
S. Henderson, J. Holland, S. McGrellis, S. Sharpe and R. Thomson (2007) *Inventing Adulthoods: A biographical approach to youth transitions* (London: Sage Publications Ltd).
S. Holloway and G. Valentine (eds) (2000) *Children's Geographies: Playing, living, learning* (London: Routledge).

L. A. Jensen and J. J. Arnett (2012) 'Going global: New pathways for adolescents and emerging adults in a changing world', *Journal of Social Sciences*, 68, 473–92.

G. Jones (2009) *Youth* (Cambridge: Polity Press).

P. Kellock [the Asquith Group] (2005) 'Local investment, national returns: The case for community support for early school leavers; A report on the national youth commitment partnerships and project' (NSW: Gebe, *Dusseldorp Skills Forum*).

K. Lloyd, M. Harrington, R. Hibbins, A. Boag and M. Cuthill (2005) 'Is it fun to be young on the Gold Coast? Perceptions of leisure opportunities and constraints among young people living on the Gold Coast', *Youth Studies Australia*, 23, 22–7.

H. Matthews and M. Limb (2003) 'Another white elephant? Youth councils as democratic structures', *Space and Polity*, 7, 173–92.

S. Miles, P. Axel, B. Stauber, A. Walther, R. M. B. Banha and M. C. Gomes (2002) *Communities of Youth: Cultural practice and informal learning* (England: Ashgate Publishing Ltd).

K. Schilt (2003) ' "I'll resist with every inch and every breath": Girls and zine making as a form of resistance', *Youth and Society*, 32, 71–97.

J. P. Singh (2007) 'Culture or commerce? A comparative assessment of international interactions and developing countries at UNESCO, WTO, and Beyond', *International Studies Perspectives*, 8, 36–53.

J. P. Singh (2010) *International Cultural Policies and Power* (Basingstoke: Palgrave Macmillan).

T. Skelton and G. Valentine (eds) (1998) *Cool Places: Geographies of youth cultures* (London: Routledge).

S. Smail (2011) 'Gold Coast "the crime capital of Australia" ', *ABC News*, http://www.abc.net.au/news/2011-07-21/gold-coast-becoming-crime-capital/2803830 (accessed 20 October 2012).

E. Soja (1996) *Thirdspace: Journeys to Los Angeles and other real-and-imagined places* (Victoria: Blackwell Publishing).

R. Stimson and J. Minnery (1998) 'Why people move to the "sun-belt": A case study of long-distance migration to the Gold Coast, Australia', *Urban Studies*, 35, 193–214.

Tourism Queensland (2012) 'Gold Coast famous for fun', http://www.visitgoldcoast.com (accessed 25 October 2012).

WCCD (1996) *Our Creative Diversity: Report of the world commission on culture and development* (W.C.C.D.) (Paris: UNESCO).

R. White and J. Wyn (2004) *Youth and Society: Exploring the social dynamics of youth experience* (New York: Oxford University Press).

P. Wise (2012) 'Solar flow: The uses of light in Gold Coast living' in A. Ballantyne and C. L. Smith (eds) *Architecture in the Space of Flows* (London; New York: Routledge).

S. Zukin (2010) *Naked City: The death and life of authentic urban places* (New York: Oxford University Press).

16
Learning in/through Public Space: Young Girls and Feminist Consciousness-raising

Maria Rodó-de-Zárate and Mireia Baylina

Introduction: An educational journey to empowerment and social action

> We are a collective of feminist women who come together to raise our own consciousness and try to show others the inequalities and violence that women continue to suffer because of the patriarchal system, which assigns specific roles to the female sex and others to the male sex, given men the dominant place in society and relegating women to second place, dependent on them. We want to put an end to the physical, psychological and moral violence that women suffer in everyday life.[1]
>
> Acció Lila

This chapter seeks to explore how the young girls of a feminist group think and act politically in their urban environment, and specifically how, through their experiences, they manage their intersecting oppressions and look for strategies to combat them. The aim is to show how they think reflectively about their experiences in the public space, manage their intersected oppressions and find individual and collective strategies to struggle transform or resist. Through their awareness of their oppression and understanding themselves as a political issue in a process of consciousness-raising they become empowered both personal and collectively. The way they share their personal experiences, develop their own tools to strengthen them and take actions to make them known are processes and practices of informal education important to be considered.

The study focuses on discussion groups held with *Acció Lila* ('Purple Action'), a group of about 10 white girls aged 16–21 years living in the city of Manresa (Barcelona province). This collective was born out of the need that a group of girls had to raise their consciousness of the gender oppression they suffered, to train themselves to understand the power mechanisms that

Figure 16.1 Acció Lila's performance against traditional gender roles for the 8th March, Manresa
Source: Col·lectiu Feminista Acció Lila – http://acciolila.blogspot.com.es

affected them and share their experiences. From these reflections came the need to take their struggle to the streets, carrying out all types of public activities (performances, video showings, talks, spreading their ideas with posters and banners, concerts) and dealing with diverse topics such as sexuality, work, personal relationships, gender stereotypes, standards of beauty, and so on (Figure 16.1).

Their main space of interaction is the *Ateneu Popular La Sequia*, a squatted house in the Manresa city centre where they carry out all different types of cultural, leisure and political activities.[2] This self-managed project of squatting is led by an open assembly and with the goal of responding to the city's lack of spaces for young people, becoming a place to plan and live out new forms of entertainment, alternative means of communication, and alternatives to the capitalist consumer society.

The chapter is framed into the studies of young people's use of public space from a gender perspective, which are very scarce in Catalonia and Spain, and are in the minority in the international context (Rodo-de-Zárate, 2011). On one hand, the literature on youth participation in urban public space shows that this relationship is complex and controversial.

While the street is a space where young people find freedom and is especially relevant during this time of constructing identity and needing to find spaces far from the adult gaze (Gough and Franch, 2005; van Lieshout and Aarts, 2008), public space is also an *adultified* space: it is constructed by and for adults and is produced as an adult space. Given adults' spatial hegemony (Valentine, 1996) young people are excluded from a space that is understood to be civic and supervised by the presence of adults who define and control it (Collins and Kearns, 2001; Driskell et al., 2008; Chiu, 2009).

Furthermore, being present in public streets is not the same for young women as it is for young men. The heteropatriarchy determines roles for each gender and disciplines their bodies so that they behave appropriately in public spaces. For example, the fact of girls being seen in the street has specific repercussions for their experience in that space, since their bodies are sexualised by the male gaze in public spaces (Hyams, 2003). Their uses of public streets will also vary according to their perception of fear, which is entirely marked by gender and determines one's experience of the city and freedom of movement (Koskela, 1997; Pain, 2001).

Recent developments of the geographies of children and youth are concerned about what counts as educational spaces. In this sense, many scholars recognise that educational spaces are essentially modified by wider social processes and they focus into the nature of sociospatial relations with different learning spaces as well as young people's identities and experiences (Hyams, 2000; Nairn, 2003; Holloway et al., 2010). By focusing on young voices and subjectivities we will find knowledge about their current and future liveworlds. Thus, taking into account young people as knowledgeable requires research that links an inward-looking focus on educational spaces with an outward-looking approach that assesses their importance to other time/spaces (Holloway et al., 2010). In our case study, young girls' learning process is an original and efficient form of informal learning, understood as the learning that takes place beyond classrooms and outside courses (Jeffs and Smith, 2005) and more precisely, of self-education, which involves a deliberate effort to learn and often some planning (Jeffs and Smith, 2005). Young girls take care of their own education: they take themselves to places where they expect learning will occur; they seek out books or people whom they judge will aid their learning; they enter into 'conversations' with others, either the writers of the books they study or those they observe and converse with. This process has a conscious base (learning-conscious) that sometimes consist of organised training actions and also more spontaneously ones (acquisition learning) through the creation of a supportive environment (Jeffs and Smith, 2005). However, beyond thinking that takes us forward, we deal with self-education, that is about development and growth. *Accló Lila* develops activities that are intended to stimulate their thinking and foster their learning.

The chapter is divided into five sections: an introduction to the study and the theoretical framework; the methodology, based on Participatory Action Research and the process of consciousness-raising; the relationship between the feminist group with the urban space of reference, Manresa; the analysis of the process of self-education, taking into account the non-hierarchical organisation of the group, and the learning practices and areas; and finally, some final thoughts that try to collect the main contributions of this chapter in regard to the processes of self-education of a feminist group and to the studies on youth and urban public space from a feminist standpoint.

Methodology

In keeping with the parameters of Participatory Action Research (PAR), the study took on a collective focus that involved the persons being 'studied' in the research (Cahill, 2004). Five discussion sessions were held in an effort to bring to light the participants' own defence and action mechanisms. Beginning with personal experience of daily life and making it a shared experience through reflective discussion, the research process itself was emphasised, with the intent of converting personal experience into a collective political conscience using a process of *conscientição* (conscientisation or consciousness-raising) described by Paolo Freire as the deepening of conscientisation, which in turn is characteristic of those who emerge from reality (Freire, 1970). This process is the creation of an awareness that participants utilise for self-empowerment but also to find solutions to the problems they confront.

Using this phenomenological approach, which takes personal lived experience as the starting point for research, emphasis is placed on transgression (both individual and collective and both everyday and organised) to break the cycle of victimisation, since the approach is not only focused on the oppression experienced but also on the type of response. It begins with the conviction that 'people are able to resist the construction of expectations about practice through place by using places and their established meanings in subversive ways' (Cresswell, 1996, p.22) and that even though the surroundings restrict and shape subjectivity, young people have the capacity to negotiate their social condition using what Cahill calls *street literacy*, the 'dymamic processes of experiental knowledge production and self-construction in a specified context, public urban space' (Cahill, 2000, p.252). Therefore, the emphasis is placed on the capacity of young women to transgress in these spaces and to manage their oppressions, based on their lived experience.

Determining factors for the study were previous personal knowledge of the group in question and the environment in which it moves, as well as similarities in age, gender identity, sexuality, background, class or political connections that could be established on the basis of feminism or ideological proximity (explicit factors). If research on young people must be alert to power relationships and ethical questions about dealing with this age group (Hopkins, 2010), in this case, thanks to relationship bonds, a climate of trust and respect was created that allowed a high level of delving into the questions posed and a careful research process, attentive to the power relationships that could arise.

The space of trust and respect created among all participants made it possible to address the study questions in an open manner, paying attention to the needs of each individual. Even so, the three- to seven-year age difference between participant and researcher was evident in the joint discussions, which made it impossible to completely erase the difference between the two. There is often a tendency to victimise young people with (or about) whom research is done, treating them as vulnerable persons who must be empowered (Hopkins, 2010) or to whom theoretical or practical knowledge of the processes of collective liberation are to be transmitted. In this case, the participants themselves were carrying out collective processes of empowerment through training and reflection about their experience as women within *Acció Lila*. Therefore, we also wanted to point out how young people, and these young women in particular, already have their own forms of developing their identities, strategies, consciousness, and reflections on overcoming the oppressions they suffer.

Acció Lila and the city: The need to be there, the discomfort of being seen

> Ayla: I think we have been out on the street very little and really, if you do an event at the Ateneu you'll get the people who always come to the Ateneu. So, to reach the majority of the population, the majority of the men and women of Manresa, you won't be able to do that if you don't get out on the street. Lots of times we don't go out and we really should get out there more.

Everyday political action by *Acció Lila* is not directed at public institutions or the local government, but rather directly at the citizenry. Apart from all of the work of learning and reflection done internally as a collective, the basis of their feminist activism, their transformational objective is to provoke changes in their immediate surroundings. And therefore they need to be present out on the street, where this possibility exists. In this way, the public space becomes the political arena in which to demand their rights, make public their proposals, and communicate with the rest of the citizenry.

However, their position in the public space, as a collective, is not only a space with possibilities and a political tool but also a place of oppression. Their political voice on the streets is neither neutral nor disembodied: it comes from a particular body that is loaded with symbolism, that of young girls. This diverse but adultified and androcentric space leaves very little room for the feminist political expression carried out by a group of young women. As Ruddick argues, 'city space has been gendered in a way that tends to exclude women from the public space realm, or to include them only in highly scripted and delimited roles' (Ruddick, 1996, p.135). The discomfort of being observed or watched in the public space by a gaze that is both adult and *masculinist* not only determines their experience of the public space at the personal level but also conditions their collective political activity. Both their age and gender are strongly marked by a lack of political authority; while age serves to stigmatise ('people think we're going to do something bad'), gender is utilised to ridicule or undervalue. To this we add the stigma that weighs down feminism and the difficulties that accompany a defence of radical postures on sexual and gender liberation and the situation becomes even more complex.

> MRZ: How do you feel in the public space?
> Lara: Different. People look at us like we're... strange, watching (us)...
> Àfrica: And you have to explain everything. Any time you do something that's outside of what's normal that's not what you're expected to do, they look at you and it's as if...
> Gemma: Well, we're young but look, if we have seen a problem that exists then maybe you can open for them... shine a light and change their thinking...

These girls find themselves caught between, on one hand, the need for public visibility and the communication of ideas to effect social change and, on the other hand, the discomfort caused by their lack of political authority when the voice comes from a particular body.

> Àfrica: What we have to do, above all, is train ourselves.

Given this situation, strengthening the collective voice through self-affirmation and empowerment, both personal and collective, is essential. They share personal experiences of oppression and, aware of the lack of knowledge about the causes of the situation in which they find themselves, they train themselves using various tools that they themselves prepare: discussions of particular texts, reading groups, film discussions, invited guest speakers, participation in events held by other feminist groups, joint discussions with other collectives, and so on. Their personal and collective empowerment, that strengthens them to be able to go out into the public space and raise their voice, is their own awareness of their oppression, understanding themselves as their political issue.

The process of self-education

For the members of *Acció Lila* training in feminism is something they don't find along their formal learning paths. It has to be deliberately informal. The first action taken in their training is to create the group. The fact of meeting and creating the group is the first step in a chain of learning that involves a variety of spaces, times, and activities. *Acció Lila* is the group, and as such is fundamental to their efforts to strengthen and empower their actions, both at the personal and collective level.

Within the group, the effort invested in learning is fundamental to their daily lives, as important as their 'action' itself, to the extent that training and action continuously complement and nourish each other. The girls reflect great motivation and need to learn, both for themselves and for other girls, and for society as a whole. Initially, they see training as an act of internal consistency and conscientisation. Teaching themselves about what interests them and what they need gives them the basic confidence to affirm themselves personally and as a group, to establish the necessary coherence between what they think, what they do, and how they live, and to empower themselves to take action. This high level of motivation leads not only to deliberate actions to prepare themselves, but also to an extraordinary capacity to absorb everything they see and experience at any time and in any place, and to share that with each other.

Self-management and non-hierarchical relationships

The fundamental pillar of how the group functions is the weekly two-hour meeting, at which they discuss questions of training and preparation as well as the steps needed to organise the activities and political actions they plan to be involved in. This is the physical meeting space that allows them to develop trust relationships and stimulates collective reflection and discussion. These meetings are conducted on the basis of self-management and non-hierarchical relationships between group members. They are careful about the interpersonal dynamics at meetings and moderate them by taking turns to speak and making 'rounds' so that all voices are heard and at the same level. Division of tasks and a commitment to 'horizontal production of knowledge' (as opposed to 'top-down' instruction) makes it possible to share what they know without allowing certain voices to systematically dominate the rest of the group. Some of the girls prepare topics for discussion, but this is a rotating role to avoid establishing fixed individual roles. All of the girls are about the same age (17–21 years old) and have similar levels of experience with feminist politics, which facilitates this type of group functioning but also limits their possibilities of addressing or resolving their doubts about the topics they work on: 'We had a lot of questions we couldn't answer. We missed having somebody who could guide us.' Despite this problem, they also see that 'doing this by ourselves means that we are all at the same level, we trust each other, we are capable of organizing ourselves, we realize that there are other points of view besides what you've been told...nobody from outside tells us "what's what"...'.

Therefore, organising their own meetings and managing their own learning process is what makes their horizontal structure possible, avoiding power relationships and hierarchies. Collective consciousness-raising based on experience is what leads to their empowerment. Their learning process reflects the ideas that Freire called conscientisation:

> One of the reasons of this research is precisely the consciousness of knowing little about oneself. When they recognise themselves in this situation of dramatic ignorance, they put themselves as a problem, they inquire, they answer and their responses lead them to new questions.
>
> (Freire, 1970, p.16)[3]

Learning practices

One of the group's standard learning practices is looking for texts by well-known authors to discuss. One or two of the girls take responsibility for finding the texts to be read and discussed once a month. They look for readings on topics that they consider 'priority' or interesting, and they make their choice by consensus after doing an 'opinions round'. So far this year they have discussed feminist theory, feminist economics, sexual-affective relationships and transexuality. At first they focussed more on the oppression of women and now they are deepening their understanding of a broader perspective on patriarchy. The current economic crisis has also 'made us shift more toward anticapitalism' as they see increasing social inequality, underground economy, and so on. Looking towards the future, they plan to work on sexual and reproductive health and to develop their ability to express themselves in public speaking. In general, from an ideological point of view, they look for readings that look at feminism through an anticapitalist lens. Nonetheless, they also recognise that 'when you choose a text, you can't really be sure what you'll get out of it'.

Based on what they learn from their discussion of each topic, they normally plan an action, either on the street or at the *Ateneu*. They complement their readings with viewing of videos that interest them on the same topic, which they post to the *Acció Lila* Facebook, and they invite someone with expertise to provide a good explanation of the topic they are working on. They are aware that this is the theory and that in practice they can't always do all three of those things because they organise many actions during the year that also demand a lot of their time.

When they have vacation time they get together at one of the girls' home and spend two days on group-building and training sessions. For this period of togetherness and learning, each girl takes charge of preparing a topic and documentation about a woman author. Having time to spend together is freeing for them and allows more and better in-depth attention to their topics of discussion at the same time they continue to build group cohesiveness. These days are especially useful when someone new joins the group because newcomer integration is much easier in this context.

Welcoming new members to the group is another important training action, both for newcomers and for those who have participated for a longer time. Although there have been no major changes in the composition of the group and growth does not seem to be a primary objective, during the first three years some new members have joined. For them, and for those who might join in future, there is a small committee of two members who take charge of this question and have developed, with group consensus, a dossier of basic materials (definitions of feminism, sex, gender, patriarchy, etc.) so that the newcomer can follow the group discussions as soon as possible and the dynamic is not affected unnecessarily.

Another, more spontaneous, training strategy is the distribution of attendance at events of interest. Given the quantity of events that occur, especially in Barcelona, and their limited mobility options due to restrictions because of school, funds or age, the girls divide up their presence at events and then comment virtually, for immediacy, or at the next meeting. These activities include participation in some festivals, such as a bookstall for *Sant Jordi* (St. George's day, a Catalan national holiday that is also the 'Day of the Book'), that allows *Acció Lila* to learn and become better known. As they put it: 'we don't go there to sell things, we go there to grow'. This activity is an example of how 'much learning takes place without being consciously organized' (Jeffs and Smith, 2005).

Learning in/through spaces

The geographies of their learning are diverse and complex. Their normal meeting space is the *Ateneu* on Sunday afternoons. The fact that most of them study outside of the city during the week requires that they find a time and space on the weekend, and this is ideal – once they have tended to their other social commitments, such as youth groups (which some of the girls lead)[4] or sports (some girls participate in team sports and have games or practice sessions). The fact that this is a space managed by young people gives the girls great freedom to decide what events they want to hold there, who can attend, and it is where they find a safe space for their ideological affinity. This allows them to create an environment that is very favourable to the kind of training practices they engage in. At the same time, it gives them contact with other young people organised into other groups, stimulating their knowledge and critical thinking. In this sense, they are engaging in incidental learning, which simply occurs but is not 'casual'; rather, it is a consequence of mental preparation in a space that favours learning.

Social networks have also allowed them to create a new social meeting space. Facebook enables them to overcome their space-time limitations and communicate in a way that is both permanent and ongoing. They have established both an external and internal Facebook account, and also a blog[5] they do not use very much. The external Facebook page[6] helps them become better known, publicise their activities and get external feedback. The internal Facebook is where the members make comments and share news, ideas, opinions about events they have attended, everyday experiences, and is also where they can continue their Sunday meetings when they go on too long.

The city where the girls live, Manresa, is not for them a primary site for training and preparation (although a variety of training opportunities are developed there). Manresa is the city where they live, hold meetings, go out with friends, but with regard to feminist training they say that 'if anything happens in Manresa we're the ones doing it'.[7] They are very conscious that they have to go to Barcelona; they look to the city and see themselves reflected there. Curiously, living on the periphery gives them an advantage because they have to leave home to study beyond secondary school. This leads to a certain diaspora for academic reasons to different Catalan cities, which enriches the group. As they express it, 'it opens a lot of doors'.

The public space, as a training space, is a place for the observation of reality, a work camp for their research, a place to confront their own experience and find diversity. Most of all, it is the place where they bring to fruition what they have worked on and, therefore, is where they make manifest their commitment to social change. In their actions the girls come face to face with the reactions of their fellow citizens and when this causes conflict it increases the learning opportunities offered by the public space as a meeting place.

Final thoughts

The *Acció Lila* process of training and conscientization is carried out in a horizontal manner, beginning with in-depth reflection on the experience of oppression they want to understand. This would be one of the training objectives for *Acció Lila*: to understand their oppression, seeking out texts and other materials that help them to understand how the mechanisms of power work, what the dynamics of patriarchy are, and, finally, how to make sense of their own experiences and understand the social and political causes. However, the objective is not simply to know and understand but to take steps towards liberation, learn to empower themselves, understand the mechanisms of oppression so they can free themselves. Although this could be a personal objective for each of the girls, the collective component of their learning is crucial. It is through sharing the experience of oppression, the discomfort and rage, that they will also be able to share their response and the processes of emancipation. Their meetings are therapeutic in the sense that they make sense of their experiences of oppression and can relate their own identity to the social processes (Cahill, 2007).

As a political collective focussed on action, training not only has the function of personal or collective liberation, there is also a clear social change objective: to change themselves to change society, to learn so they are more able to transform their surroundings. Training, then, is the fundamental and basic tool that *Acció Lila* members use to give authority to their collective voice. Being young women puts them in a position of inferiority and lack of authority that they replace with political awareness and with reasoned arguments.

Learning occurs for *Acció Lila* within the framework of a spiral process. Between the need to empower their political voice in an adult-centered public space and the discomfort that results from the lack of authority attributed to voices housed in the bodies of young women, training becomes vital and essential. Self-management of this training not only empowers and raises consciousness but also creates shared discourse and strengthens their position for a return to the public space. The process is a spiral because the public space gives them a measure by which to assess their personal and collective confidence as well as the opportunity to learn from reality itself and from encounters with others. They continue their training as part of a continuing process of increasing learning and political awareness.

Without tutors, guides, or even clear points of reference, the training process used by *Acció Lila* is exceptionally horizontal and is based on the will to know and the need to learn. It is clearly a process of conscientisation that has emerged from the experience of oppression. For that reason, this study has also been based on a research process that simply encourages discussion and reflection. Although the methodology was based on the Participatory Action Research approach, the role of the researchers was minimal, allowing the girls' own way of working and learning to guide the topics of research. This approach to 'investigation' (participatory and action-oriented by definition) was used to work in public spaces, while always attempting to respect the *Acció Lila* dynamics of discussion, reflection and, finally, production of knowledge. It show how these young women are able to manage their oppressions and find political responses to them, but also shows how authority or the effect of a political voice in the public space varies according to the physical body from which it emanates; this fact demonstrates how opportunities for participation in political debate and the exercise of citizenship is not given to neutral individuals but rather that each body, with all of its attributes, occupies a particular place in the structures of power. But these feminist young women create platforms from which to make their voice heard and to express themselves with self-affirmation from their position. They do not need anybody in a place of privilege to give them a voice. They already have a voice. All they need is that we listen.

Acknowledgements

The research which this article draws has been funded by the Ministerio de Ciencia e Innovacion of the Spanish Government (grant number

CSO2009-10913). We would like to thank the members of *Acció Lila* for their time, enthusiasm and engagement with this research. Thanks also to the people from the *Ateneu* for letting us carry on the research within it.

Notes

1. Part of the *Acció Lila* manifesto, excerpted from the group's blog: http://www.acciolila.blogspot.com/
2. *Ateneu Popular la Sequia* is a house that was squatted in September 2009 by a group of young people in Manresa. The name reflects a traditional cultural space, the *atheneum* in Latin, but is 'the people's cultural space' and is named 'The irrigation ditch' (*sequia*).
3. Our own translation from the original in Portuguese.
4. Some of the girls work as leaders of these organised groups for children and adolescents.
5. http://www.acciolila.blogspot.com.es/
6. http://www.facebook.com/accio.lila
7. There is another feminist group but the girls have less contact with them because 'they're a lot older'.

References

C. Cahill (2000) 'Street literacy: Urban teenagers' strategies for negotiating their neighbourhood', *Journal of Youth Studies*, 3, 251–77.
C. Cahill (2004) 'Defying gravity? Raising concoiusness through collective research', *Children's Geographies*, 2, 273–86.
C. Cahill (2007) 'The personal is political: Developing new subjectivities through participatory action research', *Gender, Place & Culture*, 14, 267–92.
C. Chiu (2009) 'Contestation and conformity: Street and park skateboarding in New York city public space', *Space and Culture*, 12, 25–42.
D. C. A. Collins and R. A. Kearns (2001) 'Under curfew and under siege? Legal geographies of young people', *Geoforum*, 32, 389–403.
T. Cresswell (1996) *In Place, Out of Place: Geography, ideology, and transgression* (Minneapolis: University of Minnesota Press).
D. Driskell, C. Fox and N. Kudva (2008) 'Growing up in the new New York: Youth space, citizenship, and community change in a hyperglobal city', *Environment and Planning A*, 40, 2831–44.
P. Freire (1970) *Pedagogia do oprimido* (Rio de Janeiro: Paz e terra).
K. V. Gough and M. Franch (2005) 'Spaces of the street: Socio-spatial mobility and exclusion of youth in Recife', *Children's Geographies*, 3, 149–66.
S. Holloway, P. Hubbard, H. Jöns and H. Pimlott-Wilson (2010) 'Geographies of education and the significance of children, youth and families', *Progress in Human Geography*, 34, 583–600.
P. E. Hopkins (2010) *Young People, Place and Identity* (New York: Routledge).
M. Hyams (2000) 'Pay attention in class...[and] don't get pregnant': A discourse of academic success among adolescent Latinas', *Environment and Planning A*, 32, 635–54.
M. Hyams (2003) 'Adolescent Latina bodyspaces: Making homegirls, homebodies and homeplaces', *Antipode*, 35, 535–58.

T. Jeffs and M. Smith (2005) *Informal Education: Conversation, Democracy and Learning* (Nottingham: Educational Heretics Press).

H. Koskela (1997) ' "Bold walk and breakings": Women's spatial confidence versus fear of violence', *Gender Place and Culture*, 4, 301–14.

K. Nairn (2003) 'What has the geography of sleeping arrangement got to do with the geography of our teaching spaces?' *Gender, Place and Culture*, 10, 67–81.

R. Pain (2001) 'Gender, race, age and fear in the city', *Urban Studies*, 38, 899–913.

M. Rodó-de-Zárate (2011) 'El jovent i els espais públics urbans des de la perspectiva de gènere: Un estat de la qüestió des de la geografia', *Documents d'Anàlisi Geogràfica*, 57, 147–62.

S. Ruddick (1996) 'Constructing difference in public spaces: Race, class and gender as interlocking systems', *Urban Geography*, 17, 132–51.

G. Valentine (1996) 'Angels and devils: Moral landscapes of childhood', *Environment and Planning D: Society and space*, 14, 581–99.

M. van Lieshout and N. Aarts (2008) 'Youth and immigrants' perspectives on public space', *Space and Culture*, 11, 497–513.

17
Leading the Way: Youth-Led Non-formal Learning in the Girl Scouts

Denise Goerisch

Recently, the US government identified the lack of financial literacy skills in formal educational institutions as a wide spread problem in the productivity and economic growth of the nation (GSSD, 2011). American youth are, thus, inadequately prepared to become engaging citizens in a global economy. As financial literacy skills are no longer emphasised in American primary schools, children and young people (as well as their parents or guardians) must seek out alternative spaces of non-formal education such as youth leadership organisations like the Girl Scouts. For the past 100 years, Girl Scouts have sold their famous cookies in neighbourhoods and in front of grocery stores, raising millions for the organisation. Unlike other youth organisation fundraisers, the Girl Scouts of the USA (GSUSA) recently transformed the cookie sale into an educational programme focusing on five fundamental business and leadership skills: goal-setting, decision-making, personal relationships (i.e., people skills), money management and business ethics. The organisation defines the fundraiser as an educational programme rather than a sale, emphasising its educational aspect instead of its primary function of earning money. The Girl Scout cookie programme thus claims to empower girls and young women by providing these much-needed financial literacy skills; however, many of the values expressed within the non-formal educational space of the cookie programme promote a vision of citizenship that relies on neoliberal ideals such as participation in free markets and community management. While non-formal educational spaces within the cookie programme have the potential to empower girls by providing vital business and leadership skills rooted in financial literacy, these spaces reproduce neoliberal constructions of civic engagement which complicates the organisation's message of *girl power*.

Based on a research project conducted from 2010 to 2012, this chapter examines how neoliberal citizenship is constructed within non-formal educational spaces within the Girl Scout cookie programme. Non-formal educational spaces have the potential to be transformative, especially if young people take on an active role in the creation of such spaces. Despite the potential for transformation, I argue here that neoliberal ideologies concerning youth, gender, citizenship, and education within the context of the cookie programme often counters the Girl Scouts' vision of scout-led activities as a transformative leadership and educational experience. This chapter relies upon data collected from an in-depth ethnographic study concerning older girl scouts in San Diego, California. For this study, I employed several qualitative methods, participant observation, focus groups, and informal and formal interviews. The cookie programme has a number of different resources available through the San Diego Council website for both girls and volunteers, including guidebooks, worksheets, websites, slideshows and videos, which I reviewed extensively.

Much of the research associated with this project was conducted during the 2011–12 cookie seasons.[1] Through connections previously established with the organisation, the Girl Scouts of San Diego Council granted me access to cookie-related events, including volunteer trainings and leadership events, as well as two scout-led events which are the focus of this chapter. I was invited by the local council to join, as an adult volunteer, a Senior scout troop which held a cookie-selling training workshop for Brownies (between the ages of seven and eight) in early January 2011, a few weeks before the start of the 2011 cookie season, as well as a similar 'Cookie Kick-Off' rally held in early 2012.[2] In both the three-hour training workshop and rally, the Senior Girl Scouts used the five essential life and business skills outlined in guidebooks to present the cookie programme to over 70 seven- and eight-year-old Brownies during the 2011 workshop and to over 150 girls (ranging in ages from five to nine years old) in 2012.

Neoliberal citizenship within non-formal educational spaces

Formal education (i.e., in-school curriculum) traditionally serves two functions: (1) preparation for civic life and (2) preparation for the workforce (e.g., financial literacy) (Nocon and Cole, 2006). However, as schools in the United States become more dependent on state funding based on standardised test scores, practical life skill sets are no longer offered in formal educational spaces. The reproduction of neoliberal citizenship within formal educational spaces is a significant area of research within geography (Hankins and Martin, 2006; Mitchell, 2006; Pykett, 2009; Thiem, 2009; Staeheli and Hammett, 2010; Hammett and Staeheli, 2011). However, due to the increasing presence of non-formal educational spaces in the United States, geography needs to further examine how non-formal educational spaces perpetuate neoliberal ideals concerning citizenship. Non-formal education is characterised as 'a non-curriculum form that can make a significant contribution to the development of a more convivial public life' (Bekerman et al., 2006, p.3) and is seen as a great contribution to American education systems, especially with regard to citizenship development (Schugurensky, 2006).[3] These spaces can be seen as transformative or empowering for young people as they can provide them with the tools to become agents of change (Zoerink et al., 1997). As such, non-formal educational spaces at the very least complicate constructions of youth citizenship and civic engagement. In doing so, two conflicting forms of citizenship emerge: one based on engendering socio-political change (i.e., 'agents of change') and the other reproducing neoliberal ideals (i.e., 'citizens in the making').

Definitions of citizenship constantly shift and are highly contested (Staeheli, 2011). Traditionally, citizenship is conceived as bestowing certain political, social and economic rights onto groups. Youth are generally excluded from this definition as the attainment of societal rights is seen as a marker of adulthood; therefore, children and young people are seen as 'citizens in the making' rather than as citizens or social actors in their own right (Aapola et al., 2005). As the recent youth-led social movements in Europe, the Middle East and United States have demonstrated, young people are increasingly exercising their rights as citizens and engendering economic, political and social change at the local and global level. But the citizenship practiced on the streets of the city can be perceived as being different from the citizenship that is traditionally conveyed in both formal and non-formal educational spaces, such as those in the Girl Scout cookie programme, which critics suggest is a form of neoliberal citizenship or at the very least reproduce a 'citizens in the making' discourse (Taft, 2010; Mills, 2013).

Neoliberal citizenship produced in formal educational environments encourages participation in free markets and community management, which reflects the shift towards the privatisation of once public services and maintains the State's status quo. Recently, the State has pushed neoliberal ideals onto young people to aspire to become self-reliant citizens (Brown, 2011). For example, in many American high schools, service learning has become a popular pedagogical tool to teach young people citizenship and leadership. However, service learning is often criticised as it emphasises direct service, especially in areas from which the State withdraws public services, rather than allowing young people to become engaged citizens acting to advocate alternatives (Kahne and Westheimer, 1996). With the deregulation of the State and the privatisation of public services, the burden of social responsibility falls onto communities and their citizens. When communities or citizens cannot fulfil this burden, volunteer organisations like the Girl Scouts must address the needs of the community, which may not be necessarily met due to lack of resources or leadership (Salamon, 1999; Fyfe and Milligan, 2003). While volunteer organisations have potential to act as sites of active citizenship for their members (see Milligan and Conradson, 2006), the constructions of citizenship reproduced within non-formal educational spaces need to be further examined.

The Girl Scouts has a long history of presenting itself as an organisation that allows girls to become self-reliant and independent, qualities that were cited by many of the girls in this study and that highlight the organisation's mission of girl empowerment (Miller, 2007; Proctor 2009). However, I question whether scout-led activities such as the ones organised by these older scouts complement the organisation's message of empowerment or if neoliberal assertions of American individualism are re-packaged as *girl power*.

Discover, connect, take action: Girl power, leadership and neoliberal citizenship

Over the past two decades, there has been an increasing presence of girl-centric empowerment movements in the United States and beyond. Girl empowerment can be defined as girls having the access and capability to engage in projects that work to change the discursive and material context of their everyday lives (Currie and Kelly, 2006). Popularised in the 1990s by academics and various media outlets, the term 'girl power' was coined to express girl-centred empowerment movements (primarily based in the West) which were rooted in self-exploration, independence and personal strength. While the term has become somewhat passé, girls from all around the world are taking action against social institutions to redefine hegemonic constructions of girlhood and femininity in order to attain equality. Recently, several American teenage girls spoke out against the 'whitewashing' of beauty and egregious use of airbrushing in magazines, most notably *Seventeen* and *Teen Vogue* (Brown, 2012). Additionally, girls are becoming increasingly politically active, not only engaging in local political issues but also participating in global arenas such as the UN Commission on the Status of Women and the Girls 20 World Summit. The Girl Scouts as an organisation has always concerned itself with allowing girls to 'discover, connect, and take action' in their communities, and more recently around the world.[4] For example, GSUSA recently created a model, as outlined in the guidebook, *Financial Empowerment* (2012), to help girls obtain empowerment through financial literacy via the cookie sale: '(Financial literacy + Business Skills + Innovation) × (A Leadership Lens) = Entrepreneurship and a Better Place!' (p.10). Innovation in this equation refers to girls finding creative solutions to pressing social issues. Giving girls the knowledge to become financially literate and involved in their communities is indeed laudable; I do question the Girl Scouts' claim that girls can be empowered by reproducing neoliberal ideals about women's participation in community management. The cookie programme aids girls in achieving girl power as demonstrated through the organisation's attempt to equate financial literacy, leadership and community management with girl empowerment. Financial literacy can be perceived as empowering young people, especially in these dire economic times; the older scouts in the study often commented on how invaluable the cookie programme has been in their financial education. However, many found leading the workshop and rally to be a much more transformative and empowering experience as they believed they were making a positive impact on the lives of younger scouts by instilling in them a sense of financial empowerment.

Non-formal educational spaces have the potential to be incredibly validating, as many older scouts have noted their experiences as such and teaching girls financial literacy is indeed praiseworthy, but the Girl Scouts' formula to achieving girl empowerment is seemingly rooted in neoliberal ideologies.

In 2012, GSUSA CEO Ana Maria Chavez proclaimed the year to be 'The Year of the Girl' in honour of the organisation's hundredth anniversary and to raise awareness about the lack of female leadership in the United States. The organisation has identified financial empowerment as a key component of its main objective of increased girl and woman leadership. While connections to capitalism and free enterprise are apparent in the model described above, the Girl Scouts also believe that scouts should be using their cookie money to fund innovative solutions to pressing social issues to achieve girl empowerment. This is further reiterated in the new series of guidebooks and badge books, entitled *The Girls' Guide to Girl Scouting* (GGGS), which emphasises empowerment through girl leadership in scouts' communities. The badges are divided into five categories, including two focusing on the cookie programme. Each badge ends with a reflective activity where girls spend time to plan how to turn their badge-work into a take action project to find sustainable solutions to their community's problems to create lasting socio-political change (GGGS, 2011). This ideological shift is representative of the *can-do girl* (Harris, 2004), a girl who strives to make positive and significant change in her community. However, some have criticised the Girl Scouts as teaching girls to merely learning to cope with societal problems, rather than promoting change, through a guarded and protected construction of neoliberal citizenship and civic duty (Taft, 2010). Both the *can-do girl* and social band-aid constructions of citizenship are present in the cookie programme, as illustrated in the guidebooks and the actions of the scouts and volunteers. Therefore, the citizenship developed within scouting complicates constructions of youth as either 'citizens in the making' or as 'agents of change'.

In claiming that the GSUSA is reproducing a 'citizens in the making' ideology, I do not suggest that older scouts do not feel empowered by engaging in service-oriented activities. Non-formal educational spaces enable young people to become empowered as they provide youth opportunities that encourage creativity and change rather through activities (Batsleer, 2008). While this might be true of some non-formal educational spaces and this is often promoted in scouting, feelings of girl empowerment are complicated by the overwhelming sense of duty and obligation expressed by older scouts to complete civic activities in their communities, especially within the scouting community. In doing so, this construction of neoliberal citizenship presented in the cookie programme potentially prepares girls to bear the 'triple burden of labor' experienced by many women in a post-industrial and neoliberal economy (Moser, 1993).[5] The Girl Scouts may be transitioning to a model of citizenship that embraces change on a larger scale and enables girls to take on a much more political role in their communities; however, a neoliberal discourse based on service, rather than change, is still reproduced by scouts and volunteers in non-formal educational spaces such as the girl-led cookie programme workshop and rally.

As described above, *GGGS* emphasises girl leadership in scouts' communities by engaging in long-term change rather than teaching girls that service and philanthropy are a panacea for pressing social issues. This ideological shift is presented in many of the badges in the new guidebooks. For example, the 'My Portfolio' badge encourages older scouts to create a 'handout that tells parents how the cookie sale helps girls develop business skills, then distributing it at a council event' (p.4), and the 'Customer Loyalty' badge suggests older scouts brainstorm 'with younger Girl Scouts about how they can build customer loyalty for their cookie sale' (p.4). However, it seems doubtful as to whether handing out fliers or brainstorming marketing strategies can create long-lasting change in the scouting community. These suggested activities reinforce the neoliberal ideologies that the Girl Scouts seek to move beyond from as they prepare children to engage in free market capitalism and enterprise. These activities seemingly perpetuate hegemonic constructions of children as 'citizens to be' rather than engaging social actors capable of making sustainable change. Even though the Girl Scouts may be directing scouts to a model of citizenship focused on long-lasting political engagement, constructions of citizenship based on neoliberal ideals concerning civic participation are still present throughout the non-formal educational spaces of the cookie programme.

Rather than simply handing out fliers or discussing marketing strategies with younger scouts, the Senior Girl Scout troop I followed took it upon themselves to educate younger scouts in the practice of selling cookies. As part of a requirement to earn their Silver Award, the second highest award in the American Girl Scouts, the Seniors created a three-hour workshop that outlined the five fundamental business and leadership skills of the cookie programme. The Silver Award gives older scouts the opportunity to showcase their leadership and demonstrate their determination and dedication to improving their community, whether it is within scouting, in their neighbourhood, city or beyond (Silver Award, 2012). Faith, who was a high school freshman at the time of the workshop, detailed the origins of the workshop:

> and the idea that our brownie cookie workshop, didn't it start off with us like just looked at the sheet for the five skills? And we're able to come up

with a way that we can teach people these skills and it turned into this workshop and Girl Scouts taught us to think of new and creative ways to get an idea or a product out.

(Focus Group, 7 May 2011)[6]

The older scouts came to the conclusion that due to the introduction of a new cookie programme, leaders of younger scouts may feel overwhelmed and may not be able to dedicate enough time to educate their scouts. Additionally, the older scouts recognised a general lack of council support regarding the new cookie programme guidelines and literature. It is also interesting to note that Faith equates the dissemination of knowledge with marketing, which alludes to the further commodification of education in the United States. Ashley, a 15-year-old scout, noted that as a troop they are 'making other kids' lives a bit easier with understanding cookies' (Personal Interview, 13 June 2012). Ashley as well as the other Seniors genuinely believed they were improving the Brownies' personal well-being and creating a space that encouraged Brownies to reach their full potential not only as top cookie sellers but also as leaders in their own right, within their troops and communities.

Teaching can be an empowering and liberatory experience (Freire, 1973; hooks, 1994). The Seniors felt empowered by their teaching experiences in the workshop and rally by sharing their knowledge of cookie salesmanship. These educational spaces can be communal spaces in which knowledge is exchanged between the instructors and the students (hooks, 1994). In the workshop and rally, Brownies learned how to become expert cookie sellers while the Seniors gained invaluable life and leadership skills. Many of the older girls cited wanting to complete the Silver Award as they believe it would look impressive on their college applications, but many wanted to complete their Silver Award based on personal feelings of good will and personal fulfilment. The Seniors also noted that 'helping others' and 'being kind-hearted' are inherent qualities of being a 'good' Girl Scout and that it is their duty to help those both in and out of the scouting community. It is admirable for teenagers to be taking on a leadership role within a non-formal educational space; this role potentially prepares them for their future as bearers of the triple burden of labour.

Several scouts commented that they felt empowered knowing that the skills they gained from teaching younger girls would be put to use in their future adult lives in both the workforce and at home. While 'getting a good job' is a common aspiration for young people, they also desired emotional stability (Brown, 2011). For the teen girls in this study, many envisioned becoming happy, productive adults due to their leadership experiences in scouting. For example, Cassia, another 15-year-old scout, noted that the cookie workshop was particularly rewarding as she gained invaluable work and leadership experience. She felt the workshop and scouting in general prepared her to accomplish her life goals of becoming a music teacher and good mother. When asked what the Seniors gained from their workshop experience, Ashley agrees that the workshop and Girl Scouts, in general,

> really sets you up for your future and like that's the whole thing about Girl Scouts you're always planning for the future whether it's to go sell a box of cookies or to go get into the best college you can get into and use all these skills that you use since you were really little and be able to [use] them throughout your whole future and become very successful in life.
>
> (Focus Group, 7 May 2011)

As to her own personal future goals, Ashley, who expressed an interest in working with children in the future (as a sports medicine specialist), believes that 'working with kids is just a lot of fun and you get enjoyable things out of it' (Personal Interview, 13 June 2012). She illustrates here that happiness and success are intimately linked to women's roles as caregivers. The Girl Scouts, whether intentional or not, essentialises women's future roles as potential caregivers by extending the private space of home or domestic space into the public space of the community or cityscape.

Service, rather than sustainable change, was stressed throughout the workshop and rally. Bearing the triple burden is widely experienced by many American women thus; girls are learning to juggle multiple responsibilities and obligations at a very young age within scouting. Many of the badges associated with domestic labour have been replaced with badges that emphasise social justice or environmental science; however, the scouts and volunteers in this study encouraged younger girls to perform gendered forms of reproductive labour within their communities. During the decision-making session in the workshop, Izzy and Anna provided a few example service projects that Brownies could potentially complete with their cookie money, including volunteering at a breast cancer walk, feeding the homeless or spending an afternoon helping out at Ronald McDonald House.[7] They then asked the Brownies to draw a picture of a service activity. The Brownies drew pictures of giving toys to children in a hospital and making 'diamond-shaped' pancakes for the homeless. At the rally, Erri led another decision-making activity wherein Juniors threw a frisbee to one another and whoever caught it would make a suggestion for a service activity (Figure 17.1). Many scouts, again, suggested feeding the homeless or hosting a toy drive, while a few mentioned donating pet supplies to animal shelters. It is commendable for young girls to become involved in their communities and to be introduced to important issues such as women's reproductive health, poverty and child mortality; however, engaging in these types of service projects potentially encourage girls to reproduce not only forms of neoliberal citizenship rooted in service rather than social change but also gendered notions of care.

Figure 17.1 Girls learning to make 'good' decisions at the cookie-sale rally

The service projects discussed during the decision-making sessions were exclusively associated with care and reproductive labour such as food preparation or taking care of a sick child. Interestingly, neither the older scouts nor the Brownies (or Juniors) suggested projects that revolved around current environmental or political issues, such as trail maintenance or increasing voter registration (both popular American Boy Scout service projects). This suggests that girls are socialised to *belong* in private, feminine spaces associated with the home or domesticity rather than public, masculine-associated spaces such as nature and politics. Again, it is important for girls to learn about community citizenship, especially as it helps girls develop empathy and there is potential for girls to develop leadership skills; however, girls are taught, perhaps unwittingly, that a woman's place is not necessarily on the trail or in politics but rather in the community as a caregiver. The community thus becomes an extension of the home within the context of the cookie programme. This is particularly counter-intuitive to the organisation's current 'Year of the Girl' campaign to increase girl and women leadership nationwide, as Chavez has cited on multiple occasions the lack of female presence in all branches of the US government. Additionally, the activities suggested by both younger and older scouts emphasise short-term fixes rather than thinking about long-term change. Many of the proposed activities do not involve engaging with the benefiting populations whom the girls are providing services for, rather almost all the activities involve donation instead of interacting with the intended benefactors.[8] This creates a contradictory message for girls regarding community leadership, one that suggests that the act of giving (or purchasing) connotes good leadership and citizenship rather than discussing the potential impacts of engaging in long-term change. This is not to argue that creating long-lasting change automatically equates to empowerment and participating in service projects gives scouts a false sense of agency or autonomy. Rather, a closer examination is needed of how neoliberal spaces, particularly youth-led informal educational spaces, impact young people's sense of empowerment and agency.

Perhaps, one way to examine the impact of the neoliberalisation of informal educational spaces is to see how empowerment and feelings of self-reliance are used to justify the deregulation of services like education. Empowerment rhetoric, in neoliberal discourse, has emerged to replace State dependence (i.e., welfare) (Sharma, 2008). For example, the workshop was considered to be a success by the troop with the troop leader receiving many emails from satisfied Brownie leaders complimenting the Seniors' ability to teach (and lead) dozens of Brownies. The older scouts expressed how proud and happy they were to be able to accomplish such a feat, especially as most teenagers (or adults) would not be able to lead almost 100 Brownies. The success of the workshop did not go unnoticed by the local council. The council now wants service units to host their own cookie workshops so as to alleviate some of the responsibility and cost from council.[9] The council product sales manager even commented that by giving more control over the cookie programme to volunteers, the council was empowering volunteers. By granting volunteers the ability to self-govern or control their own cookie programming, the council no longer has to bear the responsibility or cost of such programming for scouts and therefore contributes to the further neoliberalisation of education in the United States.

Conclusion

There is a need for educational programmes such as the Girl Scout cookie programme, as children and young people have limited access to financial literacy education within formal educational institutions in the United States. The informal educational space of the cookie programme enables girls to gain invaluable financial skills that can translate into multiple spaces of their lives. In this current time of economic duress, many girls commented on the need of educational spaces that prepares them for their future adult lives. However, the cookie programme prepares girls for more than just their financial futures. The cookie programme grants older scouts with the opportunity to take on leadership roles in the sale by instructing younger scouts how to be proper economic citizens as well as learning early on that American women must bear the triple burden of labour. The Girl Scouts has always been praised as an organisation that teaches girls to be self-reliant, which is a vital trait to possess, but further research is needed to examine how self-reliance is represented as being synonymous with empowerment within youth organisations, especially as many organisations are co-opted by neoliberal ideals and policies to replace important educational services. Therefore, the objectives of these spaces need further examination as many reinforce neoliberal ideals concerning women, caregiving and community management.

Acknowledgements

I would like to thank the Summer Academic Working Group, Dr Leslie Kern, Marta Jankowska and Zia Salim for their invaluable feedback and guidance.

Notes

1. Traditionally, the cookie season begins in late January and ends in mid-March; however, in colder regions of the United States, the cookie season is held during the Fall.
2. Seniors range in age from 14 to 15 years old.
3. Non-formal and informal learning differ. I use non-formal learning to describe the space of the cookie programme because it is more structured, given the extensive guidebooks and literature provided for girls and volunteers. The teen scouts also created a space that while filled with 'fun and whimsy' slightly mirrors formal educational spaces in terms of its structure.
4. 'Discover, Connect, and Take Action' is the motto for leadership within the Girl Scouts.
5. The triple burden of labour consists of (1) reproductive (childcare, domestic labour, etc.); (2) production (paid work in cash or kind); and (3) community management (maintaining the welfare of the community) (Moser, 1993).
6. Pseudonyms were used for participants.

7. Ronald McDonald House is a children's hospital and hospice centre, primarily funded by McDonald's that provides medical services and support for children and their families.
8. This is partially due to liability or insurance issues. For example, many San Diego animal shelters will not allow children to handle animals while volunteering.
9. A service unit is a smaller geographic area in the council that is governed by high-ranking volunteers.

References

S. Aapola, M. Gonick and A. Harris (2005) *Young Femininity: Girlhood, power and social change* (New York: Palgrave Macmillan).
J. Batsleer (2008) *Informal Learning in Youth Work* (Thousand Oaks: SAGE Publications).
Z. Bekerman, N. Burbules and D. Silberman Keller (2006) *Learning in Places: The informal education reader* (New York: Peter Lang).
G. Brown (2011) 'Emotional geographies of young people's aspirations for adult life', *Children's Geographies*, 9, 7–22.
M. Brown (2012) 'We've done our homework- now it's time for teen vogue to do theirs', http://www.sparksummit.com/2012/09/24/weve-done-our-homework-now-its-time-for-teen-vogue-to-do-theirs/ (accessed 5 December 2012).
D. Currie and D. Kelly (2006) 'I'm going to crush you like a bug: Understanding girls' agency and empowerment', in Y. Jiwani, C. Steenbergen and C. Mitchell (eds) *Girlhood Redefining the Limits* (Montreal: Black Rose Books).
Financial Empowerment (2012) *Financial Empowerment K-12 Program* (New York: GSUSA).
P. Freire (1973) *Pedagogy of the Oppressed* (New York: Seabury Press).
N. Fyfe and C. Milligan (2003) 'Out of the shadows: Exploring contemporary geographies of voluntarism', *Progress in Human Geography*, 27, 397–413.
GGGS (2011) *The Girl's Guide to Girl Scouting: Senior* (New York: GSUSA).
Girl Scouts San Diego (GSSD) (2011) *What Can a Cookie Do? More than you see: 2012 Cookie program guide for troop leaders*.
D. Hammett and L. Staeheli (2011) 'Respect and responsibility: Teaching citizenship in South African high schools', *International Journal of Educational Development*, 31, 269–76.
K. Hankins and D. Martin (2006) 'Charter schools and urban regimes in neoliberal context: Making workers and new spaces in metropolitan Atlanta', *International Journal of Urban and Regional Research*, 30, 528–47.
A. Harris (2004) *Future Girl: Young women in the 21st century* (New York: Routledge).
b. hooks (1994) *Teaching to Transgress: Education as the practice of freedom* (New York: Routledge).
J. Kahne and J. Westheimer (1996) 'In the service of what? The politics of service learning' *Phi Delta Kappan*, 77, 592.
S. Miller (2007) *Growing Girls: The natural origins of girls' organizations in America* (New Brunswick: Rutgers University Press).
C. Milligan and D. Conradson (2006) 'Contemporary landscapes of welfare: The voluntary turn?' in C. Milligan and D. Conradson (eds) *Landscapes of Voluntarism New Spaces of Health, Welfare and Governance* (Bristol: The Policy Press).
S. Mills (2013) 'An instruction in good citizenship: Scouting and the historical geographies of citizenship education', *Transactions of the Institute of British Geographers*, 38, 120–34.

K. Mitchell (2006) 'Neoliberal governmentality in the European Union: Education, training, and technologies of citizenship', *Environment and Planning D: Society and Space*, 29, 389–407.

C. Moser (1993) *Gender, Planning, and Development: Theory, practice, and training* (London: Routledge).

H. Nocon and M. Cole (2006) 'School's invansion of "after-school": Colonization, rationalization, or expansion of access?' in Z. Bekerman, N. Burbules and D. Silberman-Keller (eds) *Learning in Places: The informal education reader* (New York: Peter Lang).

T. Proctor (2009) *Scouting for Girls: A century of girl guides and girl scouts* (Santa Barbara: ABC-CLO).

J. Pykett (2009) 'Making citizens in the classroom: An urban geography of citizenship education?' *Urban Studies*, 46, 803–23.

L. M. Salamon (1999) 'The non-profit sector at the crossroads: The case of America', *Voluntas*, 10, 5–23.

D. Schugurensky (2006) ' "This is our school of citizenship": Informal learning in local democracy', in Z. Bekerman, N. Burbules and D. Silberman-Keller (eds) *Learning in Places: The informal education reader* (New York: Peter Lang).

A. Sharma (2008) *Logics of Empowerment Development, Gender, and Government in Neoliberal India* (Minneapolis: University of Minnesota Press).

Silver Award (2012) Silver Award Website, http://www.girlscouts.org/program/highest_awards/silver_award.asp, date accessed 1 June 2012.

L. Staeheli (2011) 'Political geography: Where's citizenship?' *Progress in Human Geography* 35, 393–400.

L. Staeheli and D. Hammett (2010) 'Educating the new national citizen: Education, political subjectivity and divided societies', *Citizenship Studies*, 14, 667–80.

J. Taft (2010) 'Girlhood in action: Contemporary U.S. girls' organizations and the public sphere', *Girlhood Studies*, 3, 11–29.

C. Thiem (2009) 'Thinking through education: The geographies of contemporary educational restructuring', *Progress in Human Geography*, 33, 154–73.

D. A. Zoerink, A. H. Magafas, and K. A. Pawelko (1997) 'Empowering youth at risk through community service', *Child and Youth Care Forum*, 26, 127–38.

18
iLearn: Engaging (In)Formal Learning in Young People's Mediated Environments

Gregory T. Donovan

The broad embrace of proprietary education, play and communication media among US youth means their daily experiences now generate 'big data' flows that are mined by states and corporations alike. Young people thus develop within ubiquitous ecosystems of information, yet rarely are they involved in the production and governance of such ecologies. In this chapter I unpack the formal and informal learning taking place in young people's mediated environments to discuss how such learning can assist the development of more open and participatory information ecologies. Through an analysis of my interviews and collaborative research and design with youth, I critique the pedagogy of proprietary media and call for more age-inclusive participation in the production of everyday media.

The proprietary quality of most information ecologies means corporations with various levels of national and international regulation typically own them. As youth learn to text, email and search, their mediated identity configurations link up with informational modes of socioeconomic production. This creates what I call a 'proprietary ecology' where most young people have broad experiential learning regarding the consumer's end of the interface but are left mystified as to what's going on behind the interface. By means of digital enclosure (cf., Andrejevic, 2007; Boyle, 2008), such as online censorship, intellectual property and service agreements, privately owned interfaces are designed as two-way mirrors for producers and mirrors for consumers.

Through an analysis of the MyDigitalFootprint.ORG Project, I take a critical approach to understanding the mutual shaping of people, place and media through the learning experiences of youth situated within this proprietary ecology. The MyDigitalFootprint.ORG Project began by interviewing 15 young people aged 14–19 from New York City to compare and contrast their privacy, property and security concerns in mediated environments.

Five of these interviewees ranging in age from 15 to 19 then participated as co-researchers in a Youth Design and Research Collective (YDRC) to analyse concerns that emerged from interviews through the collaborative design of an open-source social network. In taking a medium as our message and method, co-researchers took on the role of social network producers to gain perspectives otherwise mystified to media consumers.

The project took a participatory action design research (PADR) approach to understand and engage young people's formal and informal learning around matters of privacy, property and security. A PADR approach combines participatory action research (PAR) and participatory design (PD) to investigate and involve the people, places and media that afford mediated experiences. PAR represents an epistemological stance within academic inquiry that 'assumes knowledge is rooted in social relations and most powerful when produced collaboratively through action' (Fine et al., 2003, p.173). Such a stance helps investigate the environments of youth as relational and contextual phenomena that are constructed at multiple scales throughout the life course (Cahill, 2004; Hopkins and Pain, 2007). PD is primarily concerned with how to involve everyday people in the practice of design (Bannon and Ehn, 2012). In a digital context PD 'shares some theories and methods with user-centred design and interaction design, but the main thrust is on democratic and emancipatory practice' (Greenbaum and Loi, 2012, p.81).

Instead of producing new knowledges through proprietary means that are mystified to all but their proprietors, a participatory approach opens up regimes of ownership and governance by involving 'users' in the means of production. With information systems now a critical component of contemporary urban infrastructures, PADR has been drawn on increasingly to understand and engage urban development according to community interests and concerns (cf., Foth and Adkins, 2006; Bilandzic and Venable, 2011). In the context of young people's learning, this means taking seriously the knowledge gained from routine mediated practices while also developing a medium and method through a collaborative process that values their situated interests and concerns.

At the empirical core of the MyDigitalFootprint.ORG Project was my collaborative work with the YDRC, who were asked to reflect critically on their daily experiences as social network users to design an open-source social network. Their informal practices of emailing, texting, commenting, searching and sharing amidst evolving identity configurations guided the social network's design. Our workshops began with tutorials on information architecture, internet governance, qualitative research methods and ethics, open-source software and universal access to enhance the YDRCs consciousness in mediated environments as well as to provide the literacies necessary to design a social network. I draw from this experience-oriented design process to unpack how the YDRC negotiated global, national and

intimate matters of privacy, property and security. I also draw on my interviews with young people to situate my analysis and discuss how interviewee
concerns were revisited and analysed during six workshops with the YDRC
at the CUNY Graduate Center in Midtown Manhattan.[1] I begin by outlining the matters of concern that our work focused on before discussing the
psychosocial aspects of young people's evolving identity configurations and
how engagement in media production shaped this evolution in relation to
privacy, property and security matters.

Matters of concern

The YDRCs formal school-based education around media was predominately
framed in terms of how they should not steal content or internet connections, how they should not access certain websites at school or home, and
most importantly how someone was always watching and waiting to catch
them if they did something wrong. This comported with references to 'the
government', 'the police', 'a librarian', 'mom', 'some evil genius', 'a preda-
tor' and other actors routinely named by interviewees as potential spies
monitoring their mediated behaviours. As these statements suggest, formal
education for most US youth is focused largely on protecting and policing
their engagements with media, typically motivated by parents' and teachers'
sincere concern for a child or student's safety. Yet, it provides little in the way
of media literacies from which to negotiate a social network in an informed
way, let alone design one.

Being taught how to stay safe or out of trouble was discussed by the YDRC
as more than an annoyance. Such education was considered a distraction
from what they wanted to be learning and what they felt would be empowering to learn. In contrast to their formally structured education, the YDRC
found value in the informal ways their interactions with and within social
networks and other social media helped them learn about themselves, their
peers, and local as well as translocal cultures. I use 'informal' here to distinguish this mode of learning from more formalised school-based modes
of learning. In this sense, informal learning still accounts for the quite
formal ways proprietary media, such as Google or Facebook, encourage particular modes of searching and tagging even if one chooses to reject such
encouragement.

In our first workshop, the YDRC discussed the 'tech geeks' in their schools
who they felt held much power because they were able to technologically
outsmart teachers and administrators. These 'tech geeks,' for example, were
discussed as among the first to figure out a way around school filters and
to share this knowledge with other students. Such knowledge, according
to the YDRC, gave these 'geeks' a degree of power within their respective
schools. The linking of knowledge with empowerment through these discussions motivated the YDRC to build a social network so that they might

gain a better understanding as to how media operated in their environment. The designing of a network thus became as much of an end itself as whatever additional meaning it took on while in operation.

Boundaries and boundary-makings of development

Interviewees and the YDRC were engaged in what Erikson (1982) defines as the adolescent stage of development when identity formation emerges as an 'evolving configuration' (p.74). Erikson is eager to note, and I to emphasise, that identity is not configured during this stage of development, rather it is a configuration that evolves throughout the life course. While configuration begins well before adolescence, it is during this stage when one begins to configure their identity in relation to broader societal norms and expectations. Adolescence is a formative stage in identity development when young people begin to learn and play out social practices in line with what Erikson (1982) calls 'the ethos of production' (p.75). 16-year-old Melanie's experience searching for and listening to music highlights how social production, evolving identity configurations, and proprietary media intertwine in practice:

> [YouTube] helps you see things that are going around, or music that like people are playing, clicking a lot … if it's a nice music and it's like really cool, everybody is clicking it. It kind of like makes you go 'oh, this is so nice, everybody know this music' … So you know, you kind of like listen a lot and you know the lyrics and you might sing it, sing at some places. You might go to your friend 'oh, do you know this music? Everybody listen to it.'

Melanie goes on to explain that often she first hears music on TV then uses Google Search to ultimately find the song or artist on YouTube:

> I have this channel MTV … it shows you those kind of new music that comes up, or the old music, and all that. So you know these people that you're going to search for. And, you search them. Sometimes you don't get their name, so you put the one sentence of the – like this music that would say 'you're cooler than me,' right? So you put 'you're cooler than me,' and then they'll show you the name of the song – and, you know, you click.

How Melanie comes to know and like music situates how corporate platforms such as Google, YouTube's parent company, facilitate familiar forms of identity configuration in relation to social norms with a proprietary twist. What content Google allows on their servers as well as what forms of research and participation they afford through their interface is oriented by Google's interest in generating profit. What 'everybody is clicking' on YouTube and what Melanie sings the lyrics to when out with friends is shaped as much by her desires and peers as Google and MTV. For youth, both people and media function as peers in shaping their tastes and thus identity configuration.

Melanie's experience situates how routine interactions generate exchange value for Google while fostering particular practices that sustain broader socioeconomic development. This bolsters Erikson's (1982) association of adolescent development with an ethos of production while also suggesting youth are particularly sensitive to, and early indicators of, evolving work roles:

> A certain hierarchy of work roles has already entered the playing and learning child's imagination by way of ideal examples, real or mythical, that now present themselves in the persons of instructing adults, and in the heroes of legend, history, and fiction. (p.75)

What it means to be a 'tech geek,' student, daughter, social media sensation, or Silicon Valley mogul enters the informational imagination of youth, and influences the identities they affiliate with or repudiate. Likewise, the repudiations and affiliations of youth in turn shape what modes of development are materially and socially sustained.

Wilson (2009) offers a rereading of the cyborg metaphor's operation in the field of geography to describe an 'ontological hybridity' that is 'about contingent beings and about forms of becoming that challenge dualist narratives, like human/machine, nature/society and the virtual/real' (p.499). Along with this ontological hybridity, Wilson calls for more attention to the epistemology of cyborg geographies by researching both 'boundaries and boundary-makings' (p.500), and thus both ways of becoming and knowing in hybrid configurations of people, place, and media. It is precisely these boundary-makings that the analytical pairing of development and development helps bring into focus (Katz, 2004); yet boundaries and boundary-makings are also what become so difficult to ascertain in opaque and seemingly ubiquitous proprietary ecologies. If, as Erikson (1982) argues, negotiating the boundaries between an 'inner space' and a 'social space' is central to configuring one's identity, then demystifying the boundaries and boundary-makings in and around these spaces is central to understanding the development of adolescents in relation to broader socioeconomic development.

Lewin (1997) argues that people must be understood as operating within a 'life space' defined by the sum of all psychological factors experienced at a given time; most notably factors such as 'needs, motivation, mood, goals, anxiety, and ideals' (p.210). Lewin discusses the life space as relationally defined through an evolving 'boundary zone' that mediates a person's interactions with a 'multitude of processes in the physical and social world' (p.210). Thus, the scope of a person's situated experience at a given time – what people, places, and things they do and don't interact with at some level – shapes the boundaries of their life space and thus the form of their becoming. This boundary-making, as Wilson (2009) reminds us, is an epistemological act in cyborg geographies and, as Erikson (1982) reminds us, a psychosocial act of identity configuration. Thus, I argue these boundary-makings are acts of both knowledge production and identity configuration, which evolve around matters of privacy, property, and security within the life space of young people coming of age.

Situating privacy, property, and security

Interviewees, as well as the YDRC, felt more experienced than their parents or teachers in the affective and fulfilling qualities of social networks as well as the unpleasant and unwanted ones. The YDRC had fun browsing photos of themselves, friends, and even strangers on Facebook. They also expressed concern that someone 'creepy' could be looking at their photos or the photos of friends and family. Concerns were also raised that they could lose control of their online representations by losing control of what photos of them get posted where and when. Co-researchers often instructed each other that the present posting of a photo of oneself to Facebook could come back to haunt them later in life if found by a college or employer.

Although these concerns were felt and often noted, some YDRC members would still take photos of themselves or others during workshops and instantly upload them to Facebook. Even co-researchers who at times discouraged others from 'always uploading photos' would at other times participate in this very practice. The YDRC were experienced in the nuanced and often contradictory emotions and practices that come with participating in proprietary social networks. They understood desiring interpersonal engagement and social exposure while simultaneously desiring personal privacy and tight control over their mediated representations. This contradictory life in mediated environments undergirded the informal learning of co-researchers and provided them with a common experience that they often felt was not shared with adults. It was frequently noted that parents, teachers, and other adults lacked a common sense that they and their peers shared. This is not to suggest that these adults are naive, but that interviewees and co-researchers often perceived adults to be less experienced with media and thus more naive than themselves; an ironic inversion of the formal education they received.

Disclosures of managing a parent's engagements with the internet to ensure a certain degree of personal privacy were common among interviewees, as in this example from 14-year-old Orlando:

Well, like my mom is kind of annoying how she like – like she's a great person, but how sometimes when she gets on Facebook, she'll just start clicking. So, if she sees anything that I've been tagged in, she'll click on it and she'll go through the whole album.

Not wanting his mother to see every photo of him that gets posted to Facebook, but also not wanting to hurt his mother's feelings by 'defriending' her, Orlando configured his mother's Facebook privacy settings to enhance his own privacy:

So, what I did was I went on her – when she went to the bathroom and she was on Facebook and I went on there and I went into my profile and I said 'hide all posts.' So, I don't think she can see it, but I asked her 'would you be mad if I defriended you' and she'd be like 'yeah!' But it's so obvious if you block someone, it's even just like defriending them.

In changing his mother's privacy settings to 'hide all posts' from his personal account, Orlando remains his mother's 'friend' but she no longer sees the photos, comments, and status updates associated with his account in her news feed.

Alternatively, 15-year-old Megan was concerned that her mother's online shopping and bill paying practices could result in the theft of her mother's identity:

I think I'm really concerned about, like, for my mother. Since she uses – like she uses online to pay her bills and things.... I order on Forever 21 and I was about to enter her credit card number that, you know, how sometimes it's saved already? like it's in the box under it? And so... that wasn't the card I was about to use, and I was like 'it shouldn't have been saved'.

When entering her mother's credit card information to buy clothes online, Megan's web browser began to automatically fill-in the information for another one of her mother's cards. This auto-fill feature is common among browsers and, in this case, the browser had stored the credit card information that Megan's mother had previously entered. Whether this storage of information was intended or unintended, Megan found this concerning and informed her mother how to prevent the browser from saving such information in the future to protect her mother's privacy and financial security.

Despite feeling they knew more than others, interviewees and the YDRC did not feel totally in control within mediated environments. Frequent references were made to what they perceived as their personal failure for relying too much on 'the internet', 'Facebook', or 'texting'. They expressed guilt for getting wrapped up in gossip, peer-monitoring, and socialising online. This sense of failure and guilt was rooted in a belief that they could be doing more productive things with their time. Interviewees saw the internet as a relatively unknown and highly addictive assemblage. The expressed guilt around this felt ignorance and addiction was a tacit awareness that this assemblage was produced and that by understanding its production one could better control their own privacy, property, and security – or those of others, such as parents.

I hasten to add that aspects of this guilt are socially encouraged among youth through the ways proprietary services overwhelm their users with many complicated but weak privacy settings that become easier to avoid, and feel bad about, than actually configure. In this sense, young people are guilted into accepting responsibility for not knowing how to overcome obstacles that are designed to discourage controlling their privacy. Even as this guilt is encouraged and misplaced, it remains a desire to know more and do better than one currently feels to be the case. In this sense, the guilt expressed by interviewees and co-researchers was somewhat aspirational. If they didn't care to know more or feel more in control, then a sense of apathy and not guilt would have been expressed. Despite popular stereotypes of 'apathetic youth,' interviewees and the YDRC were interested and concerned.

Towards the beginning of every workshop we took time for members of the YDRC to raise any issue or share any media they desired. This was typically a website, video, song, or an idea that was related to something we previously discussed or that a co-researcher wanted us to discuss. In our second workshop one co-researcher raised the 2011 uprisings in Egypt and Libya that were, at the time, heavily reported in American media: 'That guy in Egypt – it keeps happening in different countries. Libya, too'. The others quickly joined the discussion to talk about the ways social media was being used, with one YDRC member noting how the governments in each country were 'shutting down the internet'. Notably, the victims and criminals in this discussion were muddled with another co-researcher commenting on Muammar Gaddafi as 'a good guy, everything I hear is that he's a good guy' and another on Hosni Mubarak as 'a good leader, but he's just been there too long.' That the YDRC consisted of self-identified Muslims and Christians, some of whom were born in Africa and Asia, appeared to give them more information or at least a different perspective from what was being communicated through American media. When one co-researcher noted that 'everything they had heard' indicated Gaddafi was 'a good guy', it was clear this wasn't heard on the local or national news but from within their respective communities.

I took this as an opportunity to generally outline how the Egyptian government shut down the internet by instructing ISPs operating within the country to close their Border Gateway Protocols (BGP) and thus cut off most data flows going in and coming out of Egypt's geographic borders. While sympathetic to the rebels in each country, the shutting down of the internet was discussed amongst the YDRC as inevitable and something to be expected when public uprisings take place. That it wasn't a violent act by these states, in and of itself, also made it more tolerable to the YDRC. With legislation being considered in the United States that would provide the executive branch with these same abilities to shut down the internet during a state of national emergency, I asked the YDRC how they would feel about their president having the same power.[2] The YRDC largely, and rather quickly, concluded that if the president felt it was warranted it would be OK to shut down the internet. Their reasoning was presented along the lines of 'if shutting down the internet could have prevented 9/11, then why wouldn't you shut it down?' They specifically noted that they 'trusted Obama' suggesting that who held the office of the president had much influence in their conclusion.

I then asked how long should the president be able to shut down the internet in an attempt to prevent another 9/11. There was a pause before one YDRC member cautiously stated, 'until night time – I think'. Another member decided they could go a week if necessary, but the rest agreed even a full day without internet access was too long. They reasoned that the loss of connectivity would cause so much disruption to their lives and those of others that it would create a national emergency far greater than the one it was intended to prevent. In connecting their experiences with those elsewhere, the YDRC reconsidered such affairs transpiring in Egypt and Libya within their own daily practices and recognised a mutual affinity for freely communicating with and within information ecologies.

Jeffrey (2013) argues the technological mobilisation of youth during the Arab Spring occurred 'outside formal party politics, institutional bodies, and readily identifiable social movements' (p.149) to afford 'new ecologies of youth protest.' Although seeing empowerment in such ecologies, Jeffrey notes the capacity of states to regulate access to the internet and thus complicate such mobilisation. Shutting down the internet in Egypt and Libya did complicate the mobilisation of young people in each country, yet this act and the global attention it provoked also ironically expanded such ecologies of protest. Considered practically, and in the context of their own lives, shutting down the internet for days no longer seemed like a justifiable proposition for most of the YDRC. The internet, in this case, helped provide a translocal gateway for co-researchers and countered the common social admonitions they encountered that framed the internet as a gateway to disengagement and distraction. The YDRCs opposition to the practices of Mubarak and Gaddafi did not emerge from formal or readily identified geopolitics, but rather an intimately understood injustice.

Conclusion

Young people are a highly sought after consumer demographic in the US economy. According to Harris Interactive (2010), US youth aged 8–24 have a collective annual spending power of $239 billion that continues to increase despite decreases among other demographics as a result of rising unemployment and reduced wages. As adults spend less on themselves, they continue to spend more on their children and the children of others. This socially positions youth as objects of significant market interest that are embedded in proprietary ecologies to influence and aggregate their consumption patterns. This strategic embedding also places youth in an environment fraught with phenomena such as cyberbullying, sexting, intellectual property disputes, data mining, and national cybersecurity; each mediating the life space of youth during early stages of identity configuration. This positioning does not make them more endangered or empowered than any other age group, but it does put them at the fore of socioeconomic restructuring.

In workshops the YDRC regularly alluded to the notion that the internet was not a natural phenomena and thus did not have to be taken as is. Co-researchers often cited 'a man' that made the internet, 'that guy' who started Facebook, or 'a terminal somewhere' that facilitates all internet-based communication. Although communicated with a vague vocabulary, this conveyed a limited consciousness of people and places that were involved in the boundaries and boundary-makings of their mediated environment. Co-researchers were not sure how the internet worked, but their experiences informed them that there was indeed work involved. More empowering relationships with and within information ecologies were possible through more critical participation. Even this limited consciousness of media production provided us a framework for such engagement as we could then began to research how some of these people and places operated.

Like other young people, interviewees and the YDRC were informally learning to use search engines; to collaboratively develop coding schemes through tagging, ranking, and categorising practices; to compose and publish their own content on multiple platforms; and to share and discuss various information asynchronously and in real-time. Learned practices such as these were drawn on in my work with the YDRC to develop the literacies necessary for designing and governing a social network. In learning how to be productive with information, the YDRC developed skills and insights for reorienting media production towards their own situated interests and concerns.

Taking the medium as our method demystified the YDRCs interactions in proprietary ecologies by producing new ones in a more open ecology. This provided opportunities and vocabularies for imagining how the platforms and practices that sustain proprietary ecologies could better address situated matters of privacy, property and security. As Cahill (2007) argues 'engaging young people in research helps challenge social exclusion, democratise the research process, and build the capacity of young people to analyse and transform their own lives and communities' (p.298). Considering the MyDigitalFootprint.ORG Project, I argue that engaging youth in media design builds critical capacities for participating in informal acts of every-day research and learning. If proprietary ecologies are the means by which states and corporations complicate and co-opt Jeffrey's (2013) 'ecologies of youth protest', then critical engagement with such privatisation opens up such ecologies to the mutual subjectivities and shared goals of the young people participating in them.

Notes

1. Co-researchers consented to the recording of workshops but collectively decided that direct quotes used in future analysis were to be attributed to 'members of the YDRC,' a 'co-researcher,' or 'the YDRC'. Asmaou, Kaitlin, Rose, Saif, and Yvonne all felt comfortable publicly identifying themselves as the YDRC (see http://mydigitalfootprint.org/ydrc/) yet they didn't want to have individual quotes or actions attributed specifically to their names. In the case of interviewees, pseudonyms are used to maintain their anonymity.
2. At the time, the bill being considered was the Cybersecurity Act of 2009. Although this bill did not pass, it continues to be proposed with various modifications during each legislative session of the US Congress.

References

M. Andrejevic (2007) 'Surveillance in the digital enclosure', *The Communication Review*, 10, 295–317.

L. J. Bannon and P. Ehn (2012) 'Design: Design matters in participatory design', in J. Simonsen and T. Robertson (eds) *The Routledge International Handbook of Participatory Design* (New York: Routledge).

M. Bilandzic and J. Venable (2011) 'Towards participatory action design research: Adapting action research and design science research methods for urban informatics', *The Journal of Community Informatics*, 7, http://ci-journal.net/index.php/ciej/article/view/786/804

J. Boyle (2008) *The Public Domain: Enclosing the Commons of the Mind* (New Haven: Yale University Press).

C. Cahill (2004) 'Defying gravity? Raising consciousness through collective research', *Children's Geographies*, 2, 273–86.

C. Cahill (2007) 'Doing research with young people: Participatory research and the rituals of collective work', *Children's Geographies*, 5, 297–312.

E. H. Erikson (1982) *The Life Cycle Completed* (New York: W.W. Norton & Company).

M. Fine, M. E. Torre, K. Boudin, I. Bowen, J. Clark, D. Hylton, M. Martinez, 'Missy', M. Rivera, R. A. Roberts, P. Smart, and D. Upegui (2003) 'Participatory action research: Within and beyond bars', in P. Camic, J. E. Rhodes, and L. Yardley (eds) *Qualitative Research in Psychology: Expanding perspectives in methodology and design* (Washington, DC: American Psychological Association).

M. Foth and B. Adkins (2006) 'A research design to build effective artnerships between city planners, developers, government and urban neighbourhood communities', *The Journal of Community Informatics*, 2, 116–33.

J. Greenbaum and D. Loi (2012) 'Participation, the camel and the elephant of design: An introduction', *CoDesign: International Journal of CoCreation in Design and the Arts*, 8, 81–5.

Harris Interactive (2010) *Trends & Tudes: YouthPulse 2010*, 9, http://www.harrisinter
active.com/vault/HI_TrendsTudes_2010_v09_i02.pdf

P. Hopkins and R. Pain (2007) 'Geographies of age: Thinking relationally', *Area*, 39, 287–94.

C. Jeffrey (2013) 'Geographies of children and youth III: Alchemists of the revolution?' *Progress in Human Geography*, 37: 145–52.

C. Katz (2004) *Growing Up Global: Economic restructuring and children's everyday lives* (Minneapolis: University of Minnesota Press).

K. Lewin (1997) *Resolving Social Conflicts: Field theory in social science* (Washington, DC: American Psychological Association).

M. W. Wilson (2009) 'Cyborg geographies: Towards hybrid epistemologies', *Gender, Place & Culture*, 16, 499–516.

Part V
Conclusion

our view, could be fruitfully developed as future lines of academic inquiry. Some of these future directions may also enable critical reflection among policy-makers and practitioners: writing as academics, we would not seek to determine the practical implications of this book, but do, in our fourth theme, suggest ways in which academics, policy-makers and practitioners might collaborate around issues pertinent to informal education.

Pushing the boundaries of informal education

Several chapters in this book engage critically and directly with definitions of informal education. As we recognised in our introductory chapter, within youth work and education studies, this impulse is far from new. Yet, given the relative lack of geographical and historical research on informal education, the chapters in this book have sought to engage with questions of the *boundaries* and *contexts* of informal education in new ways. Perhaps most significantly, taken together, they have charted a range of important linkages between informal education and its constitutive 'others': non-formal, alternative and formal learning. In some cases, these linkages may be practical, as educators seek to 'up-scale' communities of learning beyond the immediate confines of a school, youth centre or community space (Sadlier; Kraftl). In other cases, these linkages may be political, tacking together places quite distant and distinct from one another through unified, emancipatory goals that extend across space (Dickens and Lonie). Elsewhere, these same political goals may extend across time, as, for instance, styles of feminist-inspired youth work so prevalent in the 1970s re-emerge through new social media (Spence). Elsewhere again, some chapters have witnessed micro-scale practices within formal educational institutions such as schools, using recent theories from social and cultural geography to examine how bodies, emotions and material (physical) spaces may both enable and foreclose possibilities for informal education (Bowlby et al.; Aufseeser; Davies).

While in themselves representing important standalone studies, the chapters in this book also offer starting points: a series of critical questions and conceptual tools for interrogating how, where and when the geographies and histories of informal education might matter. Future research on informal education, perhaps in the many other geographical and historical contexts *not* considered in this volume, might deploy similar conceptual frameworks as those briefly listed above. More programmatically, future research could consider the *larger* spatial and temporal scales that work, recursively, to produce what appear to be 'local' and 'immediate' experiences of informal education. Such a programme of work – 'upscaling' informal education research – is important for three reasons. First, because scholarship on youth across many disciplines has tended (at least until recently) to focus upon local scales to the detriment of theorising youth agency beyond the neighbourhood (Ansell, 2009; Hopkins and Alexander, 2010).

Second, because informal education is most commonly understood to be both (temporally) imminent and (spatially) immanent to everyday life – life experienced in terms of local and immediate concerns (or, to put it crudely, 'where young people are at'). Yet, as the chapters in this volume show, informal education is often constituted by – and constitutes – 'larger'-scale processes, such as collective youth political agency, educational restructuring and deprivation. We turn to these three processes in the next section of this chapter, since it is our conviction that geographers and historians have a particular role to play in broadening the scope of informal education research. Third, because informal education might continue to have an important, if not always predictable, role to play in reconceptualising formal educational curricula in various geographical contexts: not least as new internet technologies enable ever more diverse and flexible forms of computer-mediated learning within and beyond schools (Edwards). We very briefly examine this issue later in this chapter.

Collective youth political agency: Educational restructuring and deprivation

As we noted in our introduction, informal education has always involved political – and in some cases utopian – imperatives. Often, the driving force of informal education is to start from the 'here and now' of young people's everyday experience, but with the ultimate goal of provoking some form of consciousness-raising among young people about their 'place' in the wider world. Several of the chapters in this volume exemplified diverse forms of consciousness-raising – in public spaces (Sadlier; Ditton; Rodó-de-Zárate and Baylina), online (Donovan), intentional communities (Donnachie) and various statutory or voluntary youth work contexts (Dickens and Lonie; Spence; Bradford; Mills; Bannister; Kyle; Goerisch). However, there is a difference between those moments when consciousness-raising leads to implicit, latent political *impulses* among a 'target' group of young people (Zembylas, 2013), and those moments when such impulses spill over into identifiable, active expressions of youth political *agency* that may in some instances extend beyond that target group. In other words, several of the chapters in this volume note the potential for informal education to lead to something 'bigger': perhaps inciting forms of protest, activism or participation that challenge the status quo; perhaps sowing the seeds for inter-regional or inter-national collaboration between diverse groups of young people with similar political concerns (Jeffrey, 2013); or, perhaps, inciting communities of professional practice that extend beyond local spaces of informal education (Donnachie).

These latter kinds of political agency, which inevitably extend beyond the local, immediate context of informal education practice, have tended to attract less attention in previous scholarship. We would argue that future scholarship on informal education, childhood and youth could have a key role to play in theorising and exemplifying youth political agency at a range of inter-linked spatial and temporal scales. Four specific contributions – or questions – spring to mind, in this case inspired by recent social-scientific work on children and young people's agency.

- First, there has been gathering accord across a wide range of disciplines that there is a need to pay greater attention to the *diverse* forms of young people's *political agency* (Hopkins and Alexander, 2010; Sloam, 2012; Kallio and Häkli, 2013). Some such studies examine young people's agency in formal education contexts. However, in what ways could young people's involvement in informal education – whether driven by professionalised youth work or informal peer-to-peer learning – complement and extend our understandings of the ways in which young people may act politically?

- Second, for many years, youth scholars have promoted young people's *participation* in civic life and decision-making (e.g., Davis et al., 2006). However, in what ways do informal education practices complement or challenge our (academics') assumptions about youth participation? Can informal education enable participatory processes that extend beyond the inevitable local scale at which most youth participation occurs? More pragmatically, can informal education approaches challenge the rather formulaic, narrow, adultist forms of participation that occur within so-called participatory process in formal school settings (e.g., den Besten et al., 2008)?

- Third, it has been argued that education scholars – particularly in geography – view *educational restructuring* as derivative of 'wider', neoliberal restructuring. Yet several studies have begun to posit an inverse or more recursive relationship: where certain aspects of educational change may also drive housing, employment and investment priorities in neoliberalising contexts (e.g., Hanson Thiem, 2009). However, in what ways do informal education practices – which often seek to work against the (neoliberal) status quo – operate recursively with/in processes of neoliberal restructuring? Do they reinforce predominant doxa by training young people in life skills that enable them to construct themselves as the flexible labourers of the neoliberal future? And/or does informal education enable young people to engage in forms of political agency – perhaps in alliance with adults – that enable new versions and visions of life-itself, beyond the neoliberal horizon, to be imagined (Kraftl, 2013)?

- Fourth, it has been argued that conceptual affinities for immediate emotions, affects and everyday practices have diverted attention from longer-standing and more widespread forms of *deprivation* affecting young people (Mitchell and Elwood, 2012). Significantly, some of the chapters in this book begin to demonstrate the imbrications of emotions such as love (Sadlier) and pain (Rodó-de-Zárate and Baylina) with broader processes of social change (Braidotti, 2011). However, regardless of one's conceptual standpoint, what potential is there for scholars to 'up-scale' informal education research by considering the opportunities and challenges constituted by informal education for addressing social or economic deprivation? To what extent can long-standing scholarly debates about social justice be bolstered by attention to the multiple scales of (collective) youth political agency that might be engendered by informal education?

Technologies of informal education

A further way in which informal education research may be 'up-scaled' is via greater attention to contemporary information and communication technologies. Selected chapters in this volume (Donovan; Spence; Edwards) offer critical analyses of the intersections between informal education and information technologies (especially new social media). Significantly, however, many of the other chapters in this volume barely mention such technologies, if at all. This could be for any number of reasons: perhaps young people and informal educators do not have access to such technologies in the contexts in which they work; perhaps information technologies are (or are deemed to be) irrelevant to the particular informal education activities in which practitioners are engaged; perhaps young people or practitioners seek deliberately to avoid such technologies as some kind of political statement; perhaps, for these reasons or others, scholars do not seek in their research questions to interrogate the role of contemporary information technologies.

Yet, it goes without saying, the above are all assumptions that maybe challenged in any number of contexts. Returning to youth political agency, many studies (including some in this volume) demonstrate the significance of new social media, in particular for tacking together diverse groups of young people from around the world in collective praxis (Jeffrey, 2013). Increasing access to the Internet around the world means that it becomes harder to sustain a 'digital divide' between rich and poor, although some stark differences may persist. At the same time, any critical perspective must recognise the inevitable hyperbole and polemic that accompanies both the rather celebratory and doomsaying narratives surrounding young people's use of technology (Thrift, 2003). Thus, we are not arguing for a wholesale 'shift online' by scholars of informal education. Rather, we suggest a cautious, critical engagement that teases out the *relative* role and significance of information technologies in informal education. Selected chapters in this volume offer starting points: yet, arguably, there are many opportunities for critical research about the intersections between informal education and, especially, new social media.

The role of academics and 'public' informal education research

In closing, we want briefly to raise the question of the role of academics in informing debates about informal education beyond the academy. The majority of the contributors to this book are located in university departments, although several also have backgrounds in informal and/or formal education, youth work, volunteering with youth organisations and other forms of professional or voluntary practice with young people. Clearly, a key role for academics is to offer theoretically informed, empirically rich, robust research on informal education – the like of which we hope is represented in this book. We hope that the examples and theorisations of informal education presented in this volume will be read and interpreted by practitioners and students of informal education, and that the book offers an engaging resource for thinking reflexively about the parameters of their work – not least in terms of the variability of informal education over space and time.

The above aspirations notwithstanding, there may be a sense in which academics could offer (a little) more. There have been repeated calls – of different textures – to make academic research 'public' in more explicit, active ways: in calls for 'public geographies' (Fuller and Askins, 2010), 'public sociologies' (Burawoy, 2005) and 'public histories' (Ashton and Keen, 2012). While critics suggest (contra Burawoy) that many academics *have* sought, for many years, to make their work public in a variety of ways (public history being a good example), there have been compelling calls for academics to broaden the styles in which they engage diverse possible publics for their research (see Fuller and Askins, 2010, for an exhaustive and inspirational list). Summarising three such possibilities, Ward (2007) notes how academics might:

- engage in *participatory action research*, through which research 'participants' become more equal contributors, with a stake in asking research questions, carrying out research and, therefore, carrying forward its 'results' into their everyday lives and communities;
- involve themselves in *dialogue with policy-makers* – not simply offering a summary of research 'findings' or recommendations, but fostering ongoing conversations about a particular project before, during and after that research takes place;
- aligning (critically and reflexively) with *activists*, or positioning themselves as *activist-academics*, such that their research skills become a cipher through which they can actively support community, pressure or protest groups.

Of course, scholars of informal education may seek other ways to engage publics – or may not directly seek to do so at all. Indeed, a choice *not* to insist upon one's research being instantly badged as 'useful' is in itself a central component of academic research, which may, ultimately (and perhaps iron-ically), lead to research becoming more 'useful' to diverse publics than had been anticipated (Horton and Kraftl, 2005)! Nonetheless, it strikes us that there are broad political, pedagogical and conceptual congruencies between many childhood and youth scholars and those practicing informal edu-cation, some of which are apparent in this volume. Therefore – where appropriate – we would encourage academics and informal education practi-tioners to consider into what productive *alliances* they might enter in order to forge future investigations of the role of informal education across diverse spaces and times.

References

N. Ansell (2009) 'Childhood and the politics of scale: Descaling children's geographies?' *Progress in Human Geography*, 33, 190–209.

P. Ashton and H. Keen (2012) *People and Their Pasts: Public history today* (Basingstoke: Palgrave Macmillan).

R. Braidotti (2011) *Nomadic Theory* (New York: Columbia UP).

M. Burawoy (2005) 'For public sociology', *American Sociological Review*, 70, 4–28.

J. Davis, M. Hill, K. Tisdall and A. Prout (2006) *Children, Young People and Social Inclusion: Participation for What?* (Bristol: Policy Press).

O. Den Besten, J. Horton and P. Kraftl (2008) 'Pupil involvement in school (re)design: Participation in policy and practice', *Co-Design*, 4, 197–210.

D. Fuller and K. Askins (2010) 'Public geographies II: Being organic', *Progress in Human Geography*, 34, 654–67.

C. Hanson Thiem (2009) 'Thinking through education: The geographies of contem-porary educational restructuring', *Progress in Human Geography*, 33, 154–73.

P. Hopkins and C. Alexander (2010) 'Politics, mobility and nationhood: Upscaling young people's geographies', *Area*, 42, 142–4.

J. Horton and P. Kraftl (2005) 'For more-than-usefulness: Six overlapping points about children's geographies', *Children's Geographies*, 3, 131–43.

C. Jeffrey (2013) 'Geographies of children and youth III: Alchemists of the revolution?' *Progress in Human Geography*, 37, 145–52.

K. Kallio and J. Häkli (2013) 'Children and young people's politics in everyday life', *Space and Polity* 17, 1–16.

P. Kraftl (2013) *Geographies of Alternative Education* (Bristol: Policy Press).

K. Mitchell and S. Elwood (2012) 'Mapping children's politics: The promise of artic-ulation and the limits of nonrepresentational theory', *Environment and Planning D: Society and space*, 30, 788–804.

J. Sloam (2012) 'Introduction: Youth citizenship and politics', *Parliamentary Affairs*, 65, 4–12.

N. Thrift (2003) 'Closer to the machine? Intelligent environments, new forms of possession and the rise of the supertoy', *Cultural Geographies*, 10, 389–407.

K. Ward (2007) 'Geography and public policy: Activist, participatory and policy geographies', *Progress in Human Geography*, 31, 695–705.

M. Zembylas (2013) 'Mobilizing "implicit activisms" in schools through practices of critical emotional reflexivity', *Teaching Education*, 24, 84–96.

Index

CPSIA information can be obtained
at www.ICGtesting.com
Printed in the USA
LVOW03*2120280116

472648LV00009BA/33/P